① religion 3   March 8
Russian Tea①   No risk
drop - two way half side & Jersey's

② Pemberton's
      Feb 8

THRUST AND COUNTERTHRUST

THRUST

and

COUNTERTHRUST

THE GENESIS OF THE
CANADA-UNITED STATES BOUNDARY

by

H. GEORGE CLASSEN

LONGMANS CANADA LIMITED

Longmans Canada Limited
55 Barber Greene Road
Don Mills, Ontario

Acknowledgements

The author's thanks are due to the Royal Society of Canada for permission to quote from an article by William F. Ganong in the Society's 1901 *Transactions*; and to the Clarendon Press, Oxford, for permitting the use of an excerpt from the *Dictionary of National Biography 1912-1921*.

Printed in Canada
by McCorquodale and Blades Printers Ltd.

Contents

With 5 maps by the author

Foreword

To modern civilized man, boundaries between nations are so obvious a feature of international relations that he can scarcely conceive a world where they did not exist, or where they existed only in embryonic form. Yet the sharp, fixed boundary on the surface of the earth is, anthropologically speaking, of recent origin, and it took a long time until it became universally accepted.

This statement does not contradict findings published recently that man, along with practically all animals, "defends a territory." Animals and early men defend, or defended, territories, vague territories, insofar as these were ecologically useful. The territories claimed and defended could, and generally did, change from generation to generation, and often from season to season. Modern civilized man, by contrast, defends (or pretends to defend) a sharply defined territory because it is historically *his*, and boundaries are meant to last forever.

Parallel with the growth of this new attitude toward men's territories ran the growth of a new concept of men's belonging. Men were no longer asked *of whom* they were born, but *in what place*. Concomitantly, they were no longer subject to the laws of their fathers, but to the laws of the territory in which they happened to find themselves.

The old concepts are not entirely dead; they survive in vestigial form among diplomatic and military personnel stationed abroad. Nor is it certain that they will not have a resurgence.

These fundamental considerations are essential for understanding the forces at work in the thrust and counterthrust that shaped the boundary between the British territories and the United States. For Britain had, to a much greater degree than the new republic, retained the old concepts of men's territories and men's belonging. It was interested not in the *possession* of land, but in certain *uses*; and paramount among these uses was that of passage. Also, Britain was most anxious to have its laws follow its subjects, wherever they might be; the United States was no less anxious to make its laws reign over all men found within its territories, whoever they might be. The tiresome quarrels over British impressment of seamen and inspection of cargo, live and dead, were nothing but another aspect of the clash of the old and new concepts.

Crudely put, Britain wished to exercise *some* rights, or privileges, *anywhere*; the United States wished to exercise *all* rights *somewhere*. Britain never gave up the practice of searching ships anywhere in the world, and if the United States ceased to protest it was only because it had turned from an enemy into an ally.

Here, in the North American wilderness, two traditions met, the one coming from the Indo-European rangers of the plains, the other from the soil-tillers of Mesopotamia and Egypt.

Neither side, of course, adhered to this or that concept wholly or consistently. It was rather a matter of priorities and of emphasis — which is true of all human affairs.

The span of this book embraces the genesis of the boundary between the United States and the territory that is now Canada, but which, during most of the boundary-making, was British North America. This is an important distinction. The understanding of history is not advanced by extending modern political conditions and attitudes several hundred years into the past.

This book was written in Ottawa by a Canadian, and it is therefore natural that British and Canadian original sources should have been consulted more extensively than American ones, and that the actions of British and Canadian statesmen and soldiers should have received slightly more attention than those of their United States counterparts. This statement, however, must be qualified. A look at the bibliography at the end of the book will show that most of the books and articles cited were written by Americans; some by Canadians; and a very few by Englishmen. Thus a preponderance of unpublished British sources was balanced by a preponderance of published American sources. This was not done by design; the bibliography reflects the attention the boundary has received from historians of the three countries concerned. It is regrettable that English historians have neglected the making of the Canada-United States boundary. Being farther from the scene and less involved emotionally, they would probably have composed less biased accounts than their colleagues on this side of the Atlantic.

This is not a history for historians. It is meant to be read — and, perhaps, enjoyed — rather than studied. For this reason I have omitted footnotes. The advantage of including them appeared greatly to be outweighed by the burden they impose on most readers. The copious quotations in this book and other references to the utterings of historical figures would have necessitated a veritable forest of bothersome numbers. I have also learned that the presence of such a growth is no guarantee against misquotation and misinterpretation.

The views expressed in this book are my own. Official sanction was neither sought nor received, and it is in any case doubtful that a modern official viewpoint exists in respect of any of the issues considered here. Anyone wishing to change the Canada-United States boundary will have to look for new disputes; the old disputes have served their time. They have not, however, exhausted their usefulness for the enlightenment of our contemporaries, nor, by a long shot, for their entertainment.

Note on Boundary Determination

Since portions of this book deal with the technical aspects of surveying, a short description of longitude and latitude and their relation to boundary determination may be helpful.

The entire course of the Canada-United States boundary is now fixed and described in terms of geographical co-ordinates, *i.e.,* by latitude and longitude. Since the boundary consists entirely of straight courses, it is necessary only to fix the points at which these courses change direction, called "turning-points." For greater precision, however, the length of the courses and their azimuths (in this case, direction referred to south) are also inscribed in treaty documents in Ottawa and Washington.

As is commonly known, latitude defines the north-south position of any point between the equator and the North or South Pole. It is measured in parallels, the spaces between which are further subdivided into minutes, seconds, and fractions of seconds. The determination of latitude is relatively simple, and has been made at least since the late Middle Ages. It was found early, for example, that the North Star maintains a position almost exactly over the North Pole. The farther south an observer moves from the North Pole, the closer the North Star moves toward the horizon. Latitude, therefore, corresponds roughly to the angle formed between a horizontal line and a line aiming at the North Star. Although various corrections and refinements were introduced from time to time, the principle of latitude determination through the history of the boundary remained the same.

Longitude defines the east-west position of any point in relation to some arbitrarily chosen north-south line — commonly the line running through Greenwich near London. Longitude is measured by meridians, the spaces between which are again subdivided into minutes and seconds. The difference is that while the degrees latitude and their subdivisions are all of the same size, the degrees longitude decrease from the equator to the poles, where the meridians converge.

The principle of longitude determination is also simple, and consists in the discovery of the time difference between the base meridian and the point to be fixed. As the earth turns on its axis, any fixed point in space — *i.e.*, any star — will be seen to travel from east to west. By noting the time a particular star requires to travel from its overhead position in, say, London to its overhead position in Ottawa, geographers can determine the time difference and therefore the number of degrees longitude between the two points. The prerequisite for such observations, however, is knowledge of the exact local time of both places. The observer at Ottawa will either have to have a clock brought from London showing London time, or a time signal from London via telegraph or radio.

Radio had of course not yet made its appearance during boundary-survey days, and only in a few cases was it possible to use telegraph lines, as for example at the start of the forty-ninth-parallel survey in 1872. The surveyors therefore had to rely on the transportation of clocks — chronometers — from point to point to establish time differences. Since much of this travel was through wilderness, the chronometers were shaken up and their accuracy suffered. It was better if longitude could be determined by tying in visually with some point whose co-ordinates had been fixed in favourable circumstances over long periods. In the survey of the eastern boundary, Quebec City served as such a base point.

In one instance, however, neither the transportation of a chronometer nor a tie-in with a previously determined point was possible

— the first determination of the 141st-meridian boundary on the Yukon River. Recourse had to be had to a timepiece in the sky — the moon. Since the moon, in a period of roughly twenty-eight days, makes one complete circle in the heavens around the earth, it forms, as it were, the hand of a giant clock. By carefully observing the moon's position in the heavens the local time at Greenwich can be determined. This, compared with the easily ascertainable local time at the observer's point, enables him to determine his longitude. This method can be fruitful only with complex star catalogues, precise instruments, and the most painstaking and repeated observation.

Many portions of the Canada-United States boundary were defined by arbitrary lines rather than natural landmarks — the forty-fifth-parallel boundary in the East, the forty-ninth-parallel boundary, the 141st-meridian boundary in Alaska. But even where the boundary was in the first instance defined by landmarks such as rivers or watersheds, it was subsequently described in terms of geographical co-ordinates.

The fixation of all boundary points by latitude and longitude has the inestimable value that boundary commissions are no longer dependent on natural or artificial landmarks or maps to mark the course of the boundary. If monuments are obliterated or rivers change their course (as, for instance, in the construction of the St. Lawrence Seaway) the position of the boundary can quickly be re-established from the co-ordinates. These are very exact; in most cases they are determined down to hundredths or thousandths of seconds. One hundredth of a second latitude is approximately one foot, and one hundredth of a second longitude, along the forty-fifth parallel, is approximately eight inches.

This does not mean that the position of each boundary monument has been determined by independent astronomical observations. Rather, their positions have generally been calculated from distances and directions of adjacent monuments. The entire boundary is enveloped in a grid of geodetic triangulation, a rigid skeleton like the girders of a bridge. This, in turn, is tied in with the over-all continental geodetic grid which has its base and focal point at the North American Datum, Meades Ranch in Kansas, whose astronomic position has been determined with the greatest possible exactitude.

Much of the boundary runs through water, and although it is evidently impracticable to mark its turning-points by monuments or buoys, they are nonetheless tied into the boundary grid as firmly as those on land. This is generally achieved by setting up range marks on shore. By lining up with two pairs of such range marks right and left, an observer on the water can easily find the desired boundary point. Where the land is not easily visible, water boundaries are fixed by co-ordinates alone.

CHAPTER ONE

Bugles on the St. John

On May 8, 1828, a strange trial was taking place in the New Brunswick Supreme Court in the provincial capital of Fredericton. There were the three judges — Chief Justice John Saunders, Justice John Murray Bliss, Justice Ward Chipman — the jurors and court officials; and the accused, John Baker, in rough frontiersman's dress, a settler from the upper St. John River.

After the preliminaries, the clerk of the court began to read the indictment.

York, to wit. The jurors of our Lord the King, upon their oath, present, that John Baker, late of the parish of Kent, in the county of York, laborer, James Bacon, late of the same place, laborer, and Charles Studson, late of the same place, laborer, being persons greatly disaffected to our said Lord the King, and his Government, within this, His Majesty's Province of New Brunswick, and being factiously and seditiously disposed, on the fourth day of July, in the eighth year of the reign of our said Sovereign Lord George the Fourth, with force and arms, at the parish aforesaid, in the county aforesaid, did, amongst themselves, conspire, combine, confederate, and agree together, falsely, maliciously, factiously, and seditiously, to molest and disturb the peace and common

1

tranquillity of this Province, and to bring into hatred and contempt our said Lord the King, and his Government, and to create false opinions and suspicions in the subjects of our said Lord the King, and of Royal Power and prerogative of our said Lord the King within this Province.

While the clerk droned on, John Baker could reflect on the curious and ill-fated circumstances that had brought him, a citizen of one of the United States of America, into this odd conflict with a European monarch. Not that he had not had time to reflect on this before, for he had been in and out of prison at Fredericton for over seven months, ever since he was pulled from his bed by an armed sheriff's posse on September 25, 1827, and carried down the St. John River to the New Brunswick capital. They had not caught Bacon and Studson, the men accused with him. They would not have caught him either, had they not sneaked up on him silently in the gray light of dawn.

> . . . did erect, and cause to be raised and erected a certain flag staff, and did thereon place a certain flag . . .

It was the Fourth of July, and Baker and the other Americans in the Madawaska Settlements on either side of the St. John had erected a liberty pole and hoisted on it a crude American flag sewn by Baker's wife Sophie. The French farmers, watching the strange proceedings, had been puzzled but friendly, politely accepting the drink of rum offered to them. In the evening a ball was held in Baker's house, and many of the French settlers and their womenfolk had come to dance in the warm midsummer night.

> . . . applied to divers liege subjects of our said Lord the King, and then and there presented to the same subjects a paper writing. . . . By the said paper, they, the said subjects, would bind themselves to oppose the execution of the laws of Great Britain . . .

That was the compact the Americans had drawn up the following day, to give formal significance to the occasion, and which the French had been invited to join. It was an agreement that the settlers would adjust all their differences amongst themselves, without recourse to the New Brunswick authorities, and was intended to ward off the interference of the latter.

. . . and that they had mutually entered into a written agreement to keep the same flag there, and that nothing but a force superior to their own should take it down; and further, that they considered, and had a right to consider, themselves then and there on the territory of the said United States; and that they had bound themselves to resist by force the execution of the laws of Great Britain among themselves.

Alas, the patriotic fellowship had been short-lived. Scarcely more than a month after the Americans had, in the tradition of William Tell, sworn to uphold one another against the hirelings of a foreign monarch, one of the settlers applied to the New Brunswick magistrate to help him collect a five-dollar debt from a fellow American. It was not always easy to square patriotism and gain along the disputed frontier, as Baker knew from personal experience. The British officer appeared to execute the writ, but the Americans rallied at his sight and drove him from the settlement, forcing him to yield up the debtor, and shamed the latter into paying his debt.

Even without that, however, word of the Fourth of July had got about quickly along the St. John valley, and the more the affair was viewed in perspective the more ominous it seemed. Baker became frightened, and he and his neighbour James Bacon made the arduous trip through the wilderness south to the Maine capital of Portland, where they obtained an interview with Governor Enoch Lincoln, asking for his protection. The Governor was glad to see his brave countrymen upholding the honour of the Stars and Stripes along the northern reaches of the state, and assured them of his support, but also warned them to be cautious. A few days after their return to Madawaska, Baker was arrested.

The New Brunswickers were not used to handling this sort of business. Sheriff E. W. Miller of the county of York, charged with executing the arrest warrant, started up the St. John River in a barge full of able-bodied men. It was more of a punitive expedition than the quiet, swift, and sure pounce that Lieutenant-Governor Sir Howard Douglas had in mind. He sent a messenger on horseback after the barge, but Sheriff Miller was stubborn. He had been authorized, he said, by the legislative council to proceed as he did.

Only after a second messenger confronted him with unmistakable orders did the law-enforcement officer divest himself of most of his retinue. Drawing near to the scene of the crime, however, he again began to accumulate a posse, and when he knocked on the door of the Baker family, after lying in wait through the night, he had fourteen men to back him up.

Baker gave himself up without a struggle, but the flotilla of canoes had hardly left the Mariumticook Brook that flowed past his house when the American flag once more fluttered in the breeze, hoisted defiantly by Sophie Baker.

At the time of his arrest John Baker had lived on the upper St. John for seven years. He was born in the village of Moscow, Somerset County, District of Maine, in 1787, and at the age of twenty-nine he went to lumber in the province of New Brunswick and later in Lower Canada. In 1820 he moved in with his brother Nathan who had set up as a squatter on the spot where the Mariumticook flowed into the St. John. Nathan Baker and two other Americans, John Harford and his son John Harford Jr., after lumbering and farming on the Kennebec River in Maine, had made their appearance on the upper St. John in 1817. Nathan soon began to prosper, thanks to a deal with a St. John lumber merchant named Samuel Nevers, who acted as his grubstaker and protector. In 1821, however, Nathan died, and John, still a bachelor, took over his brother's business and married his brother's widow.

The Americans — by 1827 the number of their homesteads had risen to about twenty-five — were not the first to establish themselves on the upper St. John River. The first settlers had drifted into the area late in the eighteenth century, and they were "Acadian" French. In 1790 some fifty of them obtained a land grant from the Lieutenant-Governor of New Brunswick, and another grant was made in 1794. In the year of Baker's arrest they numbered about two thousand. Their rude farms were strung out on either bank of the St. John for forty miles, the centre of the settlement being the mouth of the Madawaska River flowing into the St. John from Lake Temiscouata. From the Madawaska River the settlement got its name.

Though the Americans claimed to have settled on unoccupied land above the French farms, their arrival was not welcomed. In 1818 one of the Acadians, a captain of militia, complained to the New Brunswick authorities in Fredericton that "several American families arrived amongst us from the Kennebec River, who would have many of the inhabitants of this district believe that the jurisdiction of the United States is in force."

In time, the two sides settled down to a half-wary, half-friendly *modus vivendi*.

The first prosecution witness was George Morehouse.

> I am [he said] a Justice of the Peace for the county of York, and reside in the parish of Kent, about thirty miles below the Grand Falls. That part of the country where the French and the Americans were has been invariably under the jurisdiction and laws of this Province since I knew it. I have been in the constant habit, as a magistrate, of sending my writs and warrants there, and no objection was made to the service of them till last August.

In July, Morehouse said, he had received word from another New Brunswicker living at Madawaska, Francis Rice, a militia officer and a man of some influence, that seditious practices were going on in the settlement.

> I accordingly proceeded to Madawaska on the seventh of August, and arrived at the place where Baker's house is situate, and went into the house of James Bacon, and asked him to let me see the paper which had been handed about for signature. He said he had it not. I then went to Baker's house. I told him it was reported that he had drawn up, and circulated among the settlers, a paper, the purport of which was that they were American citizens, and had bound themselves to resist the execution of the laws of Great Britain. He said he did not know whether it was in his possession or not. We proceeded together to his house; between his residence and the mill, there is a new house, where ten or twelve Americans were assembled. When we got there, Baker took two or three aside, and consulted with them for a few minutes; he then came back, and said to me, "Mr. Morehouse, I have consulted with the committee, and we have determined that you shall not see this paper." I observed, when I went there, a flag staff erected. There was then

no flag on it, but after coming out of Bacon's I observed a flag hoisted — a white flag, with an American eagle and a semicircle of stars, red. I pointed to the flag, and asked Baker what it was. He said, "The American flag, Mr. Morehouse. Did you never see it before? If not, you can see it now." I required him in His Majesty's name to pull it down. He replied, "No, I will not. We have placed it there, and we are determined we will support it, and nothing but a superior force to ourselves shall take it down. We are on American territory, Great Britain has no jurisdiction here."

After Morehouse's evidence, Francis Rice was heard. He corroborated Morehouse. After this, several of the French Madawaskans told how the Americans had tried to make them sign the compact, and how they had refused. Others told how they had been obstructed by the Americans in their official duties. The mail courier Peter Soleste recited how, while proceeding up-river in his canoe, he had been threatened by Baker. Two Englishmen who were acquainted with Madawaska testified that the settlement had always been under British administration. Perhaps the most damaging evidence, apart from Morehouse's account, came from a man not connected with Madawaska — the county registrar of deeds, who produced a receipt to show that, three years ago, Baker had appeared before him at Woodstock to claim the special bounty on grain raised on newly cleared land, an incentive to settlers. By making such a claim, and taking the money, Baker had automatically acknowledged that his land was in New Brunswick.

But when it was his turn to testify, he declined, saying only that he considered himself an American citizen, living on American territory, not subject to the jurisdiction of the court.

After deliberating one hour, the jury brought in a verdict of guilty. The court thereupon adjourned for five days to give the judges leisure to consider the punishment.

They had much to think about, for they knew much — about Baker, about the Madawaskans, and, above all, about the disputed boundary. They were all sons of United Empire Loyalists, as were their fellow New Brunswickers, and they knew that on them were the eyes of men who had fought the War of 1812 and who had heard from the lips of their fathers of the glories and iniquities of the American Revolution. They knew that the threads of the Baker case reached to the state house in Portland and to the Castle of St. Louis in Quebec, to Washington on the Potomac and to London across the sea.

None, in fact, was more conversant with the boundary history than Justice Ward Chipman Jr., who had been British agent of the Joint British-American Boundary Commission which had tried, and failed, to settle the disputed line in accordance with the letter of ancient treaties. Yes, ancient, because when the boundary commissioners tried to take their stand on the Treaty of Paris of 1783, the formal instrument governing the division of British and United States territory, its fragile fabric quickly gave way and they were plunged into a welter of dusty parchments, the diplomatic accumulation of centuries.

It was a novel and uncomfortable experience for British diplomacy to make a treaty with a rebellious colony turned into an independent republic, and the natural inclination was to get the distasteful business over with as quickly and cleanly as possible. To conduct the peace talks on the part of Britain Lord Shelburne, the Colonial Secretary, pitted against the American delegation in Paris an elderly Scottish merchant named Richard Oswald. He was, Shelburne wrote to Benjamin Franklin, "a pacifical man . . . conversant in those negotiations which are most interesting to mankind." Franklin agreed. Later observers were to deal less kindly with the British negotiator, and one American judgment was that

> of all the remarkable incidents in this remarkable transaction, nothing now seems so difficult to account for as the mode in which Great Britain pursued her objects by negotiation. The individual pitched upon to deal with the United States was a respectable and amiable private gentleman, nominated at the suggestion of Dr. Franklin, with whom he was to treat, because he thought he would get along easily with him; but by no means a match for a combination of three men such as Franklin, Jay, and John Adams.

One of the principal charges made later against both Oswald and the British Government of the day was that he failed to define properly — or advantageously, as the case might be — the boundary from the Atlantic Ocean to the Great Lakes. Henry U. Addington, a British diplomat who was called on to wrestle with the boundary almost half a century later, wrote:

> I have perused Mr. Strachey's papers, which only go to prove extreme debility and precipitation on the part of the ministry and idiotic imbecility on the part of Mr. Oswald. It is rather hard to find oneself called upon to make good the flaws left in the original Treaty [of 1783] by the incapacity or dishonesty of the Butchers concerned in it.

But the charge of poor boundary-making would scarcely have impressed Oswald himself, for that gentleman was toying with vaster issues and was prepared to yield up not just a piece of forest wilderness but all of mainland North America.

To the modern reader, especially if he is a Canadian, such a possibility must seem absurd, perhaps monstrous. But in 1782 it was neither. What was left in British hands of North America seemed of little direct value; only a few thousand Englishmen lived there, dispersed among the French of the lower St. Lawrence, and in Nova Scotia (which then included New Brunswick). Shelburne had a grander vision: to conciliate the new republic by a liberal peace, and thus to salvage if not the form at least the substance of British economic — and perhaps even political — hegemony. Neither he nor Oswald could yet foresee the vigorous and independent development of the United States, nor the dramatic effect which the influx of Loyalists would have on the remaining British colonies. Still, when Oswald acknowledged that Franklin's demand for all of the mainland was perfectly clear and satisfactory, Whitehall reined him in, and stiffened its case with the dispatch of further emissaries to Paris.

At length the Americans contented themselves with the precise territories of the rebellious colonies along the Atlantic seaboard; farther west the bargaining narrowed to a choice of two lines: either a water boundary along the St. Lawrence River and through Lakes Ontario, Erie, Huron, and Superior, or the forty-fifth parallel all the way. The second choice would have thrown what is now southern Ontario into the United States, and northern Michigan, Wis-

consin, and Minnesota into the possession of Britain. The first line
was chosen, and its eastern portion was defined

> *by a line to be drawn along the middle of the river St. Croix from
> its source directly north to the . . . Highlands, which divide the
> rivers that fall into the Atlantic Ocean from those which fall into
> the river St. Lawrence; [then:] From the northwest angle of Nova
> Scotia, viz., that angle which is formed by a line drawn due north
> from the source of the Saint Croix River to the Highlands; along
> the said Highlands . . . to the northwesternmost head of the Con-
> necticut river; thence down the middle of that river, to the forty-
> fifth degree of north latitude until it strikes the river Iroquois or
> Cataraquy [St. Lawrence].*

Scarcely was the ink dry on the treaty when its phrases were put
to the test by geographical reality, and found wanting in clarity.
Loyalists were settling in what they assumed to be the southern
extremity of the new province of New Brunswick, recently detached
from Nova Scotia. The Americans in that vicinity protested, and it
turned out that no one could show with certainty which of the two
larger streams emptying into Passamaquoddy Bay, an inlet of the
Bay of Fundy, was the St. Croix of the treaty. The name "St. Croix"
was not in use locally; it had been bestowed by Samuel de Champlain early in the seventeenth century, but had not gained wide
acceptance, and the two streams in question were known to the settlers by their Indian names, the western one being called Schoodic
and the eastern Magaguadavic. The usage of the day, however, was
to transcribe, from parchment to parchment, and from century to
century, the precise phrases and terms used in ancient royal charters,
grants, and treaties. Diplomacy was made in European drawing-
rooms, and it was easier to copy venerable documents than to survey
hundreds of miles of primeval wilderness infested by warlike Indians, and also more prudent politically.

It is true that the treaty-makers had seen the name "St. Croix"
on a map, compiled by the famous cartographer Mitchell in 1755,
but the map was too inaccurate to provide the answer. In the
absence of proof each side attached the name "St. Croix" to the
river it considered most advantageous, the Americans claiming the
Magaguadavic for their boundary, and the British the Schoodic.

It will be seen by reference to the words of the treaty that this disagreement put into question not only the territory between the rivers themselves, but a sizable strip of land between two straight lines running "due north" from their respective sources. The eastern line cut through New Brunswick midway between Fredericton and Woodstock.

The dispute, through seaward extension, also came to include the islands in Passamaquoddy Bay, along with fishing rights, and it grew too large to be handled by local authorities. The matter was discussed for several years between London and Washington, and the way to adjustment was finally opened through a treaty signed in 1794 (known afterwards as Jay's Treaty) which provided for the appointment of a mixed commission that was to examine the local geography and to determine the application of the Treaty of 1783.

The commission was set up in 1796, and consisted of three members. The British member was Colonel Thomas Barclay, one of the most prominent men in the Atlantic colonies. Barclay, born in 1753, fought with the Loyalist forces during the Revolutionary War and later emigrated to Nova Scotia, where he became leader of the Loyalist party and speaker of the House of Assembly. In 1799 he returned to the United States as British consul-general in New York, a post he held until his death in 1830. He was thus one of the few Loyalist refugees who, in a manner of speaking, managed to have their cake and eat it too. One of his sons, Anthony, born in 1792, was to play a prominent role in another boundary dispute to be described in another chapter.

The United States member of the commission was Daniel Howell, professor of law at Brown University, Rhode Island. The third, "neutral," member was Egbert Benson, a judge of the New York Supreme Court, chosen jointly by Barclay and Howell. The choice of the American was made palatable to Barclay by Benson's being his friend and distant relative. Each side also had an agent, or executive officer, the British agent being Ward Chipman Sr. (the father of the Judge Chipman who was trying John Baker), solicitor-general of New Brunswick, and the American agent being James Sullivan, attorney-general of Massachusetts.

The commissioners elicited contradictory information from local Indians as to the identity of the river named St. Croix by Champlain. It was not until Ward Chipman had excavations made on Dochet Island, in the Schoodic River, and unearthed regular piles of brick — the actual remains of a camp erected in 1604 by de Monts, Champlain's chief — that Benson gave his vote for the British claim.

The dispute then moved on to the source of the St. Croix, the quondam Schoodic. The river was found to have two main branches, each issuing from a separate chain of lakes. Luckily, the selection of one of them as the St. Croix proper had the fortuitous effect of sorting out certain controversial grants made to British and American settlers in ignorance of the boundary line, and a compromise became possible. "A yellow birch tree hooped with iron" marked the river's source and put an end to this contentious episode.

The dispute over the Passamaquoddy islands, however, was to drag on through the War of 1812, and to become exacerbated by providing a refuge for tax-dodgers and smugglers who resisted and intrigued against both governments — the first, but by no means last, such occasion in the history of the boundary. The islands were finally apportioned by compromise in 1817, pursuant to the Treaty of Ghent, of which more will be said later.

Thus, though the St. Croix and Passamaquoddy controversies lasted long and were difficult to settle, they had little if any effect on the general political relations between Britain and the United States. The same cannot be said about that line which was to start at the source of the St. Croix and to run northward till it struck "the Highlands, which divide the rivers that fall into the Atlantic Ocean from those which fall into the river St. Lawrence."

Though the commission under the Jay Treaty had been limited to the St. Croix River, its members were keenly aware that their decision as to the source of the river would have far-reaching consequences on the location of the boundary farther north, and they naturally speculated as to the extension of the "line drawn due north" and "the northwest angle of Nova Scotia" (now New Brunswick), where it was to turn westward. The American agent Sullivan incautiously expressed the belief that it might be difficult if not impossible to find highlands that would fit the intent of the Treaty of 1783, and in the early years of the nineteenth century British and American diplomats considered setting up another joint commission to determine that question. Nothing of that sort was done, however, until the peace negotiations in Ghent that were to end the War of 1812.

The British representatives at Ghent were no longer so casual about geography as their predecessors at Paris had been thirty-two years before. Their greater geopolitical awareness derived from the campaigns of the war, and from sundry communications and petitions from the colonial authorities in North America. Among these was one from the legislature of New Brunswick praying that the Prince Regent might, in the impending peace negotiations,

> direct such measures to be adopted as he may think proper to alter the boundaries between those [United] States and this Province, so as that the important line of communication between this and the neighbouring Province of Lower Canada, by the River St. John, may not be interrupted.

Though neither the authorities of New Brunswick nor anyone else yet knew precisely how far north the due-north line might eventually run, enough was known of the area's topography to raise strong fears that it would cross both the St. John and the Restigouche and stop short only of running down the slope to the St. Lawrence.

The British peace negotiators accordingly intimated to their American counterparts in the summer of 1814 that they wished a "revision of the boundary line . . . merely for the purpose of preventing uncertainty and dispute." The Americans pricked up their ears. They had thought the boundaries were not an issue in the war, and pressed for details. The British admitted that they were seeking "such a variation of the line of frontier as may secure a direct communication between Quebec and Halifax." The Americans retorted that this amounted to cession of the northern part of the District of Maine, and rejected it. In vain did the British attempt to cover their tracks by suggesting that the boundary was so vague that the territory they sought might well be British by right. The words "revision" and "variation" clearly announced an admission which could never be retracted.

A few months later the British found that they had been dealt a trump, in the occupation by British forces of the Maine coast down to the Penobscot River. They immediately played it by introducing the principle of *uti possidetis*, according to which each belligerent retains possession of whatever territory he happens to hold at the end of hostilities. Once this was accepted, they thought, they could then exchange the occupied territory for that which they really wanted.

The Americans rejected this gambit also. They could take this attitude because Britain was war-weary and deeply entangled in the final debacle of Napoleonic Europe. Wellington declined to have anything to do with the North American war unless given large quantities of men and matériel, which the Government was not prepared to grant. The Foreign Secretary, Lord Castlereagh, wrote in September, 1814:

> Looking to a continuance of the American war, our financial state is far from satisfactory. We shall want a loan for the ensuing year of £27,000,000 to £28,000,000. The American war will not cost us less than £10,000,000, in addition to our peace establishment and other expenses. We must expect, therefore, to have it said that the property tax is continued for the purpose of securing a better frontier for Canada.

The purpose evidently not being such as to rouse the British taxpayer to sacrificial enthusiasm, the Treaty of Peace and Amity signed on Christmas Eve, 1814, left boundary definitions pretty much as they had been in 1783. It attempted, however, to turn confusion into order by separating the various sections of the line into neat compartments, and providing that (a) each section should be surveyed and determined by a joint commission, and (b) if there were any points on which the commissioners and their respective governments could not agree, these were to be submitted to "a friendly sovereign or State" for arbitration. Article 4 of the treaty covered the islands in Passamaquoddy Bay; Article 5 covered the boundary from the source of the St. Croix River to the River St. Lawrence; Article 6 covered the boundary through the upper St. Lawrence and Lakes Ontario, Erie, and Huron; and Article 7 covered the boundary through Lake Superior and thence to Lake of the Woods. Beyond that was no man's land.

The British commissioner under both Articles 4 and 5 was again Thomas Barclay, with Chipman Sr. as agent, Chipman Jr. as co-agent, and Joseph Bouchette, surveyor-general of Lower Canada, as surveyor (under the Fifth Article only).

The American team under Article 5 consisted of Cornelius P. Van Ness, of Vermont, as commissioner; William C. Bradley, agent; and John Johnson, chief surveyor.

The commission held its first meeting at St. Andrews, New Brunswick, in September, 1816, and its second at Boston in June, 1817. At the second meeting it was agreed that the first survey should be that of the due-north line starting from the source of the St. Croix, to be undertaken jointly by Johnson and Bouchette.

Although it was not for the surveyors to decide where the highlands of the treaty were, and where the north line was to end, they could hardly help being infected with the spirit of rivalry and contentiousness prevailing in any boundary commission. In this game of nerves Johnson proved to be Bouchette's master; it was told that on Sunday mornings, while the survey parties rested, he would poke about the neighbourhood and climb trees and draw imaginary highlands, sorely confusing his colleague.

The Chipmans were also dissatisfied with Bouchette's professional abilities, though whether this dissatisfaction had a genuine basis or not is hard to say. At any rate he was eased out of the commission in 1818, and the job of chief surveyor for the British commissioner was given to the Provincial Secretary of New Brunswick, William Franklin Odell. Odell and Johnson continued to survey the north line until it struck the Metis River, a small tributary of the St. Lawrence.

Farther west the forty-fifth-parallel boundary was old enough to have been surveyed back in 1774 when it still separated British colonies. For the most part it went through sparsely populated and unimportant country, but where it cut across Lake Champlain the United States had built a fort known as Rouses Point, just south of the old line, at a cost of $1,000,000. In 1818 two astronomers, Dr. Johann Ludwig Tiarks and Ferdinand R. Hassler, for Britain and the United States respectively, discovered to their consternation that the old line was too far north, and that the true forty-fifth parallel would make of the expensive fort a gift to Britain. They cautiously kept their discovery from the public and communicated it only to the agents of the commission.

The commissioners met several times during the surveys, and on May 24, 1821, they got together in New York to hear the arguments of their agents as to the proper course of the boundary line. By that time everyone concerned was well aware that the opinions of the agents were far apart. Barclay had, in fact, predicted disagreement in 1816 when acknowledging his appointment to Lord Castlereagh, who had cheerfully written that the job would be so simple as to involve only technical decisions.

Nowhere did the two sides differ more radically than on the locations of the "Highlands." Bradley maintained that, to fulfil the prescription of the treaty, the due-north line must run 143 miles to the watershed between the St. Lawrence and the Restigouche rivers. The line must then meander westward along the edge of the St. Lawrence watershed more or less parallel to the great river. (Bouchette later claimed that such a line would run within 9½ miles of Rivière-du-Loup and within thirty-three miles of Quebec City.)

Ward Chipman maintained that the north line must stop at a small though prominent mountain, known as Mars Hill, within forty miles of the source of the St. Croix, *i.e.*, well south of the St. John. The line should then trend westward along the watershed between the St. John and the Penobscot and Kennebec. He defended his choice by saying that the treaty definition did not mean that the north line had to reach the precise point at which the highlands divided the waters, etc.; it merely had to reach the highlands themselves. In any case, Mars Hill was more of a "highland" than the nondescript swamp country above the St. Lawrence.

This led to a protracted wrangle, liberally interlarded with quotations from ancient and recent grants, charters, and treaties. Neither side would yield a foot.

The two sides also disagreed on the other portions of the line under Article 5. While Barclay would select the chain of Connecticut Lakes, joined by the Connecticut River itself, as the northwesternmost head of that river, the United States commissioner chose a more westerly branch known as Indian Stream. As to the forty-fifth parallel, Chipman quite naturally opted for the true parallel as determined by Tiarks and Hassler, which would give Rouses Point to Britain. Bradley, not finding a convincing rebuttal, wished to hold the matter in abeyance.

The meetings of the commission became steadily more quarrelsome and bitter, and ended on April 13, 1822, bequeathing the dispute to the two governments.

Who was right on the major point, that of the "highlands" — Chipman or Bradley? The Americans evidently thought that they had an ironclad argument. They fastened especially on the watershed proviso, and maintained that the treaty divided rivers into two classes only — those flowing into the St. Lawrence, and all others. They ridiculed Chipman's "highlands" because they merely separated rivers all flowing into the Atlantic. They were also able to point out that the description of the Treaty of 1783 was practically a verbatim repetition of earlier proclamations separating British colonies, where it had been quite clear that the southern boundary of Canada, *i.e.*, Lower Canada, was the St. Lawrence watershed.

But Chipman was an eloquent and intelligent man, and his arguments were not wholly without persuasion. He, too, claimed that the treaty created two classes of rivers — those falling into the Atlantic, and all others. And neither the Bay of Fundy nor the Gulf of St. Lawrence was the "Atlantic." He fastened on the idea of "highlands" rather than "watershed," and made some points on that score. He was able to produce some grants according to which Nova Scotia had anciently been considered to extend right across the disputed territory, and asserted that the latter had always continued under the jurisdiction of Great Britain.

Yet when we consider the matter in perspective and without national prejudice we cannot fail to see the justice of the American claim. The eminent New Brunswick historian and scientist William F. Ganong, who went into the dispute more thoroughly than any man before or since, summed up the question in a passage that is difficult to improve on and is therefore worth quoting *in extenso*:

> In the light of the documents of the time, of the maps, of our knowledge of the negotiations leading up to the treaty, of the character of the negotiators of the treaty, of the legal boundaries of Nova Scotia, Massachusetts, and Quebec, when all were under one government, there seems no doubt that the negotiators did choose the old line between Massachusetts and Nova Scotia and hence had to run the boundary as the Americans have always claimed. It is a fact that the boundary between Massachusetts and Nova Scotia did, in pre-revolutionary times extend to these highlands. This was through no virtue or merit of Massachusetts nor the reward of any exertion of hers, but purely the result of the way in which the boundaries happened to be drawn by the authorities at a time when both were under the same government, and when it appeared to matter very little to which of the two portions of the Empire this small portion of unsettled wilderness belonged. In other words, it was a pure piece of luck for Massachusetts that at the time of the revolution her boundaries did extend so far north. It turned out, however, that this luck-boundary of Massachusetts, of no particular consequence before the revolution, became of immense consequence to Great Britain after it, for it happened to cut across the invaluable line of communication between two of her remaining provinces, and, indeed, for a part of the year, across the only communication of one of them with Great Britain. The territory in question, therefore, while of very slight value to Massachusetts [and later Maine], who had there no settlers and no interests, was of immediate and immense importance to Great Britain. Great Britain then hoped to secure a readjustment in this region for an equivalent elsewhere, but Massachusetts showed from the very start that she intended to insist upon her pound of flesh. The consideration of the great value of the region to Great Britain for her communication from province to province, and its comparative worthlessness to her, weighed not in the least with Massachusetts [and her offspring, Maine], nor would it weigh with any other nation of the time, nor with any nation to-day; for nations, in their dealings with one another are not guided by the commend-

able Christian sentiments expressed in the preambles to their
treaties. All of the men interested in this subject in New Brunswick, and the British government itself down to 1814, appear to
have taken it as a matter of course that so anomalous an arrangement from the point of view of convenience could be in some way
adjusted by negotiation on the basis of *quid pro quo.* But all such
hope was dispelled by the preliminaries to the Treaty of Ghent,
and it became evident that if Great Britain was to preserve her
interests in this corner, it must be by her wits. With nations the
end usually justifies the means, and here was a case in which the
end must have seemed to the British particularly justifiable.

Thomas Barclay and the Chipmans were less than sincere in that
they pretended to demand as a right what they craved as a convenience; but pretence has ever been of the essence in international
bargaining, and recourse to it is dictated by circumstances.

Even while the surveys were still going on, however, a political
event occurred which, though superficially unrelated to the boundary dispute, was to have a great and ominous influence on it: the
transformation of the northern district of Massachusetts into the
state of Maine, on March 15, 1820. Like most new-born political
entities, Maine was eager to prove her mettle and to make her
name, and the unsettled northern boundary was a ready-made issue.
It was, therefore, not long before state agents began to prowl about
the disputed territory, seeking by various ways to fortify the state's
claim. They took a census, they made land grants, and they encouraged the settlers to take official business to the state legislature at
Portland.

Such designs, of course, could prosper only if there were Maine
citizens residing in the disputed area, and the discovery, in the mid-
eighteen-twenties, of the handful of American settlers in Madawaska naturally gladdened the hearts of Maine's authorities.

But if the recent arrival of Americans strengthened the claim of
Maine, did not the older French community strengthen the claim
of Britain? Not at all, said the men of Maine; because these Frenchmen, or Acadians, were "neutrals," fugitives "stimulated by their
repugnance to the British," a "distinct race, a people by themselves,"
"without any sympathy" with the government of New Brunswick,

"a primitive population" acknowledging the patriarchal power of their religion and no other.

The New Brunswick authorities did not see it that way. They declared that the Madawaskans

> have received grants of land from the Government, and have, from the beginning, been enrolled in the militia; that they have voted at elections for the county of York; have applied to the Provincial courts for redress in all suits of law; and have been subject to all the duties, and exercised all the privileges, of other inhabitants of the Province.

A fairly balanced opinion comes from a later American observer, who wrote with the detachment of hindsight:

> There is little doubt that the Acadians knew very little of the new republic, and what little they knew would not make them anxious to take residence within its borders. . . . They were self-governing and desired to be let alone.

Governor Lincoln received the first news of John Baker's arrest in a complaint mailed from one of the northern post offices. Lincoln was then thirty-eight years old, and in his second year of governorship. He hailed from Massachusetts (where his brother Levi was Governor) and had sat for eight years in the United States House of Representatives, as a somewhat colourless lawyer.

Lincoln immediately dispatched a letter to the Lieutenant-Governor of New Brunswick, asking for an explanation of the arrest. Douglas coldly replied that it would be improper for him to enter into discussions infringing on international relations.

Douglas, a redoubtable warrior, had of course expected a sharp reaction from Maine when he ordered Baker's arrest, but the prospect had not deterred him. "If Baker had not been proceeded against," he later informed the Colonial Office, "or if the proceedings against him had been abandoned, our actual possession and jurisdiction [of Madawaska] would have been entirely subverted."

Sir Howard Douglas, like most colonial governors, had been rewarded with his post for military services. Born in 1776, he first set foot on North American soil in 1795, after suffering shipwreck and narrowly overcoming a mutiny. He served in Lower and Upper Canada, and one winter distinguished himself by skating all the way from Montreal to Quebec City to attend a ball, an exploit that cost a fellow officer who accompanied him his life. He married in England in 1799, and had six sons and three daughters. During most of the Napoleonic Wars he was busy as a military instructor, though he participated in the Peninsular Campaign. He was appointed Lieutenant-Governor of New Brunswick in 1823.

Having been rebuffed by Douglas, Governor Lincoln applied for assistance to the United States Government. At the same time he appointed a prominent citizen of Maine, Charles Daveis, to travel to New Brunswick as his agent to obtain information and, if possible, Baker's release. President John Quincy Adams, in turn, also appointed an agent, S. B. Barrell. The two men reached New Brunswick in the late fall of 1827. On the diplomatic front, the United States Secretary of State Henry Clay requested the British Minister Sir Charles Vaughan to intercede with Douglas, but Douglas was backed by London.

Douglas, true to his stand, refused to acknowledge Daveis, though he permitted him to visit Baker, who was lodged in Fredericton debtor's prison, a British institution later to be immortalized by Dickens. (By an ill-starred coincidence, a £230 debt from Lower Canada had just then caught up with Baker, so that he would have been in debtor's prison anyway.) Daveis did his best to cheer Baker up, and to stiffen his resolve against acknowledging British authority. Beyond that he could do little but submit a report to Governor Lincoln, couched in extremely anti-British terms.

Barrell, the federal agent, carried an introduction from the British envoy and got a friendly reception from Douglas. He also saw Baker, and made a trip up to Madawaska where he interviewed numerous settlers. On his return to Washington he too submitted a report, but it was of a very different tenor from Daveis's. It was, in fact, so damaging to Maine's pretensions in Madawaska that it might well have been composed by Douglas himself. Barrell stated that the French Madawaskans had uniformly acknowledged British jurisdiction; that the rule of Britain in the disputed area had been just and restrained, even to the extent of ceasing to make land grants to her own subjects so as not to prejudice the boundary question; that the Americans both in Madawaska and farther south, on the western branches of the St. John, were interlopers and opportunists, who sought British legal aid in debt collection when it suited them, and refused British jurisdiction when others tried to collect from them. As far as Baker himself was concerned, Barrell turned up the curious fact that in 1825 Baker had actually been on a trip south to Fredericton to seek naturalization as a British subject when he happened to meet two official land agents, from Maine and Massachusetts, who practically bribed him with a promise of a deed to his homestead (which Baker knew he could not get from the British) to make him turn back and retain his American citizenship. (The agents had been on their way to Madawaska for the express purpose of asserting the American claim by granting pre-emption deeds in the disputed territory. Douglas, who soon learned of these grants, several times complained about them to the Colonial Office.)

The failure of its intervention produced in the Maine Government a sense of helpless anger. In his annual message, on January 3, 1828, Governor Lincoln hinted that even war with Britain might not be far off.

> If that melancholy result of human frailty shall be produced . . . the seaboard, and the interior of Maine, will be the one a line of maritime invasion and the other of excursions and incursions according to the emergencies relating to our defense.

Hinting at the British occupation of northern Maine in 1814, he exhorted the citizens "not to admit any repetition here of such scenes as occurred during the last war."

Meanwhile, Baker's wife and children were without income, and to help them the state granted them $212. The money was later reimbursed to Maine by the Federal Government.

In Fredericton, justice took its leisurely course. Baker was arraigned for trial at the February session of the Supreme Court, pleaded not guilty, and asked a postponement of the trial to obtain witnesses and counsel. A little later he posted bail of £100.

And now the trial had been held, and Baker had been found guilty.

Five days later the judges of the New Brunswick Supreme Court returned to the courtroom and sentenced Baker to two months in prison, and to pay a fine of £25, and to remain in prison until the fine was paid. It was a surprisingly mild sentence, considering the charges; but the trial had served its purpose, and there was no need to be vindictive. It was, Lieutenant-Governor Douglas wrote to his superiors, "a trial conducted in all respects in a very liberal and satisfying manner."

But Baker, still glorying in his fame and the official backing of his Government, continued impenitent. "He now states he will not pay his fine," Douglas reported, "& that he will leave his case, & trust to his liberation entirely to be brought about by the measures of the Government of the United States." The Colonial Office, willing to see the matter closed, authorized Douglas to remit the fine, but the Governor was adamant. It was not until October, 1828, however, that Baker despaired of official succour and, growing weary of his jail (which, admittedly, was of the worst description) paid his fine and went home to Sophie and the children.

By that time the flag-raising in Madawaska was fading into the background in Maine and New Brunswick, for the battle over the boundary had shifted to another stage. It has already been noted that the Treaty of Ghent provided for the reference of unresolved boundary disputes to "a friendly sovereign or state," but after the final stormy meeting of the Boundary Commission in 1822 four years passed before this clause was acted on. Albert Gallatin, a prominent American politician of Swiss birth who had been one of the negotiators at Ghent, was sent to London in 1826 to attempt a settlement of the differences in bilateral negotiations. When this proposal failed, arbitration by a neutral was agreed to on September 29, 1827, (in the same month that Baker was arrested). The following June, William, King of the Netherlands, was chosen as arbitrator. (The Netherlands then comprised Holland, Belgium, and Luxembourg.)

The convention of arbitration was received with equanimity in

New Brunswick, but in Maine it aroused feelings even more vexatious than the Baker incident. Arbitration seemed synonymous with compromise; it meant to deliver the clear-cut boundary question into the long-fingered hands of shifty European intrigants and their Machiavellian diplomacy. It meant, also, the encroachment of federal power upon states' rights. Governor Lincoln summed up such sentiments in a sarcastic letter to President Adams:

> It would be unsuitable for me to comment on the dispositions or talents of foreign Sovereigns or States, but it is not in cold blood that I can anticipate the committing of the destinies of Maine to an irresponsible arbiter to be found in a distant land. . . . [Arbitration] is the delegation of Sovereignty to a despot.

Lincoln's dislike of arbitration was not abated by an incautious remark by Gallatin (who was preparing the United States case) that "an umpire, whether King or farmer, rarely decides on strict principles of law; — he has always a bias to try if possible to split the difference." In any case, the Maine Governor advised the President, "it is not believed that either the treaty-making or executive power of the United States extends to the cession or exchange of the territory of any state."

The sentiments expressed by the Governor were shared both by the legislature of the state and the citizenry in general. They were taken seriously even by Sir Howard Douglas, who voiced the belief that, if the case went against Maine's claim, the state would rebel and imperil "the very existence of the Union."

Historians like to amuse themselves and their readers by recalling the low expectations and prices often attached to certain pieces of real estate which, a century or two later, turned out to be of immense value. The twenty-four dollars for which Peter Minuit bought Manhattan Island from the Indians is part of folk-lore. Perhaps less sensational, but not less amusing, are the opposite cases. Thus it is somewhat difficult for us to appreciate the extravagant expectations entertained by Maine officials concerning the disputed backwoods, which Governor Lincoln hailed as

> a wild and fertile territory, embracing about six millions of acres. It is not necessary now to speak of its distinguished natural advant-

ages, which impart to it the capacity of sustaining some hundred thousand yeomen. Valuable, or rather invaluable, as it is . . .

To New Brunswick, as we have seen, and to Britain the disputed territory appeared in a different light. Its natural resources in soil and forest were modest beside its strategic value. In winter, when the broad St. Lawrence estuary became an icy wasteland impassable to shipping, the only communication between the Maritimes and the rest of British North America lay via the frozen roadway of the St. John River, for there was as yet no road. As late as 1842, when the mail coach and horses started to break through the river ice in spring, men would shoulder the bags and scramble along the shore and through gaps in the woods as best they could so that vital messages would get through between Quebec City and Fredericton. The route went up the St. John valley as far as the mouth of the Madawaska, where it turned north to Lake Temiscouata and on to Rivière-du-Loup, thence to Quebec City.

The arguments were to be submitted to the King of the Netherlands exclusively in writing, and both sides left no stone unturned and no document unstudied to present as convincing a case as was humanly possible. On the British side, the submission was prepared in the Foreign Office with the assistance of Ward Chipman Jr., who had gone to London in the winter of 1828-29, joined later by Sir Howard Douglas himself, who insisted on having a hand in the business. The British looked forward to the arbitration with reasonable confidence, not only because the procedure itself was prone to compromise but also because the Netherlands was traditionally within the British sphere of influence, and the Dutch king dependent on British support.

The preparation of the United States case was in the able hands of Albert Gallatin, assisted by William Pitt Preble. Preble, a former justice of the Maine Supreme Court, rejoiced in the title of "Envoy Extraordinary and Minister Plenipotentiary of the United States near the Government of the Netherlands," though, judging by his subsequent conduct, the title "Ambassador of Maine" would have been more appropriate. His view of the case was summed up in

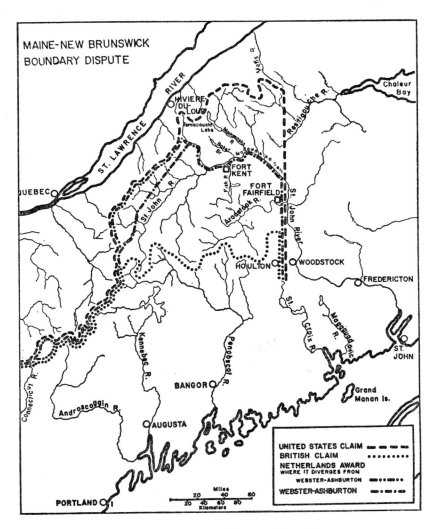

Maine-New Brunswick Boundary Dispute

1829 when, on a tour of his native state, he assured his country-men that

> while streams and rivers maintain their course, preserving their accustomed channels, and mountains and highlands maintain their place sustained by their ancient foundations, the character of the claim [of Maine] will remain written on the face of the earth itself by the finger of heaven.

Flowery words, perhaps; but they had their roots in a proposition that was beautiful in its stark, literal simplicity, geopolitical considerations notwithstanding. Just as the ancient Jews recoiled in contempt and horror from the Hellenistic sophistry of Father, Son, and Holy Ghost, and clung to the God Who is One God, so also the rugged men of Maine would with truly fundamentalist zeal scorn the subtleties and artifices of British diplomacy and, year after year, proclaim the one and only true boundary covenanted in 1783.

To assist him in delivering the United States case at The Hague, Preble prevailed on President Adams to appoint none other than Charles Daveis, who had reported in vitriolic terms on Baker's imprisonment. Maine's claim could not have been in better hands if the state legislature had repaired to The Hague in a body.

But the British were not caught napping, either. Their case was delivered at The Hague by Dr. Tiarks and a Foreign Office official named William Pitt Adams (the name William Pitt was obviously popular on both sides of the Atlantic); and Douglas, overcoming the dainty scruples of Lord Aberdeen over admitting so special a pleader, also procured an authorization to proceed to the Netherlands capital, where he then procured an audience with the king. There he slyly dropped into the royal ear a few well-chosen words as to Gallatin's supposed readiness to "split the difference." As to W. P. Adams, he too was wondering aloud whether the arbiter might not find a *"tertium quid,"* a compromise that would give to Britain half of the St. John valley. He feared, however, that Preble would not go along with such a solution.

The British and the United States cases and countercases were submitted to the King of the Netherlands in 1830, and while the advisers of the king were examining them, an event occurred which none of the statesmen had foreseen. On William's birthday, August 24, 1830, a rebellion against his throne began in the southern part of the country, and by December its break-up into two separate and independent states — Holland and Belgium — was internationally recognized. William retained Holland only.

Shortly after, on January 10, 1831, the king handed down the arbitration award. It was a lengthy and involved document written in French, but its gist was clear: finding that neither the American nor the British claim was in exact agreement with the treaty, and that the treaty was, furthermore, incapable of implementation, a conventional or compromise boundary should be adopted. This boundary should run along the due-north line as far as the St. John River; then up that river as far as the mouth of the St. Francis River; up that river to the St. Lawrence watershed; along that watershed to the head of the Connecticut River proper, and down that river to the forty-fifth parallel. As to the parallel, the king recommended that a new line be surveyed, but that the Rouses Point fort should in any case remain in the possession of the United States.

As soon as United States Minister William Pitt Preble received the award he went into action. He first of all protested the decision to the Dutch Government on the ground that the arbiter had exceeded his terms of reference. (In reporting this to Washington, he commented blandly: "I am fully aware that I have assumed some responsibility; at the same time, I am also aware that the government of the United States are not at all committed by any act of mine.") He then dashed off a confidential report to the government of Maine, speeding it on its way via Liverpool and New York. Finally, he dispatched the text of the award to Washington, on a leisurely and circuitous route through France and New Orleans.

Elaborating on his rejection of the award in a private letter to his friend, Governor Samuel E. Smith of Maine (Governor Lincoln had died in October, 1829), Preble wrote:

The revolution in France and the troubles in Belgium left to the government [of the Netherlands] not even the show of independence, but, drawing aside the veil of form, exhibited King and Court as the humble, entreating, subservient dependents of Great Britain. . . . So much, however, had been said by courtiers and others of the King's integrity and sense of justice, that, contrary to my own internal conviction, I suffered myself to hope even against hope. . . . In the meantime events continued to transpire and the instances of quibbling, evasion and petty cunning which came to my knowledge exhibiting a mind mistaking puerile subterfuge for great sagacity and bad faith for policy taught me how little the United States, under existing circumstances, had to expect from his Majesty's integrity and sense of justice.

Though it may have ill behooved Preble to charge subterfuge, his accusation concerning William's pro-British bias was not perhaps without a grain of truth. Though the boundary the king had recommended left the United States with almost two-thirds of the disputed territory — and by far the most valuable portion in soil and timber — he did give Britain precisely that which W. P. Adams hoped he would, namely the coveted line of communication. (It may be amusing that, immediately after he completed his mission to The Hague, Douglas was instructed by the British Government, in collaboration with that of Holland, to make a secret inspection tour of the Dutch defences against a possible Belgian rebel invasion. London was obviously thinking of shoring up the Dutch monarchy should this become necessary.)

It was therefore not surprising that Foreign Secretary Lord Palmerston, on February 9, 1831, notified the British Minister in Washington that Britain accepted the Netherlands award without hesitation, and hoped that the United States would do the same.

Washington learned of the award from European newspapers some time in February, but there was no word from the United States Minister. It could, however, see an augury of things to come in the ominous subterranean rumblings in Portland, erupting finally in a resolution which roundly rejected the Netherlands award and notified the Federal Government that Maine would have no part of it. Finally, on March 16, 1831, the long-delayed dispatch arrived at the State Department, over two months after the announcement of the award at The Hague.

Years later it became known that President Andrew Jackson was disposed to accept the award as definitive, without referring it to the Senate. He was, much to his subsequent regret, dissuaded from doing so by party friends who feared that acceptance would result in the overthrow of the Democrats in Maine, and Jackson needed every bit of support in the national bank issue.

The chances of the award in the United States Senate looked fairly bright. Senator Tazewell, chairman of the foreign-relations committee, was strongly in its favour, as were other influential senators.

In mid-July, 1831, Preble arrived in New York on leave of absence, and hurried on to make a personal report — not indeed to the President, but to the Governor of Maine in Portland. When he did come to the federal capital it was as Maine's special representative to influence developments in the United States Senate. The debate in that body dragged on far into 1832. To increase the possibility of acceptance Palmerston went so far as to suggest the award might be modified according to mutual convenience. The Federal Government, anxious to do its part, obtained from Maine a free hand in the disputed territory in return for deeding over to the state a choice parcel of public lands elsewhere. (This deal was not ratified, however.) Preble was lobbying against the award with might and main, sending to Maine dramatic daily bulletins on the progress of the debate. Gradually, the tide of amendments and resolutions turned against the award, and it was finally rejected in July, 1832, on the ostensible ground that it exceeded the arbiter's terms of reference.

In the meantime, Maine had launched an action calculated to destroy the conciliatory spirit then prevailing between the two national governments, and to forestall the implementation of the award by a *fait accompli*. As far as New Brunswick was concerned, the moment seemed propitious, for the resourceful Sir Howard Douglas had relinquished the lieutenant-governorship while in England, and the province was in an interregnum, being administered by a local politician, William Black.

On March 15, 1831, the state legislature passed an act incorporating the Madawaska Settlements as a town under the laws of Maine. To give practical force to this step they dispatched to Madawaska two agents, John G. Deane and Edward Kavanagh, who in the summer of 1831 made a hurried survey of the settlement, posted notices of a judicial order which required the Madawaskans to form a town administration, and left, trusting to John Baker and his fellow Americans to do the rest. The shortness of their stay may have been due, in part, to the primitive hospitality to be found among the sturdy backwoodsmen; in their subsequent report to the legislature the agents reported that a meal at an Acadian inn consisted of "rancid pork, which we could not eat, very poor butter, tea and bread middling, and potatoes good. The bill we had to pay was extravagant." In part, as we shall see, they may have had more complicated motives for their hasty departure.

In their reliance on the American settlers the Maine authorities were not disappointed. On August 20, 1831, the Americans called together a town meeting of fifty to sixty persons at the home of a French settler, sixty-three-year-old Pierre Lizotte, a man of substance and authority among his countrymen. However, two New Brunswick militia officers, Francis Rice and Leonard Coombes, were also present and tried to dissuade the French from taking part. Lizotte thereupon refused to let the assembly use his house, and the meeting adjourned to a cart in the field. Here several of the Americans were elected municipal officers in accordance with the Maine writ. John Baker, though much in evidence at the gathering, did not seek office.

Another town meeting was called on September 12, for the election of a representative in the state legislature. About fifteen Frenchmen and twelve Americans voted, the candidates being Baker and Lizotte. The latter had evidently succumbed to the prospect of legislative perquisites dangled before him by the Americans, and he was elected with twenty-one votes.

It was at just this juncture that the New Brunswick interregnum came to an end with the arrival of the new Lieutenant-Governor,

Sir Archibald Campbell. Campbell, born in 1769, was a soldier like his predecessor. Most of his campaigning had taken place in India, although, like nearly all British officers, he had got in his licks in the Peninsular War under Wellington. His most recent exploit was the subjugation of Burma in 1824-26, which had brought him great honours in Britain and, in due course, the New Brunswick appointment. Unlike Douglas, he carried over the habits of the garrison and the drill field into civil government.

Immediately upon his instalment in Government House in Fredericton, Campbell was apprised of the goings-on in Madawaska. "It is with infinite regret," he wrote to the Colonial Secretary, "that I find myself called upon — in this my first Communication, — to acquaint Your Lordship with an act of unwarrantable aggression on the part of the State of Maine." After reciting the events since the visit of Deane and Kavanagh, and emphasizing Maine's belligerence, he added:

> I cannot but feel some anxiety relative to the total inadequacy of the military means and resources of the Province. . . . The whole force at my disposal consists but of six companies of Rifles, and a very few Artillery Men, for I can scarcely consider the ill organized and worse equipped Militia . . . as coming under the head of an efficient force to take the field with. . . . At least two Regiments should be placed at my disposal.

He thus inaugurated a long series of complaints about the poor state of the province's defences.

Being, however, a man of action rather than words, he put himself at the head of an expedition and set off up the St. John River to Madawaska, to investigate the affair in person. Also up-river went a sheriff with warrants for the arrest of the men chiefly concerned in the two elections. What followed was later described to the state authorities by John Baker.

Around noon on September 26, 1831, Baker said, he saw about twenty canoes come up the river at great speed and land a short distance below his house. Knowing what was on foot, he prudently retired to the woods, leaving his wife to deal with the invaders, in whose chivalry he evidently reposed a boundless trust. Through the trees he saw men armed with muskets enter his and other houses. ("*La vice-présidente de la république, l'héroïne de Mériumticook, la Lucrèce du Madawaska, la Barbara Fritchie de l'Aroostook,* comme l'appelaient ses admirateurs et compatriotes, Madame Baker, seule, reçut froidement les visiteurs," says a French-Canadian chronicler.) After a while, Sophie Baker sneaked out to her husband and told him that several of the "town officials" had been taken prisoner, and that he, Baker, was also wanted.

While they were whispering under the trees, Baker saw a horse-boat coming up the river with more armed men. He sent his wife off to find out what these newcomers were after, and was informed that they intended to continue to the other Americans' houses farther up-stream. To frustrate their design, Baker set off through the woods at sundown and got to the up-river farms in the middle of the night. There he roused the men, and most of them took to the woods with him. They hid out for several days, after which one of the wives told them that the British had vowed to arrest them whenever they should show themselves. Thereupon Baker, without again setting foot in the settlement, made his way south to Portland to carry his tale to the state authorities, arriving in the Maine capital thirteen days later.

Actually, only four Americans were captured by the sheriff. "The Frenchmen who were overpersuaded to join them," the attorney-general reported, "have also been apprehended, but they all gave bail for their appearance at the Court and therefore were not committed." Campbell ascribed the participation of the French entirely to American instigation and was inclined to be easy on them.

> Before the intriguing emissaries of the neighbouring state appeared among them [he reported to the Colonial Office] there was not perhaps upon the Globe a more contented people than these almost unknown Acadians. . . . I had scarcely reached the Settlement ere I was apprized that the Self-Constituted American Authorities . . . had, with an excess of insolence and daring . . . actually nominated and returned a Captain of our Militia — a Frenchman named Lizotte to represent the Settlement . . . in the

Legislature of Maine — an honour which Captain Lizotte however very properly declined.

How much Lizotte's declining the honour had to do with the sudden appearance of the Lieutenant-Governor in the midst of his people is a matter for speculation. Campbell did not overstate the case when he remarked that the pressures of the boundary dispute had placed the French Madawaskans "in a cruel and trying situation."

Three of the Americans — Barnabas Hannawell, Jesse Wheelock, and Daniel Savage — were tried in New Brunswick Supreme Court on October 15 on charges arising out of the municipal election, found guilty, and fined £50 each and sentenced to three months in prison. Another trial was scheduled for February to deal with the election to the Maine legislature.

Campbell's quick and drastic action put Maine on the spot. Governor Smith was well aware of an understanding between London and Washington that both sides would refrain from any new attempts at exclusive jurisdiction in the disputed territory, as well as Secretary of State Martin Van Buren's request that Maine refrain from actions likely to "interrupt or embarrass" the negotiations of the Federal Government with Britain. But Campbell alone could free the prisoners, and Campbell could be got at only via Washington and the Foreign Office.

Smith therefore did an odd thing: he coupled his appeal to Washington for aid with a declaration that the state government had had nothing to do with the two elections in Madawaska and had, in fact, known nothing about them until the arrests; that the Americans in the settlement had acted entirely on their own initiative, as individual citizens; and that it was therefore up to the Federal Government to look to their liberation. This stratagem has been not unjustly characterized by one of Smith's successors as a blot on the history of the state "which we might well desire to have expunged from our annals."

The long-suffering Federal Government, through the then Secretary of State Edward Livingston, asked the British chargé d'affaires to intervene for the release of the three prisoners. This had its desired effect, and the three men were set free early in November 1831.

With this stalemate both on the diplomatic and on the local front a temporary relaxation spread over the disputed territory. The Madawaska Settlements were, it is true, incorporated as a town or parish by the New Brunswick legislature in 1833, but since this was merely one of many acts of *de facto* jurisdiction there it attracted no notice.

But the relative calm on the New Brunswick-Maine frontier was compensated by a brief but hectic interlude elsewhere along the controversial boundary.

It will be recalled that the disagreement between the boundary commissioners under Article 5 of the Treaty of Ghent had created not just one but several disputed areas. Of these, that between Maine and New Brunswick was the largest, and the narrow strip between the true and the false forty-fifth parallels the smallest. Between them lay the several sources of the Connecticut River, spread out like the fingers of a hand. The treaty required that the boundary should run from the "northwesternmost head" of the Connecticut River down the middle of that river to the forty-fifth parallel. The British, seizing on the words "Connecticut River," claimed the easternmost branch, flowing through a chain of lakes and known as *the* Connecticut River. The United States representatives, fastening on "northwesternmost," after some vacillation favoured that known as Hall's Stream.

The area embraced by the two lines had absolutely no strategic value; it was traversed by no road or trade route; it did not even contain what could properly be called a village; and its agricultural resources were meager. It was in dispute only because of the inveterate proclivity of boundary negotiators to see in the advancement of extreme claims merely the proof of duty well done.

The area had seen its first settlers at almost exactly the same time as Madawaska, except that in this case the pioneers were Americans rather than Acadians. The settlement came about through the "purchase" of enormous tracts of land (covering nearly

the whole northern half of New Hampshire) by two rival
colonization companies, one known as Bedel, the other as Eastman,
from local Indians. Since United States law did not recognize such
purchases by private bodies, the whole enterprise was illegal from
its inception, but it took many years before this became a public
issue. The two purchases overlapped almost completely; both
included all of the disputed territory, known generally by the name
of one of the Connecticut's branches, Indian Stream.

The rivalry between the two companies did not exactly favour
rapid and confident settlement, since competing agents would try to
scare off each other's customers, which in turn caused a good deal
of bad blood among the settlers themselves. It may therefore
truthfully be said that dissension and doubtful legality were the
godparents of the troubled community which grew up in the
eighteen-twenties and eighteen-thirties in this remote and rugged
piece of land.

The settlers had their first taste of official interference in the
mid-eighteen-twenties, when the state of New Hampshire started
proceedings against several of them for illegal squatting because
of the invalid Indian title, an accusation that should have been
addressed to the speculators. The farmers already felt neglected by
the two land companies (which merged in 1829), since promised
public works such as road-building had not been done, and a
general feeling of alienation induced them to look to their own
interests by setting up rudimentary public bodies. Aware that the
British authorities kept alive a formal claim to the territory, they
went so far as to appeal in 1826 to Alexander Rea, a Canadian
land agent and magistrate in adjoining Hereford, to assist them
in expanding their holdings. Rea passed the matter on to the
surveyor-general of Lower Canada — our acquaintance from
boundary-survey days, Joseph Bouchette — but nothing came of it.

In 1831 there were about seventy families in Indian Stream,
most of them living along the north bank of the Connecticut River.
In that year, the King of the Netherlands awarded the Indian
Stream territory to Britain. Though the decision was not accepted
by the United States, it made a strong impression in Indian Stream

and provided the final impetus toward a declaration of independence. The restless backwoodsmen had discovered (as has many a newer nation) that by organizing themselves into a nominally independent community they could play both ends against the middle, particularly as concerned the contraction and repudiation of debts, for the debt collector was regarded by all frontiersmen as Public Enemy No. 1.

In June, 1832, the inhabitants appointed a committee to draft a constitution and a code of laws, which was done in proper style, and on July 9 the new state was proclaimed by a vote of fifty-six to three.

The United States customs men on the spot were quick to take appropriate action, and began to levy duty on Indian Stream produce being carried to New Hampshire or Vermont. (Lower Canada had never levied duty, but this was unimportant, since the trade of Indian Stream was mainly southward.) More serious yet was the action of the New Hampshire authorities, who in August, 1834, entered the territory to collect debts. The council, the governing body of the territory, sent a protest to Washington, and was told, somewhat cryptically, that the inhabitants could not claim United States protection without acknowledging the jurisdiction of New Hampshire. The sheriffs were back in winter, and again in the spring of 1835, but were then beaten off by the settlers, who had also started to build a blockhouse for the defence of their country.

These events attracted the attention of Lord Aylmer, the Lieutenant-Governor of Lower Canada, in Quebec City, and in April of 1835 he sent a protest to the British Minister in Washington, who began discussions with the United States Secretary of State. New Hampshire, on the other hand, also took steps to strengthen its claim, and in August the state government sent a company of militia consisting of fifty men to Stewartstown, just south of Indian Stream, as a military demonstration.

Such pressures could not fail to produce in Indian Stream another phenomenon peculiar to weak nations coveted by powerful neighbours, namely the growth of factions seeking the support of

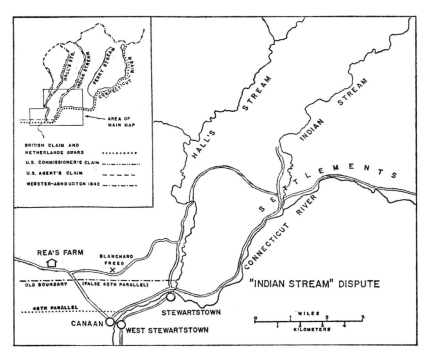

"Indian Stream" Boundary Dispute between Lower Canada and New Hampshire.

the outside antagonists. One Luther Parker, having fallen from grace in the ruling circles of the republic, plotted to invoke the authority of New Hampshire. He was opposed by Jonathan L. Knight, whose feelings leaned toward Britain, as did those of most Indian Stream inhabitants. Britain had not so far interfered in their affairs, *i.e.,* it had not sent in debt collectors. The two men came to blows, and Parker drew a butcher knife, though apparently without seriously wounding Knight. Knight complained to Rea in Lower Canada, and Rea did two things: he had Parker arrested and taken to jail in Sherbrooke, where he was later freed for lack of a true bill; and he also forwarded a petition to the Lieutenant-Governor requesting British protection for Indian Stream. Word was passed back to Rea from Quebec that "legal protection" would be given to the inhabitants of Indian Stream, and Rea, after calling a public meeting on September 26, 1835, passed the assurance on to the Indian Stream residents and advised them to choose magistrates under British law.

These activities did not sit well with the New Hampshire patriots, and they struck back in mid-October. The Indian Stream settlers were in the habit of getting their merchandise and their liquor at a general store and tavern run by Josiah Parmelly and Nehemiah Joy in Canaan, Vermont, just across the river from both New Hampshire and Indian Stream. The storekeepers had unsuccessfully tried to collect a debt from John H. Tyler of Indian Stream, and a warrant for Tyler's arrest was placed in the hands of a New Hampshire sheriff. The sheriff entered Indian Stream, and with the aid of two men, one of them a resident of the place, arrested Tyler. They had not got very far with their prisoner, however, when they were stopped by nine settlers of the pro-British faction, who by various threats persuaded the sheriff to release Tyler.

Three or four days later Tyler visited Rea and swore out a complaint against the three men who had tried to carry him off. The one who was a resident of Indian Stream, by the name of Richard J. Blanchard, was arrested on Rea's warrant on the morning of October 22 by two Canadians, Zebulon Flanders and Zacheus Clough, and Tyler. They had the more reason to go after

Blanchard as he had previously been of the pro-British faction and among the signers of an anti-New Hampshire petition. Loyalties in Indian Stream bent with the wind.

As the three men were marching their prisoner toward Rea's they were joined by several others of the pro-British faction, for a rumour had got about that the New Hampshirites would try to rescue Blanchard. To elude interceptors, they took a back road leading directly from Indian Stream across the mountain into Lower Canada, and had safely got into British territory within sight of Rea's farm when they were cut off by nine or ten men on horseback, armed with muskets, bayonets, and pistols. By threatening violence they freed Blanchard, and his former captors continued dejectedly on their way to Rea's, where they proceeded to swear out depositions.

Meanwhile the armed posse, with the liberated Blanchard, had made its triumphant arrival at Parmelly and Joy's tavern in Canaan, Vermont, where a large crowd from New Hampshire had begun to gather. Rum and patriotic discourse flowed freely, and it was not long before many of the men felt that the opportunities for glorious action had not been exhausted. The militia captain from Stewartstown, James Mooney, was among them, as was the deputy sheriff who had been frustrated in the arrest of Tyler. The sheriff was offering five dollars for Tyler's recapture. This meant another foray into Lower Canada. It was by this time late afternoon, and the assembly at the tavern had swelled to about one hundred — mostly armed, as it included a good number of Mooney's militia.

The distance from Canaan to Rea's place across the line was only about one and a half miles. Rea had just finished taking statements from the dozen or so men gathered in his house and they were leaving when one of them came running back, yelling, "They're coming!"

"Who's coming?" Rea asked.

"The New Hampshire fellows!"

Rea looked out the window and saw two horsemen drawn up on the highway talking to some of his friends. Carefully leaving his heavy walking-stick behind — he had a limp and was sometimes known as "Old Pumplefoot" — he stepped outside and walked toward the group, shouting at the riders to get off the King's highway and be gone. When he came closer he recognized them as Ephraim Aldrick and Miles Hurlburt, the former from Indian Stream and the latter a resident of Colebrook, New Hampshire. Hurlburt was pointing a brass-barrelled pistol. As Rea came up to them, Hurlburt levelled the gun at him and told him to stand off, "or, God damn you, I'll blow you through." To which Aldrick added, "Rea, you had better stand off, or he'll do you an injury."

This infuriated the magistrate, for Aldrick had been one of the pro-British faction in the disputed area, and had signed the petition to the Lieutenant-Governor. "If you have influence with this drunken fellow," Rea told Aldrick, "take him and yourself peaceably away over the line."

Aldrick told him to go to hell.

Rea then turned to one of his companions, a part-time Canadian peace officer by the name of Bernard Young, and commanded him to arrest Aldrick. Young took hold of the bridle of Aldrick's horse. Aldrick quickly pulled from the folds of his coat a cavalry saber and brought it down on Young's neck — though apparently not with the edge — hurling him to the ground. Almost at the same time some in Rea's party started to throw stones at the two intruders, Hurlburt fired his pistol, and Rea made a grab for Aldrick's bridle. The bullet hit Young in the thigh and passed through one of his testicles, and Aldrick made another pass with his saber and cut a gash in Rea's head. Having thus violently repulsed their would-be captors, Hurlburt and Aldrick wheeled about and started off toward the border. At this moment, however, the rest of the New Hampshire party, on horses and in wagons, appeared round the bend of the road, and the two returned to the attack.

Rea's party, being outnumbered and, of course, completely unarmed, dispersed in all directions. Rea himself went through a gate in his fence and made off across the field into a wood as fast as his lame leg would carry him. As he was running across the field Aldrick pulled the trigger on two pistols, but neither would fire, and disgustedly he threw the guns after the fleeing Rea and took up pursuit on foot. He caught up with the hapless magistrate at the edge of the wood, where Rea had stumbled over a log. Seizing the prone man by his neckerchief, Aldrick lunged at him with his saber, but Rea twisted around in time to seize the blade and turn it aside so that it plunged deep into the ground.

Aldrick tried to pull out his saber, but the fear-crazed Rea hung onto the blade with such desperate strength that it would not budge. Frustrated, Aldrick kicked and trampled the magistrate, swearing that he would have his heart's blood. By this time several other men of the New Hampshire party had come up, and they calmed Aldrick sufficiently to release Rea, whom they carried off as their prisoner. Covered with blood and dirt, and too exhausted to make much further protest, Rea was put on a wagon and taken to Canaan. No further attempts were made to recapture the fleeing Tyler.

The return of the posse with its blood-smeared prisoner at Parmelly and Joy's tavern provoked a mixed reaction. The more boisterous among the New Hampshirites rejoiced that they had in their power the man whom they considered the instigator of dissension and pro-British agitation in the disputed territory, but most of the calmer men thought matters had got out of hand. While Aldrick kept shouting for free liquor and a confused debate was taking place inside the tavern, Rea recognized among the mob several Vermonters who seemed disposed to help him. When the New Hampshirites attempted to take him out of the house to carry him to Colebrook jail, he caught hold of the arm of one of the Vermonters, who in turn hung on to the store counter, and after some tug-of-war Rea was permitted to be taken to an adjacent room where his wounds were looked after.

Night had now fallen. The excitement and inebriation subsided, the mob dispersed, and the magistrate was able to return home unmolested. There he found the unfortunate Young abed in great pain, and another two weeks went by before he could be moved to his own home. He never regained his former vigour.

On November 13, 1835, the adjutant-general of New Hampshire ordered Captain Mooney to occupy Indian Stream. Arriving in the territory a little before dawn with fifty militiamen, he surprised the defenders and captured their leaders. Those of the settlers who still retained pro-British sentiments were harassed by arrests and searches, and their womenfolk manhandled, until they pulled up stakes and took refuge in Canada.

The affair came at an awkward time for the Canadian authorities. The unrest that was to result in the Rebellion of 1837 was already in the air, and they did not want to risk the consequences of a border war. London had to content itself with vigorous diplomatic protests.

As to the victims of the fracas — Rea, Young, and some others — agitation for redress continued in Lower Canada for at least twenty years. Various small sums were eventually paid to them — Rea got £500 in 1853 and Young £250 — but there was probably no case in the history of the boundary where Britain failed more signally to sustain its adherents.

In New Brunswick the middle eighteen-thirties were characterized by a growing dissension between Lieutenant-Governor Archibald Campbell and the elected legislature over the disposition of the public revenue. Campbell believed that he was, at the very least, entitled to a veto on all expenditures. He especially resented the niggardly attitude of the people's representatives toward the militia, a matter that was naturally close to the heart of a martinet. Nor did he endear himself to London by his repeated complaints that he was hobbled by the military command in Halifax, and that the regular troops in his province were utterly insufficient. In 1836-37 matters reached the point where the New Brunswick legislature requested the Colonial Office to recall Campbell, and he left in May, 1837.

To fill the vacant post, the Colonial Secretary picked the Lieutenant-Governor of Prince Edward Island, Sir John Harvey. Harvey, born in 1777, had distinguished himself in the War of 1812, especially by storming the American camp at Stoney Creek, routing a force which outnumbered his own four to one. He served in North America until 1828, did a stretch as inspector-general of police in Ireland, and was sent to Prince Edward Island in 1836.

He was a large, florid man with a large family and an expansive style in both private and public affairs. He looked upon his appointment to the larger colony and the larger responsibilities in the face of American ebullience as eminently suited to his talents and accomplishments.

If anything marred this perfect suiting of man to task, it was the lack of military authority, which rested in the hands of the Lieutenant-Governor of Nova Scotia, Sir Colin Campbell, a friend and protégé of the Duke of Wellington. In what may pass as a fine example of early-Victorian officialese, Harvey informed the Colonial Secretary shortly after his arrival in Fredericton:

> I will not affect to conceal from your Lordship my impression that the selection, however accidental, for the Government of this Province of a Military Officer whose name is not unknown to the Military Annals of the United States, in connexion with many of the most successful defensive operations of the War which was entered into by that Government for the express object of extending its Territorial Possessions by the acquisition of the Canadas, may perhaps be a circumstance not ill calculated to check or render cautious the exertion of any overt Act of actual aggression upon a Territory in the charge of an officer who had, during the late War, acquired a character for promptness & Energy, some portion of which he might still be supposed to retain — but my Lord, so soon as it is publicly known that this officer does not possess the Military Authority enjoyed by his immediate and all his Predecessors & that he is merely entrusted with the administration of the Civil Affairs of the Colony, I am induced to apprehend that the knowledge of the circumstances may encourage measures of petty aggression which might otherwise not be attempted.

As it happened, a measure of petty aggression had been afoot in Madawaska for some time when Harvey wrote. One of the unorthodox financial legacies of Andrew Jackson was the "distribution of the surplus revenue" of the United States to individual states and citizens — a gambit that might engage the attention of modern Social Credit politicians — and the prerequisite for distribution was an accurate census. The state of Maine accordingly seized the opportunity to send into the disputed territory a census-taker by the name of Ebenezer S. Greely, who promised householders up to $3 each. Greely's census-taking and his promises soon brought about the normal reaction from the local New Brunswick magistrates, and he was arrested in Madawaska on May 29, 1837, and conveyed to Woodstock to be put in jail. The Woodstock sheriff, John Winslow, took a shrewd, hard look at his prospective prisoner and refused to lock him up. When upbraided for his action, Winslow replied that Greely had been suspiciously co-operative; he was practically eager to be jailed. If the Governor wanted Greely in jail, Winslow's twelve-year-old son could recapture him.

But the law-enforcement authorities of Fredericton were not impressed by such subtle reasonings, and when Greely again took up his work they had him rearrested on June 6 and conveyed to prison in Fredericton. By this time Harvey, too, was beginning to smell a rat, or rather two rats: Greely was quite likely sent by Maine as bait to provoke New Brunswick reaction and Washington counter-reaction; then again, the census might be "so far connected with Lower Canada as to be intended as a Diversion in favour of the Papineau Party by preventing Reinforcements of Troops being sent from Nova Scotia or from hence into the Province." This, of course, was a reference to the incipient rebellion in Lower Canada.

Maine reacted sharply. The state militia was ordered to hold itself ready "to bring forth military power" in supporting the claim to the disputed territory, and Washington was requested to intervene on Greely's behalf. This effected Greely's release on August 8. He returned to his home in Dover, Maine, and was promptly told to go back to census-taking in Madawaska. Nothing loath, he set out for the third time, and was for the third time arrested. This time it took longer to spring him, and it was not until February, 1838, that he was able to leave the New Brunswick capital — his jailers were extremely lenient with him and allowed him many liberties — and travel back to Augusta. (Augusta became the seat of the state government in 1832.) There the new administration of Governor Edward Kent (born 1802) pushed through a legislative resolve granting $500 to Greely for his trials and tribulations, and $675 to the Madawaska Americans, of which John Baker got the lion's share of $350. These sums were later reimbursed by Washington.

As to the French Madawaskans, Greely's forays left no appreciable effect. After making a tour of the settlements in September, 1837, Harvey was able to report that "nothing could exceed the enthusiasm of their Loyalty." He took back with him an address of welcome composed in French by the Madawaska priest Antoine Langevin, which said, in part:

> *Nos désirs et nos vœux sont de rester unis à l'Empire Britannique; mais nous voudrions aussi, jouir des privilèges dont jouissent tous les Sujets de Sa Majesté; et que le gouvernement, dans sa sagesse put de quelque manière faire dispraître les craintes et les appréhensions que nous avons d'être un jour annexés à une République étrangère où nous ne voyons aucune sécurité pour nos usages, non plus que pour notre Religion, nous prions donc très humblement votre Excellence de porter son attention sur ce Sujet.*

There was one other piece of boundary controversy that Harvey was called on to dispose of soon after his appointment. A group of businessmen in Quebec and New Brunswick had hit upon the idea — perfectly natural in itself — of building a railway from the lower province to St. Andrews, to be known as the "St. Andrews and Quebec Railroad." Unfortunately, such a line was feasible only if it passed up the St. John valley through the disputed territory, and it is a measure of Lieutenant-Governor Sir Archibald Campbell's narrow nationalism that he did not see anything incongruous in such an undertaking, even though he had angrily protested the construction of a road by Maine from Houlton to the Aroostook. He did, in fact, further the railway scheme by helping to obtain Treasury authorization for the expenditure of £10,000 on a survey, and in the summer of 1836 he sent an army engineer to make a confidential inspection of the proposed route. Such goings-on did not long remain secret, and the strong and justified objections of the United States caused Harvey, in concert with the Colonial Office, to instruct the railway promoters to suspend their activities.

At the onset of winter, 1837, such questions seemed no longer important, for the Rebellion was in full swing in Lower and Upper

Canada, and the authorities everywhere in British North America thought of little else but the volatile emotions of the subjects in their care, and the harrowing possibility of sympathetic intervention from south of the border.

On the first count, at least, Harvey had no fear: "The universal feeling of Loyal Enthusiasm which pervades the People of this Province is scarcely to be described." Having been allowed the military command in New Brunswick (though still subordinate to Sir Colin Campbell in Halifax), Harvey offered the Governor-in-Chief of British North America whatever militia he might want, and he also dispatched two regiments of regulars to Lower Canada. The soldiers were marched on the frozen St. John through the disputed territory, a fact which was carefully communicated to the United States Government. Washington raised no objection. Harvey himself obeyed a summons to visit the Governor-in-Chief, the Earl of Durham, in Quebec in the summer of 1838, by which time the rebellion had been overcome in the Canadas, and there were only border raids to worry about from fugitive "Patriots" and Irish-American sympathizers.

In the disputed territory itself there was a new development, or, more exactly, an old practice developing into new prominence. This was illicit lumbering.

Contrary to the propaganda of Maine colonizers, the disputed territory had few areas suitable for agriculture. But, being remote and generally without legal protection, it had preserved intact extensive stands of virgin timber along the rivers, where it was easy to cut and float. Lumber had always been the mainstay of New Brunswick's economy, especially for export to Britain. (Sir Howard Douglas continued to fight for the retention of tariff preferences for North American lumber long after his term of office in New Brunswick.) As the forests receded along the lower St. John, the woodcutters moved up the river and its tributaries, especially the Aroostook, deep in the disputed territory. These activities were frowned on by New Brunswick authorities. They issued no licences to cut lumber in the disputed area, and a "Warden of the Disputed Territory," James MacLauchlan, was appointed specifi-

cally to police the woods and to seize illicit lumber, proceeds from
its sale being put into a "Disputed Territory Fund." Unfortunately,
the illegal lumberers, a tough lot composed of small farmers and
squatters out of luck or out of favour with the law and the debt
collectors, were abetted by the large lumber merchants both in St.
John and in Maine, which helped to make MacLauchlan's a
thankless and ineffective task.

Unlike New Brunswick, the state of Maine did on occasion
issue licences to cut lumber in the disputed territory, as it also
granted titles to squatters, but there were few American citizens
among the illegal lumberers. Not only was the disputed territory
much more easily penetrated from the New Brunswick side, but the
only manner in which lumber could be brought out was by floating
it down the St. John River through British territory. Also, the
farmers of Maine may have scorned the relatively meager pickings
to be had from this extremely arduous work, which was traditionally done in winter. Maine was even then more populous and
prosperous than New Brunswick. The 1830 census showed
400,000 inhabitants of the state, who were to increase to 500,000
a decade later. In New Brunswick, the 1834 census showed
120,000 inhabitants; by 1840 this number may have grown to
150,000.

The illegal lumbering began to attract public attention in Maine
in the late eighteen-thirties and the fact that it was carried on
almost entirely by British subjects rather than by an enterprising
advance guard of Lincoln's hundred thousand yeomen made it
seem especially obnoxious. It was reported that the lumber cut in
the disputed territory during the winter of 1837-38 amounted to
ten thousand tons.

The fall election of 1838 brought an upset in Maine: the Whigs
were defeated, and the Democrat John Fairfield (born 1797) was
chosen Governor of the state along with a Democratic majority in
the legislature. (Harvey, reporting the event, noted with a chuckle
that the total votes cast in the election exceeded by ten thousand the
entire population of the state. Nonetheless he foresaw advantages
for New Brunswick from the Democratic victory, since it brought

Augusta politically into line with moderate Washington. He had yet to learn that on the boundary issue, party labels made little difference in Maine.)

On December 14, 1838, the land agents of Maine and Massachusetts jointly appointed an agent, George W. Buckmore, to travel through the valley of the Aroostook and Fish rivers (both western tributaries of the St. John) to obtain first-hand knowledge of the illicit lumber business. The reason for the joint appointment was that Massachusetts, when agreeing to the excision of Maine from its territory, had retained certain proprietary rights in the public lands of the younger state. Massachusetts therefore also retained a direct interest in the settlement of the boundary, though it never rose to the fervent pitch of Maine.

Buckmore, on his return, made a report to his immediate superiors and to Governor Fairfield. In it he gave a detailed account of men and ox-teams at work along the various rivers, and estimated the value of the timber expected to be cut by the 200 to 250 depredators during that winter at $100,000.

The year 1839 thus opened under different auspices in Augusta and Fredericton. Sir John Harvey, having recently witnessed the political turmoil in the Canadas, was cheered by the peace prevailing both among the people of his own province and along the disputed frontier, and expressed these feelings in a warm speech from the throne at the opening of the provincial legislature on January 15.

> I offer you my congratulations on the state of the Province, in which tranquillity and good order, security of person and property, plenty and contentment, may be said to prevail to a degree for which we cannot be too thankful — more especially when we contrast our situation with that of our Sister Provinces in North America.

And in a letter to the Colonial Office he reported with satisfaction on the friendly communication he had received from the new Governor of Maine, and put forth a feeler for a new departure in boundary diplomacy:

> I have, accordingly, no apprehensions of any very violent measures being adopted by that Body [the legislature of Maine] or at

all events of their being followed up by any immediate overt acts. . . . I have good reason for believing that if I was authorized to enter into certain unofficial communications with Individuals of the Government & Legislature of that State such is the Confidence which they appear inclined to repose in me . . . that I should not despair of being enabled to relieve the Question of much of the embarrassment by which it is at present surrounded.

It was the first version of a theme that was to recur, stubbornly, throughout Harvey's correspondence for two years: a belief that, if given a free hand, his prestige, charm, and political dexterity exerted through informal, individual contacts would enable him, and him alone, to "handle" the seemingly intractable politicians of the neighbouring state, and especially the Governor, whom he firmly believed to be of conciliatory disposition obscured only by the blustering self-seekers around him. In short, it was almost the precise parallel to the attitude exhibited in more recent times by an American president toward Joseph Stalin, except that its results were incomparably less baneful.

Even as Harvey was basking in contentment and optimism, the Maine legislature was meeting in secret session to plan action on the Buckmore Report. On January 24, 1839, Governor Fairfield put his signature to a secret legislative resolve

that the land agent be, and is hereby, authorized and required to employ forthwith sufficient force to arrest, detain, and imprison all persons found trespassing on the territory of the State, as bounded and established by the Treaty of 1783; and the land agent be, and is hereby, empowered to dispose of all the teams, lumber, and other materials in the hands and possession of the trespassers . . . by destroying the same or otherwise.

To give effect to this resolve, the state land agent, Rufus McIntire, was instructed to join forces with the sheriff of Penobscot County, Major Hastings Strickland, and Captain Stover T. Rines of the state militia. Together they collected a posse of about two hundred men and set out for the disputed territory along the road recently built from Houlton to the Aroostook. They carried with them a sufficient number of small arms and a brass six-pounder.

For several days their progress was satisfactory. They stopped all lumbering in their path, arresting ten of the British loggers and dispersing the rest. As they advanced toward the Aroostook, where most of the lumbering was going on, McIntire, no longer concealing his intention (which would in any case have been useless, since news travelled with great speed through the backwoods) sent word to MacLauchlan, the warden, that he would like to meet him for a conference at the confluence of the Aroostook and the St. John.

Harvey got wind of the Maine posse early in February, and sent up MacLauchlan to check on the confused rumours reaching Fredericton. When no word came (MacLauchlan was not noted for haste) the Lieutenant-Governor dispatched a trusted aide, Captain John Hawkshaw of the Royal Engineers, who left Fredericton for Woodstock on February 14. A few days earlier Harvey had taken the precaution of sending a request to Sir Colin Campbell in Halifax for a regiment of the line, preferably the 23rd.

In the meantime, however, other men had drawn conclusions and proceeded to act with a swiftness that was beyond both Harvey and McIntire. The illicit lumberers on the Aroostook, seeing their livelihood systematically destroyed and their companions carted off to prison, were naturally overcome by a wave of fear and outrage. Most of them retreated north-eastward before the slow advance of the posse, leaving behind look-outs who supplied them with quick and reliable information on McIntire's moves. When it had become plain that the posse would not stop until it had dispossessed every last one of them, they decided to make a stand and fight.

To equip themselves, they drove to Woodstock on the night of February 11, broke into two warehouses, and carried off a quantity of militia small arms stored there. These they took to the mouth of the Aroostook in New Brunswick (*i.e.,* the very locality where McIntire expected to meet MacLauchlan). The following night their look-outs reported that the posse had encamped near the confluence of the Little Madawaska and the Aroostook, but that several of its leaders, preferring the comforts of a log house to those of a winter bivouac, had quartered themselves in the home of a settler by the name of James Fitzherbert. A lumberer named Asa

Shaw then called for volunteers to make the capture, and out of about forty men gathered there fifteen or eighteen agreed to go along on two sleds, vowing to take on the entire Maine posse if necessary.

As it turned out it was not necessary. They achieved complete surprise in surrounding and entering Fitzherbert's house. Their joy was great when they discovered that their bag included McIntire himself, along with Thomas Bartlett, a draftsman, and Gustavus Cushman, legal adviser. Also caught up in the raid were two men who had no official connection with the posse — Colonel Ebenezer Webster, a lumber entrepreneur, and a Captain Pillsbury. McIntire later stated that when, on awakening, he found himself face to face with one of the gang's leaders and asked him by what authority he was acting, the man pointed a musket at his chest and said, "This is our authority."

The five prisoners were bundled onto the sleds and driven off towards Woodstock. Pillsbury, not being connected with the posse, was released, and Webster would perhaps have been released also, had he not irritated his captors by his hostile attitude. On their way to Woodstock the lumberers met Captain Hawkshaw.

The first news of these events reached Harvey in a report from John Winslow and R. Ketchum, respectively sheriff and militia commander of Woodstock. The report, dated February 12, told of the raid on the arms warehouses and gave the strength and position of the Maine posse, but not as yet McIntire's capture.

Harvey immediately issued a proclamation:

> Whereas I have received information that a party of armed persons, to the number of two hundred, or more, have invaded a portion of this Province, under the jurisdiction of Her Majesty's Government, from the neighbouring State of Maine, for the professed object of exercising authority, and driving off persons stated to be cutting timber therein; and that divers other persons have, without any legal authority, taken up arms with the intention of resisting such invasion and outrage, and have broken open certain stores in Woodstock, in which arms and ammunition belonging to Her Majesty were deposited, and have taken the same away for that purpose, — I do hereby charge and command all persons

concerned in such illegal acts, forthwith to return the arms and
ammunition so illegally taken to their place of deposit, as the
Government of the Province will take care to adopt all necessary
measures for resisting any hostile invasion or outrage that may be
attempted upon any part of Her Majesty's territories or subjects.
And I do hereby charge and command all magistrates, sheriffs, and
other officers to be vigilant, aiding and assisting in the apprehen-
sion of all persons so offending, and to bring them to justice. And in
order to aid and assist the civil power in that respect, if necessary,
I have ordered a sufficient military force to proceed forthwith to
the place where these outrages are represented to have been committed, as well to repel foreign invasion, as to prevent the illegal
assumption of arms by Her Majesty's subjects in this Province. And
further, in order to be prepared, if necessary, to call in the aid of
the Constitutional Militia Force of the Country, I do hereby charge
and command the officers commanding the first and second battalions of the Militia of the County of Carleton forthwith to proceed as the law directs, to the drafting of a body of men, to consist
of one-fourth of the strength of each of those battalions to be in
readiness for actual service, should occasion require. . . .
— 13 February 1839.

Despite the brave face put on his proclamation, Harvey was
extremely uneasy about the state of New Brunswick's defences, as
he confided to the Colonial Office:

This Province being at this moment without any other Garrison
of Her Majesty's Troops than a Company of Royal Artillery and
a very weak Regiment of Infantry, viz., the 36th, just arrived from
the West Indies, not healthy, improperly equipped, & necessarily
unfitted for the exposure to the Severity of a Winter Service . . . &
in number, of effective men, not capable of producing 300. . . .
I have ordered a draft of 850 Militia, as well for the protection of
the Queen's Store & Barracks at this place [Fredericton], at St.
John and St. Andrews, as for the purpose of cooperating with Her
Majesty's Troops in advance. These consist of about 200 of the
36th Regiment with three Field Guns at Woodstock and the Grenadier Company of that Regiment at the mouth of the Aroostook.
The whole under the command of Lt. Col. Maxwell of the 36th
Reg^t, who has also by my authority called out 300 militia.

As to the protection of Madawaska, Harvey wrote to Sir John
Colborne, the Governor-in-Chief in Quebec, that it might be best to

occupy the settlement by a detachment from that city. It will be noted that Harvey made no move to send any troops across the St. John to confront the Maine posse.

On February 18 he dispatched a letter to Governor Fairfield, protesting the activities of the posse and adding that

> if it be the desire of the State of Maine that the friendly relations between Great Britain and the United States should not be disturbed, it is indispensable that the armed force from that State now understood to be within the territory in dispute be immediately withdrawn, as, otherwise, I have no alternative but to take military occupation of that territory, with a view to protect Her Majesty's subjects, and to support the civil authorities in apprehending all persons claiming to exercise jurisdiction within it.

To show, at the same time, his conciliatory intentions, Harvey released McIntire, Bartlett, Cushman, and Webster (all of whom had been duly committed to jail in Fredericton) after having them acknowledge a document which read, in part:

> Whereas the offence wherewith you stand charged has been pronounced by law officers of this Province as one rather against the law of nations and treaties than against the municipal laws of this country, and as such must be referred for the decision of Her Majesty's Government, you are hereby required to pledge your parole of honor to present yourselves at Fredericton, in this province of New Brunswick, whenever such decision shall be communicated or you shall be otherwise required by or on the part of this Government.

Their boisterous captors, having blown off steam, had returned the stolen arms and melted away. Many of them trickled back into the Aroostook valley, where they continued to be a thorn in the back of the posse.

As to public opinion in New Brunswick itself, it was in a state of high excitement, tinged with triumph at the lumberers' successful sally. The *St. John Observer* exulted:

> Already [Maine's] *preliminary* heroes have cut a preeminently ridiculous figure; although they may have captured two or three astonished unarmed lumberers and a few peaceable oxen, yet it was but the sting of a gnat on the lion's nose; the stalwart lumberers

of New Brunswick's forests were not to be insulted with impunity, and with the magic celerity of Harlequin's wand the redoubted leaders of the invaders were pounced upon, snugly nestling together *in one bed,* and ingloriously led away in triumph to durance vile!

And the paper warned the authorities of the state: "Should they still persist in their absurd operations . . . they will soon find to their cost that the *nemo me impune lacessit* is not an empty sound from the mouth of the British Lion."

The capture in the wintry woods was indeed too funny to be taken with proper gravity anywhere. It was soon told and retold in greatly embroidered versions up and down the Atlantic coast, and doggerels were being sung in taverns, one of which went:

> Run, Strickland, run,
> Fire, Stover, fire!
> Were the last words of McIntire.

If the mood of New Brunswick was high excitement, that of Maine could be described only as fury rampant. The capture of McIntire had thrown the posse into confusion and humiliation, and when the unsuspecting MacLauchlan came looking for his missing co-conferee, he and a companion were arrested in revenge and taken to Bangor. Strickland himself went galloping off to carry word to Augusta, and on February 15 Governor Fairfield informed the legislature that the posse, bereft of its civilian head, had dug in at its last camping-place in expectation of a full-scale British attack as threatened in Harvey's proclamation. Three days later he told the legislature that he had appointed a new land agent, Charles Jarvis, and that

immediately upon receipt of this extraordinary document, I took measures to hasten the departure of the [new] land agent's party, understood to have been assembled at Bangor, awaiting orders, and numbering between four and five hundred men; and also issued an order to Major General Isaac Hodsdon, of the third division [state militia], to detach one thousand men . . . who were to rendezvous at Bangor, and then proceed, at the earliest possible moment, to the place occupied by the [old] land agent's party, on or near the

Aroostook River. . . . I also despatched a special messenger with a communication to Major Kirby, of United States Artillery, commanding Hancock barracks, at Houlton, informing him of the facts, and asking his cooperation with the troops under his command.

(This co-operation was not forthcoming. The Houlton garrison, consisting of 118 artillery officers and men, was then the only body of United States regulars in Maine. It never left its barracks during the entire crisis; nor did it comply with a request from the Governor for the loan of some artillery. The garrison did, of course, occupy the strategically most important point on the Maine-New Brunswick frontier, and by its presence alone could be considered to be lending support to Maine's effort.)

On the same day, the state legislature authorized the executive to spend $800,000 for military purposes — eighty times the amount originally budgeted for the posse, and far exceeding anything the state could reasonably afford to spend. (The New Brunswick legislature, more prudent, put at Harvey's disposal "the available means of the province.")

On February 21 Fairfield was able to inform the lawmakers that the posse on the Aroostook numbered 750. Learning of the release of the imprisoned McIntire and companions, he also ordered the release of MacLauchlan and his friend on the same conditions. He and his fellow politicians were, however, stung by Harvey's new threat of February 18 to occupy the disputed territory and to arrest the posse, and military preparations continued apace.

They were ardently supported by the Maine press, on both sides of the political fence. The manner in which McIntire had been captured and conveyed to jail seemed particularly insulting. The *Bangor Whig* exclaimed:

> Just look at the contrast! The British land agent [MacLauchlan] was brought here in a coach with four horses, a prisoner, carried to the Bangor House, and invited to one of the best rooms of the House, and received the best of fare, while our Agent was dragged on a horse sled to Fredericton and incarcerated within the walls of a prison. Should not such treatment cause the blood of every American to boil with indigation? . . .

> We have remonstrated and entreated long enough and to no purpose. We now appeal to arms. . . . Be the issue what it may, upon this question the whole State is united to a man, and will carry into the conflict its undivided energies.

To make its mobilization complete, the Maine government authorized the drafting of a total 10,343 militia officers and men, mostly to be held in reserve. Volunteers and adventurers flocked to the threatened region from all over New England, some of them carrying the old muskets left from the Revolutionary War and 1812. In Bangor, the marshalling point for the campaign, twenty men were casting bullets at the local foundry. The streets were filled with men in and out of uniform, horses, artillery, wagons, onlookers, peddlers. The local correspondent of the *Portland Advertiser* reported:

> The appearance of our city has been more warlike today than ever. The Kennebeck detachment was all supplied with new arms. . . . They have been showing themselves off in fine military style. The pomp and circumstance of glorious war has been enacted in every street.

The poets rose nobly to the occasion and supplied the troops with marching songs such as the following, to be sung to the tune of "Auld Lang Syne":

> We're marching on to Madawask
> To fight the trespassers;
> We'll teach the British how to walk —
> And come off conquerors.
>
> . . . .
> We'll feed them well with ball and shot,
> We'll cut these Redcoats down,
> Before we yield to them an inch
> Or title to our ground.

Another song proclaimed:

> The Aroostook's right slick stream
> Has Nation sights of woodlands,

And hang the feller that would lose
His footing in such good lands.

And all along the boundary line
There's pasturing for cattle;
But where that line of boundary is
We must decide by battle.

Governor Fairfield, addressing the assembled troops, voiced the awful premonition that "perhaps before this moment, your soil has not only been polluted by the invader's footsteps, but the blood of our citizens may have been shed by the British Myrmidons." Desertions were reported from the ranks of the British regulars on the frontier, "and some of these liberty-loving fellows," a paper wrote, "have already enlisted in our companies. The 'stars and stripes' will coax many of Her Majesty's subjects to their ample folds." At Houlton, militia trainees were using an effigy of Queen Victoria for target practice, an indignity for which General Hodsdon apologized to Harvey.

Nonetheless, the voice of pacifism was also heard, timidly, in the land, and the Reverend Caleb Bradley, having received the call to the colours, poured out his loathing to his diary:

> O, what madness! . . . Has it come to this — must we be sacrificed to gratify the wicked ambition of unfeeling demagogues who happen to be in authority. . . . Both our political authorities are mad — and worse. I abhor their doings in this respect! O, contemptible, contemptible, disgraceful, horrible, abominable!

Both Harvey and Fairfield had, immediately after the outbreak of the crisis, sent couriers to Washington, where the news of the trouble in the woods caused bewilderment. Henry Fox, the British Minister, and John Forsyth, Secretary of State, had been exchanging ineffectual memoranda on the boundary question, each hoping that the other would weary of the verbal battle and surrender. Forsyth (born 1780) was a Georgia party politician whom President Van Buren had installed in the State Department as a reward for services. He was a tall, handsome man, a *bon vivant* and facile orator, but inclined to be peremptory in negotiation and reportedly an Anglophobe. His counterpart in London was the formidable and aggressive Lord Palmerston, of whom German wags said, *"Hat der Teufel einen Sohn, so ist er sicher Palmerston."*

Nonetheless, Fox and Forsyth did manage to agree that the confrontation in the north could bring nothing but embarrassment to either side, and on February 27, 1839, they signed a joint memorandum which contained the directive that the British officers would not seek to expel the Maine posse from the valley of the Aroostook; but that the government of Maine would, voluntarily and without needless delay, withdraw the posse from the disputed territory. Any future action against trespassing lumberers should be taken "by concert" between Maine and New Brunswick.

The document had a fine statesmanlike ring to it, but that anyone in Washington, the President not excluded, could thus command the "voluntary" withdrawal of Maine was really too much to hope for. In present times, when the Federal Government can, and does, cow recalcitrant states into obedience by the manipulation of a vast array of subsidies and military investments, it is difficult to imagine a period when such means were not readily at hand.

Equally difficult for the modern reader to imagine is the deep and abiding animosity felt by most United States citizens toward Great Britain throughout the nineteenth century. Even their common tongue seemed at times merely to make it easier for the two nations to trade insults, and their common cultural heritage served but as a whetstone to sharpen the points on which they differed.

Thus it was not surprising that Congress saw in Harvey's military moves the threat of British aggression, and on March 3 passed a bill authorizing the President to accept the services of any number of volunteers not exceeding fifty thousand, and

> to complete the public armed vessels now authorized by law, and to equip, man, and employ, in actual service, all the naval force of the United States; and to build, purchase, or charter, arm, equip, and man such vessels and steam-boats on the Northern Lakes and rivers whose waters communicate with the United States

and Great Britain, as shall be deemed necessary to protect the United States from invasion from that quarter.

To defray the costs, the President was authorized to spend ten million dollars.

The bill, as Fox noted with considerable perturbation, was passed in the House of Representatives by 201 votes to 6, and received unanimous approval from the Senate. He wrote to Palmerston:

> It is impossible not to behold therein the evidence of a jealous and unfriendly intention towards Great Britain. A greater parade of preparation need scarcely have been made if Great Britain had declared a desire to reconquer the United States as British colonies.

He was aware, however, that the execution of the act was conditional on future British aggression, and he also expressed the hope that "the prudent and pacific nature of the President . . . and his well-known friendly feelings towards England, will go far to strip the Act of the offensive and mischievous character."

The precautionary measures taken by Congress must also be viewed against the smallness of the standing military forces of the United States. The strength of the regular army in 1839 was only 10,691, and that of the navy 7,676 — less, for example, than the forces of Denmark.

The Congressional debates naturally inflamed the war fever, always ready to break out at the slightest provocation. The Washington correspondent of the *New York Herald* reported early in March:

> This topic now absorbs every other subject. . . . At the soirées in the hotels, along the avenues, in the lobbies, nothing is heard but questions and conversation on Maine. Even among the pretty women there is a strong warlike disposition. The naval and military officers here are fierce for war.

The *New York Gazette* reporter wrote:

> It is popular here with all parties to go to war. It is thought chivalrous and patriotic — and, as everybody knows, it is popular to declaim in favor of war. . . . To belong to, or to have any sympathy with, the "Peace Party" will ruin a man onto his third and fourth generation.

All this was still unknown in England. The New York-Liverpool packet took six weeks at best for the return voyage, and the burden of decision fell on the shoulders of Fox and Harvey. Colborne in Quebec exercised only a loose control over his Lieutenant-Governors, and though the supervision from London was much closer, the British representatives in North America could not hope to obtain timely instructions from home in an event like this. Even by April 4 Harvey's latest Colonial Office mail was dated January 4.

From Sir Colin Campbell in Halifax, his immediate military superior, Harvey got much advice — most unwelcome advice — but not the troops he asked for. Campbell scoffed at Harvey's obsession with the security of the backwoods communication to Quebec. The war, if it came, would be fought out elsewhere, he said. In the meantime he forwarded to Harvey a couple of companies from the 69th Regiment, which, like the 36th, had just been transferred from the malarial West Indies. More helpful was the response of the Governor-in-Chief, Sir John Colborne, who dispatched to Madawaska the entire 11th Regiment, six hundred strong, under its commanding officer Colonel Goldie. The soldiers were greeted with mixed enthusiasm by the loyal French settlers; much as they welcomed protection against American encroachment, they could not help fearing for the virtue of their womenfolk.

Mixed feelings were also noted farther south. Harvey's first proclamation produced a small rush of militia volunteers in Woodstock, and Colonel Maxwell of the 36th was moved to tell them: "You will again prove what I have so often heard of the New Brunswickers — that they have bodies of adamant, and souls of fire!" A few days later, when the call-up did come, he again found occasion to laud the men — for their "useful and unremitting zeal during last night when endeavouring to secure wretches who, at the moment of emergency, have been trying to abandon their Colours." Obviously the martial fire was not burning in all New Brunswickers with equal brightness.

Meanwhile the Maine posse had further strengthened its Aroostook camp (dubbed "Fort Fairfield") by wooden fortifications, as well as by posting strong patrols along the road from Houlton.

Houlton itself was crowded with militia units, perhaps fifteen hundred strong. Harvey's own forces were drawn up in a wide arc from Woodstock to Madawaska, following the course of the St. John River. At Woodstock, facing the American strongpoint of Houlton, Colonel Maxwell disposed of a total force of 550, made up of most of the 36th Regiment, the two companies of the 69th, about three hundred "tolerably well trained" militia, with two twelve-pounders and one six-pounder. At the mouth of the Aroostook, facing Fort Fairfield, and at the Tobique River there were a grenadier company with a six-pounder and fifty militia. At Grand Falls, Harvey had posted a light company of the 36th Regiment, a six-pounder, and a few militiamen. At Madawaska, there was of course the 11th Regiment supplied from Quebec but temporarily under Harvey's control, encamped mostly on the north bank of the St. John, though a 150-man detachment also occupied a barrack on the south side of the river. With his forces thus disposed, and suitable provision made for efficient courier service, the Lieutenant-Governor of New Brunswick could draw an easier breath and await developments.

These came with the appointment by President Van Buren of General Winfield Scott as special emissary to the state of Maine and mediator in the boundary dispute.

Scott, born in 1786 on the estate of his family near Petersburg, Virginia, was then the most prominent military man in the United States. He began his military service near New Orleans and, in the War of 1812, was instrumental in bringing some skill and vigour into the faltering American front, especially along the Niagara River. He was taken prisoner by the British, but released, had several narrow escapes in battle, and, with the end of the war, had become a popular hero. He then engaged in military instruction and in temperance work, and was later called to that duty which was the most common one for United States military in the nineteenth century — Indian pacification. Here he quickly proved to be the man of the hour, and his great gifts as a mediator and pacifier were put to even greater use in 1838, when he was charged with preventing American and Canadian exile raids on Upper and Lower

Canada in the wake of the Rebellion. Ceaselessly travelling up and down the border, helped by his great popularity and renown, he managed to prevent a serious conflict between the two nations.

When the President called him to Washington to entrust him with the mission to Maine, Scott had no illusions about the task awaiting him. "Mr. President," he said, "if you want war, I need only look in silence. The Maine people will make it for you fast and hot enough. I know them; but if peace be your wish, I can give no assurance of success. The difficulties in the way will be formidable."

The basis of his instructions was the Fox-Forsyth memorandum of February 27.

Scott's arrival in Maine early in March, 1839, brought embarrassment at first. Aware only of his fame as a war hero, the populace regarded him as a heaven-sent leader to help them drive out the British. This turned to disillusionment and consternation when his true intent became apparent. In Augusta he discovered that the chief obstacle to moderation was the bitter rivalry between the dominant Democrats and the opposition Whigs, each ready to reproach the other with softness toward the British. Scott (who happened to be a confirmed Whig himself) "took up his quarters at the same house, in Augusta, with his Excellency and other leading Democrats, and sat in the midst of them three times a day at the same public table. By degrees he won their confidence," as he later recalled in his memoirs.

After winning their confidence he tried to have them accept the Fox-Forsyth agreement, but he could not prevail on them to withdraw the entire posse and thus lose face all around. Finally there emerged a compromise proposal which the state authorized General Scott to submit to Harvey. ("All the details of the negotiation cannot yet be given," Scott wrote in the eighteen-sixties. "There was, however, no bribery.") On March 21 Scott wrote to Harvey that, if Harvey would declare that

> it is not the intention of the Lieutenant-Governor of Her Britannic Majesty's province of New Brunswick, under the expected renewal of negotiations between the Cabinets of London and Washington, on the subject of the disputed territory, without renewed instruc-

tions to that effect from his Government, to seek to take military possession of that territory, or to seek, by military force, to expel therefrom the armed civil posse, or the troops of Maine,

the Governor of Maine would, on his part, declare that

it is not the intention of the Governor of Maine, without renewed instructions from the Legislature of the State, to attempt to disturb by arms the said province, in the possession of the Madawaska Settlements, or to interrupt the usual communications between that Province and Her Majesty's upper Provinces. . . . With this understanding, the Governor of Maine will, without unnecessary delay, withdraw the military force of the State from the said disputed territory, leaving only, under a land agent, a small civil posse, armed or unarmed, to protect the timber recently cut, and to pre - vent future depredations.

The next move was now up to Sir John Harvey. As it happened, he and General Scott were not at all strangers. They had served opposite each other in the Niagara campaign, where they had formed that peculiar type of mutual chivalrous regard which seems to have been possible only in the romantic climate of the early nineteenth century. Again according to Scott, whose great sense of dignity and decorum, like that of Charles de Gaulle, allowed him to speak of himself only in the third person:

Harvey and Scott being leaders, and always in front, exchanged salutes several times in the field, and once, when out reconnoitring, Scott's escort cut off the Englishman from his party. A soldier, taking a deadly aim, would, certainly, have finished a gallant career, if Scott had not knocked up the rifle — saying, Don't kill our prisoner! But though a prisoner for a moment, Harvey, by a sudden movement, spurred his charger and escaped into a thicket. . . . This was the second time that he had escaped from captivity, and Scott now gave strict orders never to spare again an enemy so active and dangerous.

Another time, Scott noticed in the possession of an American soldier the uniform coat of a British staff officer and a portmanteau marked "Lieutenant-Colonel Harvey." He bought the items, and found in the coat pocket a miniature of a young lady. Scott lost no time in sending these things back to their rightful owner. The miniature, of course, turned out to be that of Harvey's young bride, at that time still in England.

The two men kept up an irregular correspondence after the war, and its effusive sentimentality cannot but induce slight discomfort in the modern reader who is accustomed to different language from military men. In January, 1839, Harvey congratulated Scott on his appointment to the northern frontier, and invited him to visit Fredericton. On March 12, while Scott was labouring in Augusta, Harvey even went so far as to apologize to him for the stiff note which he had sent to Fairfield with the threat of military occupation. He implied that he had merely put on record his instructions from London, without any personal intention of carrying them out.

It was therefore not surprising that Harvey accepted Scott's armistice proposal with alacrity, and sent his agreement by return mail.

General Scott was delighted.

> To this most desirable result [he wrote Harvey] it cannot be doubted, my dear Friend, that we have smoothed the way—whereby you may have lost a Peerage, and I a vote of thanks with a Gold Medal which we might respectively have won on the battlefield.

As to Harvey (who had a tendency to be what the Germans call *überschwenglich*), his feelings flowed over. Rushing off a report on the peaceful solution of the crisis to Lord Glenelg in London, he suggested that "if any expression or distinctive mark of the Queen's approbation could correctly be conveyed to be conferred upon General Scott it would be more gratifying to me than if conferred upon myself." To which Glenelg replied, drily, that such a distinction would not be judicious, as "the General would probably be embarrassed rather than gratified by such a communication which could scarcely fail to expose him to invidious remarks." Nonetheless, Whitehall approved of the agreement, as did the Governor-in-Chief, Sir John Colborne, who had no doubt now that the Maine volunteers would retire from the Aroostook and that "the Boundary Question will be submitted for the arbitration of Louis Philippe," King of France. Where he had picked up that last bit of prescience is not clear.

The agreement was interpreted by the diplomats to mean that Maine would retain control in the valley of the Aroostook, and New Brunswick in that of the upper St. John, without implying any permanent rights.

The time had now come to dismantle the military buildup. On March 27 General Harvey appeared at Woodstock and reviewed a parade of the regulars and militia, after which he ordered the latter disbanded. In the evening a sumptuous banquet was held in the small town, and the toasts reverberated late into the night.

The redisposition of the regular forces, however, required careful planning. Harvey had no hesitation in withdrawing the 11th Regiment from Madawaska and sending it back to its barracks in Quebec. He was, as he wrote to London, influenced by three considerations: first, to return to Sir John Colborne a force he could ill spare; second, "to produce as powerful a moral effect upon the French Canadians [of Lower Canada] by the prompt return to Canada of the Detachment"; third, to show to Maine that he meant to fulfil his part of the agreement. At Woodstock, however, he retained a strong wing of the 69th Regiment with some artillery and militia, and at the mouth of the Aroostook and at Grand Falls he also left smaller forces with some field guns. All these posts were on undisputed New Brunswick territory. Both Harvey and his predecessor had fought so long for their establishment as permanent strong-points that his reluctance to abandon them was understandable.

This, of course, left the Madawaska Settlements without a single British soldier or militiaman (Harvey had not thought it politic to call out the French settlers). But on that score he had no fears. With strong British posts both at Woodstock and Grand Falls it would have been military folly for Maine to attempt an attack on the settlements, as its long and precarious supply line through the wellnigh roadless wilderness could easily be cut. As early as February 26, 1839, Harvey noted that, although Maine was full of excitement, he had private information that there was no intention of pushing the posse beyond the valley of the Aroostook. A week later he wrote to Colonel Goldie, then still at Madawaska:

When I applied to Sir John Colborne for a strong Detachment to be sent from Quebec to Madawaska, I had every reason to apprehend that it was the intention of the State of Maine to dispute the possession of that part of the St. John with us. . . . I have managed, however, to protract the crisis to a season of the year [*i.e.,* spring] when the invasion of the Madawaska Settlement from the valley of the Arestook by the Eagle Lakes may be considered as almost impracticable from the risk which the invading Party would incur of having its retreat cut off by the breaking up of the Winter Roads.

(Sir John Colborne, not susceptible to such geographical considerations, had placed three months' provisions for the 11th at Rivière-du-Loup.)

On March 11 Harvey repeated his assurance to Goldie that the Maine militia would not dare to approach Madawaska in anything but overwhelming strength — a most unlikely contingency. By March 18, three days before the "armistice," he reiterated:

My hope and belief are that the [military arrangements] will be so far satisfactory that we shall be relieved from all idea of any intention on the part of the State of Maine of undertaking so wild a crusade as a design of pushing on to the upper St. John; *any* Troops attempting that operation looking to the State of Communications could only be regarded as "Enfans Purdues" [*sic*].

It was in the first days of April, after the 11th Regiment had been withdrawn and Harvey had settled back into the routine of civil administration at Fredericton, that this confident mood was shattered, as disturbing rumours reached him about the appearance of armed Maine militia on the Fish River. The Fish River flows northward from the Eagle Lakes into the St. John, about twenty miles above the mouth of the Madawaska. It is definitely not in the valley of the Aroostook.

Harvey first flared into hot anger — compounded, no doubt, by guilt feelings — and fired off a message to the hapless MacLauchlan threatening dismissal for not keeping him informed. He also ordered a detachment of the 69th Regiment to hold itself ready to march to Madawaska to protect the settlers and the mail service. At the same time he delicately complained to General Scott about the apparent breach of their agreement by the state of Maine, underscoring his own friendly disposition by taking a swipe at "the extraordinary speeches of the Tory Leaders" in England, which had "raised the hopes of the War Party." Scott replied that the stab toward Madawaska was, no doubt, the work of a subordinate officer and would surely be discountenanced by Governor Fairfield. This somewhat calmed Harvey, who was always ready to believe in the essential goodness of man. (Scott later paid him the two-edged compliment that "Sir John Harvey was too elevated a character to be fastidious about non-essentials.")

It was even at this moment not too late to intervene physically at the Fish River. The Maine party, not at all self-assured, had first pitched camp nine miles from the river's mouth, and a timely occupation of the latter spot by a British guard would have been effective, justifiable, and not likely to provoke a clash. Instead Harvey dispatched to Maine his commissioner of Crown lands to try to persuade McIntire ("a moderate and sensible person") to use his influence to have the Fish River detachment recalled. McIntire, not batting an eye, allowed that the leader of the detachment had in fact exceeded his instructions; but, once encamped at the Fish River, he might as well remain there. The mouth of the river was, after all, really above the Madawaska Settlements. This, on reflection, struck Harvey as not an unreasonable argument. There were, he found, practically no French Acadians living above the Fish River on the south bank of the St. John. He therefore informed the Colonial Office:

> So long as no encroachment takes place below these points, I am not aware that we could justly complain of any actual infringement of the Letter of the Agreement. . . . No national rights can possibly have been compromised by these unauthorized Acts.

The Maine posse, finding itself unmolested, had in the meantime moved down to the Fish River's mouth, where it proceeded to erect a powerful blockhouse, named Fort Jarvis (later Fort Kent), defended by cannon. It was never to be dislodged.

What neither Harvey, nor Colborne, nor even Campbell understood was that the canons of military strategy made no sense in the struggle for the disputed territory. Harvey especially was much exercised by such matters as dependable supply lines, strategic deployment of troops, security of flanks, freedom of manoeuvre, etc. Had it come to battle he could reasonably expect his forces to slaughter Maine's Army of the Aroostook, not to speak of the sitting-duck detachment at Fish River. But of course it did not come to battle; battle meant national war from Boston to New Orleans, and that was something else.

Maine cared little about safe supply lines or the other subleties of the military art. The Maine politicians were children of the wilderness, squatters all or sons of squatters. They knew that if you coveted a piece of virgin land you went and squatted on it and let the legal froth take care of itself. Accordingly, they went and squatted, first on the Aroostook, then on the Fish River and thus on the upper St. John. With this, *de facto* control of the western water-shed of the St. John passed from New Brunswick to Maine, and the Scott-Harvey Agreement, at first blush a confirmation of the *status quo ante bellum,* turned out to be an instrument of surrender.

It was so interpreted by some of the Lieutenant-Governor's political foes in New Brunswick. Even while he was still celebrating the conclusion of the "armistice" an anonymous writer in the *St. John Observer* charged that Harvey had not only "virtually ceded the larger part of the territory in dispute, but has forfeited the confidence of the Loyal Inhabitants of this Province."

The Marquis of Normanby, who in the spring had succeeded Glenelg as Colonial Secretary, found himself constrained to approve of Harvey's withholding troops from Madawaska, especially in view of Campbell's incessant sniping from Halifax against any troop deployment west of Fredericton.

For some time, however, Harvey's intimate correspondence with Scott and his frank and trusting communications to Fairfield and other Maine politicians had caused growing irritation in London, and on April 16, 1839, Normanby wrote:

> I entirely agree with my predecessor's views as to the serious inconvenience which would arise from any unauthorized corres-

pondence between yourself & individual Citizens or Public Functionaries of the State of Maine on this question. . . . It appears to me scarcely less essential that you should abstain with regard to any inhabitants of New Brunswick or the other Provinces. . . . The negociation can be conducted only by Her Majesty's Ministers.

The injunction was repeated on June 6, and coupled with a didactic observation on Harvey's habit of giving spur-of-the-moment advice on the settlement of the boundary dispute:

> Perhaps you will allow me to suggest the advantage of digesting your views on this subject into a single comprehensive paper, instead of embodying them in the order in which they occur to your mind in separate despatches.

By the late fall of 1839 it had become apparent that Fort Jarvis was exerting psychological pressure on the French inhabitants of Madawaska, and the shifting back and forth of blame between Harvey and Campbell grew more acrimonious. Harvey reproached Campbell with having prevented an adequate display of military force, and Campbell, behind Harvey's back, called him a hothead and made mock of the inglorious Scott-Harvey Agreement. Fox, the British Minister at Washington, sent a formal protest over the blockhouses both at Fort Fairfield and at Fort Jarvis to Secretary of State Forsyth, saying that these strong-points were hardly in the spirit of an undertaking merely to prevent lumbering. Forsyth, after secretly admonishing Fairfield, justified Maine's fortifications by pointing to the rambunctious New Brunswick loggers who one night in September had rushed up to Fort Fairfield firing off all sorts of stolen arms.

Plainly, something had to be done to restore ebbing British influence in the disputed area. On November 2 Fox urged on Harvey the reoccupation of the barracks in the Madawaska Settlement to ward off American encroachments. Harvey, reluctantly, requested the Governor-General to send in two companies.

The man now guiding the affairs of British North America was Sir Charles Edward Poulett Thomson, who had succeeded the brief tenure of Lord Durham in the fall of 1839. Thomson (born 1799 and thus Harvey's junior by twenty-two years) was the son of a well-to-do English merchant. In addition to participating in the family business he took a hand in politics and entered Parliament at the age of twenty-seven. At thirty-five he became president of the Board of Trade. He was a vain man but a hard worker and a successful and efficient administrator, and for his achievements in post-rebellion reform in the Canadas was made Lord Sydenham in August, 1840.

Thomson took a much closer interest in New Brunswick than Colborne, and Harvey soon felt the reins tightening.

The Governor-General was ready for Harvey's long-delayed request for troops. Being less apprehensive about Maine's feelings than the Lieutenant-Governor of New Brunswick, and beyond Campbell's veto, the Quebec authorities had quietly constructed groups of barracks at both ends of Lake Temiscouata and improved the road from the lake to the Madawaska Settlements. The construction was started by Colborne in spring, 1839, and completed by Thomson in the fall. A small corporal's guard was stationed at the lake throughout the summer and fall to take care of the barracks and stores, and in November and January, after Harvey's request, two companies of the 11th Regiment — 175 men in all — were moved in. The reasons for thus quartering the soldiers at Temiscouata rather than the Madawaska Settlements were probably these: less likelihood of a clash with Maine's posse; less reason for Maine to complain; less chance of friction with the settlers, and desertion — and, therefore, better discipline; better control from Quebec.

Palmerston had also been laying the groundwork for a new diplomatic offensive by dispatching to the frontier two surveyors, Richard Z. Mudge and G. W. Featherstonhaugh, who were to go over the disputed territory once again in search of suitable highlands. Harvey, well enough acquainted with the geography of the region, allowed himself the irreverent comment that the success of the survey would be "a misfortune rather than an advantage." This may have got back to Palmerston; at any rate, the irascible Foreign Secretary in August, 1840, suggested to his colleague of the Colonial Office that "the less Sir John Harvey occupies himself with the Boundary question the better, as his views and notions upon that question appear . . . by no means calculated to advance British Interests or to facilitate a satisfactory arrangement of the matter."

By that time Featherstonhaugh and Mudge, who understood politics at least as well as surveying, had come up with the discovery of "an uninterrupted line of Highlands and true axis of elevation" precisely along the line of the British claim. Since any modern topographical map will show these "uninterrupted Highlands" to be entirely chimerical the report cannot rank as a high point in British survey history. Harvey, in a letter to Fox, now hailed it as "triumphant, stunning." Sir Howard Douglas, safe in his post as High Commissioner of the Ionian Islands in far-away Corfu, could afford to be less flattering as to the probable effect of the survey on the boundary dispute: "It puts that question," he advised Whitehall, "should this Report be adopted, in a state further from settlement than ever."

The report was soon buried in the files. It had no influence whatever on the boundary settlement.

In the state of Maine, as Harvey had feared, the military occupation of Lake Temiscouata caused protests. Maine merchants who travelled between that state and Quebec soon brought accurate news of the troop movements, supplemented and confirmed on February 27, 1840, by an official intelligence agent sent north expressly for that purpose by Governor Fairfield.

(Not the least curious aspect of the border strife was this casual and untrammelled traffic of men, merchandise, and information across the frontier. Even at the height of the crisis, in the spring of 1839, neither mail nor freight traffic was interrupted, and the garrison of the Fish River blockhouse regularly obtained its supplies from Quebec via the British-garrisoned route.)

The agent, after making his business known to the commanding officer at Temiscouata, got full and courteous answers to all questions. The only prerequisite, it seems, was complete guilelessness. By contrast, it was reported with satisfaction by the New Brunswick press that "a Yankee doctor, who was travelling under pretence of selling medicines, with a phial in one hand and a rifle in the other," had been arrested in Woodstock.

Fairfield went so far as to ask the Federal Government whether, in its opinion, the *casus belli* provided for in the act of Congress of March, 1839, had not now arisen. He also bitterly complained to Harvey about the Temiscouata force. Harvey, incapable of enduring the burden of distrust, forgot the Colonial Secretary's injunctions and wrote Fairfield that the troops had not been sent by his authority.

A net had now begun to envelop Sir John Harvey, woven of the contrary dictates of heart and duty, and every impulse enmeshed him further.

In March, 1840, he was told to make no move in the boundary dispute without instructions from the Governor-General, and in July Poulett Thomson himself made a tour of his eastern dependencies and inspected the boundary area. A ray of light briefly lit up the gathering doom in the early fall of the year, when Harvey's long-time military thorn in the flesh, Sir Colin Campbell, departed from Halifax and was replaced by a civilian. This transferred the military command in New Brunswick *and* Nova Scotia to General Harvey, but it brought him little profit.

On November 3, 1840, Francis Rice, one of the magistrates who kept an eye on Madawaskan affairs, wrote to MacLauchlan that in mid-October the Americans had held a "town meeting" at the house of a French settler, near the Fish River blockhouse. They had elected town officers and "John Baker, the well-known agitator of Madawaska," had been moderator for the day. "After they had finished the meeting," Rice concluded, "they fired three discharges from a field piece, hoisted the American flag, drums beat, music played, and a general rejoicing took place."

Rice was instructed by MacLauchlan to watch any further such meetings, and he learned that another one was scheduled for November 2. This, it turned out, was for voting in the 1840 presidential election — the election which resulted in the Whig victory and the elevation of Harrison to the presidency. Rice duly presented himself at Fort Jarvis and was warned by the commandant, Stover Rines, not to interfere on pain of arrest. Rice reported:

There were about one hundred persons present, principally Americans, there were a few French Canadians [*i.e.,* not of the original Acadian community] of the lower class. . . . I then stood up and said: "As the Queen's civil officer and in Her Britannic Majesty's name, I protest against your proceedings and meetings as unlawful, illegal, and uncalled-for." I was then ordered out of the room, or rather taken out by the arm, by Captain Ryans [*sic*], when I was roughly used by John Baker, Joseph Wiles, and others. Baker made different attempts to strike me, but was prevented by Captain Ryans. Captain Ryans also stated publicly at the meeting, that if any peace officer of New Brunswick should attempt to arrest any person, or serve any writ, or exercise any fact of jurisdiction whatever, from the Madawaska River upwards, that he should arrest them, and send them off to Augusta prisoner.

It was by all odds the ugliest American demonstration yet. Harvey, bursting with indignation, rushed off a request to Sydenham-Thomson on November 13 to station troops in Madawaska itself, including the south bank of the St. John. The following day he reinforced his appeal with a recommendation "instantly to order & to commence the erection of two strong Block-houses one on the heights commanding the entrance of the Madawaska River & the other directly opposite to 'Fish River.' "

But as usual his militancy was short-lived. The latest issue of the British Blue Book on the boundary dispute just happened to come into his hands, and he read and reread avidly the letters, memoranda, and reports from both sides of the ocean. Seeing his own name mingled so familiarly with those of the great of this world he once more succumbed to the spell of international politics. What a calamity if this grand pattern were riven by a rash counsel! Perhaps, instead of risking "the outcry of 'military occupation,' " it would be wiser to do things the casual, unobtrusive way — like Maine. On November 17 Harvey dispatched another message to Sydenham, suggesting that no troops be moved into Madawaska, as he had come to the conclusion that it would be better to use a posse of armed labourers to guard the settlement.

The letter came too late; Sydenham had already given the order for troops to move into Madawaska.

This threw Harvey into a state close to panic. On December 9 he sent MacLauchlan in person to Montreal to convey his objections and motivations to Sydenham. (MacLauchlan, well remembering former slights at the hands of his chief, conveyed a good deal besides, some of it unflattering to Harvey.) At the same time, and without waiting to hear from Augusta, or for that matter from Montreal, Harvey wrote to Governor Fairfield apprising him of the movement of troops into Madawaska and his own opinion that a civilian posse would do, and giving assurances that he had already asked the Governor-General to withdraw the troops, a request which His Excellency would no doubt comply with forthwith. To Sydenham he repeated his request for the troops' withdrawal and complained:

> I had no idea that the movement of the troops would have been made so suddenly, on the contrary I had supposed that as suggested on a former occasion they would have been put at my disposal but not *actually moved* without further communication.

Shortly afterward Harvey was gravely informed by his legal experts that the arming of a civilian posse was quite outside the legal usages of Britain.

The storm was now ready to break over Sir John Harvey's head. On December 28 Sydenham dispatched a long, angry report to the Colonial Office, citing Harvey's record of chronic "vacillation" and "supineness" in the face of Maine's encroachments, and topping it off with an account of the Lieutenant-Governor's bad faith in going behind Sydenham's back to reassure and almost to conspire with the Governor of Maine.

On February 23, 1841, Harvey received a weighty dispatch from Lord John Russell, the new Colonial Secretary. It started out by raking him over the coals for his failure to heed well-meant and oft-repeated warnings not to dabble in the perilous game of international diplomacy, and wound up by saying:

> It cannot but be disadvantageous to the Queen's Service that the Governor of a Foreign State should be induced to conclude that on a matter of so much importance any difference of opinion, or any want of consent, had arisen between the Governor General

of British North America and the Lieutenant Governor of one of the British Provinces. . . . The interests of Her Majesty's Service require that you should no longer continue in the administration of the Government of the Province of New Bunswick.

It was a stunning blow. In vain did Harvey plead for reconsideration, in vain did he cite his distinguished military record, the successful administration of New Brunswick civilian affairs, his forty-seven years in government service, his age, his large family, his straitened circumstances. Whitehall would not be moved.

It was only bitter irony that he should be honoured by a letter from the newly elected Whig Governor of Maine, Edward Kent, expressing the great appreciation in which Harvey was held by the people of that state and the general relief that "rumors" about his recall were apparently untrue.

In New Brunswick itself the dismissal was received with regret. Harvey, with his policy of live and let live, had made far more friends than enemies, and the legislature voted him a farewell present of a service of plate worth £1500.

Only just before his departure from Halifax in late spring, 1841, did the Colonial Office respond to Harvey's plea for "an early nomination to an honorable & lucrative Command" by notifying him of his appointment to the governorship of Newfoundland, the equivalent of Siberia.

(All's well that ends well. Harvey went on to become Lieutenant-Governor of Nova Scotia, where he died in high honour and esteem at the age of seventy-four. A few months after Harvey's dismissal Sydenham fell from his horse and died.)

The new Lieutenant-Governor of New Brunswick, Sir William MacBean George Colebrooke, took over his duties on April 27, 1841. Colebrooke (born 1787) had been Governor of the Leeward Islands in the Caribbean. A few days after assuming his post in Fredericton he was able to report to London that James Mac-Lauchlan had arrested John Baker and three others for having enticed several soldiers from the British detachment in Madawaska to desert to the American side. Baker and one of his hired men were convicted and fined £20 each, despite Baker's refusal to acknowledge British jurisdiction. Captain Rines of the Fish River fort (now named Fort Kent in honour of the new Whig Governor) was said to be implicated in the desertion.

Otherwise the disputed frontier was relatively calm during the rest of 1841 and the spring of 1842. MacLauchlan, still Warden of the Disputed Territory — though his jurisdiction had shrunk a good deal since 1838 — continued to attempt to prevent illicit lumbering, with no better success than before. On the diplomatic level, Fox was notified in June, 1841, by the new Secretary of State, Daniel Webster, that the President proposed to relieve the civil posse of Maine by placing small detachments of United States troops in Forts Kent and Fairfield, "it being understood that the detachments of British troops will be continued in their present position on the left or north bank of the St. John River."

Palmerston immediately objected to such a further legitimization of the Fish River strong-point and the freezing of British occupation on the north bank of the St. John. Fox accordingly submitted to Webster that in any new arrangement the Fish River post must be abandoned altogether. Washington had no ears for such proposals, and on September 17, 1841, Fort Kent was taken over by United States regulars consisting of one captain, two non-commissioned officers, one physician, and sixty-five enlisted men.

Sir Richard Jackson, who had been Commander-in-Chief of the Forces in British North America under Sydenham and had become Acting Governor-General after the latter's death, then ordered a seven-man detachment of the Madawaska garrison to cross the St. John and to establish itself in the barrack on the south bank. It was the first time that British soldiers had set foot on the opposite bank of the river since March, 1839, and it was clearly a case of locking the barn after the horse had been stolen.

If there was any belligerence on the British side, it was displayed by the loggers and farmers. The displaced squatters who had shot up the night at Fort Fairfield in 1840 tried to burn down the stockade, equally ineffectually, in the summer of 1841, and an American survey which busied itself about the old north line in 1840 and 1841 was a few times fired on by angry settlers. No one got hurt in any of these demonstrations.

The breakthrough in the boundary stalemate was due to domestic political upheavals in Britain and the United States. In Britain the Liberal Government of Viscount Melville was replaced by the Conservative one of Sir Robert Peel in the fall of 1841, and the belligerent and unyielding Palmerston was replaced as Foreign Secretary by the conciliatory and patient Lord Aberdeen.

The changes in the United States were more complicated. The new political era under the widely trusted and respected Harrison, which the Whig accession of 1840 had seemed to presage, dissolved in bickering and confusion when the President died a month after his inauguration. Vice-President Tyler, on whom the presidential office now devolved, turned out to be a most unorthodox Whig. In fact, so much was he at odds with the other top politicians of his party that the entire Harrison Cabinet resigned in protest, with the exception of Webster, who was determined to hang on to his high office, second in importance only to the coveted and elusive presidency.

In the spring of 1839, while the boundary crisis was at its peak, Webster, then a senator, had made a tour of England in which he combined financial business with pleasure. He was already famous then, and was received everywhere with much cordiality. This helped to turn him into something of an Anglophile — he was certainly so regarded by Fox. "Mr. Webster continues in office," he wrote home in September, 1841, "mainly, if not solely, on account of the critical and dangerous state of the questions at issue between the United States and Great Britain." He added: "His temporary continuance in office, at this moment, is favourable to Peace." A firm and peaceful hand was needed more than ever, since, in the wake of Whig disarray, the Democrats recaptured the government of Maine, with Fairfield once more at the head of the state. The return of the Democratic Party in Maine, Fox wrote, was unfavourable to the progress of the boundary negotiations.

The negotiations Fox had in mind had been suggested by Webster himself, and with Aberdeen guiding British foreign policy a favourable response seemed likely.

British-American relations were at this period bedevilled by the post-rebellion border raids, and particularly by the case of the *Caroline*. The *Caroline* was a small American steamship in the Niagara River which had been taken over by rebel sympathizers who used it for supporting their guerilla warfare. To stop this, a band of volunteers crossed over from Canada on December 29, 1837, drove off the crew, killing one of them, and sent the vessel to its destruction down Niagara Falls. Some time later a Canadian named Alexander McLeod boasted in a New York tavern that he had been the man who killed the American. This set off a long and extremely emotional court case as well as a diplomatic quarrel that came at least as close to provoking war as the boundary. Fortunately, McLeod's boast was proved to be false.

As soon as the McLeod case was out of the way, London let it be known that it was prepared to send over to the United States a special envoy to negotiate with Webster a settlement of the entire disputed boundary, from the eastern seaboard to the Pacific, along with other outstanding conflicts on land and sea.

The envoy chosen by Peel and Aberdeen was Lord Ashburton, born Alexander Baring in 1774. He was a scion of the enormously rich and influential house of Baring, which had extensive holdings in the United States. While residing in that country as his firm's representative, young Baring married Anne Louise, eldest daughter of William Bingham of Philadelphia, a member of the United States Senate. Through her he came into possession of extensive tracts of land in the state of Maine. He had also been one of the most lavish and enthusiastic hosts of Daniel Webster in England in 1839, and a negotiator who was more *persona grata* to the United States Government could scarcely have been found in all of Britain.

Nonetheless, Ashburton could never be confused with Richard Oswald, a man of similar background sent to settle the North American boundary sixty years earlier. Ashburton had sat in the House of Commons from 1806 to 1835. He was an arch-conservative and opposed reform to such an extent that a public outcry frustrated his appointment to a Duke of Wellington Cabinet. Unlike other conservatives, he combined a thorough loathing for

popular assemblies — whose rule he regarded as that of the
irresponsible mob — with a sound appreciation of their power, and
he was keenly cognizant of American political practice. As an astute
and knowledgeable negotiator he yielded to none, and his friendly
ties with America did not lessen a determination to drive the best
possible bargain for Britain.

As to the polemical capacities of Webster, they are of course
legendary and need no further emphasis. The two men were
therefore worthy antagonists.

The issue of the Maine-New Brunswick boundary was not,
however, for these two men alone to resolve. Webster knew from
the beginning that his toughest bargaining might not be with
Ashburton but with the politicians of Maine.

On January 28, 1842, shortly after news of the proposed
Ashburton appointment reached Washington, Fox reported to
Aberdeen:

> I have had a long interview this morning with Mr. Webster.
> The result of this interview is very satisfactory — and as far as
> any thing in this country can be reckoned to depend upon the will
> of the Federal Government — the Mission of Lord Ashburton
> seems likely to be attended with the happiest consequences. Mr.
> Webster desires me to assure Your Lordship that the United States
> Government have received the announcement of Lord Ashburton's
> appointment with much pleasure, as a proof of the earnest wish
> of Her Majesty's Government to terminate as speedily as possible
> the existing differences: that the appointment of the Mission, and
> the choice of the individual, are equally satisfactory.

The Minister warned, however, that the negotiations might easily
be ruined by "the most worthless and disreputable portions of the
community." These apprehensions were fortified when Fox was
told in an interview with President Tyler that the United States
negotiating team would include representatives from Maine and
Massachusetts who could, of course, exercise a veto.

Ashburton received his formal appointment on February 8,
1842. In his instructions concerning the boundary from the St.
Croix to the St. Lawrence he was told to base himself on the
Netherlands Award. He was still at sea, however, when the

formidable Duke of Wellington, still the undisputed military expert of Britain, prevailed on Aberdeen to revise the instructions so as to secure a wider strip of land south-east of Quebec City. Aberdeen reluctantly sent a letter after Ashburton, saying:

> The geographical features of the Country appear to offer no natural frontier, or strong line of defence; and the most indispensable condition for the security of our North American Possessions is to be found in a direct and constant communication between Quebec and the Sea at the Port of Halifax . . . during that period of the year when the St. Lawrence is rendered inaccessible.

Ashburton was therefore permitted to yield Rouses Point and the Indian Stream territory if he would thereby secure a line running up the St. John River from its junction with the St. Francis to its source. (This would add a strip about twenty-five miles wide to the line of the Netherlands Award for a distance of about a hundred miles.)

Ashburton arrived in Washington on April 4 and reported to Aberdeen that he was very well received by press and politicians alike and was renewing "old personal intimacies" with some of the congressmen. "I am inclined to believe that the Cabinet, which has no supporting party in either House of Congress, think that a complete and satisfactory settlement with me is to give them popularity: a circumstance which, if true, is of good augury." If there was anything seriously to worry about it was the northern state: "The Maine Legislature is a wild and uncertain Body; the unbounded Democracy is always best propitiated by violent measures."

Then, however, he came to his revised instructions, and his genial optimism vanished. He was an old man and wise, who had come out of retirement to extract his country from one more quandary; he had no career to worry about and would not let his task be wrecked by other men who, though also old, were not equally wise. What he had to say to Aberdeen on that point is worth quoting if only as a fine example to modern negotiators bedevilled by a wayward home office.

I now proceed to state plainly and undisguisedly what occurs to me on this subject of the Maine Boundary, and the condition which I think we are likely to obtain. What we should like to have is one thing; but to a compromise there must be two Parties, and our other Party in this case is a jealous, arrogant, democratic Body. You may, it is true, from motives of expediency, refuse to treat; but this Mission, in the face of the Publick, implies a readiness to settle differences on terms which reasonable men shall say are fair and honorable. If I leave this country throwing all our relations with it into confusion, because I had insisted on a larger portion of this disputed Territory than we had at one period of our Negotiations been willing to accept, and which our Adversary had always refused to give, the consequences could not fail to be that the whole Union would indignantly take part with Maine, and we should pass for a Power having trifled with and insulted the Country. . . . I am not denying that it is most expedient to obtain by every possible exertion the Boundary deemed desirable by the opinions you send me of the highest military authorities. . . . [But] strange as it may seem the almost universal American opinion, whether of Parties politically friendly or otherwise to us, is adverse to our claim.

That last tinge of sarcasm was hardly intended for Aberdeen alone, nor was the warning that should Ashburton's mission fail — which was certainly likely if he was forced to adhere to the revised instructions — "you must expect an irregular skirmishing Border encroachment, which if not resisted brings our power and authority into contempt, and, if resisted, brings on probably a general War."

As to the disputed territory itself, it was worth nothing. He had, Ashburton said, visited the St. John valley many years ago and he was sure that once the boundary was defined excitement in Maine would speedily die down and "this miserable region will not be cultivated to any extent for the next century" — a prophecy that proved correct.

Ashburton's letter resulted in another modification of his instructions. He was now told that he could yield on the upper St. John but that he should at least try to exclude the United States from all of Madawaska by drawing a chord across the great arc of the St. John in that area.

Though Ashburton arrived in the United States early in April, full-dress negotiation on the Maine-New Brunswick boundary did not begin until June. The reason was that the Maine legislature had to be called into session to work out the terms on which the state commissioners would take part in the bargaining — which, as the legislators well knew, must entail a surrender of their claim to the line of 1783. During this time, however, Webster and Ashburton were not idle. They had, of course, other problems to discuss; and even in 1841 Webster had begun to bring pressure to bear on various key politicians in New England, his home area, in regard to the boundary. "The interest of both parties," he wrote to Augusta in December, "undoubtedly requires a compromise, and I have no doubt that the position which Maine has assumed is the only obstacle to bringing about such a compromise." To sweeten the pill the Secretary of State hinted broadly that Maine could expect to be recompensed for any sacrifice of territorial claims by British concessions elsewhere, and by a substantial indemnity.

When the situation still looked far from promising in May, 1842, Webster and Ashburton indulged in a stratagem about which all participants have understandably been reticent, and for which even now the evidence is only circumstantial.

One of the reasons for the boundary dispute was the lack of maps that could reliably be said to have been marked by the negotiators. Various maps were known to exist, but the lines traced thereon disagreed in important respects and their authenticity was doubtful. In the winter of 1840-41 the American historian Jared Sparks learned that Benjamin Franklin, one of the negotiators of 1782-83, had marked the boundary line on a map for the French Foreign Minister. Sparks accordingly made a search of the Foreign Ministry archives in Paris and in no time at all discovered a French map of North America whereon a United States-British boundary was entered with a strong red line, just as Franklin had said. The line gave all of the disputed territory — and more — to Britain.

Sparks naturally kept quiet about his discovery, especially as he had doubts about its authenticity. He had seen other maps in the British archives, and those maps agreed with the American claim.

Nevertheless, the Paris map was an important document, and in 1842 Sparks sent a partial copy of it to Webster, with the comment that, although the coincidence was curious, there was no "positive proof" that the map was that of Dr. Franklin.

Webster was delighted. Here was a proper bugaboo to put the fear of God into the obdurate men from the Pine Tree State — if only Sparks could be persuaded to carry the map, and the word, to Maine and Massachusetts in person. It turned out that Sparks could be persuaded, if Webster would pay his "expenses." These were going to be considerable, and the Secretary of State did not dispose of that sort of a slush fund. Perhaps Ashburton . . . ?

Webster accordingly approached the British negotiator, intimating that he needed a goodly sum of money, and that it would be wisely and usefully spent. Precisely for what purpose he did not, apparently, reveal; but Ashburton trusted his friend, and paid £2,998, which was then turned over to Sparks. "I have some reason to suspect that Webster has discovered some evidence, known at present to nobody," Ashburton wrote privately to Aberdeen, "but favorable to our claim, and that he is using it with the Commissioners [from Maine and Massachusetts]. I have some clue to this fact and hope to get at it."

He did not get at it while the negotiations were in progress. But the pressure had been sufficient to persuade Maine and Massachusetts to agree to partition, and to instruct their delegations accordingly. The Maine delegation included the ever aggressive William Pitt Preble, as well as Edward Kavanagh, who helped to get up the first Madawaska "town meeting," and ex-Governor Kent. Ashburton thought that the Maine commissioners were reasonable men, with the exception of Preble. Nonetheless, "I do not despair that we shall get the better of his very rooted prejudices."

The negotiations were first carried on through the exchange of notes which reviewed the history of the dispute and recapitulated some of the old arguments. Ashburton opened the bargaining by offering the St. John to its source (as demanded by the British military), making, however, a southward deviation to include the entire Madawaska Settlements, then along the St. Lawrence watershed and the old, false, forty-fifth parallel so as to give Rouses Point to the United States. In return Ashburton had originally been disposed to surrender also the narrow strip lying between the north line and the St. John, but anguished objections from New Brunswick soon disabused him of any such notions.

By the end of June Ashburton wrote optimistically to Aberdeen that the negotiations would probably conclude in another ten days, and that he would obtain the St. John all the way. Almost on the same day, Webster wrote to the American Minister in London that

> our movement for the last ten days, if any has been made, has been rather backward. The boundary is by no means in a highly promising state — so many difficulties arise, not only between us and England, but between us and the commissioners, and the commissioners of the two States themselves.

The last was a reference to Massachusetts' greater willingness to compromise. Two weeks later, when Maine rejected both Ashburton's chord to save south Madawaska, and the St. John to its source, Ashburton too became gloomy. "I fear [the settlement] may be on rather less favorable terms than I had given your Lordship to expect," he wrote. He was keenly disappointed that he could not extend British jurisdiction over the southern bank of the Madawaska Settlement and thus prevent the splitting-up of the French community. It was here that Harvey's failure to guard against the American advance to the Fish River told on the negotiations. Ashburton's claim to all of Madawaska would have carried much more weight, and would have been less obnoxious to Maine, had he been able to point to continuous and undivided British occupation of both banks.

Having made almost no progress in their written exchanges, Webster and Ashburton then decided to continue with less formal oral discussions, and on July 29 Ashburton was able to report that the boundary had been settled and that a treaty would shortly be signed.

> I had hoped to retain the upper part of [the St. John River] as a boundary. At this point I made my stand for some time, but finding the Maine commissioners obstinate, supported by all their

deputation in Congress, and, as I believe, really ready to return home *re infecta,* I yielded to the mediation of a third party [President Tyler] and consented to an intermediate line between the Highlands, as claimed by America, and the River. It will be seen that it removes the boundary completely from the crest of the Hills over-looking the St. Lawrence to their feet towards the River St. John, and that in no part will it run nearer than 50 miles from Quebec.

This, of course, had the ironic result of leaving John Baker's farm in British territory:

> Agitators on the part of Maine and the Maine Commissioners fearing that his situation as a British subject might expose him to difficulties, made every effort to throw his property within the Maine line. . . . I got over the difficulty by a voluntary promise, not put into the Treaty, that, if Baker wishes to leave the Province, and is not able at once to find a purchaser for his property, it shall be taken over at a reasonable price.

It was only at this stage that Webster showed Sparks's red-line map to Ashburton, who admitted that, had he seen the map earlier, he would certainly have stood on his first proposal.

As to the state of Maine, its delegates could be persuaded to acquiesce in the boundary line only after a stipulation was put into the treaty draft that Maine and Massachusetts would each receive $150,000 from the Federal Government (not from Britain) and that Maine would in addition be reimbursed for its military expenditures. (This reimbursement was to come to $286,934.79.) Also, Maine citizens were to have the same rights in floating lumber and agricultural produce down the St. John as British subjects. Even so, the outcry in Maine was great, and one of the papers expressed the general consensus when it complained that the delegates had been forced to agree only because they were "surrounded by difficulties, importuned by gentlemen from all parts of the Union, receiving no support from our Massachusetts co-proprietors of the disputed territory, and more than all, most basely betrayed by the secretary of state."

The treaty, signed in Washington on August 9, 1842, defined the boundary as follows:

> *Beginning at the monument at the source of the river St. Croix*
> *. . . ; thence, north, following the exploring line run and marked*
> *by the surveyors of the two Governments in the years 1817 and*
> *1818 . . . to its intersection with the river St. John, and to the*
> *middle of the channel thereof; thence, up the middle of the main*
> *channel of the said river St. John to the mouth of the river St.*
> *Francis; thence, up the middle of the channel of the said river*
> *St. Francis and of the lakes through which it flows, to the outlet*
> *of the Lake Pohenagamook; thence, southwesterly, in a straight*
> *line, to a point on the northwest branch of the river St. John,*
> *which point shall be ten miles distant from the main branch of the*
> *St. John, in a straight line; . . . thence, in a straight line, in a*
> *course about south, eight degrees west, to the point where the paral-*
> *lel of latitude of 46°25′ north intersects the southwest branch of*
> *the St. John's; thence, southerly, by the said branch, to the source*
> *thereof in the highlands at the Metjarmette portage; thence, down*
> *along the said highlands which divide the waters which empty*
> *themselves into the River Saint Lawrence from those which fall*
> *into the Atlantic Ocean, to the head of Hall's Stream; thence, down*
> *the middle of said stream, till the line thus run intersects the old*
> *line of boundary surveyed and marked . . . previously to the year*
> *1774, as the 45th degree of north latitude . . . to the Iroquois*
> *or St. Lawrence River.*

The treaty thus gave to Maine less territory than the Netherlands Award that the state had rejected so angrily; but it did give more to the states of New Hampshire and New York, the first-named being the larger beneficiary with the 150-square-mile Indian Stream territory. Webster could point out to Maine that its seven thousand square miles, out of the total twelve thousand, were, agriculturally speaking, "equal in value to four-fifths of the whole." Together with the money grant and the equal use of the St. John River, this was not a bad bargain.

It was for these reasons that the treaty was assailed in New Brunswick. It is worth noting, however, that New Brunswick almost immediately got into a quarrel over its new boundary with Lower Canada, and defended its claim with the selfsame historical arguments previously employed against it by Maine.

The treaty also provided for a joint survey and demarcation of the new boundary line, and, since the negotiators had been careful enough to seek professional advice in writing their definitions, this was now merely a technical task. (Ashburton's other boundary negotiations, partly successful and partly not, will be dealt with in subsequent chapters.)

Before the treaty could become law it had to be ratified. This was a simple enough formality in Britain, but in the United States Senate the document got a rough going-over from a last-ditch minority. Thomas Hart Benton, a stalwart expansionist, accused Webster of "victimizing that deserted and doomed State," Maine, and James Buchanan said Ashburton's claim was a "bold and bare-faced pretension." As to the supposed Franklin map, which Webster confidentially exhibited to the senators, Benton put no stock in it — "solemn and mysterious humbuggery . . . awful apparition." Nonetheless the treaty was ratified on August 20, after only a four-day debate, by a vote of 39 to 9.

Ratifications with Britain were exchanged in London on October 13. Although Parliament was not in session, Palmerston at once mounted a virulent attack on the treaty in a friendly newspaper, calling it "Ashburton's Capitulation." Privately he wrote to a fellow Whig, Lord John Russell, that it was important to place objections to the treaty on record now, so that, if difficulties over it should develop, the Whigs could say "we told you so." He went on:

> We ought never to have allowed the Americans, for instance, to set foot north of the St. John. . . . Why did we throw Rouse's Point at their heads, even without its being asked for? Never was there imbecility like that of Ashburton, if it was nothing worse.

John Russell, too, thought that Ashburton had made "about as bad a treaty as it was possible to make. . . . I fear Baring and Co., and the land sharks of Maine will be the only gainers."

Since in 1831 Palmerston, as Foreign Secretary, had been willing to accept the Netherlands Award, his new opinion could not carry much conviction.

When Parliament opened in the spring of 1843 he returned to the attack by impugning Ashburton's motives and capacities, along with those of the Peel Government. Peel responded by pointing to

1831 and by exhibiting an old map which, he said, had only recently come to his knowledge (but which was well known to Palmerston). One of the famous Mitchells, it had a strong red line, marked "Boundary as described by Mr. Oswald," corresponding precisely to the American contention. The map had a better claim to authenticity than that used by Webster, and proved that Britain had made an excellent bargain.

Additional evidence in support of the United States claim was discovered as recently as 1933, in the shape of a map in the Madrid archives. The map had been sent to Madrid by Count de Aranda, the Spanish Minister in Paris in 1782, with a note saying the boundary on it (following the American claim) had been entered by John Jay after agreement had been reached with Britain.

The time had now come to divide up the "Disputed Territory Fund," the proceeds from seizures of illicit lumber accumulated in New Brunswick by James MacLauchlan. It took several years of niggling and haggling among the several governments, until the matter was adjusted in 1846. Miller says: "The amount paid over to the agent of Massachusetts for the use of the two States was $14,893.45 (£3,723 8s 3½d currency); the bonds delivered came to £8,700 2s 10d, subject, apparently, to credits of £2,113 3s 1d."

As to John Baker, now in his fifty-fifth year, he at first thought of taking up Ashburton's offer of purchase and moving to Maine. Then, however, he seems to have become reconciled to living out his life under the British Crown. He died a resident of New Brunswick in 1868. Many years later, the government of Maine bethought itself of the state's once-famous son, and had his remains transferred for reburial in the Protestant cemetery near the town of Fort Fairfield. Over his new grave it erected a modest memorial bearing the inscription:

> Erected by authority of a Resolve of the Legislature of Maine A.D. 1895, to commemorate the Patriotism of JOHN BAKER a Loyal son of Maine in maintaining the Honor of his Flag during the contentions on the disputed Territory 1834-42.

The last dates appear to rest on an error; the logical choice, as concerns Baker himself, would be 1827-42. With a little effort the gravestone can be located by the cemetery caretaker.

Baker's descendants, however, became solid and loyal New Brunswickers and Canadians. One of his grandsons, Colonel Jesse Wheelock Baker, was a member of the provincial legislature.

Fort Fairfield itself has long since disappeared, but the Fort Kent blockhouse still broods somberly over the mouth of the Fish River. It is now used by the Boy Scouts.

The survey and demarcation of the boundary were carried out by British and American teams from 1843 to 1845. The British commissioner appointed for that purpose was Lieutenant-Colonel James Bucknall Bucknall Estcourt (born 1802), and the United States commissioner was Albert Smith. Each of the commissioners had a staff of astronomers, surveyors, axemen, and other helpers, that of Estcourt sometimes swelling to five hundred.

All survey and line-cutting operations were preceded by careful astronomic determinations of important points along the boundary, especially at angles. Since the determination of longitude depends on extremely precise measurement of time, and since telegraph lines for the transmission of time signals did not as yet exist, time differences between points were established by the transportation of chronometers by canoe and sled. Wagons were useless for this purpose, not only because roads were scarce but because the shaking of the wagon would have thrown off the chronometer rate. So accurate were the astronomers and surveyors that when two parties were converging through the forest from points sixty-four miles apart — along the so-called South-west Line — they missed each other by only 341 feet, corresponding to less than one half-second of time.

The whole chain of astronomical stations had of course to be connected to some point tying in with the world-wide geodetic network. This was Quebec City. Here is how the *International Boundary Commission Report* issued 1924 describes the manner in which this was done:

> As it was desired to connect the station on the Northwest Branch [of the St. John] astronomically with Quebec, Lieutenant Pipon . . .

proceeded to Quebec, where he occupied a station on the Plains of Abraham. Captain Robinson moved his instruments from the Northwest Branch to a near-by hill, called Lake Hill, which was connected with the Northwest Branch by triangulation.

About 20 miles from Lake Hill, in the direction of Quebec, a range of hills could be seen, and it was rightly supposed that these would be visible from Quebec. To the highest of these, Captain Robinson sent Sergeant McGuckin, of the Royal Sappers and Miners, with a party of laborers and the necessary camp outfit. From the Lake Hill station a heliostat was kept reflecting in the direction of this hill to enable Sergeant McGuckin on his arrival there to be sure he was on the one chosen.

When he had reached the hill and found, on climbing a tree, that he could see back to Lake Hill and forward in the direction of Quebec, he had his party cut down the timber on top of the hill, leaving only one tall tree standing in the center of the clearing. The limbs and branches were cut off this tree and near its top was fastened a small pulley, through which was run an endless rope with a conical tin cup attached. A charge of gunpowder, weighing from one-fourth to one-half pound, was wrapped in paper and put in the cup with a piece of touch paper, which was lighted, and the cup was quickly hoisted to the top of the tree where the charge exploded. The cup was then hauled down again and the operation repeated.

Sergeant McGuckin had orders to fire these charges every 10 minutes between 8 and 10 o'clock in the evening. He was informed by signals from Lake Hill when Lieutenant Pipon at Quebec was ready to observe. At the beginning and end of each evening's program two rockets were fired, which were found to be more difficult to observe than the bursting charges.

To retrace and clear the north line from the St. Croix to the St. John was a difficult job because the old cut was hard to find and easy to confuse with other exploratory cuts. Farmers who had their own axes to grind did not help matters by leading the surveyors down the wrong tracks.

Wherever the boundary passed through forest, the axemen cleared a thirty-foot strip, or "vista." In the St. John River itself the boundary was generally made to follow the deepest channel, which was important in the apportioning of islands. The most tedious part was the Highlands Line, where the boundary was required to follow the watershed between the St. Lawrence and the rivers flowing south. It was primeval wilderness of the most inhospitable type. Estcourt had instructions not to insist on too fine a separation, but Smith was a perfectionist and made the line wind most carefully around the smallest rivulet or swamp. To lay down the watershed line, prominent summits were first selected. So that the surveyors and axemen would not veer off in the wrong direction as they were feeling and slashing their winding way from one summit to the next, a hornblower would be stationed on the summit they were heading for with instructions to emit a blast every few minutes.

All supplies had to be packed in on men's backs. Estcourt remarked in his reports to Lord Aberdeen:

> This labor was severe, and it was difficult to induce the men to continue it, through the discouragement of fatigue, bad or hot weather, and paths which soon became deep and muddy. Many men would undertake the work, perform one journey, become discouraged, and give up.

The entire boundary from the St. Croix to the St. Lawrence turned out to be 670 miles long; of this, 179 miles was formed by rivers.

Two types of hollow cast-iron monuments, made in Boston, were used to mark the boundary. At the thirteen main angles, ten-foot monuments were set up, with six-foot markers for the other 760 points. Transportation of these heavy objects to the line was one of the least agreeable tasks of the operation.

The whole job demanded a great deal of planning and foresight, such as in the placing of supply depots and caches and the distribution of work parties so that many tasks and many parts of the boundary would be attended to simultaneously. Even military campaigns in North America seldom had cause to stray far from civilized territory. But boundaries nearly always plunged far into the untrodden and unfriendly interior.

Owing to delays in the appropriation of money the American team had to curtail its work, and the larger share fell to the British, who, under Colonel Estcourt's leadership, drove on with military precision and unflagging perseverance. Their relations with their American counterparts were harmonious throughout, and no differences impeded their joint progress. There was, in fact, an uncanny measure of agreement in some of their technical data, giving rise to the suspicion that they had accepted each other's findings without checking.

Lord Aberdeen, the Foreign Secretary, was highly pleased with the efficiency of the survey — even though the difficult terrain had caused greater expenditures than expected — as well as the good relations between the commissioners. "I can scarcely bestow too much praise on the energy and resolution with which the work has been conducted and executed," he wrote Estcourt on January 3, 1845.

The two commissioners concluded their work by publishing, on June 28, 1847, a concise joint report. With it the dispute over the boundary from the source of the St. Croix to the St. Lawrence was formally laid to rest.

There was an unhappy postscript for Estcourt. Sent to the Crimea during the Crimean War of 1854-56 as supply officer, he was widely — though apparently unjustly — blamed for the sufferings of the ill-prepared British Army during the first winter at Sebastopol. Shortly afterwards he caught cholera, and died in camp in his fifty-third year.

CHAPTER TWO

Through Rivers, Lakes, and Plains

Where Lake Ontario, the last and easternmost custodian of the water moving in stately procession through the Great Lakes, passes on its fullness to the St. Lawrence River, it does not pour out through a single channel but through a picturesque and far-flung archipelago. This archipelago is known to boaters and vacationers as the Thousand Islands. Actually the figure is an understatement: the number of isles and islets is about fifteen hundred.

On one side of the river is Canada, on the other the United States. Where would the "middle" be between the two shores?

And yet when the commissioners, under Article 6 of the Treaty of Ghent, set out to find the middle and to lay down on charts the boundary, the Thousand Islands proved to be one of the minor difficulties of a strange and troublesome eight-year safari through lakes, rivers, and portages, attended by farce and misfortune, stylish high living and dismal grubbing, high-flown eloquence and petty bickering.

We have noted in the preceding chapter that in the peace negotiations at Paris in 1782-83 the American negotiators offered the British a choice of two boundary lines west of the St. Lawrence:

either along the forty-fifth parallel all the way to no man's land, or through the middle of the Great Lakes and their various links to the Lake of the Woods. Either of these lines implied the sacrifice by Britain of a large territory lying between the lakes, the Ohio, and the Mississippi, and counted as part of Canada since the Quebec Act of 1774. The sacrifice was made, but not without protests from the colonies. When the boundaries came up once more for bargaining in 1814, the merchants of Upper and Lower Canada presented a joint memorial to Sir George Prevost, Governor-in-Chief, suggesting that "the madness and injustice of the Government of the United States . . . have now placed within the reach of the British Government the reparation of a most gross and extraordinary error in the negociation and treaty, at the close of the American War," and that the new boundary to be imposed on the republic should run "from Sandusky, on Lake Erie, to the nearest waters falling into the Ohio, then down that river, and up the Mississippi, to the mouth of the Missouri — thence up the Missouri to its principal source." The merchants did not, however, want this additional piece of land for colonization — even the most optimistic booster of the day could not see it as a home for the white man — but recommended that it be reserved "wholly for the Indians" — and, of course, British trade.

Ghent did not change the boundaries, and the definitions of 1783 remained in force. The British and American negotiators of the Peace of Paris had thought that they had to do no more than repeat on parchment what Nature had so plainly inscribed on the globe. They stipulated that the water boundary between the newly formed United States and the remaining British colonies should run, from the point where the forty-fifth parallel struck the St. Lawrence,

> *along the middle of said River into lake Ontario; Through the middle of said Lake until it strikes the Communication by Water between that Lake and Lake Erie; Thence along the middle of said Lake until it arrives at the Water Communication between that Lake and Lake Huron; Thence along the middle of said Water Communication into Lake Huron; thence through the middle of*

said Lake to the Water Communication between that Lake and
Lake Superior, thence through Lake Superior Northward of the
Isles Royal and Phelipeaux to Long Lake, Thence through the
middle of said Long Lake and the Water Communication between
it and the Lake of the Woods, to the said Lake of the Woods,
thence through the said Lake to the most Northwestern Point
thereof, and from hence on a due west Course to the River
Mississipi.

The Mississippi was the western limit of the United States.

The War of 1812 had demonstrated, however, that Nature had
written with a broad and streaky brush, and in the Treaty of Ghent
(which also provided for the determination of the eastern boundary
considered in the preceding chapter) due cognizance was taken of
this in the words:

Whereas doubts have arisen what was the middle of the said
Rivers, Lakes and water communications, and whether certain
Islands lying in the same were within the dominion of His Britannic Majesty, or of the United States: in order therefore finally to
decide these doubts, they shall be referred to Two Commissioners.

The commissioners were to survey, first, the line from the forty-
fifth parallel and the St. Lawrence to the St. Mary's River (Article
6 of the Treaty of Ghent), and, second, through the St. Mary's
River to the most north-western point of the Lake of the Woods
(Article 7).

In accordance with this treaty, Britain appointed as its commissioner John Ogilvy of Montreal, and the United States General
Peter Buell Porter of New York. Each was to have an agent, or
executive officer, but the British did not get around to appointing
one until 1818. His name was John Hale; the United States agent
was Colonel Samuel Hawkins. There were also astronomers and
surveyors, most famous among them the explorer David Thompson,
who had already made a name for himself by traversing the North-
west down to the Pacific.

Ogilvy, who was born about 1769 in Scotland, came to Canada
approximately in 1790, formed a partnership with several merchants in Montreal, and through various mergers rose to high

position in the North West Company, the chief rival of the Hudson's Bay Company. Through his work in the fur trade he was well acquainted with the lake and river routes that were to form the boundary, as well as with the organization of travel through that wilderness. A surgeon who joined the commission some years later said that "there was about him, I am informed, an unusual amount of public spirit and talent; but he was variable, apt to be obstinate in trifles, and immediately afterwards too pliant in matters of importance."

Porter, born 1773, was a lawyer and politician in New York State, owning a large house and estate on the Niagara River. Since 1810 he had been developing properties in that area. A member of the United States Congress from 1809 to 1813, he was a leader of the "War Hawks" who preached the conquest of Canada. During the War of 1812 he commanded a force of volunteers and Indians. His house was occupied and sacked by British soldiers. He was described as an impressive figure, highly intelligent, and a good speaker, but many people considered him self-seeking and covetous.

The two commissioners held their first meeting in Albany in November, 1816, and decided to start their survey the following spring. Meanwhile Hawkins, who looked upon his post as a fine political plum, decided to make a quick preliminary review of the eastern portion of the boundary area. He set out in company with a major of the Topographical Engineers, and the two of them, *"bons vivants* and *bons companions,"* as one of the American surveyors, William Bird, was to recollect later, turned the trip into a pleasure junket that yielded many empty bottles but little practical information. "All they did," Bird remarked, "amounted to nothing except to alarm the settlers along the lines."

When the parties assembled at St. Regis, New York, in the late spring of 1817, the American establishment amazed by its opulence both the British and the local Indians, who tilled their plots under the care of a French-Canadian priest. Each of the officers and surveyors in the American party had his own tent, with servants, secretary, cook, waiter, boatmen, etc., that of General Porter generally being styled The Marquee. Elegant dining, visiting, hunting, and regular receptions and entertainments for the leading citizens in the small towns along the upper St. Lawrence were the order of the day, with a bit of official business thrown in here and there. The high point of the social season was the arrival, on August 1, of President Monroe and *entourage,* to view the progress of the survey and to look about for fortification sites.

Not the least curious personage in the American encampment was a gentleman who, strictly speaking, had no business there but who was to become extremely important in the course of events. This was Major Joseph Delafield, a young extrovert who, driven by boredom and curiosity, had used his acquaintance with both Porter and Hawkins to wangle an invitation to go along for the fun of it. Delafield kept a voluminous diary in which he noted down social and geographical details (but few of the work itself), always keeping a sharp eye out for American interests as against those of Britain. At St. Regis he was shocked to hear the Indians talk French and see them hoist a British flag, all under the influence of French priests and occasional gifts of gunpowder from the British military. He figured that given fifty dollars to spend on powder and trinkets, he would easily make the Indian village thoroughly American.

But more exciting things were on foot. It became clear from the beginning that Commissioner Porter and his agent were completely at odds as to their respective duties and privileges, each claiming that it was his prerogative to direct the American surveyors. Delafield, being friendly with both antagonists, played a double confidant with great gusto, until at length things got to the stage where collaboration between Porter and Hawkins became impossible, and the only way out was for both officials to absent themselves from the actual survey. This left the field to Delafield, and it was not long before he was made acting agent, and then agent, of the United States commission, with Hawkins completely out of the picture and Porter following events from afar and giving his signature to proposals advanced by Delafield. To the latter's credit it must be said that he was a tireless and ever enthusiastic worker and a zealous patriot, but for whose perseverance the American side might have floundered.

Meanwhile, however, the commissioners were faced with the problem of deciding how to interpret the expression "through the middle." They agreed on one principle — that the boundary should everywhere run through water, and that if an island was found in the middle, the line should run around it. But on which side? On that where the river was wider, or where it carried the most water, or where the best ship channel was? These questions were never threshed out in principle, and the commission proceeded from island to island, judging each case on its merits. "Conflicting interests and opinions had to be adjusted and concessions made by each," says Bird. "In this manner they proceeded, keeping a sort of debit and credit account of quantities [of acres] in the doubtful islands."

Such problems did not become pressing at once, because the commission decided, wisely, to survey the first portion of the boundary area before making final decisions on the line itself. In the first two summers, 1817 and 1818, they finished the St. Lawrence River, and in 1819 they did the Niagara River and made a start on the Detroit. It had been stipulated by the governments that the total expenses were to be shared equally by both nations. The arrangement required a good deal of international harmony; and, as far as the sixth Article was concerned, this was generally achieved. Usually the two parties proceeded along the boundary in leap-frog fashion, each checking the other's work. In winter they would retire from the field and draw maps and square accounts in their home offices, Montreal and New York.

The two governments had not, however, expected so thorough a survey, the first such joint venture — and critics both in Congress and in Whitehall soon demanded a more modest effort. Though they did not prevail against the professional arguments of the astronomers and surveyors, finances remained a sore point, especially with the British Foreign Office. Ogilvy had become accustomed to the enterprising ways of the fur business, and he chafed constantly under the close bureaucratic supervision of desk-bound penny-pinchers in London. In March, 1818, he felt bound to protest against insinuations that his expenditures were "irreconcilable" with Foreign Office regulations, adding:

> I have executed the Duties of my Office in good faith under what I conceived to be a direct Authority. I have acted without an Agent at a time when Colonel Hawkins the American Agent attended the Board with an establishment which caused an extra expense to the American Government of £1,000 to £1,500 Sterling. I have personally superintended the active operations of the Board to accelerate the Business and with my own Money defrayed all expenses . . .

Nonetheless his troubles continued, and he never knew whether and when he would be reimbursed for his advances.

Ogilvy could not think of carrying out so weighty a task without his personal supervision, and his bark canoe was a familiar sight to the surveyors and astronomers. In October, 1818, he reported to Castlereagh that the work during the preceding two summers had been carried on

> with a degree of zeal and industry which I am satisfied cannot be surpassed. . . . The survey will comprize, within a distance of one hundred Miles, not less than Twelve Hundred Islands and perhaps more. In carrying on the above service much arrangement and management are necessary which render my superintendance indispensable and a great deal of troublesome and vexatious Business is unavoidably borne by me. The whole Season is passed under Tents upon uninhabited Islands where consequently every article of Provisions must be supplied from a distance and the Surveyors being out in boats all day the hardships and privations to which all the Persons employed are exposed induce me not only to allow them very ample Rations of Provisions but also to afford them all the little comforts that can be procured, though these are necessarily very limited.

And, anticipating mockingly raised eyebrows among the London scribes:

> One article among the contingent charges, as it may be thought too much of a Luxury I shall notice namely Umbrellas, but these are required to screen the Surveyors and their Instruments from the Sun while they are observing.

As if to underline London's lack of understanding of North American money matters, Ogilvy's secretary and one of the assistant surveyors resigned early in 1819 because they considered their pay too low. Later that year the entire survey staff quit, and astronomer Thompson, bound to Ogilvy by old fur-trade associations, had to carry on alone for a while.

As far as the Detroit River, nature had been rough on the survey parties, but it had not been dangerous. The swampy lowlands of that area, however, bred fever against which the medical science of the day had no drugs. On October 17, 1819, John Hale, the recently appointed British agent, wrote to Lord Castlereagh:

> I have a very painful duty to perform. . . . Commissioner John Ogilvy . . . died at Amherstburgh in Upper Canada of a Fever which prevails so frequently upon the marshy shores of Lake Erie, and which had previously rendered every Individual in the camps of both Commissioners incapable of keeping the field any longer . . .

Ogilvy had died on September 28, and Hale waited until the return to winter quarters in Quebec before he reported to London. Others were quicker. Thomas Barclay, commissioner under Articles 4 and 5, read of Ogilvy's death in a newspaper in New York on October 11, and sat down at once to put in his bid with Castlereagh:

> In the event of your Lordship being at a loss to name a proper person to succeed Mr. Ogilvy, permit me to say, that my son Mr. Anthony Barclay, who was Secretary under the 4th Article of that Treaty [of Ghent], is in point of Talents, and every other necessary Qualification, perfectly competent to execute the duties.

Barclay's letter must have reached London before Hale's. Thomas Barclay's stock in London was high, and his wish was granted.

Anthony Barclay, who had studied law in England, had then just turned twenty-seven. He was appointed commissioner under Articles 6 and 7 on January 10, 1820. Anthony was in New York with his father when he received the commission, and he set out for Canada soon after. Throughout the fall and winter, Hale, who himself harboured hopes of being named commissioner, had had to carry on alone.

Anthony Barclay's *modus operandi* was quite different from Ogilvy's. He was the staff officer, the diplomat and administrator. In usually indifferent health, he rarely visited the field but kept moving about the eastern United States, whence he directed a steady stream of correspondence to his field party, the United States commissioner, and the Foreign Office. He was trained as a lawyer and schooled in his father's formal habits, so it was not surprising that he and the London bureaucrats should hit it off from the start; but David Thompson the explorer also showed himself satisfied with the instructions of his new chief and wrote that "far more progress has been made in the late Summer [of 1820] than during any preceding year. This is to be ascribed, probably, to a new system, of surveying in two parties, which in the prosecution has been attended with harmony and success."

To help in the survey of Lake St. Clair and Lake Huron, Hale in the fall of 1819 had ordered from the naval dockyard at Kingston "a Decked Vessel capable of accommodating the whole Surveying party, so as to enable them to avoid encamping upon the Swampy shores of the communication [between Lakes Huron and Erie] and to navigate in safety Lake Huron," explaining to London that "the want of such a Vessel was seriously felt upon Lake Erie; and to that circumstance the loss of Mr. Ogilvy's life may in some measure be attributed." He also pointed out that the American party already had a schooner at its disposal, the *Ghent*.

The schooner was built and launched in time for the 1820 field season. It was christened *Confiance* and did service on Lakes St. Clair, Huron, and Superior.

The commissioners had decided to settle outstanding boundary problems under Article 6 of the Treaty of Ghent before moving on to the survey under Article 7. They arrived at an amicable compromise concerning the doubtful islands in the St. Lawrence by giving Grand (or Wolfe) Island near Kingston to Britain, and the Long Sault Islands near Cornwall to the United States.

Barclay was later attacked for the relinquishment of the latter, especially Barnhart Island, by certain business interests in Upper

Canada. He justified his decision by pointing to the greater value to Britain of Grand Island:

> This island lies in the River St. Lawrence, immediately and in full view of the Dock Yard, and Fortifications and Town of Kingston. In point of extent and fertility, also, it is the first island adjacent to the Boundary. It contains 31283 Acres. His Majesty's Dock Yard at Kingston is the most important establishment in those provinces, and I deemed it an object of primary consideration, to secure every thing which might preserve, or contribute to, its advantages. I succeeded in inducing the American commissioner in appropriating this momentous island to Great Britain.

As to Barnhart, the story was altogether different:

> It is a fact, I believe, very notorious, that these islands have served as the principal depots for smuggling along the whole Frontier. I should be sorry to be able to assert that any of the Memorialists, who certainly inhabit that vicinity, were concerned in such illegal and un-loyal traffic: but I do not hesitate to say, that, after the imposing style of this "Memorial of the Undersigned Magistrates and Inhabitants of the Eastern District of Upper Canada," some surprize would be excited by a knowledge of the weight of character of some of those who subscribed.

Strategic considerations were also uppermost in the minds of both commissioners when they had to apportion four islands in the Detroit River — Fox, Sugar, Stony, and Bois Blanc. Each side felt it had a good claim to all four of them, though the British claim was stronger. Each side was fearful that the other intended to place batteries on any of the islands it could obtain. Only Bois Blanc, however, was an island in the true sense, the other three being "mere specks"; it was also closest to the British shore. After much argument back and forth and diligent consultation with London ("the American Commissioner declares that he dare not shew his face in Washington if he should resign the United States claim") Barclay was at last authorized to yield all but Bois Blanc Island. With this the boundary under Article 6 was settled in its entire length, the agreement being concluded on June 18, 1822.

Meanwhile, the surveyors had moved on to St. Mary's River, joining Lakes Superior and Huron, and were soon nosing about

Lake Superior's western shores and up the rivers.

Here civilization was left behind, and the survey parties began to penetrate into a wild domain of fur traders, half-breed *voyageurs,* untamed and unpredictable Indian tribes, and uncharted waters. The food became miserable; for weeks there was nothing but rancid pork and boiled flour balls, supplemented with such fish and game as the men might catch or barter from the Indians. Mosquitoes were thick and furious, and portages were many and excruciatingly tough.

Although the top officials hibernated comfortably in large cities, some of the surveying staff were left to winter in Fort William, a post of the North West Company, where the dreary monotony was relieved only by occasional dances:

> There are 2 fiddles and a triangle here [wrote an American surveyor] and every fortnight since the first of November has been distinguished by a ball. The women and children amount to about thirty, and with our establishment there are as many men. They dance Scotch reels and are as merry as can be. The Northwest Company encourage these dances to keep their men in spirits.

But what was worse than physical trials, the harmony and give-and-take which had characterized the proceedings of the commission broke down, and soon the two sides were far apart and bitterly divided not only over the proposed course of the boundary — that would have to be argued out later — but about the areas to be surveyed.

The reason was that the treaty-makers of 1783 had relied entirely on the Mitchell map, whose inaccuracies had already bedevilled boundary commissioners farther east in their search for the true River St. Croix. Unlike the boundary between New Brunswick and Maine, however, that west of Lake Superior had no documentary history. It was, so to speak, created out of nothing by Franklin, Oswald, and their colleagues in Paris. In Lake Superior and the territory west of it, the Mitchell map showed some strange and wonderful features that could not be identified on the ground. Most notable were the non-existent "Isles Philippeaux" just east of Isle Royale, and the equally non-existent "Long Lake" in the approximate position of Pigeon River, both of them cited in the treaty. Also, a fairly large river was shown flowing from the Lake of the Woods into Lake Superior, whereas the two lakes actually belong to different watersheds.

At first both parties were concentrating on the exploration of the Pigeon River route to Rainy Lake as the most likely "Long Lake." But in 1825 the British commissioner diverted his surveyors to the western end of Lake Superior and up the St. Louis River. This evoked angry objections from Delafield, the American agent, who refused to have any part of such a survey, on the well-founded suspicion that Barclay intended to claim the St. Louis as the boundary. Delafield, being powerless to stop Barclay, began to look for a counterweight to this extravagant British claim, and seized upon the next convenient water route north of Pigeon River, the Kaministikwia and Dog rivers. And, in case this did not suffice to bring the British to their senses, he held himself in readiness, as he told his commissioner, to claim a line yet farther north and east, through Lake Nipigon.

It was plain that both sides had abandoned sincere efforts to follow the treaty and were trying to seize whatever they could by pretence and sophistry.

In advancing his claim for the St. Louis River route, Barclay used the argument that the Mitchell map had been so thoroughly discredited that no part of it could be trusted, even though it showed clearly that the St. Louis River and "Long Lake" were far apart. He had a fine time dwelling on the haphazard ways in which such old maps had been compiled, from dimly perceived bits of shores and mountains and the superstitious folk tales of the natives. The Isles Philippeaux, or Phelipeaux, for example, could well be a duplication of Isle Royale or the Keweenaw Peninsula, or even the mythical abode of an Indian god:

> The Indians fix the residence of their Manitou, or Great Spirit, in fabulous spots, or in such real regions of Nature as are not subject to be frequented by man. The magnitude of the Great Lake, as they term Lake Superior, afforded them a fit habitation for

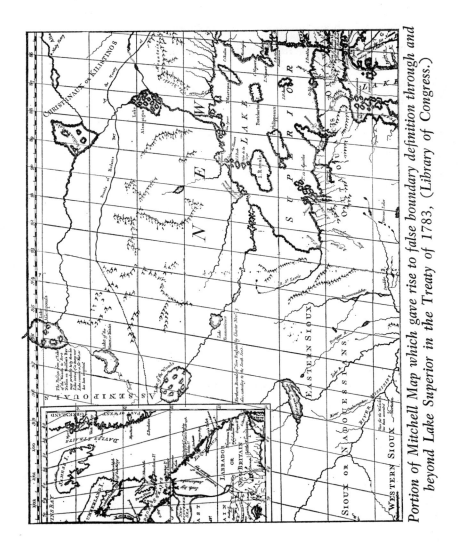

Portion of Mitchell Map which gave rise to false boundary definition through and beyond Lake Superior in the Treaty of 1783. (Library of Congress.)

Him, for they had no conception of any vessel larger than their canoes which are obliged to hug the shore.

Since "Long Lake" had proved to be non-existent, the obvious thing to look for, Barclay said, was the best and largest water communication from Lake Superior to Rainy Lake to fulfil the spirit of the treaty as embodied in the rest of the water boundary. This was obviously the St. Louis River. He justly ridiculed the attempt of Delafield to force a canoe up the Kaministikwia route to prove its passability, and emphasized the hazards of protracted portaging:

> During these delays and the consequent separation of Stores, Baggage, and Proprietors frequent losses are sustained by the depredations not only of the Natives but also of the Voyageurs themselves, whose consciences become corrupted by scanty allowances, there rendered necessary. Before the long Portages are completed, frequently some of the men are taken Sick, either from accidents or from fevers produced by fatigue and galls.

Porter, coached by Delafield, was convinced that the Pigeon River was the route intended by the treaty, but he felt it necessary to defend the Kaministikwia route to balance Barclay's claim, and came up with the ingenious notion that the "Isles Phelipeaux" did in fact exist, but to the west rather than the east of the Isle Royale; in short, in the shape of little Pie Island. Since the treaty said that the boundary should pass northward of these islands, it was obvious to him that it was meant to enter the land at the mouth of the Kaministikwia.

The reason for Barclay's sudden deviation toward the St. Louis River and the resulting dispute is, of course, simple in the extreme. That Mitchell's "Long Lake" was identical with Pigeon River and that it was the boundary intended by the Treaty of 1783 must be obvious to anyone who compares the old map with a modern one. (It may be argued that the treaty-makers would not have chosen the Pigeon River had they known that it was but a relatively small watercourse, and that it did not flow from the Lake of the Woods into Lake Superior. This, however, is no more than a speculation about motivations.) It was obvious to the Canadian fur traders as soon as the treaty was signed, and their loud protests to London were one of the reasons why Britain dragged out its promised evacuation of the Midwest. Up the Pigeon River ran the most important trade route from the Great Lakes to the Prairies. This would not normally have been interfered with by a boundary along its middle, but it happens that near its mouth the river drops down precipitous rapids, which can be circumvented only by a portage on the *southern side,* about six miles from the river's mouth.

Barclay, being a Maritimer, was not at first familiar with these details and their fateful importance to the Canadian fur trade. But as it became apparent that he might agree to the Pigeon River boundary, protests must surely have begun to pour in on him. He therefore attempted to get Porter to modify the United States claim to Pigeon River so far as to cede to Britain the small piece of land south of the river's mouth. Porter, who was probably as mindful of the interests of the underdog American fur trade as Barclay was of that of Canada, refused this request on the very proper ground that neither the Treaty of Paris nor the Treaty of Ghent nor his authority as commissioner sanctioned such a land boundary. Barclay then sought a simple stipulation that the portage, even if it were on American territory, should be free to British traders. Porter declined this also.

Anthony Barclay now found himself in much the same situation as his father on the eastern boundary, and he did not hesitate to follow in his father's footsteps by using his wits to supply the deficiency of his title. But where a vague geography and confused historical documents lent to the Mars Hill line at least the shadow of plausibility, Anthony Barclay's St. Louis River claim was palpably at war with reality. Nonetheless it was in due course sustained by the Foreign Office.

There was also trouble over the water communication between Lakes Superior and Huron, where both Barclay and Porter laid claim to Sugar Island. East of Sugar Island ran the navigable channel from Lake Superior to Lake Huron; west of the island were dangerous rapids. But a glance at the map will show that it is the western channel which is the logical line of separation. Both sides coveted the exclusive control of the ship channel, and no agreement could be reached.

Yet another place bade fair to become as contentious as any — the north-westernmost point of the Lake of the Woods.

On Mitchell's map the Lake of the Woods was represented as a perfect oval, and its north-westernmost point was simply the point farthest from Lake Superior in a straight line. It was found by the surveyors that the lake had in reality an extremely irregular shape, and that it merged almost imperceptibly into other lakes and swamps. In the summer of 1824 Thompson mapped the lake, especially its northern and western shores. On written instructions of Dr. Tiarks, who by that time had returned to England after his labours on the forty-fifth parallel, he chose several alternate "north-westernmost points," all clustered together on a western arm of the lake. The British feared, however, that the Americans would claim Rat Portage, the start of the Winnipeg River route, as the north-westernmost point. This would make the boundary bisect the lake from north to south. George Canning, the Foreign Secretary, queried the Hudson's Bay Company, as the body most directly concerned, on its opinion of the alternatives. Nicholas Garry, the company's deputy governor, replied:

> If the Boundary line which Mr. Barclay supposes will be claimed by the American Commissioner were to be acceded to, the communication between one considerable portion of the Hudson's Bay Company's Territories and the whole of His Majesty's other Indian Territory with Canada, would be entirely cut off. . . . The claim ought not, under any circumstances, to be admitted by His Majesty's Government.

To leave nothing undone to prevent such a calamity, Canning insisted on dispatching Dr. Tiarks himself to the Lake of the Woods to make exact measurements. Anthony Barclay was not very enthusiastic about the mission; he was well satisfied with Thompson's competence and he feared that news of Tiarks's arrival would stiffen the Americans. He recommended therefore that the astronomer should conceal his true object and profess to be interested

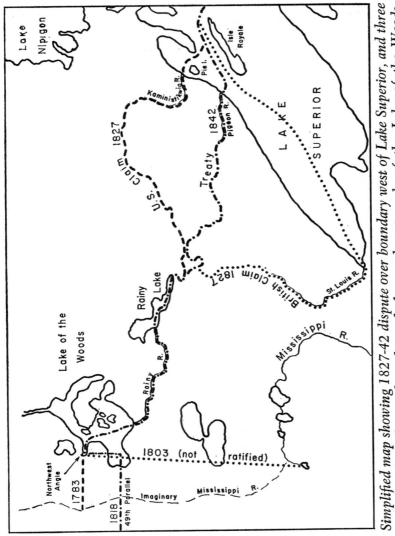

Simplified map showing 1827–42 dispute over boundary west of Lake Superior, and three stages of boundary-making beyond the northwest angle of the Lake of the Woods.

in some other point. Canning, fearing Barclay's interference, told
him to leave Tiarks alone.

Nonetheless, everything went well. Tiarks arrived in New York
in May, 1825, met Barclay, and travelled with the commissioner
to the Lake of the Woods. It was Barclay's first trip into that wilderness, and though he had planned it for some time he still regarded
it with distaste. The tour, he explained sourly to his correspondents
in cozy London, would "require my absence from the civilized
world for five months. The Lake of the Woods is removed about
Two Thousand Miles from the Atlantic." At the Lake of the Woods
Dr. Tiarks made his scientific observations with great care and
ingenuity, and in due course pronounced in favour of one of
Thompson's points. Barclay, reporting this to the Foreign Office,
remarked that Tiarks's efforts had succeeded in shifting the point
"a fraction of a mile," gaining for Britain a tiny stretch of muskeg.

The observations were accepted by Porter, and on this point at
least British worries were laid to rest.

The two commissioners made their final reports under Article 7
late in 1827, still differing on the possession of Sugar Island
between Lakes Huron and Superior, and on the line from Lake
Superior to Rainy Lake. The entire cost of the surveys made under
Articles 6 and 7 amounted to $178,102.50½, of which each nation
was required to pay half.

Whatever the legal or ethical merits of Anthony Barclay's claim
of the St. Louis River, it had its desired political and economic
effect. While the boundary was in dispute British fur traders were
able to continue to pass unhindered over the Grand Portage south
of the Pigeon River's mouth. When Webster and Lord Ashburton
proceeded to the settlement of this portion of the boundary in 1842,
they had little difficulty in deciding on the Pigeon River line, with
a stipulation that all portages be free to traders of both nations. In
the St. Mary's River, the American claim to Sugar Island was
allowed. The negotiators also reopened the boundary under Article
6 to make all channels around the Long Sault Islands free to the
navigation of both sides, a proviso that was also applied to the
River and Lake St. Clair.

Before agreeing to the Pigeon River boundary with the toll-free portage, Webster consulted Delafield and his surveyor, James Ferguson. Both replied that the territory was valuable to the fur traders, but useless for agriculture. In attacking Webster for his deal with Ashburton, the expansionist Senator Thomas Benton said that Ashburton had wanted the disputed area

> for the benefit of the fur trade, and for the consequent command which it would give the British over the Indians in time of war. All this is apparent; yet our Secretary would only look at it as a corn and potato region! And finding it not good for that purpose, he surrenders it to the British!

But to crave a piece of land for reasons other than its intrinsic value was still a novelty in American political thought.

Along the entire boundary from the St. Lawrence to the Lake of the Woods the commission had planted only two monuments — at the starting-point of St. Regis, and at the end, in the swampy brush of the North-westernmost Point, or Angle. The latter monument consisted of a pyramid of wood, the only material at hand. The commissioners had early determined to make the entire course a water boundary, and they almost succeeded, except for a few missing links on the watershed between the Lake of the Woods and Lake Superior. These short pieces of land boundary totalled only four thousand feet.

With the Webster-Ashburton accord of 1842 the boundary was finally fixed on maps and treaties and forgotten. Fur traders, missionaries, and Indians went their accustomed way, forest fires blackened the bush, rot, ice, and floods ate into the old wood, and before long the North-westernmost Angle of the Lake of the Woods had returned to its wild and undistinguished state.

In the late fall of 1872 the Angle suddenly awoke to new life; the tent, the canoe, the axe, the zenith telescope, the whole paraphernalia of the surveyor's craft were back, to locate and continue the long-lost thread. The surveyors had come to lay down the boundary of the forty-ninth parallel from the Lake of the Woods to the Rocky Mountains — the Great Plains boundary.

The treaty that finally established the forty-ninth parallel as the boundary on the Plains had been signed as early as 1818, while Ogilvy and Porter were still busy along the upper St. Lawrence. When the British surveyors were winding up their work in the Lake of the Woods, Anthony Barclay was all in favour of connecting the North-west Angle with the forty-ninth parallel via the stipulated north-south line; but this was not covered by the Treaty of Ghent, and neither London nor Washington was willing to go through the labour of formal negotiations for the sake of an insignificant survey.

How had this gap between the Angle and the Plains boundary come about? The question opens a whole Pandora's box of confusion, misconception, intrigue, and accident that is not only curious and often amusing but also illustrates well the workings of North American geopolitics at the end of the eighteenth and the beginning of the nineteenth century.

The Treaty of Paris of 1783 said that the boundary was to run from the North-west Angle "on a due west course to the river Mississipi; thence by a line to be drawn along the middle of the said river Mississipi until it shall intersect the northernmost part of the thirty-first degree of north latitude." Here again the negotiators based themselves exclusively on Mitchell's map. That map did not show the source of the Mississippi, for the area west of the Lake of the Woods was covered by a large inset map. Beside it, however, there was a note, reading, "The Head of the Mississipi is not yet known: It is supposed to arise about the 50th degree Latitude." Since the North-west Angle was shown in the approximate latitude of 49°30′, a line from it drawn westward would intersect the Mississippi.

However, it was well known to fur traders and some geographers even in 1783 that the source of the great river lay much farther south. The definite determination was made by David Thompson in 1798, while he was still in the employ of the North West Company. He placed the source at 47°39′. A line westward from the North-west Angle could not therefore meet the Mississippi.

The knowledge about the true source of the Mississippi penetrated into British diplomatic circles together with the protests of the fur trade about the disadvantageous line from Lake Superior to the Lake of the Woods. Trade in western furs was the most profitable of all British North American industries; from 1783 to 1793 its annual yield was £200,000, of which about £40,000 came from pelts brought in via the Pigeon River route and the Grand Portage.

London therefore saw in the treaty error a welcome opportunity to redraw the boundary more to its own advantage. In 1792 the British Minister in Washington suggested that the sensible thing to do now was to draw the line from the North-west Angle not westward but rougly southward until it struck the Mississippi. That it should strike the river was essential, for the Treaty of 1783 had provided that the navigation of the Mississippi should be free to both nations — and how could Britain navigate the river if its territory did not extend to it? Therefore the line should not merely run to the river's source, but to that point where the river became truly navigable, *i.e.,* about the latitude of St. Paul.

President Jefferson did not admit the argument about navigability, implying that the British were cleverly trying to put the cart before the horse, and nothing came of the British-American negotiations on the gap between the Lake of the Woods and the Mississippi River until 1803. On May 12, 1803, Lord Hawkesbury, the British Foreign Secretary, and Rufus King, United States Minister, concluded in London a treaty, one of whose articles — the fifth — said that

> whereas it is uncertain whether the River Mississippi extends so far to the Northward as to be intercepted by a Line drawn due West from the Lake of the Woods . . . it is agreed that . . . the Boundary of the United States in that quarter shall . . . be the shortest line which can be drawn between the North-west Point of the Lake of the Woods and the nearest Source of the River Mississippi.

Such a line, as a modern map shows, would run almost directly south, or perhaps south-east, depending on what is understood by "nearest source."

Unbeknownst to Hawkesbury and King — such was the slowness of mail in war-torn Europe — American negotiators in Paris had on April 30 concluded a transaction with Napoleon to purchase from France its North American territory of Louisiana. The price was $11,250,000 plus an undertaking by the United States to satisfy claims of its citizens against France, amounting to $3,750,000. Interest charges brought the final price to $27,267,622.

Louisiana had a tangled history. It comprised roughly — very roughly — the watershed of the Mississippi River and had been claimed by France by virtue of discovery and exploration. It had then been ceded by France to Spain as a reward for Spanish services in the Seven Years' War, but in 1800 Napoleon compelled Spain to retrocede the territory to France, in return for a casual promise not to cede it to any third party.

The retrocession to France was kept secret at first, but rumours about it soon reached Washington, greatly alarming the United States Government. Although American sympathies lay traditionally with France, the possession of the Mississippi River route by so powerful and wilful a nation induced great fears in the western farmers who relied on their exports via New Orleans. Jefferson therefore instructed the American Minister in Paris, Robert Livingston, to attempt to purchase New Orleans and environs from France, and sent over James Monroe to help in the negotiations. To their surprise, Napoleon after much delay and uncertainty suddenly offered all of Louisiana. Livingston and Monroe, assuming an awful responsibility, bought, thereby doubling the territory of their country.

Their first thought, after buying, was to ascertain the limits of what they had acquired. The purchase agreement said that the territory sold was to have "the same extent that is now in the hands of Spain, and that it had when France possessed it, and such as it should be after the treaties subsequently entered into between Spain and other nations." When the Americans sought elucidation of this phrase they met evasive smiles. The reason was simple: Napoleon hoped to arouse disputes between the United States and Britain, to his own advantage.

The Americans were thus obliged to discover their own boundaries. This quest proved particularly quarrelsome in the east and west of Louisiana, but since those regions do not concern us we shall confine ourselves to Louisiana's northern reaches.

When the United States bought Louisiana in April, 1803, the territory had not yet been formally surrendered by Spain to France, and before the United States commissioners could take possession of it this prior transfer had to be effected. Spain, however, was unhappy about the whole deal, which it regarded as a breach of promise, and dragged its feet. The tricolour finally went up over New Orleans in November, 1803, but as late as January, 1804, the Spanish Governor was still making difficulties about the transfer to France of various outlying parts of the territory. Anthony Merry, the British Minister in Washington, reported home that the Spaniards contended that the northern boundary of Louisiana extended only

> to the Banks of the River Missouris, their Posts on which River it is well known that they have given Orders not to be evacuated, whilst it is asserted here [in United States Government circles] that the United States have a Right to whatever was formerly the Extent of the Province, which, at the same Time, they pretend to have discovered went . . . to the Source of the Mississippi to the North.

Against such Spanish tight-fistedness the French Prefect, Pierre Clement Laussat, who in line with his instructions was anxious to hand over to the United States as unrestricted a claim as possible, asserted grandly that

> the boundaries of Louisiana retroceded to the Republic [of France] are, southward, the Gulf of Mexico, westward, the Rio Bravo from its mouth to the thirtieth degree of north latitude, from whence the line of demarcation has not been determined toward the northeast, as well as toward the north, where it is lost in the vast wildernesses in which there is no European settlement and in which it seems that even the necessity for boundaries is unknown.

The wildernesses might be vast, but the necessity for boundaries was known only too well to London and Washington. When Merry took up his post in the American capital at the beginning of winter, 1803, one of his first questions to Secretary of State James Madison was why the United States Senate had not yet ratified the Hawkesbury-King convention of May last. To his surprise and, indeed, consternation, Madison replied that

> an Hesitation on the Subject had arisen in the Senate of the United States, and that the Difficulty on their Part proceeded from a Fear that the Stipulation of the fifth Article respecting the River Mississippi [*i.e.,* the line from the North-west Angle to the source of the Mississippi] might upon Examination prove to interfere with the Territory which the United States have acquired by their late Treaty with France respecting the Cession to them of the Province of Louisiana. Mr. Madison stated at the same Time that the Senate were only anxious to provide against any possible Contingency.

How, Merry wanted to know, could a boundary treaty between Britain and the United States possibly affect a deal between the United States and France? To this Madison gave no definite answer. The British Minister (a haughty aristocrat to whom the stay in plebeian Washington was a succession of tortures) therefore suspected "that Ideas of Encroachment on his Majesty's just Rights are entertained by some Persons, who have a voice in deciding upon the Question of the Ratification."

Among these persons, of course, were President Jefferson and Secretary Madison. Jefferson, whom the momentous, daring, and quite possibly unconstitutional acquisition of Louisiana had kept in a high state of excitement and almost feverish cerebration, at first blush allowed that the northern bounds of Louisiana followed "those highlands around the springs of the Mississippi to its source where we join the English or perhaps to the lake of the Woods." This could still be made to accord with the Hawkesbury-King convention. During the fall recess, however, Jefferson repaired to his estate of Monticello in Virginia, and after rummaging in his library evolved a new boundary doctrine, which he laid down in a memorandum dated January 15, 1804. Copies of the memorandum were immediately sent to the American Ministers in Madrid and Paris for their guidance.

Jefferson found that the original northern limit of Louisiana was, indeed, the Mississippi watershed. This, he contended, had been changed by the Treaty of Utrecht of 1713 between England and France. Pursuant to that treaty, commissioners were appointed by both nations, and the commissioners had agreed on a line of separation between the British and French possessions in North America which, in the Great Plains, was to run along the forty-ninth parallel.

So much for the delimitation of British-French boundaries. As to the United States, Jefferson said, it had not troubled itself greatly over such matters up to recent days.

> Without undertaking to decide what were the limits dividing Great Britain & Spain [*i.e.,* Louisiana] in that quarter, we concluded it would be safest to settle, as occasions should offer, our boundary there with both nations, on the principle of 'valeat quantum valere potest' with each.

With the acquisition of Louisiana, however, such settlements as the Hawkesbury-King convention became obsolete:

> For England holding nothing in that quarter Southward of 49° the line proposed in the [Hawkesbury-King convention] . . . is through a country not belonging to her, but now to the US. . . . It follows then that the Vth Article of the Convention of London of May 12, 1803, should be expunged, as nugatory; and that instead of it, should be substituted one declaring that the dividing line between Louisiana & the British possessions adjacent to it, shall be from the North Western point of the Lake of the Woods, along the water edge Westwardly to it's [*sic*] intersection with the parallel of 49° North . . . then along that parallel (as established by the treaty of Utrecht between Gr. Britain & France) until it shall meet the limits of the Spanish province next adjacent.

This astounding document permits several conclusions, none of them flattering to the probity of the United States Government.

1. It was the declared policy of the United States Government to make treaties in bad faith, or, in the translation of Jefferson's elegant Latin, "for what they might be worth."

2. It was likewise the declared policy of the United States to

enter into international arrangements without being in possession of the basic facts.

3. If, on the other hand, the United States Government had been aware of the British-French forty-ninth-parallel boundary, what business did it have to join Britain in drawing a line through, or adjacent to, territory which did not belong to Britain, behind the back of the rightful owner, France?

There was, of course, a precedent for a British-American agreement concerning boundaries between the United States and third parties: the Treaty of Paris of 1783. In that treaty Britain had subscribed to the Mississippi boundary and to the southern United States boundary along the thirty-first parallel, separating the United States from Spanish colonies. But that treaty was in a special category. It was no ordinary boundary treaty between independent nations, but an essential step in the process whereby the United States acquired its nationhood. If Britain defined therein the boundary between the United States and Spain, it was merely to make certain that it was not holding anything back from the newly born republic. If the Hawkesbury-King convention was a belated addition to that category (and Jefferson implied that it was, by saying it had been concluded "merely for the purpose of explaining and supplying the provisions of the treaty of 1783"), then it could not, *ipso facto,* interfere with the acquisition of Louisiana. Jefferson had certainly seen no difficulty in jumping across another portion of the 1783 boundary, the Mississippi River!

The Foreign Office was of course quite astute enough to discern in these pretensions not the desire to see historical rights confirmed but an artfully masked grab for all the territory the United States could possibly bring within its orbit. If there were any lingering doubts on that score they were dispelled by Jefferson's departure from the watershed doctrine in favour of the forty-ninth parallel only in those parts where it was advantageous to the United States; where the parallel was disadvantageous he wished the watershed line to be retained:

> It would be desirable to agree further that, if that [forty-ninth] parallel shall, in any part, intersect any waters of the Missouri,

then the dividing line shall pass round all those waters to the North until it shall again fall into the same parallel.

But few points are ever gained in international negotiations by charging the other party with insincerity. When the United States Senate in February, 1804, ratified the Hawkesbury-King convention with the deletion of the boundary article, there was not much that London could do about it. Merry in Washington did have some moments of gleeful satisfaction when Aaron Burr, the United States Vice-President, secretly began to intrigue with him for the secession of the western states and Louisiana, but nothing concrete came of that.

The most remarkable feature of Jefferson's memoir, however, is that it rests on a false premise: no boundary line, either the forty-ninth parallel or any other, was ever agreed on under the Treaty of Utrecht. Commissioners were in fact appointed pursuant to the treaty, but not until six years after, and by that time France had recovered from its defeat and was in no mood to yield anything.

The British commissioners received their instructions concerning the British boundary claim from the Lords of Trade, who did not have much to go by apart from what could be construed as the Hudson's Bay Company's hunting preserve. That was generally understood by the company to comprise the watershed of Hudson Bay. Not being sufficiently familiar with the extent of the watershed (no one was), the Lords of Trade simply opted for a line which, they fondly assumed, was far enough south to embrace any river. This was the forty-ninth parallel. The line was also far enough south to take in the entire course of the Albany River, at whose headwaters the French were understood to be building a fort. As it turned out even their farthest claim had not been far enough, for the Red River, which belongs to the Hudson Bay watershed, rises south of 46° latitude. There was, however, an escape clause — the commissioners were warned that the "said boundaries be understood to regard the trade of the Hudson's Bay Company only; that his Majesty does not thereby recede from the right to any lands in America, not comprized within the said boundaries."

Despite the breakdown of negotiations, and the above injunction, patriotic map-makers in London henceforward entered the forty-ninth parallel as the boundary between British and French possessions in the Plains, and it came to be accepted as genuine by a great many statesmen, including Jefferson. Nonetheless, Jefferson and Madison knew that they were relying on second-hand information, and Madison instructed his Ministers both in London and Paris to seek confirmation in the local archives. Their search — if they made any — was apparently unsuccessful.

In 1806 Lords Auckland and Holland and the United States plenipotentiaries James Monroe and William Pinkney negotiated and signed a convention in London for the regulation of trade and maritime rights. Early in 1807 they turned to the consideration of the still unsettled Plains boundary. This was the opportunity for the British Foreign Office to explode the spurious forty-ninth-parallel doctrine.

Nothing of the sort happened. Incredible as it must seem to us, no one in the top circles of British diplomacy appears to have known the truth about the Treaty of Utrecht. Even more incredible was the ignorance of the usually well-informed Hudson's Bay Company, the semi-public organization that was most intimately concerned with the boundary question. Everyone concerned accepted the doctrine of the old forty-ninth parallel boundary as genuine. Auckland and Holland did ask the Hudson's Bay Company to go through its archives, but they were informed that "after a diligent search no traces of the papers relative to the report of the Commissioners of the Treaty of Utrecht can be found."

The Foreign Office and the Hudson's Bay Company thus had no decisive argument to oppose to the American claim. This was not to say that the proposed forty-ninth-parallel boundary met with instant favour in London. Monroe and Pinkney reported to Washington that the boundary proposal had

> encountered much zealous opposition here, even in the form suggested by the British commissioners, from the prejudices, supposed interests, and mistaken views of many persons, an explanation of some of which will be found in an idle paper written by Lord Selkirk.

The "idle paper" of Lord Selkirk (who was promoting colonization of British North America) was a closely reasoned memorandum which attempted to show that, whatever the southward extent of the British and Canadian territories, the Louisiana Territory never extended farther north than the mouth of the Missouri River, or the forty-first degree of north latitude. But Selkirk, too, subscribed to the erroneous belief that the Treaty of Utrecht had fixed the forty-ninth parallel as the separation between the British holdings and the French colony of Canada.

The boundary article which acknowledged the forty-ninth parallel as far west as the territories of Britain and the United States extended "in that quarter" was signed, but not ratified by the United States because the convention of which it was part did not prohibit British impressment of seamen. (It must be stressed that throughout the era of the French Revolution the British-American quarrel was not primarily over the exercise of sovereignty on land, but on water.) Still, the treaty draft represented the first definite commitment of both sides to the forty-ninth parallel as a boundary, and it would have to be taken into account in a future settlement.

There remains the intriguing possibility that both sides in the 1807 negotiations were aware that no boundary had been settled by the Treaty of Utrecht, but that they preferred to let sleeping dogs lie. It is true that by exposing the falseness of the forty-ninth-parallel doctrine Britain might actually have weakened its bargaining position, and that the forty-ninth parallel is a reasonably fair compromise line between the Hudson Bay and Mississippi watersheds. If the Red River does arise south of the parallel, the Missouri has branches north of it. Although it seems hardly likely that the negotiators would have carried secrecy over into their confidential correspondence, now open to study, the notion cannot be dismissed entirely. Even if both sides had been in possession of correct historical facts, however, they would probably have been obliged to compromise on some parallel of latitude, and the forty-ninth was as good a choice as any.

With the latitude of the boundary west of the Lake of the Woods thus settled in principle, it remained only to fix its westward extent. This proved tricky, as each side tried to outflank the other. There was also another residual difficulty: the British were loath to part with their claim to the free navigation of the Mississippi, even though the source of that river was now physically out of reach. It was this claim which caused western boundary negotiations to fail at Ghent in 1814.

Finally, in 1818, another of those omnibus conventions which were the fashion in that century was negotiated in London between Albert Gallatin and Richard Rush for the United States and Frederick John Robinson and Henry Goulburn for Britain. Among other problems they also took up the still unsettled boundary west of the Lake of the Woods. The American negotiators now wished to extend the forty-ninth-parallel boundary to the Pacific Ocean, but Britain also had claims on the Pacific Coast both north and south of 49°, as did Spain and even Russia. The British also continued to cast wistful eyes in the direction of the Mississippi. In the end the two parties compromised on confirming the forty-ninth parallel to the Rockies, and leaving the Pacific watershed open to both nations for ten years. They also provided for a link between the parallel and the North-west Angle:

> *It is agreed that a line drawn from the most North Western Point of the Lake of the Woods, along the forty Ninth Parallel of North Latitude, or, if the said Point shall not be in the Forty Ninth Parallel of North Latitude, then that a line drawn from the said Point due North or South as the Case may be, until the said Line shall intersect the said Parallel of North Latitude and from the Point of such Intersection due West along and with the said Parallel shall be the Line of Demarcation between the Territories of the United States and those of His Britannic Majesty . . . from the Lake of the Woods to the Stony Mountains. . . .*
>
> *It is agreed that any Country that may be claimed by either Party on the North West Coast of America, Westward of the Stony Mountains, shall, together with it's Harbours, Bays, and Creeks, and the Navigation of all Rivers within the same, be free and open, for the term of ten years from the date of the Signature of the present Convention, to the Vessels, Citizens, and Subjects of the Two Powers.*

With this the Great Plains boundary dispute was at an end.

I have dwelt on the genesis of the forty-ninth-parallel boundary in some detail because it has been treated in a fragmentary and inconclusive manner by historians. It caused no notable local agitation — the agitation was to come later, after the boundary was an old historical fact — and did not, at that time, seem terribly important to the two governments, not at all comparable to the eastern boundary. One of the reasons for British acquiescence in 1818 in a boundary by astronomical co-ordinates was that it was simple. Robinson and Goulburn were instructed by the Foreign Office so to draw the line "as to obviate the delay and expense of a survey over a tract so little frequented and so little worth submitting at this day to any more precise delimitation than what parallels of latitude may establish." It was only when the two powers were compelled to pace out on the awesome sweep of the Prairies the curved line so elegantly limned on paper that human imagination was staggered by the task.

The survey parties which invaded the wilderness of the Lake of the Woods' North-west Angle were the advance guard of a joint British-American Boundary Commission created earlier in 1872 after several years of discussion.

The ostensible cause of the survey was the assertion by an American army surveyor, in 1870, that a Hudson's Bay Company post on the Red River was several thousand feet south of the forty-ninth parallel and thus on American territory. (The location of the parallel where it intersected the Red River had been determined several times before, the earliest being 1823 and the latest 1850, but none of the various posts planted on the banks of the river — the artery of communication from St. Paul to Fort Garry — had bilateral authority.) The true cause of the survey was the growing American immigration to the Plains, the speculative glances cast by western American expansionists on "Rupert's Land," as the Hudson's Bay Company territory west of the Great Lakes was called, and the equivocal attitude of the half-breed mainly French-speaking population of that territory.

In August, 1867, the British Minister in Washington wrote home:

> There is a considerable section of the Western population look-
> ing forward to the acquisition of the territory which includes the
> Saskatchewan River and the Red River settlement, and I foresee
> that if it is not shortly occupied with settlers who can turn its
> natural resources to account, it will be over-run by squatters push-
> ing up from Montana with whom the Hudson's Bay Company and
> the Canadian authorities will find it difficult to deal.
>
> The New York Times is supposed on these general questions
> to reflect in some measure Mr. Seward's opinions which are known
> to be strongly in favour of territorial extension for the sake of
> popularity. [Secretary of State William H. Seward had just sur-
> prised the British — and his own countrymen — by buying
> Alaska from the Russians.]
>
> Indeed I was present at a conversation lately in which Mr.
> Seward urged an American capitalist to form a company for the
> purpose of buying up the rights of the Hudson's Bay Company,
> and of thus obtaining the command of what he considers would
> be the best line for a northern communication between the Atlantic
> and Pacific Ocean.

In St. Paul, Minnesota, the well-known writer and publicist
James Wickes Taylor declared in 1868 that "our fellow citizens of
the Pacific Coast and the people of the Northwest States have
resolved that the Dominion of Canada shall find its western boundary on the 90th meridian," *i.e.,* at Fort William. (Minnesota's
population even then approached half a million; Manitoba had at
most twenty-five thousand.) A little later the United States Senate,
urged by its Minnesota members, resolved to instruct the State
Department to inquire into the possibility of buying from the
Hudson's Bay Company its enormous hunting and trading preserve
which would otherwise fall to the new Dominion. After all, the
affluent United States could offer the company a price many times
higher than the impecunious one-year-old Government at Ottawa.
Even in 1870 some congressmen still thought a boundary survey
would be a waste of money, since the whole of Manitoba would
probably be ceded by Britain to the United States at the forthcoming
international conference of 1871.

Along the lower Red River itself things were in a most precarious state in the late eighteen-sixties. The much-talked-about imminent withdrawal of the Hudson's Bay Company from the administration of Rupert's Land, extending vaguely from the Great Lakes to the Rockies, raised fear among the semi-nomadic half-breeds that this would mean the end of their free-and-easy life. Not being able to come to terms with either the company or the heir-apparent at Ottawa, they rose in rebellion in 1869 under Louis Riel. Although Riel, a French-speaking Catholic with authoritarian background, could not have much affinity with the English-speaking Protestant democrats across the line, he could scarcely refuse their enthusiastically offered moral and financial support, offered in the hope that it would pull Riel's "republic" into the larger nation in the manner of Texas and California. Also active along the frontier were the ever restless Fenians, Anglophobic Irish filibusters already met with in connection with the eastern boundary dispute.

All this agitation has led some historians to believe that the boundary was actually up for negotiation and revision, and that a slight extra push might have tipped the northern Plains into the United States. This view is overdrawn. The issues never rose above the level of amateurish speculation and intrigue, and though the survey was definitely connected with them, it had local rather than world political significance.

The transfer of Rupert's Land to Canada took place in 1869, and since the boundary to be surveyed was now a Canadian-American one, Whitehall considered that the Dominion Government ought to share both in the expenses and in the appointments. It was quickly agreed that the British expenses of the survey would be divided equally between London and Ottawa. The appointments were a thornier matter, since the Macdonald Government claimed the right to appoint the British commissioner. For that post it put forward the name of Donald Roderick Cameron, Captain, Royal Artillery.

The nomination of Cameron was no accident; he was the son-in-law of Charles Tupper, Sir John A. Macdonald's close friend

and Cabinet colleague, a former Premier of Nova Scotia, and one
of the leaders of the Conservative Party.

Cameron was born in Scotland in 1834. He had seen most of his
early military service in India, after which he was sent to Canada
where he met and married Emma Tupper. Seldom has a marriage
had so profound an effect not only on the public career of the
groom but, indirectly, on the political affairs of the country of
the bride.

Soon after his marriage Captain Cameron was appointed aide-
de-camp to William McDougall, who was being sent by the
Canadian Government to Fort Garry in 1869 to assume the
administration of Rupert's Land. That mission ended in failure and
farce, thanks to the ignorance of Riel's armed half-breeds who did
not recognize a British gentleman when they saw one, and old Dr.
Tupper liked to reminisce long after how he had personally made
the long journey to Red River to bring back his daughter to
civilization, and how he found her alone in a miserable sod cabin
haunted by the prairie wind and the odd shiftless Indian.

Now, Whitehall willing, there was to be granted to Cameron the
boon every proud man craves: to return in triumph to the scene of
his earlier discomfiture. But Whitehall had serious doubts. It
would have much preferred to send a man experienced in boundary surveys, such as Colonel John S. Hawkins, who had been
commissioner for the boundary survey west of the Rockies (to be
dealt with in the next chapter). That failing, the British Government would have liked another officer of the Royal Engineers.
Cameron, an artilleryman, could be counted on to have mastered
the essentials of geometry and topography, but not much more.
Queried as to his qualifications, Sir James Lindsay, Inspector-
General of Reserve Forces, replied with a note that said much
between the lines:

> Captain Cameron is the son in law of D[r]. Tupper, who is one
> of the Cabinet Ministers of the Dominion. He was employed in the
> Red River Territory during the troubles of 1869-70. Though I have
> seen him, I have no personal knowledge of his qualities, but I
> heard him spoken of in Canada, and by Artillery Officers as a

sharp, intelligent officer, who had considerable energy of character. It was intended by the Dominion Government to send him as the Chief of a Mounted Police Force with the Expedition [of Colonel Wolseley] to Red River. To this I objected, as I thought it necessary to make a rule that no one who had had connection with the troubles of the previous year should accompany the force. In no other way did I object to Capt. Cameron. I fully believe that he will be a useful auxiliary to the Boundary commission. I do not speak of his scientific acquirements, for of them I know nothing.

Under other circumstances, such a report would have finished Cameron's high hopes then and there, but Ottawa had its own *raison d'état*. Lord Granville thought he knew a name for it: "It would be much to be regretted if the appointment of the Commissioner on the part of Great Britain who ought for the efficient execution of his duty to be a man of scientific acquirements, were to be dealt with merely as a question of patronage."

While Ottawa pressed for confirmation of the appointment and London struggled on the horns of its dilemma, the object of all this behind-the-scenes wire-pulling, on leave of absence in London, fretted and worried. Early in 1872 he finally received orders from the War Office to hold himself in readiness to depart on March 1 — for Ceylon. Frantic wires now started to fly across the Atlantic, and on February 22 London gave in, cabling Ottawa that Cameron would be appointed, "at the proper time."

As soon as he was advised of his impending commission, Cameron submitted to the Foreign Office the names of the men he would like as his assistants. Again there was irritation, but again Cameron got his way. Lieutenant Samuel Anderson (born 1839) of the Topographical Department, Royal Engineers, was named chief astronomer, and Lieutenant Albany Featherstonhaugh (born 1840, the year his father G. W. Featherstonhaugh helped to discover the mythical "uninterrupted highlands" in Maine), also of the Royal Engineers, was made assistant astronomer. Lieutenant Arthur C. Ward was named secretary to the commissioner.

The United States commissioner was Archibald Campbell, who had behind him the survey of the western boundary. Born in 1813 (and thus twenty-one years older than his British colleague),

Campbell had graduated from West Point and had worked as a civil engineer on various public-works surveys, serving after that as a War Department administrator.

Captain Cameron left Liverpool for New York on July 9, 1872, and arrived eleven days later. In Washington he had a conference with Campbell, discussing march routes and first survey tasks, and on September 16 he arrived at Pembina on the Red River, followed a few days later by most of his men. When the two survey parties were assembled they made up a small army, with wagon trains pulled by horses, oxen, and mules, with cavalry detachments from the United States Army, astronomers, surveyors, topographers, engineers, surgeons, veterinarians, naturalists, photographers, cooks, tailors, carpenters, wheelwrights, bakers, blacksmiths, and various other trades and labourers. The backbone of the 270-man British contingent consisted of forty-four Royal Engineers. Most of the labourers came from Canada, as did the assistants to Anderson and Featherstonhaugh, the geologist George Mercer Dawson (a twenty-three-year-old Montrealer whose hunchbacked body was compensated for by an excellent mind), the surgeons, and the veterinarians.

But in frontier Manitoba the arrival of so many men and animals, and the business which they were about to undertake, got scant attention. The new province was far too busy trying to bring order into the political and social mess left by the first Riel Rebellion, which had just run its course, and to deal with the first growing pains brought on by immigration, land speculation, the uncontrolled plagues of grasshoppers, gigantic transportation problems, and poor communications with Ottawa, not to speak of the law-breakers that hung about all pioneer settlements.

The summer was too far advanced for much field work, but there was time for one important act: a joint pilgrimage to that mysterious Mecca of an earlier boundary survey, the North-westernmost Point of the Lake of the Woods, familiarly known as the Angle.

Its general vicinity was found easily enough. It was a narrow northward-reaching arm of the lake, petering out in watery bush. But diligent search failed to uncover any trace of David Thompson's wooden monument. The Foreign Office had written to the aged Anthony Barclay, still living in the United States, for detailed information as to the location and construction of the monument. Barclay replied with a description of the spot and the pyramid, adding regretfully that he could not produce the actual field notes and memoranda because these had been lost in 1864 when victorious Union soldiers subjected his home in Savannah, Georgia, to "several successive days of rapine." Help as to the location of the old Angle also came from the local Indians, who, after much beating about the bush, were at last persuaded to lead the surveyors to a depression in the swamp where the holes left by the logs of the monument could still be discerned.

The location was thus practically ascertained to the satisfaction of the British astronomer and the American commissioner, but Cameron declined to give his formal agreement. He did this because he was nourishing hopes that the Angle might with some diplomatic skill be moved so as to give a more favourable line to Britain. The anomalous situation of the Angle had of course been recognized even at the earlier survey. It was this: in its north-westward course from Rainy River to the Angle, the boundary followed the deepest channel of the lake in a winding course. From the Angle south to the forty-ninth parallel the line ran straight as an arrow, intersecting the zigzag at several points. What was to become of the small water areas trapped between zigzag and straight line? It was enough to drive a boundary surveyor to distraction. Worse yet, from the British viewpoint, the southward line cut across a peninsula projecting eastward into the lake. The peninsula was therefore American territory, accessible from the rest of the United States only by water. To British and Canadian eyes it looked like an unnecessary and perhaps troublesome oddity which reasonable persons could only wish to abolish.

This, however, was not a question for surveyors, who could do no more than follow the letter of the treaties, and on the Angle the letter was unequivocal. Astronomer Anderson was therefore annoyed with his own chief, of whom he had already begun to form an unfavourable opinion. Writing to his mother on October 24,

1872, he remarked: "Our Commissioner has so far neither turned out brilliant nor successful. He has a most unfortunate habit of rubbing everybody the wrong way without meaning anything. Poor Mr. Campbell . . . is terribly put out."

On another point, though trivial by comparison, Cameron obtained immediate satisfaction, as he reported to the Foreign Office:

> An amusing incident happened in connection with Mr. Campbell's private Cook — a discharged United States soldier. When dining at our camp and just before our projected visit to the Lake of the Woods Mr. Campbell mentioned that his cook — 'Brady' — was a fenian. I made enquiries about the man and found that he had been one of the late raiders in this neighborhood who under O'Neill and O'Donoghue had seized our custom House and the Hudson's Bay Company Post — and partially plundered the latter, and that he had been serjeant of the Fenian Guard here. Being on friendly terms with Mr. Campbell I took an opportunity to advise him to leave Brady behind instead of running any disagreeable risks which might lead to unpleasant correspondence — for however much the authorities of Manitoba would respect Mr. Campbell's office — they could not protect Brady against free anti-fenian Britishers on our side of the line. Mr. Campbell — to my astonishment — immediately flared into stars and stripes — and announced his desire to have an opportunity to find out if any one dared to interfere with a man under his official protection. A night's sleep calmed Mr. Campbell's feelings, and next day he consented to avail himself of my cook during our journey, but he did not forget to remind me frequently that my antifenianism had spoiled his dinners. 'Brady' on our return to Pembina was in the United States prison there to remain until next session, for trial on a charge of highway robbery with violence.

Cameron apparently hoped to continue joint winter surveys with the United States party; but Campbell did not perhaps look forward to long winter evenings with the abrasive British commissioner, and on December 21 Cameron wrote:

> Family attractions and possibly a desire to spin out the Commission have withdrawn the United States Party. They left along the first week of November — just as frost was setting in. On the second day after Mr. Campbell's return here he visited the Hudson's Bay Company Post to make some purchases, and I went to speak

to him as he stood at the shop counter. I was not a little surprised to hear for the first time that he and the Chief Astronomer [Captain W. J. Twining] intended leaving for the winter that evening. . . . There are two inches of ice on the inside of the window in the room in which I am writing.

If Cameron had to face ice on the inside of his window, his survey parties had no windows at all. They were facing the prairie winter in the open.

Although Cameron had not accepted the legal validity of the Angle discovered that fall, he did not object to the surveying and cutting of a meridian line south to the forty-ninth parallel. This line drove across the peninsula mentioned earlier — a distance of sixteen miles — and met the parallel in the lake. A group of about a dozen Chippewa Indians was hired to cut the meridian line, but these braves proved disappointing as labourers. They worked erratically and knocked off frequently to present new demands to management. Anderson, who supervised the operation, recalled later:

> The great talker of the party, who is well known throughout the country, began with a great flourish, and very soon disabled himself with his own axe, and eventually settled down as the cook of the party. . . . The Indians would only work on the condition that I would take care of their wives and families during their absence. . . . After living almost entirely on moose-meat and a few roots, they have an indescribable craving for flour.

And Featherstonhaugh wrote:

> After a fortnight, only half-a-dozen of these men were able to continue at work, the others breaking down through want of stamina. They were all miserably clad, and the working in the icy water of the still unfrozen swamps was very severe upon them; . . . the ground passed over was all swampy.

Having completed the meridian line, the surveyors and their axemen began to work westward along the parallel. Winter was now well advanced, but, thwarting their hopes, the muskeg refused to freeze solid because much of it was covered by a light and fluffy blanket of snow which acted as insulation. In the half-frozen swamps men sank up to their middle.

> This, with the thermometer at zero [Featherstonhaugh wrote], or but a little above it, could not fail to be a serious thing, and besides the direct suffering from the cold, many were attacked with diarrhoea, one man becoming dangerously ill with congestion of the liver.

Still they plodded grimly on, observing, sighting, marking, cutting, hauling supplies by dogsled, sleeping in tents, keeping warm as best they could at open fires. The temperature began to fall to 20° and 30° below zero Fahrenheit. At such temperatures, the British noted with naïve wonder,

> the slightest breeze produces great discomfort, and it is very difficult to pay the proper attention to surveying operations. On several occasions the eyelids would feel as if they were about to be frozen down, the ends of the lashes becoming tipped with ice; the first realization of this produces unbounded surprise to the person concerned.

But when at last the swamps froze solid, the men rejoiced and continued with new energy. Soon the cold became so ferocious that it was difficult to make the simplest observations of stars, because the lubricating oil in the instruments would freeze, as well as the oil in the lamps that had to be kept burning. Such experiences were repeated the following winter (the country was impassable in summer) when it was the turn of the Americans to confirm the British observations. An American surveyor wrote:

> The lamps burned about fifteen minutes before the oil congealed and extinguished them, hence it was necessary to have duplicate sets at the mark and about the instrument, one set being constantly by the fire. . . . If the wind blew the smoke in the direction of the instrument the observations had to cease, for the fire was essential to thaw out the lamps, keep the observer's fingers flexible, and occasionally unfasten his eyelashes stuck together with frost. The pain in the eyes, from the proximity of the cold eye-piece, was at times very severe, and occasionally brought tears, which congealed in little icicles depending from the eyelashes, and gave the face a comical look, somewhat like that on children's pictures of Jack Frost.

With the tremendous frost of midwinter came the snowstorms.

In January, 1873, there was a three-day storm during which the surveyors could do nothing but hole up in their tents and sleeping-bags and try to keep a fire going in the protection of the bush. During that storm, it was learned, eighty persons froze to death in Minnesota alone, many of them children on their way from school, and the temperature plunged to 51° below zero. The following winter the Americans, too, were caught in a snowstorm in which their tent burned down and several nearly lost their lives. Altogether it was almost a miracle that the inexperienced survey parties came through the two winters with nothing worse than frostbite.

The American party passed the winter of 1872-73 in the East, but Cameron and his young wife stayed on in his newly built barrack-town of Dufferin, named in honour of the Governor-General of Canada (on whom the flattery was lost). The house which the commissioner had built for himself and family was christened Emmadale. Christmas and New Year's Eve were celebrated with all the pomp and pleasure that could be mustered at the desolate camp, and there were ceremonious visits back and forth between Dufferin and the United States military post of Pembina.

While the winter surveys were going on, Captain Cameron had leisure to plot next summer's activities. Among the schemes on which his mind was turning was the formation of a scouting force of mounted Red River half-breeds to carry messages and to reassure their half-brothers the Indians, who would be met with on the Plains. Along with most British officers Cameron adhered to the tenet that the North American Indian felt kindlier toward British authority than toward that of the United States, thanks to the more enlightened treatment he received from the representatives of the Crown. There is evidence that this was indeed so, but it would probably be wrong to give credit solely to British gentlemanliness. The British interfered less in the life of the Indian because there were fewer settlers in British territories. Not the trader or the soldier but the homesteader was the Indian's greatest menace; military suppression was merely the corollary of settlement.

Be that as it may, Cameron was anxious to keep the British

image untarnished and separate from the American one in the eyes of the Plains Indians. This meant separation from the United States cavalry units, the only purely military force attached to the commission. (The Royal Engineers, though supplied with firearms, were busy in their various trades.) No step, he thought, would be more fatal to the "quasi-friendliness" of the British Indians than to seek protection from the United States military forces "along a line of posts periodically attacked by Indians, and the garrisons of which are virtually in a state of perpetual siege." The quasi-friendliness could not, however, be entirely relied on. Among the fiercest tribes, the commissioner noted, were the Blackfeet along the Rockies, and the Vaulteaux. Of the latter it was said that "often in the midst of starvation and privation they undertake journeys of several hundred miles on foot to surprise and scalp an enemy who is generally defenceless, and return triumphantly to perform the war dance and to shout the hideous scalping song."

Yet there was undoubtedly also a personal motive in Cameron's advocacy of a half-breed scouting troop. He was still smarting over the rejection by the War Office of his appointment as chief of mounted police for the North-west. He had gone to military school in France, spoke French, was a bit of an amateur sociologist, and prided himself on his insight into the soul of the French-speaking half-breeds. It was therefore wounding to his pride that he should have been considered *persona non grata* to the Red River people, and the proposed scouting troop was an obvious means of rectifying all that.

He succeeded in getting his recommendation approved by all the authorities concerned, and the mounted troop was duly recruited and put into service. It had the advantage of giving some of the poor and restless Red River men a chance to use their skills and to earn some cash.

Between his return from the eastern survey and the preparation for the summer work Anderson made a bit of history by determining the exact longitude of Fort Garry, or Winnipeg, by means of time signals along the newly strung telegraph wire from Chicago. This was a time-consuming and monotonous job, and not quite comprehensible to the numerous operators along the line, who broke in frequently with inopportune comments and messages.

The survey of the Plains between the Red River and the Rocky Mountains got under way in midsummer 1873, and was to last two years. It covered a distance of eight hundred miles, one-twentieth of the forty-ninth parallel's entire circumference.

It was agreed between the two parties that they would work only in summer and would progress together, each side working on a twenty-mile stretch, alternating with one another in leap-frog fashion. At each twenty-mile point, more or less, exact astronomical observations would be made, and the parallel between these stations would then be laid out with the aid of tangents, *i.e.,* straight lines at right angles to the meridian, from which the parallel would be set off, at three-mile intervals.

The astronomical observations at each twenty-mile station occupied on the average seven days, since not every night was suitable for observing, and there were always unforeseen delays and accidents.

To the seafaring British the entire expedition presented itself in the light of an exploration voyage into unknown and inhospitable waters. And in fact, the first reaction of the Englishmen on seeing the Prairies was to feel that they were at sea: "The spectator appears to be in the middle of a small circle, just as is the case at sea, and the feeling which is induced is that of an oppressive monotony." Under these circumstances, self-sufficiency was the watchword. Nothing was left to chance, and each man's daily rations were predetermined exactly: 1½ oz. dried apples, 4 oz. biscuits, 16 oz. flour, 2½ oz. cheese, 1 oz. oatmeal, 16 oz. meat (this was considered insufficient by the chief surgeon), ½ oz. pepper, ⅓ oz. salt, ⅔ oz. soap, 3 oz. sugar, 1/100 gal. syrup, 1 oz. tea, ½ oz. tobacco, and 4 oz. dried beans. Each man also got a weekly allowance of 1/200 gal. pickles and ½ oz. mustard.

To the Americans the survey was another foray into hostile Indian lands, and they accordingly put much emphasis on military escorts, supply lines and supply depots, and mobility. Sometimes the latter was not very great, as in the spring of 1874, when the American party travelled part of the way to the boundary in a river steamer up the Missouri from Bismarck to Fort Buford. The steamer, incredibly overloaded, snorting steam, smoke, and sparks from a hundred cracks, was constantly in danger of sinking, burning, or exploding, and took seven days for the trip.

On the whole, about one-third of the entire personnel were engaged in the actual observations and surveys, and the rest ministered to their needs.

It was inevitable that in a force of this size and placed under such strains, some bad apples should be discovered. Accidents and illnesses also had to be reckoned with. Dr. T. J. W. Burgess, the British surgeon, gave a medical examination to every Canadian applicant, but a few sufferers from rheumatism and other chronic ailments slipped in. It was harder to screen out men who turned to the whiskey bottle for comfort, and wellnigh impossible to prevent a good number from being infected with venereal diseases by "abandoned women" who hung about the Dufferin barracks. The most common disease was diarrhoea, followed by venereal diseases and acute pharyngitis. In one case Dr. Burgess may have made medical history by healing a skull fracture with absolute rest (a tent was built over the injured man where he had fallen), cold applications, and purgatives.

The commission's top problem, of course, was that of locomotion across the roadless, bridgeless Plains, and it was here, in the sunset of the unmotorized age, that draft animals accomplished one of their greatest feats.

Generally the British-Canadian contingent depended on oxen, and the Americans on mules. The growing fondness of the British for the powerful, lumbering cloven-feet is shown by the change in the proportion of animals from 1873 to 1874. In the first summer the British party had 100 horses, 59 ponies, and 48 oxen, with a total of 112 wagons. (Many of the horses were, of course, used exclusively for riding.) The next summer the composition had changed to 114 horses, 55 ponies, and 210 oxen, with 179 wagons. The oxen were slow, covering in a day about eighteen miles on the average, but they were very useful in roadless terrain, where their great strength compensated for their lack of speed. When their hoofs began to wear down they were shod — an unusual practice, and a tricky one, for the animal had to be thrown on its back and held firmly while the twin irons were being applied. Perhaps their greatest virtue was their frugality: on the long trek from the Red River to the Rockies and back in the summer of 1874 they covered 2,400 miles, in harness every day, with no other fodder than the coarse prairie grass and the rank water found in the muddy rivers and wallows.

The oxen and horses did not, however, stand up well to the gruelling hardships of winter in the swamps east of the Red River, where the American mules came into their own. These hardy hybrids, gorged on double rations, spent their days hitched six at a time to a heavy sled in mud and brush, and their nights standing about calmly in the open, showered with snow and buffeted by knife-like winds, while the temperature hovered around 35° below zero. At the end of the winter they were hardly the worse for wear.

The dog teams used near the Lake of the Woods were supplied and handled by Red River half-breeds. "They [the men] were lazy and unreliable," wrote the American surveyor in charge of the party, "and apparently very cruel to the dogs; but they got a great deal of work out of them, and were themselves capable of great endurance in running and possessed of enormous gastronomic powers." The dogs were fed one pound of pemmican per day, and slept in the open, burrowing into the snow for warmth.

Red River carts were tried by the commission, but the screeching wheels and axles, famous in folk-lore, broke down so often that other types had to be adopted.

In the fall of 1873 Commissioner Cameron took his family east for the winter. On his return he moved out of Emmadale and into the officers' bachelor quarters. There he spent the long winter evenings in lonely and dogmatic lucubration until February, when he again left for more civilized climes. In Ottawa things had taken a turn for the worse for his father-in-law: the Conservative Government of Macdonald had been felled by the Pacific Scandal and had been succeeded by the Liberal one of Alexander Mackenzie. Anderson took note of this development:

> We shall get on all the better for not having any backstairs influence at work. Capt. C. and the American Commissioner never agree upon anything, and it is very humiliating to find one's own superior so overbearing and continually putting himself in the wrong box.

On another occasion he wrote:

> I felt rather sorry for Captain C., for while he was here he invited nobody's confidence, never got up till eleven, shut himself up in his room all day, never went out, and we saw nothing of him except at meals. Being a very obstinate man, his obstinacy was allowed to run its course, and I found it quite impossible to do any business with him except on paper.

The business the chief astronomer was referring to included several weighty problems that went beyond practical surveying and involved not only the two commissioners but the two Governments as well. One of them was the fate of the North-west Angle and the United States enclave just south of it, and two others concerned the course of the forty-ninth-parallel boundary itself. Archibald Campbell had proposed that the boundary between any two monuments (which were about three miles apart west of the Red River and one mile apart east of it) should be considered a straight line. This would cut off minuscule segments of Canadian territory, the maximum separation between curve and line being measured only in inches, but it might save future land surveyors some trouble. It had been sanctioned by both sides west of the Rockies, where monuments were much farther apart. But Cameron would have none of it. The other problem of the parallel was that owing to magnetic anomalies in the earth's crust the precise levels being used by the surveyors to make astronomic observations for latitude were usually deflected very slightly. The result was that the line did not follow the theoretical parallel but zig-zagged a bit. The greatest such deflection was found in the vicinity of the Sweetgrass Hills near the Rockies, where it amounted to twelve hundred feet. Cameron proposed to run a "mean" parallel by averaging the zigzag line. Campbell was opposed to it.

Campbell's reasons for opposing the "mean" parallel were that it would require a great deal of extra work, and that, if the boundary monuments were obliterated, the line could not easily be relocated by local observations. This view was shared by Anderson, who informed Cameron accordingly. But Cameron was not a man to be swayed by mere practicality, and he quietly obtained the backing of the Canadian Government for his scheme before tackling the Foreign Office.

When Anderson learned of this early in February, 1874, he became alarmed and rushed off a confidential letter to his friend and fellow topographer C. W. Wilson in London, who, like Anderson, had been on the British boundary survey west of the Rockies.

> Cameron has just informed me that he has received a telegram from the Canadian Government to run a mean Parallel, instead of an astronomical Parallel. We have already run the astronomical Parallel for 500 miles, built the mounds, and I have estimated that in conjunction with the Americans we can complete the demarcation of the astronomical Parallel to the summit of the Rocky Mountains this season. . . .
>
> To mark a mean Parallel will involve another season's work going over the whole ground again, and is altogether opposed to the views of Mr. Campbell and his Chief Astronomer, with whom I am in perfect accord.
>
> Surely the Foreign Office would never consent to this much unnecessary waste of public money, merely to move the boundary mounds a few feet north and south and still be no nearer the truth. . . .
>
> The Foreign Office when they receive Cameron's report recommending a mean Parallel and backed up by the Canadian Government, will naturally think that he is acting on my advice in this specially technical matter.
>
> The Canadian Government seem anxious to prolong the work as much as possible, but that is no reason why the Foreign Office who bear half the expense should be drawn into this most unnecessary expenditure.

Wilson, as Anderson expected him to, lost no time in passing this anguished plea to the proper men in the Foreign Office, who had the good sense to seek the private opinion of the most eminent authority in the field — Astronomer Royal G. B. Airy. Airy replied that the astronomically determined parallel fulfilled, as accurately as possible, the requirements of the treaty, and that the determination of a mean line, as proposed by Cameron, was "wholly unnecessary."

When Captain Cameron's proposal reached the Foreign Office, accompanied by the assurance that Ottawa was as keen on the mean parallel as himself ("the Dominion Government . . . regard the question of cost as a matter of secondary consideration"), Whitehall was forewarned and forearmed, and got Airy to confirm his earlier opinion in a formal statement. In doing so Airy pointed out that an ideal, uniform parallel as defined by Cameron was in any case impossible to draw because of the unevenness of the terrain: a man on a hill would be farther away from the theoretical equator than a man in a valley, even though both might be exactly on a "mean" parallel. Airy added: "How the space intervening between neighbouring points is to be filled up will be a question between the contracting parties. The easiest way, probably securing sufficient accuracy, would be, to draw straight lines."

This scotched Cameron's mean parallel — the commissioner was mortified that, for all his perfectionism, he had never thought of the effect of differences in elevation. But the mildly expressed view of the Astronomer Royal concerning the line between monuments permitted him to assert his stand at least on *that* point, and Campbell, glad to obtain the larger victory, assented.

Cameron had also been compelled to come round to the acceptance of the old Angle as the north-westernmost point of the Lake of the Woods. He was finally instructed to give his agreement on May 1, 1874. But these were minor points. The major question was the American peninsula. Campbell was well aware that some move on the part of the British was afoot, and he had already intimated that there was practically no hope that his Government would yield.

Oddly enough, though the 130-square-mile enclave was virtually bare of natural resources, its position in the lake had made it serve as the eastern terminus of the so-called Dawson Road, the rough immigrant route from Lake of the Woods to Fort Garry. There was as yet no Canadian railway beyond Lake Superior, and the boat landing on the peninsula seemed important. The area was also thought of as the possible starting-point for a canal to link the Lake of the Woods and Lake Winnipeg. Furthermore — and this seemed a particularly alarming prospect to Cameron — "the district will harbour smugglers and refugees from justice who may carry on their operations with impunity, unless indeed very costly arrangements are made by the Canadian Government to meet the difficulty." The American enclave, he said, would be much in the same position as the French enclave of Chandermagore near Calcutta, "where thieves and refugees from all the surrounding country seek freedom from arrest and organize illegal proceedings."

As usual his arguments were adopted more or less verbatim by the Cabinet in Ottawa, which resolved

> that the Government of Canada (while unprepared to make any except a very inconsiderable concession to secure the readjustment) should view favourably a proposal to alter the Boundary Line . . . so as to follow the Southern course of the Lake Westwardly to the first intersection of the Coast Line with the parallel of 49° North Latitude, or that the parallel of 49° North Latitude should be adopted.

In other words, the boundary should never go farther north than the forty-ninth parallel. This would abolish the American enclave.

Before placing this gesture before the State Department in Washington, Whitehall asked Ottawa to spell out its "very inconsiderable concession" in round figures. Ottawa mulled it over for four months and came up with $25,000, or thirty cents an acre. When Secretary of State Hamilton Fish was apprised of the offer he preferred to treat it as a joke, to no one's great surprise. Nor was he inclined to sanction the elimination of the small American water areas created through the intersection of the northward zigzag line by the southward meridian line in the Lake of the Woods. The United States had never ceded any territory to anyone, and he was not going to set a precedent.

With this last outstanding issue settled, the work could be carried through to its conclusion unencumbered by further doubts, hopes, and suspicions. The letter of the treaty had triumphed along the whole line.

But to the men who laboured in the surveys and along the trails these geometrical abstractions could be little more than fleeting phantoms against the stark reality of the Plains themselves.

On and on the grasslands stretched, now flat, now gently undulating, now cut by deep ravines and river-beds, now dotted with picturesque wooded hills and lakes. In this awesome emptiness men and whole wagon trains were swallowed up as in a great, heavy stillness, in which shouts seemed to fall tonelessly to the ground like exhausted birds, and the yawning distance appeared to condemn the labouring march of the oxen to the mockery of a treadmill. But grand and terrible as the stillness of the Plains were the outbursts of primeval nature that interrupted it. Both in 1872 and 1873 the survey parties were struck by fierce "equinoctial" snowstorms around the twenty-third of September, which lasted several days and gave way, strangely enough, to a long stretch of beautiful Indian summer.

The great storm of 1873 caught the parties in the field and was heralded "by flocks of ducks and other aquatic birds winging their way southward, while at night the air was filled with wild-geese urging their flight before the tempest, and piercing the sky with harsh cries and the rushing of wings." (What modern civil servant would dare, or desire, to use such language in an official report?) In the Turtle Mountain area the commission weathered a thunderstorm such as the men had never seen before, with the fiercest of lightning and hailstones as large as small chicken eggs.

But a greater danger than the occasional storm was the periodic grass fires which occurred every summer and spread with incredible speed. The fire was not usually high or intense enough to kill men or large animals, but much gear was lost. The worst consequence of the fires was the loss of pasture. The dry grass would burst into flame at the drop of a spark: on one of the treks a labourer struck a match against the sole of his boot to light his pipe; the grass caught fire, and the blaze immediately flamed into a broad front sweeping on to the southern horizon. It was later learned that the fire had cut a swath 150 miles wide from the border to the Missouri.

After the monotonous, treeless Prairies, the romantic Turtle Mountain area brought a pleasant relief to the eye and more practical benefits, too, together with new nuisances:

> Grass, fuel, and water were abundant, but the plague of flies was almost intolerable; the horses, which could not feed properly, suffered considerably in condition, and all hands had to wear mosquito veils and gauntlets. The number of mosquitoes in the summer in these countries is quite incredible, and the reality is worse than the anticipation. It may suffice to say that oxen have been known to be choked by them, and that on a still warm night the noise they make beating against the outside of a tent resembles that of rain. The only time that there is any relief from them is in the middle of the day, when the heat of the sun prevents their appearing; a moderate breeze will also keep them quiet.

Less constant, but not less abundant when they appeared, were the grasshoppers. On the Grand Coteau the parties were overtaken by a tremendous swarm: "The ground was covered with them, and the air was so full of them that the appearance was exactly like that of a snow storm." It was the annually recurring grasshopper plague which wiped out the British party's garden at Dufferin and caused many agricultural authorities of the period to doubt that the Great Plains could ever be farmed on a large scale.

Perhaps the most impressive biological feature of the Plains was the buffaloes, which were then concentrated around the Three Buttes or Sweetgrass Hills, in the Alberta-Montana area. The American chief astronomer, Captain Twining, wrote about them:

> These buttes are the center of the feeding-ground of the great northern herd of buffaloes. This herd, which ranges from the Missouri River north to the Saskatchewan, made its appearance, going south, about the last of August. The number of animals is beyond all estimation. Looking at the front of the herd from an elevation of 1,800 feet above the plain, I was unable to see the end in either direction. The half-breeds, Sioux, Assiniboines, Gros

Ventres of the Prairies, and the Blackfeet, all follow the outskirts of this herd; but, with all their wasteful slaughter, they make but little impression upon it. It is even said by the traders at Fort Benton that the number of buffaloes is increasing, owing to the destruction of the wolves in late years.

At one point, a dense herd of buffalo came stampeding across the plain straight toward the wagon train, and the men began to fear the worst; but some half-breeds who were with them rode to meet the avalanche, shooting into its midst. This caused the herd to open up, and as it thundered past on either side the men caught sight, in the whirling dust, of whooping Indian horsemen who were chasing their plentiful prey.

Like the camel, the buffalo yielded not only meat and hide but also fuel; the chips, known to the half-breeds as *bois des vaches*, were often the only material available for keeping the camp-fires burning.

But no matter how important the buffalo were in the native ecology, they were decidedly a mixed blessing to the survey parties. One of the greatest problems on the prairies was the scarcity of drinkable water. Rain was infrequent in summer, and not only were lakes and rivers few and far between, but their water was often so strongly alkaline that men and beasts were unable to stomach it. And when the survey men did find a good pool the buffalo had often been there before them. A member of the American party wrote, with puckered mouth:

> The buffalo find every pool of water existing upon the prairie, and are in the habit of standing in them to rid themselves of the flies which are their peculiar pests. Wherever, therefore, the buffalo had preceded us we found the pools were mud-holes, which were loaded with buffalo *excreta*. Sometimes the water which we were compelled to drink, even of pools large enough to be called ponds or small lakes, was so impregnated with buffalo-urine as to partake of its color, and to be altogether disgusting to the stomach.

(By the end of the century the vast buffalo herds had vanished, and the animal was almost extinct. A few thousand are now kept in game reserves in Canada and the United States.)

Another mixed blessing was the Indians. Generally they were

friendly toward survey personnel and contented themselves with demanding food, such as tea, sugar, and flour, and they were "keen after matches"; but they could also be insolent where they outnumbered the whites, and help themselves to provisions without permission. The drawing of the boundary line intrigued them and seemed to meet with their approval, since it was obviously to their advantage, when raiding or making war, to know exactly when they crossed from one country to another and were thus placing themselves beyond the reach of law.

The sizeable military escort supplied by the Americans may have prevented molestations, such as those suffered by lonely traders. At Fort Turnay on a tributary of the Milk River in Montana an American detachment found two traders who, only the day before, had given a banquet for a party of Sioux to conciliate the Indians; these showed their appreciation by making off with all of the traders' healthy horses. In the vicinity of the Sweetgrass Hills the surveyors came across the bodies of about twenty Crow Indians who had been killed by the Blackfeet the year before after stealing some of the Blackfeet's horses. The bodies had been mutilated.

On its way home in the autumn of 1874 the commission received reports from Fort Benton that large troops of Indians planned to attack the survey train, and several thousand of them were known to be swarming about; but all went well. Such warnings were not to be shrugged off; Custer's Last Stand still lay two years ahead.

The setting up of monuments on the boundary was completed in 1875. Along the eastern portion between the Red River and the Lake of the Woods the surveyors used cast-iron pillars at one-mile intervals; through the Prairies they built earthen mounds every three miles. Each of the iron pillars was eight feet tall, the bottom half was buried in the ground, and they weighed 285 pounds each.

In the fall of 1874 the two parties began to break up. Cameron, however, stayed behind in Dufferin to look after the disposal of his barrack-town. He was not a man to shirk hardship.

With the dissolution of the British commission, long-restrained animosities were allowed to come into the open in the shape of petty bickering. Anderson, Featherstonhaugh, and one of the assistant astronomers appealed to London against Cameron's ruling that they would have to pay out of their own pockets for their horses and riding outfits, worth £47 each, as well as for marmalade and ale, which, the commissioner held, were non-regular, luxury items. London found that Cameron was correct, and the three officers had to pay. (Cameron got his comeuppance when, after his return to London, he was forced to reimburse the Crown for extra shipping and rental expenditures.)

The commissioner — who was promoted to major early in 1875 — sailed to England in the fall of that year, accompanied by his wife Emma and his four children. In April, 1876, Commissioner Campbell, too, crossed the Atlantic. After touring Germany and Austria he turned up in London in May and signed the final joint report of the Boundary Commission. With that he retired from public life. Young George Dawson published his famous report on the geography and geology of the Prairies and went on to become director of Canada's Geological Survey. Dr. Elliott Coues, the naturalist of the United States Commission, later became one of America's outstanding ornithologists.

Major Cameron also struck out for new fields of action. Predictably, he sought the aid of his prominent father-in-law, who started to pull what wires he still had in Ottawa, after his party's defeat. On July 27, 1876, Governor-General Lord Dufferin wrote privately to Lord Carnarvon, the Colonial Secretary:

> Major Cameron who conducted the Boundary Survey has just concluded his connection with the Foreign Office, and his father-in-law, Dr. Tupper, has asked me to bring the fact to your recollection, with the view of forwarding his promotion in the army, or suggesting any other recognition of his services which may be thought advisable.
>
> The proper way of proceeding would undoubtedly have been for the Canadian Government to have called your attention officially to the fact, and I made [Prime Minister] Mackenzie a suggestion to this effect to which he promised to attend, but although he admitted that some such tribute would be very proper on the occasion, I could see that the matter was distasteful to him, on account of Cameron's connection with his enemy Tupper.

On a separate sheet Dufferin appended his own opinion:

> I think some little caution will be required in this matter; it
> may perhaps be rather strong language to say that Major C's
> appointment as Commissioner was a gross political job but at all
> events it is certain that he had no claim to such an appointment
> beyond being the son in law of Tupper; and it must not be for-
> gotten that we have had reason to doubt whether his action as
> Commissioner did not tend rather to retard and impede than to
> expedite the progress of work. . . . A step in army rank . . . is
> quite out of the question in this case.
>
> I believe myself, though as an R.E. [Royal Engineer] I must
> expect my advocacy to be mistrusted, that the success of this
> difficult work was due to the science and perseverance of Capt.
> Anderson, the chief astronomer and the officers and men of R.E.
> under him and was achieved in the face of much opposition from
> the Commissioner; but this is of course only my private opinion.

Ottawa having failed him, Cameron was obliged to seek ordinary
military posting, and he thought that the war clouds over Turkey
might open up attractive prospects. He was, instead, sent to the
island of Malta to command a detachment of artillery. Fortune did
not smile on him again until Macdonald, and Tupper, had returned
to power.

These notes are relevant to our subject: While still engrossed in
his forty-ninth-parallel problems, Cameron had been pondering
those of another boundary as well, passed on to him for his estima-
tion by the Canadian Government — the Alaskan Panhandle. From
this spark a rampant flame was to spring up, whose hot breath
seared the conscience of a nation.

CHAPTER THREE

Fifty-four Forty, or Fight

On November 15, 1843, John McLoughlin, a chief factor of the Hudson's Bay Company and the man in charge of the company's business west of the Rocky Mountains, dictated a series of reports to his home office in London. In his rambling, ponderous style he surveyed the summer's operations, incidents and accidents good and bad, expectations and regrets both official and personal: The party hunting in California had made only a poor hunt, but the venture had nonetheless paid off; more trade ought to be carried on with the Sandwich Islands (the modern Hawaii); an excitement broke out among the Nez Percé and Cayuse Indians at Walla Walla; the crops at Fort Vancouver, his headquarters on the lower Columbia River, had been more abundant than ever; Adolph Karlovitch Etholine, the Governor of Sitka, capital of Russian Alaska, complained about the wheat sent to him in exchange for furs by the Hudson's Bay Company; evidence had been obtained that the murder of John McLoughlin Jr. at Fort Stikine in April, 1842, had been premeditated. At the end he added:

Last year about one hundred Americans of all ages came from

148

the States, who from the stories that had been raised without cause
against us, were rather disposed to look upon us with jealousy, but
by management, we got over it. In the Spring, a good many moved
off to Calefornia, where I understand they have got lands. This year
it is said, there are come a thousand men, women and children,
but I think, there are not so many, they came with their Waggons
from the States, to the Dalles of the Columbia, and brought a large
number of Cattle, they seem much better disposed towards us, than
those who came last year, they say that the Columbia, will be the
boundary, and that the Americans expect to be allowed to get the
North side of the Bay of St. Francisco.

Here, alluded to in routine and random fashion, were explosive
elements which in a year or two would disrupt and transform
human patterns on the Pacific Coast of North America, and echo
menacingly in the stately halls of London and Washington.

It is true that when the issue of the "Oregon country" came to
trial between the United States and Britain the chain of cause and
effect was pursued with pedantry and partiality down through the
centuries, in vain search for the proof that would, brilliantly and
decisively, establish the claim of this or that side. But these were
mere diversionary manoeuvres not only in their effect but, one
suspects, also in their intention. The fate of the Pacific slope was
decided not by abstract historical arguments but by the emotions
of the people who had a stake in it.

Old "Oregon" was a vast stage, much grander than its modern
boundaries suggest. It stretched from the forty-second degree of
latitude to the fifty-fourth, and from the crest of the Rocky Mountains to the Pacific, embracing the modern states of Oregon,
Washington, and Idaho, and the southern half of British Columbia.
And in the centre of the stage sat the post of the Hudson's Bay
Company, called Fort Vancouver in honour of the great British
seafarer and explorer who had been among the first to chart
America's north-west coast. For years it was the only secure foothold of civilization west of the Rockies, between the sleepy Mexican
mission of Saint Francis and the melancholy outpost of imperial
Russia in Alaska.

In the fertile imagination of American expansionists Fort Vancouver had long spooked as an outpost of "that mighty creation and secret engine of the English aristocracy, the Hudson Bay Company, which for power and disposition to do evil is second only to its elder sister the monstrous East India Company." It was a lowering feudal stronghold, peopled by stolid serfs and lorded over by ruthless robber barons who sallied forth every now and then to plunder the hapless savages of their furs, or, worse, to incite them against the sturdy but guileless American traders and pioneers who were battling their way west to claim their just and proper heritage, and to carry the flag of liberty and democracy to the shores of the Pacific.

Reality was different. An American clergyman who journeyed to the Pacific coast in the eighteen-thirties and later published a travelogue, left this description:

> Fort Vancouver is situated on the north side of the Columbia river, about sixty rods [a thousand feet] from the shore, upon a prairie of some few hundred acres, surrounded with dense woods. The country around, for a great distance, is generally level and of good soil, covered with heavy forests, excepting some prairies interspersed, and has a pleasing aspect. . . . The enclosure is strongly stoccaded, thirty-seven rods long and eighteen rods wide [six hundred by three hundred feet] facing south. There are about one hundred white persons belonging to this establishment, and an Indian population of three hundred in a small compass contiguous. There are eight substantial buildings within the enclosure, and a great number of small ones without.

Some years later, two British officers drew a plan of the fort. It shows no fewer than twenty-three buildings of various sizes and uses inside the palisade, and a bastion jutting from the north-west corner.

For many years the only heavy weapons in the fort were two old ten-pounders standing ceremoniously, and ineffectively, on either side of the entrance to the chief factor's residence. When the political atmosphere clouded over in the forties the bastion was added and armed with eight iron three-pounders. It was sufficient to impress the Indians; against a battalion of determined American frontiersmen it would scarcely have withstood very long.

As to the Indians, relations were close and profitable, both in business and in personal affairs. Until the early eighteen-forties there was not a single white woman in Fort Vancouver, and the traders, from chief factor to the lowliest *voyageur,* drew their female companions from among the natives of the country. This practice was traditional with the fur trade, and of the "one hundred white persons" mentioned by the good American pastor most were no doubt half-breeds. They were called "Canadians" by company officers, which meant mostly that they were the descendants of French-Canadian men and Indian women, speaking a mixture of French and English and professing the Catholic religion. They had long forgotten where they came from and cared little where they went, as long as they had plenty of game, shot and powder, a goodly portion of rum on a feast day, and a complaisant dusky maiden when the camp-fire burned low. They were bound by a lively personal loyalty to the sprawling trading empire of the Hudson's Bay Company (which shortly before had swallowed the North West Company) and by an abstract loyalty to the British Crown.

It was the first tie that often excited the righteous condemnation of United States politicians, and was capable of rousing a few twinges of conscience even among the Hudson's Bay officials themselves. The company had been formed in 1607, an age in which private and public enterprise were not so rigidly separated as now. After all, it was only in 1858 that the British East India Company finally passed out of the picture in India. Here, too, though the Government in London was always careful to make formal distinction between its own colonial territories and those held, or rather hunted, by the Bay, it had invested the senior officers of the company with essentially the same legal powers as those of British governors — in respect of the company's own employees. In effect, this gave the resident administrators of the company much the same authority as that possessed in those times by ship captains, including the right of recapturing and punishing deserters. According to the Canadian Jurisdiction Act passed by Parliament in 1803, any person whatever might arrest and carry off to Lower Canada for trial anyone considered guilty of an offence against British law in the "Indian Territories," that is, land within the jurisdiction of neither the Canadian authorities nor those of the United States. This plainly included "Oregon," and the provisions of the Act were occasionally used by the officers of the Hudson's Bay Company to rid themselves of or to discourage wrongdoers. An American magazine, the *Democratic Review,* had this to say on this point in 1843:

> The laws of this company are most arbitrary and tyrannical, and from them no appeal can be made. Life and death are in their hands, as well as liberty and slavery. They determine the pay of their servants, and withhold it at pleasure; and also set the price upon all articles of consumption, from which there is no deviation; and also upon all articles they purchase of the natives. And what is worse, the leaders of companies, and, in fact, any superior, exercises the privilege of shooting down every one who disregards their regulations.

If it was so easy to misinterpret and to misrepresent the policy of the company, it was because the company was so powerful economically, and because it operated in so remote and rude a territory.

The long arm of the company extended even to retired employees, or "servants," who had settled as farmers along the tributaries of the lower Columbia. It was against company policy to discharge servants for settlement within its own regions, and to permit the men and their families to stay McLoughlin had resorted to the subterfuge of still carrying them on his rolls.

These points are worth remembering, for it must be understood that when the crisis came there was not a British subject in Oregon whose life was not, in one way or another, interwoven with the fate of the Hudson's Bay Company.

Many travellers and adventurers visited the company's Oregon headquarters in the eighteen-thirties and eighteen-forties; it was one of the marvels of the Far West. And no sooner had the missionary, soldier, naturalist, or official tasted its hospitality and taken its guided tour than he felt an irresistible urge to take pen in hand and to astonish in turn the civilized world. Just as the grand piano in the hotel room and the birch-broom-wielding female street cleaner are seldom missing from the wide-eyed account of our modern Moscow traveller, so there were certain remarkable features about Fort Vancouver that never failed to impress: the feudal ritual of the large dining-hall, where the white-haired chieftain presided at appointed hours over an entirely male and rigorously stratified company; or the marvelously self-sufficient economy of the fort where everything, from library and drugstore to smithy, was doing an ample and well-ordered business.

Most remarkable of all was Dr. McLoughlin himself, of whom many stories have been written. He was born in 1784 at Rivière-du-Loup, and studied medicine in Quebec. He was licensed to prac-tise in 1803, but the same year he joined the service of the North West Company, which later merged with the Hudson's Bay Com-pany. He soon showed a flair for the fur business, and in 1824 he was made superintendent of the (then ailing) Columbia Depart-ment, *i.e.,* Oregon. Under his administration, and with the backing of his superiors, the remote trading post grew and flourished.

Perhaps the best and most lucid description of Vancouver society has been left by Lieutenant Charles Wilkes, a United States naval officer who led a famous exploring expedition around the world and who visited the fort in 1841. He wrote about the common meal in the dining-hall:

> All the functionaries of the Company were present, and each individual seemed to have his place assigned to him. It reminded me of the description of a feast of feudal times, for there were many "below the salt." Like all great dinners, it was stiff and formal. Sir George Simpson [the director of the company's oper-ations in North America, who happened to visit Oregon at that time] occupied the head of the table, and there were none but men present. Their wives seem to be little thought of. . . . Military etiquette prevails. The meal lasts no longer than is necessary to satisfy hunger. With the officers who are clerks, business is the sole object of their life, and one is entirely at a loss here who has nothing to do.

Even the multi-hued urchins who sprang up like the lush grass everywhere around the fort had been gathered into a tidy company to be instructed in simple arts and to provide for their own sustenance by cultivating the land: "They have planted and raised six hundred bushels of potatoes; and from what Dr. M'Laughlin said to me, fully maintain themselves."

It was, in some ways, old Sparta come to life — except that it had more than its historical share of Periœci and Helots. And across the Columbia River, which here substituted for the Corinthian and Saronic gulfs, lay Athens, the small but restless democracy of the American pioneers settled in the valley of the Willamette.

Not that the first Americans to establish themselves opposite the Hudson's Bay Company south of the Columbia were independent farmers. The American advance guard, too, was the arm of a distant but powerful organization, an organization that could claim strong popular sympathies in nineteenth-century America and England too: a board of Christian missions. The manner in which its entry into Oregon came about quickly grew into one of the cherished legends of the North-west, much like the mission of Pope Gregory the Great to Anglo-Saxon England or that of St. Patrick to Ireland. Briefly, the events were as follows.

Around 1832, four Indians, said to be either Flatheads or Nez Percés, travelled from the head-waters of the Columbia to St. Louis in order to obtain an audience with the United States Indian agent there, who was none other than General William Clark, of Lewis and Clark expedition fame. The Indians explained to Clark that they wanted the white man's holy book and instruction in his faith, of whose power they had heard from passing traders.

Their romantic quest made good newspaper copy, and before long churches as far away as New York and Boston were sparked with missionary zeal. In 1833 the Missionary Board of the Methodist Episcopal Church appointed Jason Lee, assisted by his nephew Daniel Lee, to carry the word of God to the mountain Indians who had cried the Macedonian cry. ("And a vision appeared to Paul in the night; There stood a man of Macedonia, and prayed him, saying, Come over into Macedonia, and help us." — Acts XVI: 9) Jason Lee was born in 1803 and sprang from old American stock, though he was a native of and had held pastoral office in Stanstead, Lower Canada.

To travel to their new field of labour the Lees, both still bachelors, joined the second expedition to Oregon of one Nathaniel J. Wyeth, an ambitious entrepreneur and promoter from the eastern United States who hoped to make his fortune by catching and salting the famous Pacific salmon. Entrusting most of their gear to the brig *May Dacre* which was to sail around the Horn, the men themselves rode west toward Missouri. At Independence they struck the Oregon Trail, in April of 1834, and in September of that year, after the usual tough crossing of the Rockies, they arrived at Fort Vancouver.

McLoughlin received the missionaries with his wonted hospitality and discussed with them opportunities for establishing a mission. What the Lees had seen of the wildness of the country in which their prospective flock dwelt, and of the flock itself, seemed to presage a harvest of grief rather than souls. McLoughlin needed to make only casual remarks concerning the climatic and geographical advantages of the nearby valley of the Willamette River, entering the Columbia from the south near Vancouver, for the missionaries to seize on his advice and to abandon their original intention. That there were practically no Indians in the neighbourhood now seemed almost a blessing. With the loan of seeds and animals from the Hudson's Bay Company they set up a small farming community and began to prosper reasonably well.

By 1838 the number of men connected with the Methodist mission had grown to ten, and there were six women as well (one of them Jason Lee's new wife, who died that year). There were also the families of twenty-three retired servants of the Hudson's Bay Company, and eighteen American settlers who had drifted in by various routes. Among the latter were the remnants of Wyeth's expedition — which had again foundered — along with those of other unsuccessful expeditions organized by ambitious but impractical Americans, such as the eccentric propagandist Hall J. Kelley.

Numerically and economically the American element did not as yet seem like much of a counterweight to the Hudson's Bay Company in Oregon, but politically it was already a very effective counterweight. It was not necessary that the territory be overrun with American citizens; it was necessary only that some Americans should have settled there, so that they could supply expansionist politicians back East with food for talk. Although such a role could be played with perfect passivity, Jason Lee soon went over to action.

In the winter of 1836-37 the settlement was visited by a secret emissary of Secretary of State John Forsyth, a former United States Navy purser named William A. Slacum. Slacum's job was to assess the strength of British influence in Oregon and the chances for American penetration. He did much to bolster the spirit of the Americans and helped them to obtain badly needed cattle from California. His visit also inspired Jason Lee and his fellow missionaries to draw up and circulate a petition which Lee carried east in 1838. The petition, which reached Congress through Senator Lewis F. Linn, asked for the extension of United States jurisdiction over Oregon. Slacum himself returned east in 1837 and submitted a report that extolled the value of Oregon to the United States, and attacked the Hudson's Bay Company. Speaking, for instance, of the company's hunting parties, Slacum wrote:

> Excesses, too, are unquestionably committed by these hunting parties on the Indians; and every small American party (save one) that has passed through the same country has met defeat and death. The parties being much smaller than those of the Hudson Bay Company, the Indians attack them with success; and Americans hesitate not to charge the subordinate agents of the Hudson Bay Company with instigating the Indians to attack all parties.

This statement was widely quoted and misquoted, usually without Slacum's cautious qualifications.

Both the petition and the report were of a species that flourished in the succeeding years, in various forms and degrees of accuracy. Few of these documents were as slanderous as the one tabled by Senator Benton in 1829, which charged that in the preceding twenty years the Hudson's Bay Company had been responsible for the murder of five hundred American traders and their despoliation of $500,000 worth of goods.

Wilkes, perhaps with Slacum's report in mind, wrote that a charge made against the Hudson's Bay Company

of exciting attacks on the free trappers, who are generally from our borders, is to be received with many allowances. It has been made in many cases from interested motives; and I am satisfied that nothing of the kind could emanate from Vancouver or from any of the officers. The whole conduct of Dr. M'Laughlin is totally at variance with such a course; every facility has been at all times extended to newcomers and settlers; it is sufficient that they are of good character, and the use of cattle, horses, farming utensils, and supplies, is invariably extended to facilitate their operations, until such time as they are able to provide for themselves.

Wilkes also had something to say about the mission:

During our stay at Vancouver, I had the pleasure of seeing many members of the Willamette Mission; but they were unable to give me much information. They invariably spoke of Dr. M'Laughlin in the highest terms: they were averse to his absolute rule over the whole territory, and although it was considered by them as despotic, they could not adduce any instance in the wrong application of his power. He is notwithstanding extremely unpopular among all classes of our countrymen, but for what reason it is difficult to conceive.

As to the mission itself, his judgment was equally candid:

About all the premises of this mission there was an evident want of the attention required to keep things in repair, and an absence of neatness that I regretted much to witness. We had the expectation of getting a sight of the Indians on whom they were inculcating good habits and teaching the word of God; but with the exception of four Indian servants, we saw none since leaving the Catholic Mission.

Later the lieutenant did see a few Indian boys supposedly under the training of the clergy. They were "ragged and half-clothed." Wilkes was greatly disappointed and concluded that the men of God were sadly neglecting the task in whose name fellow Christians in the United States had made many financial sacrifices.

When Wilkes visited the mission it had been swelled by the "Great Reinforcement" of 1840, consisting of some thirteen men

and seventeen women brought in personally by Jason Lee. What
with the missionaries and their helpers, the retired servants of the
Hudson's Bay Company, and a few more remnants of American
trading expeditions and other migrations, the total non-Indian population of the Willamette valley in 1841 had grown to several hundred, half of them United States citizens.

The increase in American strength and numbers was not unforeseen by the guiding spirits of the Hudson's Bay Company. The
significance of the Methodist mission had not escaped them. In
1837 a directive was issued that the missionaries were to be supplied with merchandise — at a decent profit — to discourage
American merchantmen from calling at the Columbia. The missionaries were to be treated civilly, but not to be encouraged to visit
Hudson's Bay Company posts:

> Were we satisfied that the sole objects of these Missionaries,
> were the civilization of the Natives, and the diffusion of moral and
> Religious Instruction, we should be happy to render them our most
> cordial support and assistance; but we have all along foreseen that
> the purport of their visit was not confined to those objects; but that
> the formation of a Colony of United States Citizens on the Banks
> of the Columbia was the main or fundamental part of their plan,
> which, if successful, might be attended with material injury, not
> only to the Fur Trade, but in a National point of view.

To counter such dangers, George Simpson and John McLoughlin
were summoned to London in 1838 and there helped to formulate
a policy of controlled British immigration to Oregon. British settlement was desirable also to make the rule of the Hudson's Bay Company more popular and acceptable in the eyes of British politicians
and the public. Doubts were being expressed even then whether it
was wise to leave such a vast territory to the exclusive trade of a
private concern devoted entirely to the exploitation of fur animals.
The exclusive licence of the company was to expire in 1842, but
the governing board applied for renewal five years earlier, shrewdly
coupling its request with a promise to help colonize its preserve. On
these conditions the licence was renewed.

Like all endeavours of the Hudson's Bay Company, the coloniza-

Hudson Bay tried to colonize— but was a complete failure.

tion scheme was to be rigorously planned and supervised to the last penny and the last heifer. A subsidiary was formed, called the Puget's Sound Agricultural Company, and shares in it were sold to Hudson's Bay Company stockholders. The agricultural company was to supply prospective immigrants with all the requisites for farming and receive, in turn, half of the increase from the land. It was, in short, a form of share-cropping. Immigrants were to be sought, at least at first, among the Red River half-breeds, and in due course a trek of twenty-one families — 115 persons — arrived overland.

The experiment proved a complete failure. The Red River people were not of the same timber as the self-reliant, hard-working American pioneers; the land around Puget Sound was not so fertile as that along the Willamette; the paternalism of the company discouraged whatever initiative and free enterprise there might have been. The company official who was to watch over the newcomers found them "insolent and thriftless" and was glad to see them drift south to the Willamette to join the society of the retired servants. As to immigration from Canada or the British Isles, there was no prospect of it whatsoever. The sparse population of Canada was still wrestling with its own wilderness about the Great Lakes, and for British farm labourers to undertake the long and ruinously expensive voyage to Oregon was probably the last thing to be dreamed of. The company made no real attempt to recruit British colonists, and none came.

So the Hudson's Bay Company, and its Oregon establishment, had to look entirely to the Foreign Office for the defence of their privileges; and the Foreign Office, in turn, could base its claim by occupation on little else than the operation of an anachronistic monopoly. It was an uneasy love affair which could never rid itself of a faint odour of impropriety.

 Claims by virtue of occupation were not, of course, the only or even the most important claims advanced by the two contending nations. The issues involved in the dispute were argued at great length in the diplomatic correspondence of the time, and they can be, and have been, elaborated in even greater detail by historians.

claims by U.S. + Britain

They are nonetheless capable of being summed up briefly and adequately, as has been done by Hunter Miller:

> It may perhaps be said that the chief bases of the United States claim to the Oregon country were (a) the supposed possibility that the Louisiana cession of 1803 included territory west of the Rocky Mountains; (b) the Spanish title to the Oregon country, which passed to the United States under the treaty with Spain of February 22, 1819; (c) the discovery and exploration of the Columbia River in 1792 by Captain Robert Gray; (d) the explorations of the Lewis and Clark expedition of 1804-6; (e) the fur-trading settlement established at Astoria in 1811 by John Jacob Astor, coupled with the restoration thereof by the British Government after the War of 1812, pursuant to the Treaty of Ghent; and (f) the principles of continuity and contiguity, particularly in respect of the region south of the 49th parallel.
>
> At no time did the British Government claim exclusive sovereignty over the whole Oregon country: its contention was that both Britain and the United States had rights there from which might follow division of the territory between the two powers. The British argument was grounded on (a) the Nootka controversy and the Nootka Sound Convention between Great Britain and Spain of October 28, 1790, which was considered as being in full force (though deemed by [the United States] Government to have been terminated by the war between Great Britain and Spain begun in 1796); (b) the explorations of Captain James Cook in 1778, during his third voyage; (c) the explorations of Captain George Vancouver in 1792; (d) the explorations of Alexander Mackenzie ... in 1792-93 [*i.e.,* his overland journey to the Pacific in latitude 52°]; and (e) settlement, begun with the trading post established in 1806 by the North-West Company on Fraser Lake, situated in 54° north latitude and thought to have been "the first settlement made by civilized men west of the Rocky Mountains."

Thus juxtaposed, the two series of claims appear to balance rather nicely. In reality, the British claim was always stronger than the American one in the same category, except under the principle of continuity, which was in any case of dubious validity.

The Louisiana theory was too far-fetched to merit serious attention. As to the Spanish inheritance, the United States had disputed the Spanish title to the Pacific North-west before Spain agreed to limit itself south of the forty-second parallel, and the British Foreign Office argued that the United States could not now add together that which had formerly tended to cancel out. The British explorers and traders had come onto the scene earlier than the American ones; they had been more numerous and had ranged farther, and their work had been more thorough and lasting. The "restoration" of Astoria to the United States was nothing more than a symbolic flag-raising; the place was not again occupied by Americans. Although the United States claimed, or was soon to claim, all land west of the Rockies up to the Alaskan Panhandle, American explorers and traders had never penetrated anywhere into the continent north of Puget Sound. Both Bancroft and Bemis — American historians whose qualifications to pronounce on the question are unexcelled — say that the British claim to Oregon was stronger.

The conflicting arguments had to be fought out within the framework of the Treaty of 1818 that set up the forty-ninth parallel as the boundary from the Lake of the Woods to the Rocky Mountains. That treaty, it may be recalled from the preceding chapter, also stipulated that any country that might be claimed by either party west of the Rocky Mountains should be "free and open, for the term of ten years . . . to the vessels, citizens, and subjects of the two powers."

The article was recognized as a very imperfect and temporary expedient, and efforts were continued by both London and Washington to replace it by a more definite and lasting accord. This could be accomplished only if the disputed area was first disembarrassed of the cloudy pretensions of nations north and south, Russia and Spain. Spain, in retreat on the international scene ever since Napoleon, in 1819 concluded a treaty with the United States — alluded to earlier — to limit its possessions on the north by the forty-second degree of latitude. The treaty was the work of Secretary of State John Quincy Adams and was hailed by him as "an epocha in the history of the United States," presumably opening the door for successful south-westward expansion on a scale comparable to the Louisiana Purchase sixteen years earlier. But the two cases were quite different, for Spain's claim to the North-west had never been strong, and had grown so feeble as to be in danger of extinction by default. Spain had no post anywhere north of the forty-second parallel, and there could not even be the flag ceremony so beloved by politicians. Nonetheless, Congress made the most of the treaty. A committee of the House was appointed in December, 1820, to study the situation west of the Rockies and to report on the expediency of occupying the Columbia River. Early in 1821 the committee brought in a sweeping claim to the North-west as far north as the sixtieth parallel, *i.e.*, the present northern boundary of British Columbia. Individual members of Congress also advocated settlement and occupation.

The British Minister was naturally disturbed by these declarations, but when he took his worries to Adams the Secretary of State flared into an angry vindication of American expansionism. It was as proper for the British envoy to interest himself in Congressional designs on the Pacific North-west, Adams said, as it would be for the American envoy to enter into debates concerning the Shetland Islands or New South Wales. "The United States has no claims there, but Great Britain has claims in the Pacific North-west," the British Minister remarked. Adams declared that he did not care if Britain pretended to have claims all over the globe — it was up to the United States to choose those which it would recognize. He added:

> I have not heard that you claim exclusively any part of the moon, but there is not a spot on this habitable globe that I could affirm you do not claim; and there is none which you may not claim with as much color of right as you can have to Columbia River or its mouth.

He reiterated that United States rights extended to the Pacific (or the South Sea, as he called it), and he certainly supposed that the British Government had come to the conclusion that there would be "neither policy nor profit in cavilling with us about this North American continent." The Briton asked whether "this North American continent" took in the British provinces in the east. "No," Adams replied, "there the boundary is marked, and we have no disposition to encroach upon it. Keep what is yours, but leave the rest to us."

It was the forerunner of the Monroe Doctrine, but, like that ambitious pronouncement, it too turned out to be unenforceable and was, to that extent, a liability rather than an asset. Foreign Secretary George Canning (whose successful support of anti-Spanish revolts in Latin America, to weaken Latin influence in Europe, permitted him to coin the sonorous phrase that he had "called the New World into being to redress the balance of the Old") was as tough as John Quincy Adams, and well capable of protecting British interests.

There remained, after the withdrawal of Spain, still the Russian claim deriving from the voyages of Captain Vitus Bering down the coast of Alaska and subsequent Russian exploration and settlement in that quarter. In the fall of 1821 the Tsar was induced to relieve the Russian-American Fur Company of onerous Anglo-Saxon competition by signing a ukase forbidding non-Russian ships to approach Alaskan coasts north of 51° north latitude. This was a new and menacing pretension, and had the effect of bringing Britain and the United States into a semblance of joint opposition. Its strength seemed to surprise St. Petersburg, and the Russian Foreign Ministry, well aware of Russia's naval weakness, soon let it be known that the ukase was subject to negotiation.

The differences between the United States and Britain, however, were too great to allow them to face Russia together. In his message to Congress at the end of 1823, President James Monroe proclaimed his Doctrine, aimed in part against Britain. At the same time the United States Minister in London proposed to Secretary Canning that Russian subjects were to make no settlements south of 55° and United States citizens north of 51°. This, presumably, would leave the intervening strip to Britain — if Russia consented to retreat from its announced claim; otherwise Britain would get nothing. Canning refused to be thus deprived of Britain's claim in all of the North-west down to 42°, and his negotiators at length came up with a proposal to divide British and American claims along the forty-ninth parallel as far as the Columbia River, and then down that river to the ocean. Washington offered to compromise on the forty-ninth parallel all the way to the Pacific, falling back on a proposal made and rejected back in 1818. The outcome was stalemate.

Meanwhile, however, separate negotiations with Russia had made headway, with curious results. On April 17, 1824, the United States and Russia signed a treaty designating the latitude of 54° 40′ as the line separating their respective spheres of influence west of the Rockies; on February 28, 1825, Britain and Russia signed a treaty designating the same latitude as the separation of *their* territories, but in addition defining the eastward extent of the Russian possession by a line running parallel to the coast. (This treaty and its history will be described in greater detail in the chapter on the Alaskan Panhandle.) Russia was now out of the picture also. The two chief antagonists had dug out their bone of contention; they now knew, at least, precisely over what they were quarrelling.

Negotiations between Britain and the United States resumed the following year, 1826, in London. The United States Minister again offered the forty-ninth parallel, with concession of the free navigation of the Columbia River. The British negotiators stuck to the Columbia River line, but offered, as the last resort, to satisfy the United States' desire for harbours by ceding the Olympic Peninsula. The American Minister rejected this enclave.

By this time it was mid-1827, and time was pressing, for the ten-year limit of the joint-occupancy article of the Treaty of 1818 was about to expire. Not to leave things entirely up in the air, the two parties therefore concluded, on August 6, 1827, an agreement extending indefinitely the clauses of the Treaty of 1818 concerning the Oregon country; provided that either side could terminate the agreement on one year's notice.

Although the lengthy negotiations had yielded no settlement they had at least narrowed down the area in dispute. Barring radical changes, Britain would not seriously claim the territory south of the Columbia River, or the United States that north of the forty-ninth parallel.

George Canning died on the day the agreement of extension was signed, and with his passing the offensive on the part of Britain seemed to pass also. No formal discussions concerning the Oregon boundary took place between the two nations for fifteen years, until Lord Ashburton arrived in Washington in 1842 to settle accumulated British-American jurisdictional disputes.

Soon after his arrival in the United States capital he wrote to Foreign Secretary Aberdeen:

> The Oregon or Columbia River Boundary I hope to settle satisfactorily, and by this I mean to carry our line down the river. . . . I shall make no settlement in this case on any other terms. . . . What they are principally looking to is to have a harbour. . . . The estuary to the north of [the Columbia] entered, I believe, by the Strait of Juan de Fuca, is the only good harbour on this part of the coast, and hence the obstinacy with which they have hitherto persisted in carrying the boundary line further north.

But Webster and Ashburton, who by their conspiratorial collaboration muted other obstreperous quarrels, saw a way to get rid of this one also:

> Webster . . . intimated that this [problem of harbours for the United States] might be managed if they could make a settlement of boundaries with Mexico, so as to give them the harbour of San Francisco. . . . I believed that we should make no objection to any arrangement of the kind, provided the cession by Mexico were voluntary. [And again:] This acquisition of the harbour of San Francisco seems to have been a project of some standing, for Mr. Everett [United States Minister in London] spoke to me of it before I left England. I doubt whether in any case we could interfere with effect to prevent this arrangement, unless it were attempted to be forced upon Mexico. We shall therefore probably do well to avail ourselves of the circumstances of this expectation to settle satisfactorily our own boundaries.

It soon became apparent that the "arrangement" was rather President John Tyler's project than Webster's, and that it might well entail British participation in a pressure play against Mexico not only for California but also for Texas, with definite martial overtones. Webster was not enthusiastic about this, and Ashburton was more than cool, so that the entire *quid pro quo* scheme was quietly dropped, the more so as its prosecution might jeopardize the delicate negotiations over the Maine-New Brunswick border. Also, the exploring expedition of Wilkes just happened to return to New York at the time, and its reports on Oregon gained wide attention. "The public is at present busy with the subject," Ashburton reported, "and little in a temper for any reasonable settlement."

But debate and manoeuvre were not confined to international exchanges. In 1825 the Foreign Office confidentially advised the Hudson's Bay Company to abandon its trading post of Fort George, adjacent to the old Astoria at the mouth of the Columbia River, on its south bank. The company immediately realized the implications and transferred its Oregon headquarters to a new location seventy-five miles up the river, on the north bank. It was named Fort Vancouver — as the company put it, "in order to identify our Claim to the Soil and trade with Broughton's discovery and Survey." (Broughton, one of Captain Vancouver's lieutenants, had been the first to survey the Columbia.) From then on the company formed no posts south of the river, and Simpson advised John McLoughlin to trap heavily in that area "as while we have access thereto it is in our interest to reap all the advantage we can for ourselves, and leave it in as bad a state as possible for our successors." This policy was somewhat premature.

In preparation for the negotiations of 1826-27, the Foreign Office, in its turn, sent a long questionnaire to the Hudson's Bay Company head office concerning the geography of the disputed country, which was replied to by George Simpson. Concerning the Columbia River Simpson wrote that there was simply no alternative to this waterway as an artery of commerce:

> From all the information I have been able to collect respecting Frazer's River it is not my opinion that it affords a communication by which the interior Country can be supplied from the Coast or that it can be depended on as an outlet for the returns of the interior. I will further altho' unasked take the liberty of giving it as my opinion that if the navigation of the Columbia is not free to the Hudson's Bay Company, and that the territory to the northward is not secured to them, they must abandon and curtail their Trade in some parts and probably be constrained to relinquish it on the West side of the Rocky Mountains altogether.

And if the Hudson's Bay Company left, British influence and possession left with it — that went without saying.

Throughout the succeeding years the Hudson's Bay Company kept the Foreign Office posted on developments in the disputed territory, never neglecting an opportunity to remind the politicians that it was the company alone which upheld the British flag in that distant land.

The Americans, too, had their Oregon lobby in Washington, but unlike the British one it had the great advantage of being composed of people's rather than company representatives. We have already noted the sweeping report brought in by a House committee in 1821; and bills for the occupation of Oregon kept coming up in Congress ever since then. Their first proponent and advocate was Representative John Floyd of Virginia, whose boyhood on the Kentucky frontier (his life span very nearly coincided with that of Davy Crockett) apparently imbued him with strong expansionist sentiments. When he retired from Congress in 1829, Floyd had become something of a "Mr. Oregon," a title he bequeathed to Senator Lewis F. Linn of Missouri, a state that was more closely identified with western expansionism than any other. From the same state was Thomas Hart Benton, a senator for thirty years from 1820 to 1850, also a stalwart supporter of westward progress.

Floyd's bill for the unilateral extension of United States jurisdiction over Oregon was passed, after several years' debate, by the House in 1824, but failed in the Senate. Linn's bill for the occupation of the Columbia River, the establishment of a United States Territory in Oregon, the errection of a military fort on the Columbia, the enforcement of United States revenue laws (all to be accomplished with an expenditure of fifty thousand dollars) was also voted down in the upper chamber, but he kept reintroducing it, slowly gaining sympathies and votes, in the hope that it would eventually prevail. In February, 1843, just before his death, Linn's bill passed the Senate after a heated discussion; but the House rejected it.

Memorials, petitions, and private communications advocating an aggressive policy on Oregon kept reaching Washington, and especially the men of the Oregon lobby, from the western states — Illinois, Indiana, Missouri, Kentucky, Ohio. In 1839 Jason Lee arrived with his petition for the extension of American law over the settlers in Oregon. The Secretary of War in his 1842 annual message hearkened to popular demand and recommended a line of military posts along the Oregon Trail, the extension of United States jurisdiction over Oregon, armed protection to American settlers there, and appropriations for further colonization.

All these bills, schemes, and proposals were wrecked on the same rock: American law could not be effectively enforced in a territory where the United States did not have full sovereignty. The United States could not unilaterally incorporate Oregon within the nation, since this would be tantamount to a declaration of war on Britain. Anything short of such a step, however, would make the United States legal process impossible. It was the good fortune of the American people that both in the legislature and in the executive there were always just enough men who were capable of seeing this even through the emotional fog that whirled about their heads.

But wait! Did not the United States in its dealings with the Indians possess an embryonic *ius gentium,* a jurisdictional instrument that could be applied to *people* irrespective of *territory?* Perhaps. And it is therefore not surprising that in this murky area of legality we find the only overt attempt of the United States Government to extend its jurisdiction into the disputed territory, with the appointment in 1842 of Dr. Elijah White as United States sub-Indian Agent for Oregon. There was no Indian Agent for Oregon; that would have seemed too official. The "sub" was to be the grease that was to help Dr. White to slip more or less smoothly through the net of the Treaty of 1818.

Dr. White had first made his appearance in Oregon as a member of the small reinforcement of the Methodist mission that arrived in the Willamette in 1837. Bancroft says of him:

> Dr. White was little more than thirty years of age. . . . His manners were of that obliging and flattering kind which made him popular, especially among women, but which men often called sycophantish or insincere. He was fond of oratorical display and of

society, affectedly rather than truly pious, not altogether a bad man, though a weak one.

After practising a bit of medicine in the Willamette mission, White quarrelled with Jason Lee and returned East in 1841. There his lectures on Oregon attracted the attention of Senator Linn, who called him to Washington and helped to obtain for him the appointment noted earlier. In the spring of 1842 he placed himself at the head of a 140-man emigrant train to Oregon, where he expected to represent American authority not only in respect of Indians, but also in respect of United States citizens. The trek was marked by dissension and hardship, and before it was across the Rockies Dr. White had been deprived of the command.

The chief factor in Fort Vancouver watched the yearly increase of the American settlement with a wary eye, for he was extremely conscious of its connection with annexationist sentiment in the United States, as well as anti-Hudson's Bay Company feelings both in Oregon and elsewhere. But he was also aware that nothing could be gained, and much lost, by a callous attitude on his part toward the destitute newcomers, as he explained to his superiors.

> In this Country I have always found it best to be watchful without appearing to be so, as the appearance of fear incites to aggression, and if we had refused assistance to these men, and that driven by their wants they had made an attack upon our property, for which we could never have had any redress, the world, anxious to throw discredit on all our proceedings, would have said we deserved to suffer; and if some of these Immigrants had perished, which would undoubtedly have been the case if we had not assisted them, we would have incurred such a load of odium as would have been ruinous to us. In making my selection, I chose of two evils that which appeared to me the least.

It took a great deal of explaining to put this policy over with London; the Honourable Company of Adventurers Trading into Hudson's Bay was not accustomed to see itself as a charitable institution, much less one that was duty-bound to afford aid and comfort to the avowed opponents of Britain. McLoughlin never quite succeeded in this task, either with the London head office

or with British political circles. In an apologia which he wrote after
his retirement and after the settlement of the dispute, he was to
take bitter issue with the manner in which he was rewarded for
his pains both by the settlers and by his company:

> If all the immigrants had been my brothers and sisters, I could
> not have done more for them. I fed the hungry, caused the sick to
> be attended to and nursed, furnished them every assistance so long
> as they required it, and which some have not paid to this day,
> though abundantly able, for which if they do not pay, I am answer-
> able to the Hudson's Bay Company. It may be said, and it has been
> said, that I was too liberal in making these advances. It is not so,
> but it was done judiciously and prudently. . . .
>
> It is true several thought I was too forbearing; but when I saw
> how much the good on both sides would suffer if I acted differently,
> and that a war between Great Britain and the United States might
> be caused by it, I considered it my duty to act as I did, and by
> which I think I may have prevented a war between the United
> States and Great Britain. And how have I been treated by both?
>
> By British demagogues I have been represented as a traitor. For
> what? Because I acted as a Christian; saved American citizens,
> men, women, and children, from the Indian tomahawk, and
> enabled them to make farms to support their families.
>
> American demagogues have been base enough to assert that I
> had caused American citizens to be massacred by the hundreds by
> savages. I, who saved all I could. . . .
>
> To be brief, I founded this settlement and prevented a war
> between the United States and Great Britain, and for doing this
> peaceably and quietly I was treated by the British in such a manner
> that from self-respect I resigned my situation in the Hudson's Bay
> Company's service, by which I sacrificed $12,000 per annum, and
> the Oregon Land Bill [passed by the Oregon legislature] shows the
> treatment I received from the Americans.

The justification is perhaps on the maudlin side, as were all of
the old factor's writings, but there is really little exaggeration in it.
More astounding than any other was the attitude of the Methodist
missionaries, exemplified by their quarrel with McLoughlin over
property rights at the falls of the Willamette River.

Around 1829, long before the arrival of the first missionaries,
McLoughlin had noted the water-power potential of the falls of

the Willamette (later the site of Oregon City). He had driven in his stake and made a few improvements with an idea of setting up a sawmill and in general holding the valuable location for the company. Nothing further was done for many years. In 1840 one of the newly arrived missionaries, Alvin F. Waller, proposed to set up a small mission near the falls, and McLoughlin helped him by donating land and lumber. Soon after it became apparent that Waller's intentions were mercenary rather than missionary. He tried, unsuccessfully, to take a hand in the fur business (for which he was rebuked by Lieutenant Wilkes), and laid claim to the falls. McLoughlin, seeing the drift of events, began to lay out his own claim in lots to assert his title. Waller, with the aid of his fellow clergymen, then started to set up a mill at the falls. McLoughlin countered by setting up his own mill, which, thanks to his superior resources, easily outdid that of the mission.

This infuriated Waller and his friends, and they once more initiated a petition to the United States Congress, more intemperate than any previous one, charging McLoughlin with a long list of insults and misdemeanors. They complained in particular that McLoughlin pretended to claim the falls site for himself, while actually holding it for "a foreign corporation," *i.e.,* the Hudson's Bay Company. Corporations could not, under United States law, pre-empt public lands — but United States law did not apply in Oregon. (Several American settlers refused to sign this petition.) As to McLoughlin's true intentions, it was more probable that he pretended to claim the land for the company, while actually holding it for himself, the more so as the company had indicated a lack of interest in the site.

Such pervasive — not to say perverse — ingratitude must appear as incomprehensible to us as it appeared to McLoughlin himself, and would be incredible as well, did we not see close parallels in the way many poor nations reward American foreign aid. The motive is the same: pride, pride outraged by the beneficiary's inability either to compel or to requite the generosity of a powerful benefactor. One of the men connected with the mission said later: "Many of the brethren fell into temptation after buffeting Satan some years in Oregon." There being practically no heathen to contend with, Satan must have been within themselves.

(There was another Protestant mission in Oregon which did exert itself in the conversion of Indians, though with miserable success. This was the Presbyterian establishment of Dr. Marcus Whitman east of Walla Walla. Not being connected with a settlement, it did not have the political importance of the Willamette mission. Whitman, his wife, and several others were slain in the infamous massacre of 1847 by Cayuse Indians, and others were held captive and subjected to rape and other sufferings. A party set out at once from Fort Vancouver and ransomed some fifty survivors, at considerable cost. One of those rescued, a clergyman, soon after began to vilify the Hudson's Bay Company in the usual manner. The company was never reimbursed by anyone for the ransom.)

But on McLoughlin's two-front war his position in regard to his superiors caused him easily as much grief as the settlers and missionaries. One of his children, John McLoughlin Jr. (who was of course a half-breed), after an undistinguished career in Canada and Europe, had been sent to manage the company's post on the Stikine River, which the company leased from the Russian-American Company. There he was killed in a brawl in 1842 under obscure circumstances. Sir George Simpson happened on the scene shortly after on his world-girdling tour. He quickly determined that young McLoughlin, for whom he had never had a high regard, was at least partly at fault in the drunken fracas. Also, there was the difficult matter of criminal jurisdiction, as the affair had occurred on Russian territory and the Russians washed their hands of it. Simpson therefore decided that it was best for the good of the company if proceedings were quietly dropped.

This infuriated McLoughlin. Added to certain disagreements with his head office over salary, company policy as to the use of ships rather than trading posts for bartering with the Indians, the lack of company support in the quarrel over the falls of the Willamette, and sundry other matters, it created a pool of bitterness in the old chieftain's heart at a time when his loyalty to the Hudson's Bay Company and to Britain was of the utmost importance.

It was not long before this loyalty was to be tested more directly than through letters and petitions. The American settlers, well accustomed in their home states and territories to administer their own affairs, determined to do their part toward introducing United States laws into Oregon by organizing themselves into a quasi-republic. The founding meeting took place on May 2, 1843, at a place called Champoeg along the Willamette River. All settlers of the Willamette valley were invited to attend, and the proposal to set up a local government to regulate the settlers' internal affairs was put to a vote. It was carried by the exceedingly narrow margin of fifty-two to fifty, reflecting almost exactly the nationality of the voters. It was, however, the last time that British subjects could make their weight count in public affairs; with the great immigration of that summer, they were so far outnumbered as to be reduced to impotence. Representatives of the Hudson's Bay Company did not as yet take part in the proceedings.

The reason for the French Canadians' opposition was twofold: first, the set of laws was modelled closely on the customs in the United States (more particularly, the laws of Iowa), and the settlers frankly declared through their Catholic priests that they preferred a British-style senate or council; second, the whole tenor of the new compact was in favour of United States annexation. The preamble read:

> We, the people of Oregon Territory, for the purpose of mutual protection, and to secure peace and prosperity among ourselves, agree to adopt the following laws and regulations, until such time as the United States extend their jurisdiction over us.

The compact provided for mild taxation, land tenure, the administration of justice, and a modest executive. Here Dr. White fully expected to receive his due as the anointed of the Great White Father. The settlers, however, remembering his leadership of the trek of 1842, passed him over for high office.

The "constitution" was further elaborated and extended with the arrival of even larger numbers of settlers in 1844 and 1845. The

immigration of these two years added some three thousand persons
to the Willamette community, all Americans. Practically all of them
remained south of the Columbia River, which was still considered
by the Hudson's Bay Company as the probable boundary line. But
there was the odd incident which indicated to McLoughlin and his
colleagues, James Douglas and Peter Skene Ogden, that this natural
separation of settlers and company would not continue indefinitely,
and that encroachments on the part of the American settlers on
the extensive holdings of the company must be expected. One
American immigrant attempted to set up a claim on company land
in February, 1845, greatly alarming everybody.

Against such encroachments there was no legal defence. Although
the company was capable of physically removing individual
intruders, the agitation and propaganda which would inevitably
follow must have the gravest consequences. They therefore revised
their attitude toward the upstart republic in the Willamette, which
had gained in authority and effectiveness, and in the summer of
1845 signified that the Hudson's Bay Company was ready to accede
to the constitution, provided that their loyalty to Britain be safeguarded. This was taken care of with the addition of a clause that
adherence to the Oregon laws did not affect national allegiance,
and on these terms McLoughlin signed. From now on he would
be able to apply to the settlers' executive for the removal of
trespassers.

It was a signal victory for the young American community. How
the development was viewed in London may be guessed from
McLoughlin's apologia quoted earlier; the subject will also be
touched on later in this chapter.

The mid-eighteen-forties also wrought changes in the fortunes
of the Lees and Dr. White. In 1844 Jason Lee was charged by his
superiors in the Methodist Church with gross mismanagement of
the Willamette mission (which had consumed about a quarter of a
million dollars) and with complete failure to spread the gospel. He
was relieved of his post and the mission was dissolved in the same
year. A year later he died in his home town of Stanstead. Dr.
White, the sub-Indian Agent, left Oregon in 1845. Neither of the

two men fulfilled the expectations of their official calling, but their propaganda did much to further United States involvement in Oregon.

We must now return to the larger theater of national and international politics, which we left with the fruitless outcome of the Webster-Ashburton talks on Oregon in 1842.

Ashburton had barely left Washington when Henry Fox, the British Minister, again broached the subject of the Oregon boundary with the State Department. Instead of receiving an official answer to his proposal to negotiate, he was surprised to hear President Tyler declare in his state-of-the-union message of December, 1842, that he would not delay to urge on Great Britain the importance of the early settlement of the Oregon dispute. As he made no mention of Fox's proposal, this looked suspiciously as if the President was trying to give the appearance that the initiative was coming from the United States. If anything, it seemed an attempt to delay discussions, for the United States Government let the matter rest for almost a year. In October, 1843, Secretary of State Abel P. Upshur wrote to the American Minister in London, Edward Everett, that the Oregon issue would again be taken up with Britain, and that the United States would again offer the forty-ninth parallel with navigation rights on the Columbia River. Beyond that the President was not now prepared to go. It was a mere gesture, to pass the time while the American ferment in Oregon continued.

Lord Aberdeen, the British Foreign Secretary, was willing to continue talks even on this meager basis. He recalled Fox from Washington and replaced him with Richard Pakenham, intimating to Everett that the change in ministers had been made to facilitate negotiations. He succeeded in convincing the American envoy that Britain was sincere in its desire to settle on compromise terms, and Everett responded by suggesting that the United States might go so far as to give Britain the southern portion of Vancouver Island, which would otherwise be cut off by the forty-ninth parallel. All that was needed, it seemed, was an official and definite proposal from the United States to bring the issue to a satisfactory conclusion.

This proposal never came. The United States was already in the throes of the campaign for the presidential election of 1844, and the voice of expansionism was growing louder in the land. Sniffing the wind, President Tyler in his annual message at the end of 1843 said:

> After the most rigid and, as far as practicable, unbiased examination of the subject, the United States have always contended that their rights appertain to the entire region of country lying on the Pacific, and embraced within 42° and 54°40′ of north latitude.

He spoke of a "negotiation now in progress" — which wasn't accurate — and echoed the cry of the Oregon immigrants:

> I must repeat the recommendation contained in previous messages, for the establishment of military posts, at such places, on the line of travel [*i.e.,* the Oregon Trail] as will furnish security and protection to our hardy adventurers against hostile tribes of Indians inhabiting those extensive regions. Our laws should also follow them, so modified as the circumstances of the case may seem to require. Under the influence of our free system of government, new republics are destined to spring up, at no distant day, on this side of the Rocky Mountains, and giving a wider and more extensive spread to the principles of civil and religious liberty.

The Oregon discussions were further complicated by discontinuity in the tenure of the State Department. Webster resigned as Secretary of State in October, 1843. His successor, Upshur, was killed in a naval gun explosion on February 28, 1844. He was succeeded by John C. Calhoun.

Aberdeen, who had been much encouraged by Everett's attitude, had officially instructed Pakenham to propose the Columbia River line plus free ports for the United States on the coasts north of that river; privately he wrote, in March of 1844:

> Should my apprehensions be verified [that the official proposal would be rejected by the United States Government] you will endeavour, without committing yourself or your gov't, to draw from the American negotiator a proposal to make the 49th degree of latitude the boundary, with the proviso that the ports to the south of that parallel to the Columbia inclusive shall be free ports to G. Britain. The navigation of the Columbia should be common

Tone of Am. side.

to both; and care should be taken that the 49th degree of latitude, as a boundary, is to extend only to the sea, and not to apply to Vancouver's Island.

This was practically what Everett had informally promised.

Calhoun, however, was in no hurry. This comported with his earlier views, for in January, 1843, while still a senator, he had declared:

> There is only one means by which it [the annexation of Oregon] can be done; but that, fortunately, is the most powerful of all — *time. Time* is acting for us; and, if we shall have the wisdom to trust its operation, it will assert and maintain our right with resistless force, without costing a cent of money, or a drop of blood. There is often, in the affairs of government, more efficiency and wisdom in non-action than in action. All we want to effect our object in this case, is "a wise and masterly inactivity." Our population is rolling towards the shores of the Pacific with an impetus greater than we realize.

The speech had been meant as a rebuttal of those who advocated extreme measures to end British domination — Calhoun, as a Southerner, had no desire to embroil the Union in a conflict for the aggrandizement of the North; but it was not such as to calm the fears of British statesmen.

So it was late August, 1844, by the time Calhoun announced that he was open to proposals on Oregon. Pakenham immediately tendered his official line, the Columbia River plus harbours, waiting hopefully for the Secretary of State to respond with a compromise bid. But Calhoun was not really interested in practical bargaining. He delivered his answer early in September in the form of a lengthy memorandum which, after reciting all Spanish and American discoveries in support of the American claim, and pointing triumphantly to recent American immigration to Oregon, concluded by claiming all of the territory, without even offering the standard forty-ninth-parallel line. Pakenham could do nothing but quote history in his turn, and the discussion gradually came to nought. A British proposal for arbitration was rejected out of hand. The settlement which only a few months ago had seemed so near was again receding into the distance — a distance already darkened by an approaching storm that was soon to sweep the nation.

James Knox Polk had been made the presidential candidate by the Democratic convention in May, 1844, in preference to ex-President Martin Van Buren, mainly because the latter opposed the annexation of Texas (then an independent state carved out of Mexican territory by American citizens) and of Oregon. By advocating the "re-occupation" of both Texas and Oregon, Polk neatly managed to appeal to both the pro-slavery vote (cotton-growing Texas was sure to be a slave state) and the anti-slavery vote (Oregon was slave-free; in fact, its embryo constitution forbade Negroes to enter, or remain in, the country on pain of corporal punishment). Not only did the Democrats put the annexation of Oregon into their platform — the first time a "platform" was formulated in a presidential campaign — but they declared that the annexation must cover the American claim in its entirety. This plank was popularly translated into the slogan "Fifty-Four Forty, or Fight."

Polk won handily in the fall of 1844. He was a stern man, of simple tastes, not given to flights of imagination, and somewhat suspicious of more complicated politicians.

Everything now depended on the attitude of the new American Government, and the portents were grim. Taken on its face the proclaimed foreign policy of the Democrats did not seem the wisest in the world: aggressive actions toward neighbours both north and south, while the United States Army had eighty-five hundred men and the Navy, with eleven thousand, was nowhere near a match for the world's greatest naval power. So imbued, however, were the American people with the notion that the North American continent was theirs to grasp, and so far-reaching had European acquiescence become in this doctrine, that such a policy seemed not only natural but inevitable.

Still, acquiescence went only so far, and the intrigues of the British Ministers in Mexico and Texas, as well as the lesser activities of French diplomats, had done much to arouse the Democrats against the two European powers. James Buchanan, the new

Secretary of State, wrote to the new United States Minister in London, Louis McLane:

> The interference of that Power [Britain] in connection with France to defeat the annexation of Texas, — the stream of abuse which proceeds in one unvarying current from English newspapers against our Country & its Institutions [*i.e.*, slavery], — the disposition of the two nations to intermeddle in the concerns of this Continent, & the strong suspicion entertained that they are now intriguing both in Mexico and California in relation to the latter; all these have conspired to excite American feeling against Great Britain to a very high pitch.

Such was the mood of the men who took office in Washington in the spring of 1845.

The Conservative Government of Sir Robert Peel naturally awaited the Polk Government's first steps in the Oregon dispute with a good measure of anxiety. The anxiety was fully justified when, in his inaugural speech on March 4, 1845, President Polk declared that he would

> assert and maintain by all constitutional means the right of the United States to that portion of our territory which lies beyond the Rocky Mountains. Our title to the country of the Oregon is "clear and unquestionable," and already are our people preparing to perfect that title by occupying it with their wives and children. . . . Our people, increasing to many millions, . . . are already engaged in establishing the blessings of self-government in valleys of which the rivers flow to the Pacific. . . . The jurisdiction of our laws and the benefits of our republican institutions should be extended over them in the distant regions which they have selected for their homes.

The speech aroused a storm in Britain as no other American event had done since the Canadian Rebellion and the McLeod trial. In Parliament Conservatives and Whigs were united in angry denunciation of Polk's "clear and unquestionable" claim. In the Commons Peel retorted that Britain, too, had rights in Oregon that were clear and unquestionable and would maintain them, come what may. To Pakenham, the normally pacific Foreign Secretary wrote on April 3, 1845:

Judging from the language of Mr. Polk, I presume we must expect that the American Government will renounce the treaty without delay. In this case, unless the question be speedily settled, a local collision will be liable to take place, which may involve the countries in serious difficulty, and not improbably lead to war itself. At all events, whatever may be the course of the United States Government, the time is come when we must be prepared for every contingency. Our naval force in the Pacific is amply sufficient to maintain our supremacy in that sea; and Sir George Seymour [admiral commanding the Pacific Fleet] has been instructed to repair without delay to the coasts of the Oregon Territory.

The London *Times* wrote on March 28:

In the inaugural address by the new president on the 4th of March, we find faithfully re-produced all the worst characteristics of the American statesmen who have been in power since the withdrawal of Mr. Webster from the cabinet of Washington. If Mr. Polk was chosen as the thorough representative of the party which makes slavery, repudiation, and foreign aggression its claims to distinction, we are bound to acknowledge that he has not swerved from the intentions of his constituents. . . . It may spare time likely to be consumed in a very unprofitable discussion, if we express an opinion, at least as decided as his own, that in spite of his marauders, and what he terms his constitutional rights, the territory of the Oregon will never be wrested from the British Crown, to which it belongs, but by war.

So that the United States Government and public might be apprised without delay of these sentiments the Cunard packet *Caledonia* plying between Liverpool and New York was delayed by the British Government for one day to take on board the debates of Parliament and other communications.

Also on the *Caledonia* to New York went Sir George Simpson, accompanied by his family, on a cloak-and-dagger mission.

In anticipation of Polk's more aggressive attitude on Oregon, the Peel Government, while still expecting the dispute to be settled amicably, had begun to take stock of its military position, especially in those regions were no war had ever been fought and no strategic principles had been elaborated. This applied particularly to the territories of the Hudson's Bay Company, from the Great Lakes to the Pacific, and the manpower resources of the company suddenly became an important question.

Prime Minister Peel, who consistently took a more uncompromising stand on Oregon than his Foreign Secretary, wrote to the latter on February 23, 1845:

> You seem confident that we have the upper hand on the banks of the Columbia — that the settlers connected with the Hudson's Bay Company are actually stronger than the settlers, the subjects of the United States are at present. Have you carefully ascertained this fact? If our subjects are the stronger at this present time, may not their superiority be speedily weakened or destroyed by the accession of fresh strength to the Americans?

Peel then asked Aberdeen to prepare a memorandum on the American situation for the Cabinet, with special attention to Oregon. He also suggested that it might be advisable to send a navy frigate to the Columbia River and to place some artillery on the shore.

A small British vessel, the eighteen-gun sloop-of-war *Modeste* under Lieutenant Thomas Baillie, had visited Fort Vancouver in the summer of 1844, and had been welcomed with high expectations by the officers of the Hudson's Bay Company, who thought the military display would reawaken patriotic feelings among the British subjects and dampen the aggressiveness of the Americans. In this they were disappointed, for young Baillie failed to grasp the political significance of his visit and looked upon it merely as another shore leave to be enjoyed as a welcome interruption of shipboard routine. Chief Factor James Douglas wrote about him:

> I rode with him and several of the Officers over a great part of the Wallamette Settlement, introducing them every where and showing them every thing, but they did not exhibit that degree of interest in the scene which I expected. They were all young men, and though most courteous and agreeable, had more taste for a lark than for a "musty" lecture on politics or the great national interests in question. No sir, these are not the men to come here, we want one of the American school; who thinks closely and sees clearly, from a habit of discussing great public questions. We met the anglo-Canadian Population, on a Sunday at the Roman Catholic Church,

and spent two nights under the Revd. Mr. Blanchet's hospitable roof. The Canadians without displaying much enthusiasm, nevertheless, gave her Majesty's Officers a warm reception; but Baillie did not attempt to play the envoy, or awaken feelings of loyalty and attachment to their country's cause, by one single expression of sympathy or interest about them. . . . While the American Party are pouring petition after petition into the hands of their government and keeping their national feelings alive, by a system of ceaseless agitation, we are doing nothing; British feeling is dying away so much, that Englishmen, in the Wallamette, are either afraid or ashamed to own their country.

All this had not yet penetrated to the quiet halls of the Foreign Office, but the Hudson's Bay Company head office in London was aware of it. Simpson wrote to McLoughlin on January 1, 1845, that Fort Vancouver must henceforward be considered in constant and imminent danger from "lawless aggression." He recommended strongly that no more trade goods be stored at the fort than absolutely necessary for immediate needs, and that the bulk of the goods for the Columbia River trade, which were normally shipped a year in advance of consumption, be kept at the new post of Fort Victoria on Vancouver Island (founded in 1843), and the goods for the costal trade at Fort Simpson farther north, "so as to be as much as possible out of reach of the troublesome people by whom you are surrounded at present." He likewise recommended that the furs collected from Indians and trappers be kept at Victoria instead of Vancouver, and that Victoria become the chief overseas port of the Hudson's Bay Company on the Pacific Coast.

McLoughlin's personal relations with Simpson were so bad, however, that almost any directive emanating from the latter was apt to be protested or neglected by the former, for spite if for no other reason.

The Hudson's Bay Company officers in London were thus well prepared to answer questions when Lord Aberdeen, seeking to comply with Peel's request for information, turned to the company's governor, Sir John Pelly. Pelly gave the Foreign Office an extract from Simpson's report written from Red River on June 20, 1844, which contained the statement that American influence predominated very much in Oregon and that out of a population of three thousand not more than one-third were British subjects. (This of course was too optimistic an estimate.)

Simpson himself, who happened to be in London at the time, threw himself with verve into the discussion and drew up a detailed memorandum on March 29, 1845, whose receipt by the Government coincided with the arrival of the text of Polk's inaugural address. In his memorandum Simpson said that, should the dispute over Oregon result in hostilities, it would be absolutely necessary for the protection of the Hudson's Bay Company that a small force of British regulars be stationed on the Red River, and that a company of riflemen be formed from the local half-breeds, "who are admirably adapted for guerilla warfare, being exceedingly active, and, by the constant use of the gun from childhood, good marksmen." As to the Oregon coast, it was necessary that two sailing ships of war and two steamers be stationed there for the time being; that an artillery battery be placed on Cape Disappointment, the promontory jutting out to sea at the mouth of the Columbia River; that a large body of marines be attached to the warships; and that a force of two thousand half-breeds and Indians be assembled for territorial defence.

He also had suggestions to offer concerning the boundary line. If the Oregon country were to be partitioned peaceably between the United States and Britain, the absolute minimum for Britain should be the forty-ninth parallel to the Strait of Georgia, all of Vancouver Island, and the free navigation of the Strait of Juan de Fuca. Also, an agreement would have to be made with the United States securing to the Hudson's Bay Company and other British subjects their lands in the area that would fall to the United States.

Peel and Aberdeen were sufficiently impressed by this memorandum to invite Simpson to an interview, which took place on April 2, on the eve of the Parliamentary debate on the subject. Simpson repeated and elaborated his recommendations.

The Cabinet was, however, reluctant to act purely on the opinion of a layman (and not a disinterested layman at that), and it was decided that one or two army officers be sent to Oregon to review and report on the military situation. The arrangement of this tour, which was to be kept strictly secret, was left to Simpson and the Governor-General of British North America, Lord Metcalfe.

On arrival in New York, Simpson first hastened to Washington where he had a discussion with Sir Richard Pakenham. Pakenham, who was closer to the explosive political atmosphere in the United States, became somewhat alarmed at Simpson's ambitious military schemes. He discouraged the notion of fortifying Cape Disappointment — a step that was sure to provoke United States retaliation in kind.

From Washington Simpson hurried on to Montreal, where the commander of the British forces in Canada selected two young officers to be conveyed by Simpson to Oregon, via Red River. These were Lieutenants Henry J. Warre and Mervin Vavasour. Simpson immediately took them in hand, and by the fastest possible means travelled with them to Fort Garry. On the way he plied them with information and recommendations, in both oral and written form, as to the territory through which they were to travel. It was a highly optimistic picture concerning the defensive possibilities of the vast Hudson's Bay Company territory, and it must have evoked the odd smile on the part of the skeptical professionals. On June 5, 1845, they arrived at Red River, where Simpson handed his charges over to Chief Factor Peter Skene Ogden, who accompanied them to Oregon under the guise of a hunting and exploring expedition.

Lord Metcalfe was as excited as Simpson by the prospect of action. Less than a year earlier, Lord Stanley, the Colonial Secretary, and Sir Robert Peel had been disinclined to do much about the defence of Canada in view of the colony's unsatisfactory political record in recent years. London's renewed military interest in North America now prompted the Governor-General to propose that the colonies be put in a genuine state of military preparedness, and that the Oregon territory be occupied by a force consisting of Europeans and native troops from India (where he had recently served).

Warlike notes were also sounded in the United States, but public opinion was sharply divided, the western states being generally most eager for a military solution and the eastern seaboard most reluctant to jeopardize the peace. The *Illinois State Register* declared in May, 1845:

> Nothing would please the people of the entire West half so well as a war with England; and, for our part, we think enough has been done by Parliament, and said by Sir Robert to justify Congress in declaring war against that country forthwith. . . . We are all for War! War!

The New York *Tribune* took a more sober view:

> If we mean to take possession of Oregon by force, we must begin by spending one hundred millions on a Navy capable of flogging the British Navy, so as to hold the mouth of the Columbia and Puget's Sound. . . . The next step would be to raise an army of one hundred thousand veterans and subjugate Canada. . . . All that is desirable to us of Oregon [*i.e.*, the part south of the forty-ninth parallel] is ours without a struggle; the rest is neither to be got by fighting, nor worth having at any rate.

While setting about to prepare for the worst, the Peel Government, and especially Aberdeen, continued to hope for the best. Pakenham's first personal contacts with Secretary of States James Buchanan persuaded the former that Polk's bark might be worse than his bite, and that it would be possible to do business with the new administration. Aberdeen accordingly sent the following instruction to Pakenham on April 18, in a private letter:

> If Mr. Buchanan should propose an extension of the 49th parallel to the sea, as the line of boundary, leaving us in possession of the whole of Vancouver's Island, and the free entrance into the Straits of Juan de Fuca; . . . I should not like to regard his proposal as perfectly inadmissible. It is possible that by some modifications it might be accepted, although I do not think it at all likely, and of course you will give no encouragement to the notion, but recur to arbitration in the event of our terms [the Columbia River line] being rejected. At the same time, you might send Mr. Buchanan's proposal, if made, for the consideration of Her Majesty's Government.
>
> I think it should be clearly understood that the navigation of

the Columbia should be common to both parties, and the Ports within the Straits of Juan de Fuca, and south of latitude 49° should be free Ports, by whomsoever they might be occupied.

It is worth noting that this was precisely the same hypothetical proposal mentioned by Aberdeen a year earlier in preparation for the Calhoun-Pakenham discussions, but it was hedged with considerably more ifs and buts. All of Polk's militant expansionism, all of the war clouds that had arisen in the past few months had not shifted the Foreign Secretary one bit. It had not made him more yielding, or more aggressive — only more cautious. Or so at least it seemed.

Polk's offer came on July 12, 1845, in a note from Buchanan to Pakenham. After once more marshalling all the historical arguments for the American claim to latitude 54°40′, the note concluded:

> Such being the opinion of the President in regard to the title of the United States he would not have consented to yield any portion of the Oregon Territory had he not found himself embarrassed, if not committed, by the acts of his predecessors. . . . He has therefore, instructed the Undersigned again to propose to the Government of Great Britain that the Oregon Territory shall be divided between the two countries by the forty-ninth parallel of north latitude from the Rocky Mountains to the Pacific Ocean; offering, at the same time, to make free to Great Britain any port or ports on Vancouver's Island, south of this parallel, which the British Government may desire.

When Buchanan wrote that the President would not have consented to yield the line of fifty-four forty had he not been "embarrassed" by commitments made by the previous administration, he was not being hypocritical. The offer to Britain had meant for Polk an agonizing reappraisal and had been tendered in the full awareness that it must, if accepted, bring down on his head the denunciations of some of his most loyal and fervent supporters.

Pakenham, however, could not heed such considerations. He, too, had his precedents to consider; and whatever his inclinations might be, he felt bound by Aberdeen's instructions. Buchanan's offer certainly fell far short of what Aberdeen had said might just possibly be worth referring to London for consideration, though not likely to be accepted. He therefore rejected the offer, adding that he hoped Buchanan would make some further proposal "more consistent with fairness and equity, and with the reasonable expectations of the British Government."

Polk was appalled. He had gone far, much farther than he ought to have in view of his announced policy, only to be rebuffed by a subordinate British official. In high dudgeon the President told Buchanan to withdraw even the offer of the forty-ninth parallel and to make his stand henceforward on fifty-four forty, come what might. All considered, he told his Cabinet, it was just as well that Pakenham had rejected the forty-ninth parallel. Now there need be no more compromises.

Buchanan demurred. If the President's new stand were to be upheld it would mean war. Very well, Polk replied. "If we do have war it will not be our fault." Buchanan allowed that war would probably come in any case, but that the American people would be more willing to fight for forty-nine than for fifty-four forty. The Secretary of State then drew up and delivered the note retracting the offer. Entering a Cabinet meeting, he said, "Well, the deed is done," adding that he still considered it unwise to deliver such a note in the existing state of United States-Mexican relations. Polk had no regrets.

But Aberdeen was also shocked by Pakenham's action. It was true, he wrote to him, that Buchanan's note did not meet British expectations, but the least Pakenham should have done was to keep the door to negotiations open by transmitting the offer to London. Now neither the United States nor Britain could reopen talks without loss of honour. Aberdeen also took care to communicate his feelings on that point to Louis McLane, the United States Minister. But the door was shut, and remained shut. Diplomacy had failed through inflexibility on both sides, and the two governments now began to address themselves directly to public opinion in preparation for the show-down.

Debate in Congress, formerly centred on the extension of military posts and United States law to Oregon, now began to turn on the

termination of the joint-occupation agreement as the prerequisite
for annexation. Termination required one year's notice and was
perfectly within the rights of the United States; but the purpose
for which it was to be accomplished made it look like a declaration
of war with a twelve-month fuse.

With President Polk's annual message, given on December 2,
1845, the abrogation of the agreement also became the official
policy of the United States Government:

> All attempts at compromise having failed, it becomes the duty
> of Congress to consider what measures it may be proper to adopt
> for the security and protection of our citizens now inhabiting, or
> who may hereafter inhabit, Oregon, and for the maintenance of
> our just title to that territory. In adopting measures for this pur-
> pose, care should be taken that nothing be done to violate the
> stipulations of the Convention of 1827 which is still in force. . . .
> Under that Convention, a year's notice is required to be given by
> either party to the other, before the joint occupancy shall terminate,
> and before either can rightfully assert or exercise exclusive juris-
> diction over any portion of the territory. This notice it would, in
> my judgement, be proper to give; and I recommend that provision
> be made by law for giving it accordingly, and terminating, in this
> manner, the Convention.

The crux of the matter was that the convention did not in any
way envision abrogation as a step leading to the "rightful exercise
of exclusive jurisdiction over any portion of the territory," as Polk
seemed to imply. The convention was entirely silent on the
hypothetical consequences of abrogation. Whatever course the
United States chose to adopt after abrogation became effective, it
could not be based on the terms of the convention; it could not be
based on any international law or treaty of any kind.

These implications were sharply analyzed by the eighty-four-year-
old Albert Gallatin, one of the negotiators of the Treaty of 1818, in
a pamphlet which he published early in 1846:

> It is not, therefore, on account of the intrinsic value of the con-
> vention that its abrogation is objectionable and dangerous. It is
> because nothing is substituted in its place; it is because, if the two
> Powers are not yet prepared to make a definite agreement, it

becomes the duty of both Governments, instead of breaking the only barrier which still preserves peace, to substitute for the existing convention one adapted to the present state of things, and which shall prevent collisions until the question of sovereignty shall have been settled. . . . The sudden transition, from an agreement however defective to a promiscuous occupancy, without any provisions whatever that may prevent collisions, is highly dangerous. When this is accompanied by an avowed determination on the part of the United States to assume that exclusive sovereignty which Great Britain has positively declared she would resist, War becomes inevitable.

The implications of the annual message were discussed at a Cabinet meeting just before Christmas. Buchanan, according to Polk's diary,

expressed himself decidedly in favor of making vigorous preparations for defense, and said it was his conviction that the next two weeks would decide the issue of peace or war. I expressed my concurrence with Mr. Buchanan that the country should be put in a state of defense without delay; that if peace continued the expenditure would not be lost, and if war came such preparations would be indispensable.

To a doubting congressman the President explained that

the only way to treat John Bull was to look him straight in the eye; . . . that if Congress faltered or hesitated in their course, John Bull would immediately become arrogant and more grasping in his demands; and that such had been the history of the British nation in all their contests with other powers for the last two hundred years.

Polk's declaration on December 2, 1845, did not surprise Aberdeen; almost on the same day it was made he wrote to Pakenham:

I expect a strong declaration from the President in his annual message, and even a recommendation to terminate the Treaty. I shall not at all regret this; for as the crisis becomes more imminent, the chance of settlement improves. I imagine the President and his Government are more afraid of the Senate than they are of us, and that much management is required to accomplish what they really desire. Mr. Polk may well doubt his power of obtaining the sanction of two-thirds of the Senate to any Convention which he could conclude with us. But many things may shortly occur to improve the prospect of affairs very considerably. The access of Indian corn to our markets would go far to pacify the warriors of the Western States.

The last sentence alluded to the imminent end of the Corn Laws in Britain, which will be dealt with a little later.

Aberdeen's sanguine expectation of the effects of the crisis, however, was disappointed. Soon after the presidential message, Pakenham, on Aberdeen's instructions, tried to reopen negotiations by once more offering arbitration of the dispute. He tried to meet deep-rooted American objections to such an expedient by proposing that the arbiter should be asked, first, to decide on the claims to the whole of Oregon; only if he found neither nation entitled to the whole should he be at liberty to divide the territory. It was now Buchanan's turn to reject the proposal without further consideration.

This angered Aberdeen, for arbitration was always a pet principle with him. To the American Minister he huffed darkly that while he was not giving up hope that an amicable settlement might yet be achieved, he would no longer oppose measures looking to the possibility of war with the United States, not just as concerned the defence of the Canadas but on an unlimited scale. For one thing, preparations were being made to equip thirty sail of the line, along with steamers and other vessels of war, not to mention general military armaments. McLane, aware of the British temper, had already warned Buchanan that, though the British Government might find it difficult to present the forty-ninth-parallel boundary to the public as a cause worth fighting for, if war did come "it will receive the undivided support of the British people."

Equally certain to give its support to a war against the Union was the loyal population of Canada, still smouldering over the aid and comfort afforded south of the border to the rebellion. The Kingston *News* wrote, late in 1845:

> If hostilities shall be the result, the battle must, in great part, be fought here. There may be a little skirmishing . . . in the valleys of the Columbia . . . but in this province must the full force of

war be felt. The United States have long looked with covetous eyes upon Canada. . . . War seems inevitable: even they who most fervently pray that such a calamity may be averted hardly dare entertain the hope that their wish will be gratified.

The Toronto *Globe,* clothing its animosities in the cloak of righteousness which has ever been Toronto's chief claim to distinction, said: "If war were now to take place between the two nations, Oregon would be the avowed issue, but with every man whose heart beats with freedom, the true issue would be the destruction of slavery." One prominent Montreal citizen, addressing the city's Shakespeare Club, accused the United States of having imperialistic designs on all of the North American continent, and claimed that the Americans would not rest until their grasp reached from Panama to the shores of the Arctic Ocean — a prediction that was to come true, even though not in the form the speaker feared.

Some eager militia officers in Montreal published an advertisement asking for volunteers to train under them "for the approaching war." This caused a minor sensation and was repeated, with various comments, in many American newspapers. A few days later, apparently after having been rapped over the knuckles by their superiors, the officers lamely explained that the word "war" was a misprint; it should have read "drill."

In the United States the dominant mood on the Oregon question was put into memorable words by John L. O'Sullivan, the influential editor of the New York *Morning News,* who wrote in December, 1845:

> Away, away with all these cobweb tissues of rights of discovery, exploration, settlement, contiguity, etc. . . . [The United States claim] is by right of our manifest destiny to overspread and to possess the whole of the continent which Providence has given us for the development of the great experiment of liberty and federative self-government entrusted to us. . . . It is in our future far more than in our past, or in the past history of Spanish exploration or French colonial rights, that our True Title is to be found.

On the question of war and peace the American press was divided. That Congress took a long recess after Christmas, 1845, was interpreted by Washington pundits as a sign that the politicians had no fear of war, but the Washington *Union* (regarded as Polk's mouthpiece) weighed the pros and cons and came to the conclusion that "no man can now positively say, what will be the result — whether peace or war."

The New York *Courier and Inquirer* thought England had at least as much to lose in a war as the United States:

> English manufacturers would be cut off from our cotton. English trade would be cut off from our consumption. . . . There are, it is computed, about $290,000,000 of stock of the different states now afloat. Of this amount, two-thirds are, it is quite safe to assume, held in England.

In case of war, would not the states repudiate these loans?

But war was a two-edged sword and would undoubtedly cut both ways. The New York *Post* warned:

> A war would be ruinous to the class, in this country engaged in commerce; to the inhabitants of the sea-port towns; to the cotton planter, and to all who depend upon the exportation of their surplus to Europe.

The direct antithesis to western expansionism was voiced by the New York *Journal of Commerce*:

> There is a great deal of senseless declamation to the "whole of Oregon." . . . It is, in truth, a subject of great difficulty. The evidence, even as far South as the Columbia River, is not all on one side, by a great deal. And when we come to latitude 49, the claim of England is better than our own. . . . Latitude 49 has been advocated by some of the more moderate English papers, including the *London Examiner,* as the proper boundary, and there is every reason to believe that the British Government is ready to meet us on what it deems liberal terms. . . . England is the last nation in the world that we ought to desire to measure strength with, especially at a point so remote from even the frontiers of civilization, and so accessible to her fleets.

The paper admitted, however, that "the state of public opinion is such, especially in the west, that the President and his Cabinet may be tempted to go further . . . than their own judgment would dictate."

It is possible that some of the anti-expansionist statements in American newspapers were due to British ideological warfare waged by means of business contacts and widely circulated pamphlets attacking the fifty-four-forty school. Simpson, on his journey through the United States in the spring of 1845, unostentatiously spread his propaganda in New York, and made arrangements to have a pamphlet upholding the British view published "in some of the American journals of most extensive circulation."

The Peel Government could well do with a little public-relations work. If the Polk administration had to secure its flank against the Mexican imbroglio, Peel faced extra dangers both internally and externally.

The internal danger was the Corn Laws. These laws, which regulated the export and import of grain from and to Britain, were of hoary antiquity and had come to be looked on as an essential prop by British grain growers, generally represented by the landed aristocracy. The basic feature of the Corn Laws was the fixation of a minimum price at which foreign grain could be imported; in essence, this meant a support price for the English farmer. The growing manufacturing class, however, favoured free trade, and the growing population of factory workers wanted cheaper bread. Modification or outright abolition of the Corn Laws was being advocated by an ever more influential section of the British public throughout the eighteen-thirties and forties.

Sir Robert Peel, though a Conservative and the natural ally of the landowners, had early recognized the need for Corn Law reform and had taken some steps in that direction in 1842. There was no let-up in the campaign for total repeal, and the clamour for cheaper grain became particularly strong with the outbreak of the Irish Potato Famine, causing dangerous social unrest among the poor Irish peasants. As soon as it became apparent, however, that Peel was leaning toward Corn Law repeal, he was faced with the revolt of his own colleagues who regarded any such move as a blatant betrayal of Conservative principles. As Polk had been elected to gain Oregon, so Peel had been voted into office to maintain the Corn Laws.

In December, 1845, dissension in the Cabinet forced Peel to submit his resignation to Queen Victoria. The Queen thereupon requested Lord John Russell, the leader of the Whig Opposition, to form a government. This proved impossible, mainly because of the refusal of prominent Whigs to accept Lord Palmerston as Foreign Secretary, and Palmerston's refusal to serve in any other post.

The opposition to Palmerston was closely connected with the external danger — Britain's relations with France. Palmerston, who was belligerent by nature and aggressive in his conduct of foreign affairs, had always been considered an enemy of France, Britain's greatest European rival. In the mid-eighteen-forties relations with France were particularly bad, owing to a dispute over the succession to the Spanish throne — a problem that had already plunged Europe into a long war once and would soon serve as the excuse for another. The question this time turned on the prospective marriage of Queen Isabella II, who was eighteen years of age in 1845 but had succeeded to the throne at the tender age of thirteen. King Louis Philippe of France sought to promote a marriage with one of his relatives in order to tie Spain securely to France. Britain vehemently opposed such a step. Aberdeen had managed to secure a precarious truce in the royal courting rivalry. The situation was sufficiently grave in 1845-46 for the Duke of Wellington to predict that should war break out with the United States over Oregon, France would probably join in on the American side.

With John Russell's failure to form a government, Peel was once more in office, more determined than ever to carry out his Corn Law reform. All political observers agreed that the Government was living on borrowed time.

This was the international situation at the beginning of the year 1846.

Lieutenants Warre and Vavasour, after travelling overland from Red River with their Hudson's Bay Company guide and companion Peter Skene Ogden, arrived at Fort Vancouver in August, 1845. Their journey had been rapid and efficient, as were all Hudson's

Bay Company travels, but it was obviously not in the customary military style. Ogden wrote to Simpson, from whom he had taken over the conveyance of the two intelligence agents:

> I had certainly the two most disagreeable companions, and I almost doubt you could have selected another that would have so quietly submitted as I did, but from a sense of duty I was determined not to lose sight of the object of our voyage and was silent to their constant grumbling and complaining not only about their food which was as good and abundant as any Man could wish for or desire but also in regard to promises made by you and on one occasion I was obliged to check the Engineer [Vavasour].

Immediately after their arrival the two officers outfitted themselves as civilian gentleman adventurers, down to perfume and silk kerchiefs, and set about with a good deal of energy exploring and assessing the country from a strategic point of view. To their chagrin they found Cape Disappointment already "pre-empted" by some American settlers, but the Hudson's Bay Company managed to buy it at considerable cost. Nothing, of course, was done about fortifying the promontory. The officers stayed for several months, and the report which they sent to London was an interesting and valuable document, but since it arrived too late to influence the outcome no cognizance will be taken of it.

Of greater importance to the fate of Oregon was the arrival of other official British representatives which took place in early September, 1845.

Although Aberdeen had recommended to the Admiralty that Sir George Seymour, the admiral commanding the Pacific Station at Hawaii, personally visit the Columbia to show the flag, the task was delegated to a subordinate, Captain John Gordon, commanding the fifty-gun frigate *America*. There was something to be said for this choice, for Gordon happened to be Aberdeen's brother. Serving on his ship was Lieutenant William Peel, a son of the British Prime Minister. Whatever these two men might report would doubtless find receptive ears and eyes in Whitehall.

Gordon, however, did not wish to endanger his relatively large ship in an attempt to cross the perilous sand-bar in the mouth of the Columbia River, and repaired to safe and commodious anchorage in Puget Sound. From there he dispatched Lieutenant Peel and another officer to Fort Vancouver. They carried messages to McLoughlin from Admiral Seymour and Captain Gordon, that from the admiral promising protection to the British subjects in case of need. This message was partly in response to complaints from McLoughlin that his requests for reassurance from the military in Hawaii had brought no result. The Hudson's Bay Company head office, too, had advised the chief factor that in his dealings with the American settlers he must look to his own protection.

Seymour's reassuring letter came too late; shortly before the arrival of the *America* in Oregon waters, McLoughlin and his staff had given their adherence to the Oregon constitution set up by the settlers.

Much has been made of this sequence of events by some historians. Even so careful an observer as White considered McLoughlin's adherence to the constitution a fateful step which, on being reported to London, proved to be the turning-point of the dispute by demonstrating to Peel and Aberdeen that the Hudson's Bay Company itself no longer cared about British jurisdiction. White, however, seems to have been unaware not only that Aberdeen himself had been ready to accept the forty-ninth-parallel boundary on the mainland as long ago as March, 1844, but also that Sir George Simpson, a man who commanded more attention in London than McLoughlin, had heralded the company's acquiescence in the forty-ninth-parallel line in his memorandum of March, 1845.

Whether or not McLoughlin would have joined the Oregon compact had the visit of the *America* occurred a few months earlier is debatable; it is quite possible that he would. It is true that his action was also influenced by his growing animosity toward Simpson, by his sense of personal neglect and abandonment by the company which he had served so long, so faithfully, and so well, and, perhaps, even by a desire to secure his claim at the falls of the Willamette, which, he knew, would in any case end up on the American side of the line.

Nor did the visit of the *America* strike the Hudson's Bay Company officers in Oregon as the belated answer to their prayers. That Captain Gordon did not deign to visit Fort Vancouver in person was indicative of his interest in the territory. He seems to have spent his stay in Puget Sound fishing, riding, and hunting, and there is an apocryphal story that he was so disgusted with the refusal of the Pacific salmon to rise to his fly rod that he pronounced the country "not worth a damn." Chief Factor Douglas, who was again delegated to keep the distinguished visitor company, wrote as dejectedly as he had about the captain of the *Modeste*:

> The old Gentleman was exceedingly kind, but no wise enthusiastic about Oregon or British interests. He does not think the country worth five straws and is surprised that Government should take any troubles about it. He assured me that he could not interfere, with trespassers squatting on our claims and in such cases advised a settlement by arbitration. . . . He did not appear at all friendly to the Hudson's Bay Company, and told me plainly that we could not expect to hold the entire country.

The *America* hoisted anchor in Juan de Fuca Strait on October 1, 1845, and returned to Honolulu on October 20. Lieutenant Peel was sent on to London to carry Captain Gordon's report, travelling via Central America and Havana. From the latter city he wrote to Pakenham in New York:

> May I venture to say as expressing also the opinion of my Captain that if the 49th degree be the boundary determined on, it should not include the southern extremity of Vancouver Island.

This opinion was undoubtedly conveyed to his father when he arrived in London early in February, 1846, along with the information that of the three thousand inhabitants in the Willamette valley, only six or seven hundred were "French Canadians" who "seemed to carry little weight in proportion to their number." Captain Gordon reported to the Admiralty that

> the settlers in the Wallamette or Oregon appear to live in harmony with the Hudson's Bay Company proper who seem to have treated them in the most liberal manner and I sh'd fear greatly induced the flow of Emigration the Emigrants being assured of getting all manner of supplies at their arrival.

As to McLoughlin's joining the compact of the Americans, "the policy of this measure I think rather questionable as the Company's own people were sufficiently strong to protect themselves."

Soon after the departure of the *America,* the sloop *Modeste* again sailed up the Columbia River, still under the command of Thomas Baillie. This time she stayed for a year and a half, in effect providing a military garrison for Fort Vancouver. McLoughlin, however, was to play the genial host for only a short time. In June, 1845, his executive authority had been diluted by the setting up of a triumvirate of McLoughlin, Douglas and Ogden. In January, 1846, he moved to Oregon City to occupy his claim, taking leave of absence from the company, from which he never returned to his former post, although his retirement was not made official until June, 1849.

The officers and crew of the *Modeste* tried to pass the time, and to improve their relations with the hostile American settlers, by staging several plays on board ship during the winter of 1845-46. It was not an uncommon form of entertainment on British men-of-war, though this time the midshipmen were relieved of the necessity of playing female roles by the participation of several comely damsels from the Willamette settlement. The titles of some of the plays were *Three Weeks after Marriage, The Deuce is in him,* and *The Mayor of Garratt.* The backdrop for the stage was painted by the crew.

In the spring the British naval force in the Columbia was increased by the arrival of the forty-two-gun frigate *Fisgard,* which remained throughout the summer of 1846.

Military measures were also afoot elsewhere in the Hudson's Bay Company's domain. The free-roaming Red River half-breeds, on their famous buffalo hunts, were in the habit of pursuing the herds regardless of international boundaries and had often ridden deep into United States territory. There they clashed with the Sioux Indians. To prevent their incursions the United States Secretary of War had considered ordering dragoons into the Sioux territory in 1842; and in the summer of 1845, at the very time that Warre and Vavasour were traversing the Prairies on their trip to Oregon, two companies of United States Dragoons were being moved from Fort Atkinson and Fort Des Moines into the buffalo hunting-grounds, the modern North Dakota. The cavalry caught up with the half-breeds near Devil's Lake, and the commanding officer warned them not to return.

The appearance of United States cavalry so close to the Red River settlement alarmed the Hudson's Bay Company officers and made them fear that the company posts would fall into enemy hands in case of conflict. Moreover, they were worried over the unrest among the half-breeds themselves, an early harbinger of the Riel Rebellion. The Hudson's Bay Company therefore put pressure on Whitehall to establish a military post at Fort Garry. Simpson wrote to Governor Pelly in the fall of 1845 from Montreal:

> As I consider the salvation of the Hon. Company's trade to depend on the early formation of the post, I think there is not a moment to be lost in preparing the Government upon the subject while the excitement on the Oregon question exists.

The recommendation had the desired effect, and on April 1, 1846, Pelly was informed by the Colonial Office that the troops would be sent. The matter, however, was considered further, and the contingent, consisting of 346 officers and men, did not sail until June 26, 1846.

The United States Government also made a military gesture in the direction of Oregon, though on a more modest scale than Britain. This was due not only to the smallness of the United States military establishment, but also because the danger of a war with Mexico had made necessary a concentration of forces in the South. In the summer of 1845 nearly half of the United States Army, for instance, was stationed in the newly acquired state of Texas.

On December 5, 1845, Secretary of the Navy George Bancroft sent a secret instruction to the officer commanding the United States Pacific Squadron, Commodore J. D. Sloat, on the west coast of Mexico. Sloat was instructed to keep watch on the British forces farther north on the Pacific Coast, and to detach one of his vessels for duty on the Columbia and the Strait of Juan de Fuca. There was also the following curious note:

If you have any rifles or other small arms on board your ships which can be spared for the purpose, you may permit them to be exchanged with the people of that region for wheat, flour, or other stores, taking all possible care that they fall into the hands of no one who is unfriendly to the United States.

The vessel sent on this mission was the twelve-gun schooner *Shark,* no match for the small *Modeste.* The *Shark,* under the command of Lieutenant Neil N. Howison, entered the Columbia River on July 18, 1846, and was received with great rejoicing by the American settlers, who greeted the arrival of the ship with a salute fired from a hole in an anvil.

While these military schemes were unfolding, Sir Robert Peel and his Government were engaged in a perilous gamble on the domestic plane. In this manoeuvre the press played an unusually important role. Aberdeen's excellent connection with John Thadeus Delane, the youthful (born 1817) editor of the London *Times,* stood the Conservative Government in good stead. Aberdeen had taken the most unusual step of giving Delane a scoop on the impending repeal of the Corn Laws, thereby preparing the nation through the launching of a trial balloon fashioned by sympathetic hands. It was thanks to Aberdeen's influence with Delane that the *Times* switched from an uncompromisingly militant stand on Oregon to a policy of peaceful compromise along a line closely approximating that offered by the United States.

In the first days of the year 1846, the *Times* carried three editorials on the Oregon dispute, that of January 2 openly advocating the forty-ninth parallel plus all of Vancouver Island. To political circles, this was the first clear indication of Foreign Office thinking. Lord John Russell, the leader of the Opposition, was so incensed at this hand-in-glove relationship that he was moved to complain to Queen Victoria: "The degree of information possessed by the *Times* with regard to the most secret affairs of State is mortifying, humiliating, and incomprehensible." Peel himself was constrained to warn Aberdeen on this point.

It was not, however, the political line of the *Times* itself that John Russell was quarrelling with. The Whig paper the *London*

Examiner also advocated the forty-ninth-parallel line. John Russell himself was in favour of compromise, and he took care to tell Aberdeen so. Informing Palmerston, his "shadow Foreign Secretary," of this, he wrote on February 3:

> My opinion upon the whole is that we may well and with due regard to our own interests give up the Columbia river, and I have let Aberdeen know privately that he will have no opposition from me on that ground.

The fact was that if the Conservative Party, by and large, was miscast in the role of free-trade promotion into which it had been forced by the enterprising Peel, the Whigs could scarcely renounce their own industrial origins and doctrines and oppose Corn Law repeal merely for the sake of political party strife. Corn Law repeal, however, had an intimate connection with British-American relations, for American grain growers were bound to be the most benefited by such a reform. This was well understood by Aberdeen when he wrote, in December of 1845, that the access to the British market of "Indian corn" would go far "to pacify the warriors of the Western States."

Thus it came that when the bill for the repeal of the Corn Laws (which were to be abolished in several steps, the final one to be taken in 1849) came up for second reading, on February 27, 1846, Peel's party split, 231 members voting against the measure, and 112 for it, along with the Whigs. The Government was thus saved from defeat by the Opposition — a state of affairs that could not last, as it was plain that the disaffected Tories would seize the first opportunity to team up with the Whigs to bring down the traitorous Cabinet.

The passage of the Corn Law repeal Act confirmed a new trend in British politics, favouring the Industrial Revolution, free trade, and a "Little England" that would not dissipate its strength on colonial adventures.

In this atmosphere the advocates of an aggressive policy on Oregon, who were few enough to begin with, found little public support. This applied particularly to the Hudson's Bay Company itself. It is always easier to sympathize with, and respond to, the appeals of a multitude of citizens than to those of an entrenched commercial organization. Its virtues seem to spring from self-interest, and no credit is given for them; its vices and failings seem premeditated and perverse. It also seems worth noting, in this connection, that while the American missionaries and settlers kept letter after letter and petition after petition pouring into Washington, there is no record that the British subjects in Oregon, as such, ever addressed any communication to their Government or any of its representatives, even though this practice was by no means foreign to British colonial politics.

In Washington, President Polk had his own hard row to hoe. As he had made the notice of termination of the 1818 joint-occupancy agreement his official policy, his political stature and career depended on a quick and decisive passage by Congress of the necessary legislation. Congress, however, proved refractory. There was a broad consensus that the United States had a claim to at least the larger part of Oregon, and that this claim should be made good. As to the extent of the claim and the method whereby it ought to be secured, the legislators were divided. Many of those representing the cotton-growing South and the industrial East favoured peace with Britain, and were therefore easily persuaded that the United States claim did not extend north of the forty-ninth parallel. If they could be made to vote for the abrogation of the treaty at all, they would insist on giving the law such a form as to turn it into a basis for negotiation and compromise. The so-called "fifty-four-forty men" — the septuagenarian John Quincy Adams among them — saw the termination of the treaty as the bar to further compromise.

Polk found himself compelled to go around button-holing senators to press for quick passage of the bill. He thought there was yet another reason for the senators' erratic behaviour — personal ambition:

> The truth is that in all this Oregon discussion in the Senate, too many Democratic Senators have been more concerned about the Presidential election in '48 than they have been about settling

Oregon either at 49° or 54°40′. "Forty-eight" has been with them the great question.

The debate raged from February, 1846, through March and into April, and set a record for length that was broken only by the civil-rights debate of 1964.

On the diplomatic front, Polk began to try his hand at Aberdeen's game of blowing hot and cold as the occasion demanded. Having taken an uncompromising stand in the summer of 1845, he found it hard at first to regain freedom of manoeuvre. But by the end of 1845 he had hit on a rare and long-dormant precedent of constitutional practice that gave him the desired loophole: if Britain were to make another formal proposal that seemed just barely acceptable, he would reverse the normal procedure and first submit it to the Senate for its opinion before accepting or rejecting it. McLane in London received his first intimation of such a course in a letter written by Buchanan on January 29, 1846. Buchanan repeated the same information in another letter a month later, adding, more explicitly, that the British proposal the President had in mind would be the forty-ninth-parallel line on the mainland, leaving Vancouver Island to Britain.

Both sides had now reached the point where they were seeking the same boundary line, modified perhaps by navigational and possessory rights. All that remained to be overcome were points of national honour and diplomatic etiquette. These of course were weighty enough.

On April 23, 1846, the notice of termination of the joint-occupancy agreement passed Congress, with a preamble, insisted on by the moderates, that presented it as a step toward a negotiated settlement. On April 25 the first armed clash occurred between Mexican and United States armed forces along the Rio Grande, and on May 12 the Senate formally declared war on Mexico.

The notice of termination was at once transmitted to London both by Pakenham and by Buchanan. Pakenham had spent the first months of 1846 advancing Aberdeen's scheme of arbitration over Oregon, without success. At the same time he kept sending

Aberdeen voluminous clippings from American newspapers to convey an idea of the drift of public opinion and congressional debates. Even in January he reported that the impending conflict with Mexico would bring about "the prevalence of more moderate views" in the United States. At the end of the month he wrote: "Upon the whole, My Lord . . . I should say that the appearance of things in this country has become more pacifick," and at the end of February he was able to write that the forecast Corn Law repeal had caused "a great and, I think I may say, gratifying sensation" in the United States.

The first news of the notice of termination reached Whitehall on May 15. A few days later the formal notice itself arrived, with instructions to McLane to have it presented to Queen Victoria if at all possible. It turned out to be quite impossible, but McLane was wise enough not to be put off by such high-flown trivialities. As soon as the news reached Aberdeen he had a conference with the American Minister, in the course of which he communicated the gist of a new proposal to be laid before the United States Government.

Aberdeen had, of course, expected and even awaited the notice, and had some time before mapped out his course of action. This was not too difficult, for the events and communications of the past several months had narrowly circumscribed the limits of a possible settlement. Certainly, time was pressing; Richard Crocker, a fellow Conservative and confidant of Lord Aberdeen, had told the latter in May:

> If you get 49° and the Columbia, you will have done a miracle, but I have no hope of miracles now-a-days, and I shall gladly assent to 49° and half the Straits of Fuca; but, for God's sake, end it; for if anything were to happen to Louis Philippe, we should have an American War immediately, and a French one just after, a rebellion in Ireland, real starvation in the manufacturing districts, and a twenty-per-cent complication in Income Tax — not pleasant in prospect.

Reporting on the dispatch of his proposal in the House of Lords, Aberdeen said:

I did not delay for a moment, putting aside all ideas of diplomatic etiquette, which might have led me to expect that some steps would be taken on the other side; but, without waiting for a moment, I prepared the draught of a convention, which was sent by the packet of the 18th May to Mr. Pakenham.

To Pakenham, Aberdeen wrote that, if queried on the subject by Buchanan, he was quite free to admit that the Peel ministry would probably not last much longer. This should help Polk and Buchanan to make up their minds. The ploy was unnecessary; the United States Government had already been informed accordingly by McLane. "The conduct of my predecessor and successor," Aberdeen remarked later in reference to Palmerston, "with regard to the Ashburton Treaty, had filled Mr. McLane with the greatest alarm."

Also by the packet of May 18 went McLane's report to his own Government in which he outlined the terms of the convention which would probably be proposed by Aberdeen. He added that if the United States wished to make changes in the draft it would have to hurry.

Pakenham handed the British proposal to Buchanan on June 6. It was drawn up in the form of a finished treaty, and described the boundary as running from the point where the old forty-ninth-parallel boundary terminated at the Rocky Mountains

> westward along the said forty-ninth parallel of north latitude to the middle of the channel which separates the continent from Vancouver's Island; and thence southerly through the middle of said channel, and of Fuca's Straits to the Pacific Ocean.

The whole of the channel through which the boundary ran was to be open to the ships of both parties; in navigating the Columbia River the Hudson's Bay Company and all British subjects trading with it should have the same rights as United States citizens; the possessory rights of the Hudson's Bay Company, the Puget's Sound Agricultural Company, and all other British subjects should be safeguarded.

That same day the Cabinet considered the draft and agreed that it should be submitted to the Senate for advice; the Cabinet members also agreed that, should the draft be rejected, it would almost certainly mean war, as the President could offer no modification.

There were some last-minute discussions during those days between Buchanan and Pakenham, but the latter's task had become relatively simple. It was sufficient for him to hint that any change in the draft treaty would make it necessary to consult London, for Buchanan to drop all notions of further bargaining. "If it had not been for this circumstance," Pakenham wrote to Aberdeen, "I am far from being satisfied that the matter would have been so promptly and easily settled."

It is quite probable that no British government ever turned its own impending downfall to better account in international negotiations, but in this haste there was also the seed of future trouble. That, however, belongs in another chapter.

On June 10 President Polk transmitted the draft treaty to the Senate for its advice, and, after a two-day debate, that body approved the British proposal by a vote of thirty-eight to twelve. Polk affixed his signature on June 15.

On June 25 the Peel Government fell, being defeated in a House of Commons vote on an Irish Coercion Bill to suppress peasant unrest due to the Potato Famine. Just before that, the House of Commons had finally approved Corn Law repeal.

On June 29, in the morning, Sir Robert Peel went to the palace to tender his resignation to Queen Victoria. When he returned for a last time to his office to clear out his desk he found on it a dispatch from Pakenham in Washington, dated June 13, announcing the acceptance by the Senate and the President of the Oregon Treaty, "without the addition or alteration of a single word."

In the afternoon Peel announced his resignation in the House, and read Pakenham's letter. The chamber exploded into cheers. After Peel had concluded, Lord Palmerston rose to congratulate the outgoing Conservative Government on the successful conclusion of the dispute — he who had so vehemently condemned the Webster-Ashburton Treaty, a treaty that was so much better than anything Britain could legally expect, better than what Palmerston himself had once been willing to accept, and better by all accounts than the surrender of historic priorities by the treaty just concluded. Such are the vagaries of party politics.

That evening Peel reported to the Queen:

> Sir Robert Peel, with his humble duty to your Majesty, begs leave to acquaint your Majesty that he has just concluded his speech notifying to the House the resignation of the Government.
>
> He thinks it was very well received. Lord Palmerston spoke after Sir Robert Peel, but not very effectively, but no other person spoke. . . .
>
> Sir Robert Peel humbly congratulates your Majesty on the intelligence received *this day* from America. The defeat of the Government on the day on which they carried the Corn Bill, and the receipt of the intelligence from America on the day on which they resign, are singular coincidences.

Victoria replied on July 1:

> The Queen returns these letters, with her best thanks. The settlement of the Oregon question has given us the greatest satisfaction. It does seem strange that at the moment of triumph the Government should have to resign. The Queen read Sir Robert Peel's speech with great admiration.

News of the end of the dispute was slow in reaching the locus of contention. The signing of the Oregon Treaty seems to have become known in the Columbia valley in November, through a newspaper brought from Honolulu. The British consul on Hawaii also sent an official notification to John McLoughlin. No notification was sent to the provisional territorial government.

In the meantime, Lieutenant Howison and his crew from the *Shark* had done their best to make patriotic propaganda, although it is not known whether they distributed the rifles referred to in the secret dispatch. But when the schooner set sail early in October to rejoin the United States Pacific Squadron it missed the elusive channel around the Columbia estuary sand-bar, and was wrecked. All men were saved, but everything else was lost. It was the crew of the *Modeste* — still contemplating the possibility of hostilities — which loaded its cutter with food and clothing and sped to the rescue of the American sailors, huddling cold and hungry at Astoria. Thus was effected the "reoccupation" by the United States of the only piece of ground to which that term could by any stretch of the imagination be applied.

Of all the boundary disputes, that over Oregon was by far the most complex and the most difficult to analyze for cause and effect. If the other disputes can be likened to a stage play acted out against the larger political background — necessary, to be sure, but also relatively stable and at times merely decorative — that over Oregon resembles one of those bullfights that are staged in the streets of some Spanish towns, where amateur toreros keep dashing out here and there from the crowd to have their spell of danger and glory, and disappear again into the milling mass that furnishes both spectators and participants.

There was the Hudson's Bay Company, but it did not really speak with one voice, those of McLoughlin and of the hierarchy represented by Simpson becoming ever more dissonant; the missionaries; the American fur traders and colonizers from Gray to Wyeth; the American settlers; the expansionists in the western states and the merchants in the eastern states; the domestic situation in Britain, compounded of the Industrial Revolution, the potato blight, a clash of personalities, and other things; the British-French struggle for European hegemony centring on the Iberian Peninsula; the Mexican War. Historians, who have already compiled a vast literature on the subject, are still discovering new facets and factors.

It is, therefore, tempting to avoid charges of over-generalization and simplification by apportioning blame and credit equally among all the forces involved and letting it go at that. But on closer look it will appear that what we are faced with is not a choice among a multitude of discrete factors, but the selection of a unifying principle that nourishes a number of factors, much as certain types of soil and climate nourish certain flowers. This principle, in the case of the United States, was the drive to overspread and possess the soil to the farthest limits of imagination. The exponent of the principle was the settler, the homesteader. In the case of Britain, the principle was imperial interest. The American people were interested in the Oregon country principally for its own sake; the British establishment never viewed a disputed area in such a narrow context, but in relation to the surrounding territories and even to the empire's most distant outposts.

It is true that Slacum, Wilkes, and other travellers had expounded on the strategic need for American harbours on the Pacific Coast and the consequent necessity of acquiring control of Puget Sound; and also that various politicians, Benton among them, pointed to the commercial advantage of possessing the Pacific seaboard. But while such questions may have weighed with the Government, it was not these considerations, not these images that were capable of moving the American people to sacrificial fervour. It was the image of the pioneer homesteader. It mattered little whether the image of Oregon and the American settlers in it corresponded in all respects to reality.

It has been pointed out that the entire American community in Oregon was concentrated in the Willamette valley, an area that would fall to the United States without any exertion; that they had chosen to settle there because of geographical rather than political considerations; and that the area north of the Columbia River for which various United States Governments had fought so tenaciously was one in which the settlers themselves had shown no interest. But the folks back home in Missouri and Indiana did not make such fine distinctions. They looked to symbols to inspire them, symbols they were familiar with. The right of the settler to the soil, and the westward extension of the United States in its undiminished fullness, were such symbols.

Britain was interested in the area south of the forty-ninth parallel for one reason only: the Columbia River. When it became apparent that the Columbia had been overrated as an artery of transportation — especially by the Hudson's Bay Company — relinquishment of that claim was relatively painless.

But for some of the Britons left behind in American Oregon the sequel was unhappy. McLoughlin had to fight for his claim in Oregon City to the end of his life, the pretensions of Waller and his friends having been taken over by the territorial government. The Hudson's Bay Company trade declined. Its headquarters on the Pacific was shifted to Victoria. In 1869 the company's holdings in the United States were acquired by the United States Government for $650,000, a small fraction of what the company asked.

There being no settlements in the vicinity of the forty-ninth parallel, the survey and demarcation of that boundary did not seem urgent. In 1853 the territory of Oregon was divided into the territories of Oregon and Washington. The latter included the present state of Idaho until 1863. Although the influx of settlers continued to be relatively slight (in 1850 there were only twelve hundred white persons in Washington), its momentum was increasing, and in the mid-eighteen-fifties it became apparent that the mild climate of the Pacific slope and its mineral riches would accelerate immigration even more.

In 1856 the United States and Britain made formal provision for the survey and demarcation of the boundary west of the Rocky Mountains. Britain appointed as its commissioner Captain James Charles Prevost, Royal Navy, with Captain George Harry Richards as surveyor and assistant commissioner. Early in 1857 the United States appointed as its commissioner Archibald Campbell (who was later appointed United States commissioner for the Prairie boundary survey). The two commissioners held their first meeting on June 27, 1857, on board H.M.S. *Satellite,* the ship on which Prevost had sailed from England, in Esquimalt Harbour, Vancouver Island. It became apparent that there had been a misunderstanding: while Campbell's commission empowered him to determine and mark out the entire boundary both on land and on water, Prevost was authorized only to lay down the water boundary through the Straits of Juan de Fuca and Georgia. Therefore, they confined their discussion to that quarter; the discordant sequel will be described in the chapter that follows.

On February 3, 1858, Britain appointed Captain John Summerfield Hawkins of the Royal Engineers as commissioner for the land boundary. Hawkins arrived at Esquimalt on July 12, 1858, in H.M.S. *Havannah.* He brought with him fifty-six non-commissioned officers and men. One of his men had caught yellow fever while crossing the Panamanian Isthmus and died, and several deserted on Vancouver Island. Also with his team were astronomers, naturalists, and medical officers. Charles W. Wilson, who later frustrated Cameron's "mean forty-ninth parallel," was secretary and transport officer.

The United States party had started work in 1857, and by the time the British party arrived on the scene the Americans had already determined four astronomical points on the forty-ninth parallel and made a thorough reconnaissance of the area to be traversed for a considerable distance from the shore of the Strait of Georgia.

The first meeting between the two commissioners took place on August 13, 1858, at the United States camp of Semiahmoo, where the boundary first strikes salt water. At that meeting they agreed that it would be too expensive and difficult to cut a vista throughout the whole length of the boundary.

> It was therefore agreed to ascertain points on the line by the determination of astronomical points at convenient intervals on or near the Boundary; and to mark such Astronomical Stations or points fixed on the Parallel forming the Boundary, by cutting a track of not less than 20 feet in width on each side for the distance of half a mile or more according to circumstances. Further that the Boundary be determined and similarly marked where it crosses streams of any size, permanent trails, or any striking natural features of the Country. In the vicinity of settlements on or near the line, it is deemed advisable to cut the track for a greater distance, and to mark it in a manner to be determined hereafter.

At their second meeting, held from April 16 to 23, 1859, at Semiahmoo, the British commissioner suggested a revision of the earlier agreement so as to cut the twenty-foot vista along the entire boundary, in so far as it was accessible to cutting parties, and that the line be monumented throughout, where possible at one-mile intervals. Hawkins also proposed that in the one-mile intervals between monuments the boundary be considered a straight line, which was a concession on his part.

Campbell consistently opposed thorough demarcation, and agreed to none of Hawkins's new proposals in that direction. The principle of straight rather than curved intervals — a question familiar to readers from the preceding chapter — was later adopted, however, and applied to much greater distances than Hawkins had at first contemplated.

There was only the barest essential minimum of collaboration between the two parties in the survey of the boundary. They usually worked separately, verifying one another's results by independent observations, and compromising on obvious divergencies. The area to be traversed was rugged in the extreme, being mostly mountainous and heavily forested. The boundary line was intersected by few important streams or other avenues of commerce, and at times the parties suffered serious privations. Campbell wrote later:

> The 49th parallel extends over rugged and precipitous mountains that attain great elevation and in the Cascade range on and near the boundary perpetual snow covers many of the peaks, whose northern gorges are filled up with immense glaciers. The timber on the western slope of the Cascade mountains is dense, being a heavy growth of pine and fir that in many places stands over a fallen forest not yet decayed. This is the character of the country as far east as the valley of the Similkameen River. . . . Here the timber becomes more open and surveying operations less difficult. After passing the Okinokane [Okanogan] river, which is the lowest line of the great valley between the Cascade and the Rocky Mountains, the country again becomes rough and the timber more dense. . . .
>
> It being impossible to follow the 49th parallel continuously, the line of survey was carried over the nearest practicable route for a pack trail. . . . Rough stone monuments were erected over posts buried in the ground to indicate the exact line. . . . The reconnaissance work extends over an area of about 30,000 sq. miles. . . . Trails had to be opened for ¾ of the distance travelled involving great labor in cutting, grading, and bridging to make the route practicable for pack-mule transportation. The water-courses were numerous and rapid. . . . Many of the trails opened are now travelled routes to the mines then and since discovered.

Where the terrain was flat — nearer to the sea — other hardships had to be borne. Lieutenant Wilson kept a diary, in which he described the survey party's ordeal in 1859, when work had to be stopped in the Sumas prairie in July because of the mosquito plague:

My present dress consists of a very bad jim crow, a red serge shirt with pockets, a blue serge pair of trousers, stockings and moccasins, a huge gause bag over my head, and a short pipe puffing to try and keep the 'squiters off. . . . [And later:] The mosquitoes have now regularly set in . . . washing is a perfect torture, they settle en masse upon you perfectly covering every portion of the body exposed, we sit wrapped up in leather with gloves on and bags round our heads and even that cannot keep them off. None of us have had any sleep for the last two nights and we can scarcely eat, exposing the face is such a painful operation. [Finally:] As I am now leaving the mosquito country, I may as well tell you some of the effects of these venomous little animals and pray do not think I am inventing stories to amuse you as however incredible they are perfectly true; my hands have been so swollen and stiff that I could hardly bend my joints and have had to wrap them in wet towels to be ready for the next day's work; one's hands are literally covered with them when writing and even when wearing kid gloves, the bites through the needle holes in the seams were sufficient to produce this; each mule as it is packed is obliged to be led into a circle of fires continually kept up as they are quite intractable when they are worried by the mosquitoes; two . . . mules have been blinded, and six of our horses were so reduced that we had to turn them out onto the prairie and let them take their chance of living, I never saw anything like the state of their skins one mass of sores; our tents used to be so frequently covered with mosquitoes inside and out, that it was difficult to see the canvas and the very action of getting under the curtains introduced so many that it was impossible either to kill them or sleep; even after smoking them all out in half an hour it was just the same, whatever pains we took to shut up the tent; we are all of us as you may imagine a good deal pulled down by want of sleep and continuous irritation.

In August, 1859, Hawkins left for London via Panama to carry dispatches and information concerning the San Juan dispute to be described in the following chapter. He took advantage of this voyage to stop off in Washington, where he visited the British Minister Lord Lyons in February, 1860. Through Lyons Hawkins was introduced to Secretary of State Lewis Cass. Hawkins's purpose in seeking these interviews was to complain of lack of co-operation on the part of Commissioner Campbell, and to urge that Campbell be replaced by a military man. The exact reasons for which Hawkins objected to Campbell are not made clear by the correspondence, but it appears that Hawkins was still trying to obtain United States agreement to a continuous boundary vista. His efforts met with no success.

Another of Hawkins's difficulties was a completely accidental one: his arrival in British Columbia coincided with the height of the gold rush to the upper Fraser River. Prices and wages rose to fantastic heights. Hawkins's sappers were on army pay, and luckily did not cause extra expediture, but the axemen, mule drivers, and other labourers had to be hired locally at wages never heard of by London treasury officials.

The survey and demarcation of the land boundary was finished some time in 1862. Cartographic and other office work was held up in London and Washington for many years, owing no doubt to the American Civil War. The commissioners did not hold their final joint conference until May, 1869. The minutes of that meeting, which took place in Washington, gave official sanction to lists of reference points and maps, and stated that

> it is agreed by the Commissioners that, between any two successive defined points, marked on the ground shown on the maps . . . the line of Boundary above described is to be understood to be a right or straight line; and that this rule is to apply throughout the entire Boundary without regard to the distances between the consecutive points.

These distances were in some places considerable, the longest measuring twenty-five miles. In that interval, the maximum distance between the straight line and the curve of the parallel was forty yards, being territory which Britain ceded to the United States. "We were induced to do this," Commissioner Hawkins wrote in his final report to the Foreign Secretary, "upon the consideration that it was of the greatest importance, nothing should be left for *future* discussion or settlement."

The exact length of the land boundary west of the summit of the Rocky Mountains was 409.4 miles. It had been held by Britain that the boundary described by the Treaty of 1846 extended to the eastern base of the Rockies; but Campbell's commission covered only the northern boundary of the Territory of Washington, which extended to the summit. Therefore, the joint operation ended at the summit, or watershed, of the Rocky Mountains. The boundary was established by twenty-eight astronomical stations, of which fourteen were established by the American party, eleven by the British party, and three jointly.

The first forty-five miles from the coast were marked by forty-two iron pillars, at irregular intervals. For the following 108 miles, to the Similkameen River, the boundary was marked by nineteen stone cairns as well as intermittent cuttings. This portion of the boundary ran through the Cascade Mountains. Between the Similkameen and the Columbia rivers, a distance of ninety-five miles, the commission placed sixty-nine stone cairns and one earth mound, and cut vistas "in all necessary cases." From the Columbia to the crest of the Rocky Mountains, 162 miles, there were some twenty-seven cairns. Hawkins described the final monument as follows:

> No better means for marking the eastern end of the Boundary were at command than by a dry stone pyramid of the usual description which was built as carefully as possible, and which may be preserved for many years by its protected situation on a narrow saddle with precipitous sides connecting two lofty mountains, which position will moreover serve to identify the approximate locality.

When Hawkins wrote this, the start of the prairie boundary survey was only three years off. In 1874 the survey parties ascending the Rocky Mountains from the east found the saddle described above quite easily, and the cairn placed on it in perfect condition.

Only where the forty-ninth-parallel boundary finally leaves dry land to plunge into the Strait of Georgia did the commissioners splurge on a pretentious memorial to their labour — a "substantial Granite obelisk." Its various sections, weighing a total of forty tons, were cut at New Westminster, British Columbia, in 1861. Hawkins, who had to use all his power of persuasion to obtain the necessary authorization for this project, estimated that the cost of the monument would be fifteen hundreds pounds, half of which would go to pay the stonecutters. The actual cost was $7,590.58, shared equally by both nations. A special wharf and ramp were built on the western shore of Point Roberts — the monument was to stand on a steep cliff 160 feet above the sea — and sailors and marines from H.M.S. *Grappler* helped to land and erect the noble pile. It is still standing.

CHAPTER FOUR

The Pig and the Emperor

On June 15, 1859, an American squatter named Lyman A. Cutler spied a large pig rooting in his potato patch on San Juan Island in the Gulf of Georgia. Cutler knew the pig; it had been at his potatoes before. Being a true man of the frontier, he dashed into his shack, seized a shotgun, and pursued the pig into the adjoining woods, where he shot it.

The pig (later described as a valuable breeding boar) belonged to a large sheep farm of the Hudson's Bay Company managed by Charles John Griffin. The loss of the pig was quickly noticed by its owners, and the next day Cutler was confronted by Griffin and the director of the Hudson's Bay Company west of the Rockies, Alexander Grant Dallas. Dallas, who was the son-in-law of Vancouver Island's Governor James Douglas, had happened to step off at San Juan the day of the shooting, from the *Beaver,* one of the company's trading vessels.

What took place between Cutler and his accusers is not certain, as both sides gave different stories. It appears that Cutler was berated by the company men, who may also have threatened to take him before a magistrate in Victoria. (Griffin himself was a justice of the peace and presumably could have dealt with the offence on the spot, had he wanted to take legal action.) Cutler offered to pay for the pig — though not what the company considered the animal was worth — but he also threatened to deal with any other of the company's stock in the same summary manner as he had with the pig, and declared that he would not let himself be carried before a British judge.

Cutler's behaviour was not exceptional. The Pacific seaboard in 1859 was overrun with wild men following in the wake of the gold-rush wave of the preceding year. Victoria, the capital of the British colony of Vancouver Island, had just been transformed from a sleepy handful of government and Hudson's Bay Company houses into a crowded, turbulent way station between San Francisco and the gold-fields along the Fraser River. Fights, robberies, thefts, killings were as common as traffic offences are today. The correspondent of the London *Times* reported:

> It is the San Francisco of 1848 reproduced. The same hurry-scurry, hurley-burley, dust, inconvenience, bad living, cheating, and lying. The sudden metamorphosis of a quiet little hamlet of scarce 400 souls to a huge hive of 6000 to 7000 brigands, produced by the same causes, confirms the comparison. . . . The riffraff of San Francisco congregated there.

Also congregating at Victoria were hundreds of Indians who kept streaming in from the north of the island and along the coast. The men were stealing, robbing, and drinking, and the women were begging and prostituting themselves. Every evening at seven Victoria's small police force would gather in the centre of the town, from where the constables would fan out toward the outskirts, driving the Indians before them, thus clearing the streets. Battles between rival Indian tribes were not uncommon, and were sometimes staged just outside the town. No one was surprised to come across a corpse in a lane or on the shore, and the body of an Indian woman was left floating for days in Victoria harbour.

Under the circumstances the killing of a pig did not seem an event likely to attract official notice. But it was nonetheless noticed by Governor Douglas and in due course helped to persuade him to appoint a full-time magistrate to administer justice on the Island of San Juan. The reason for this solicitude was that San Juan — along with the several other islands, such as Lopez and Orcas, which together formed the San Juan or Haro Archipelago — was disputed ground between Britain and the United States, and Douglas was determined to resist any act tending to call in question British sovereignty. The magistrate, whose name was John F. de Courcy, was appointed a few weeks after the pig incident, but he was not sent to San Juan until July 27 because the Governor waited for an opportunity to install him with proper pomp. He waited two days too many.

In the first days of July, 1859, Governor Douglas received the visit of General William S. Harney, commanding United States forces in the Department of Oregon, embracing the territory north of California and west of the Rocky Mountains. Harney was on a tour of inspection of his command, and after paying his respects to Douglas he went on to San Juan Island, where he landed on July 9 and went into conclave with the Americans. He was told about the shooting of the pig, and about other irritations between British and Americans, as well as the visits of marauding Indians. The meeting was of course quite informal and no record was kept of what was said, but one of the participants recalled later that General Harney said to the squatters, "If you will send me a petition with 28 signers I will send you a company of soldiers," or words to that effect. The general left the island the same day to return to his headquarters at Fort Vancouver on the banks of the Columbia River. He had not told Douglas that he intended to visit San Juan, and he did not inform the Governor of his visit after it had taken place.

The Americans on San Juan then proceeded to draw up their petition, which said, among other things:

> In April, 1858, the house of the United States Inspector of Customs for the island was attacked and fired into in the night by a party of Indians living on this island, and known as the Clallams, and had it not been for the timely aid of the Hudson's Bay Com-

pany, the Inspector would have fallen a victim to their savage designs. . . . Inclusive with the above dangers that we are exposed to from our neighboring Indians, we are continually in fear of a descent upon us by the marauding northern Indians, who infest these waters in large numbers, and are greatly retarding the progress of the settlement of this island.

The petition said that several Americans had already been murdered in the area by Indians. The settlers then added that according to the Oregon Treaty of 1846 San Juan Island belonged to the United States, and requested military protection. The petition was dated July 11, 1859, and signed by twenty-two persons. Before the document arrived in Fort Vancouver, however, General Harney had already taken action, and the pig slain on San Juan Island was well on its way to historical immortality.

The stage for these developments had been set by the haste and urgency in which the Treaty of 1846 was framed and concluded. The aim of the treaty was to divide British and United States possessions along the forty-ninth parallel on the mainland, but to leave Vancouver Island entirely to Britain. To define the dividing line between Vancouver Island and the mainland, the man who drafted the treaty in the British Foreign Office, having no other guide to follow, quite naturally used the "through-the-middle" principle familiar from numerous other boundary treaties concerning rivers and channels.

It was later admitted that difficulties over this all-too-simple definition had been expected. Henry U. Addington, Permanent Under Secretary for Foreign Affairs, wrote in 1854:

> At the time of the negotiation and conclusion of the Oregon Treaty it was foreseen that some difficulty might arise as to the precise line of boundary from the 49th parallel of N. Lat. in the middle of the Gulf of Georgia down the Channel to the entrance of Fuca's Strait: but this consideration being of less importance than the conclusion of the Treaty, the Treaty was concluded and signed.

It was therefore not lack of geographical knowledge alone that resulted in the unclear boundary definition. Both British and

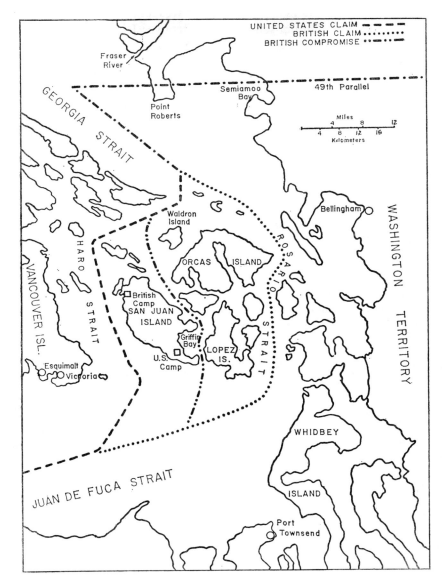

San Juan Boundary Dispute.

American negotiators knew that there was a large archipelago in the middle of the channel separating Vancouver Island from the mainland, and that this obstruction might make the search for the "middle" difficult.

George Bancroft, the former Secretary of the Navy in President Polk's Cabinet and afterwards United States Minister in London, had hardly arrived at his new post when he wrote home for a copy of "Wilkes's chart of the Straits of Haro," on November 3, 1846:

> It is intimated to me that questions may arise with regard to the islands east of that Strait. I ask your authority to meet any such claim at the threshold by the assertion of the central channel of the Straits of Haro as the main channel intended by the recent Treaty.

Now the Strait of Haro is that channel which runs between Vancouver Island and the San Juan Islands, and a boundary drawn through it would naturally leave the archipelago on the American side. The opinion that the treaty applied to the Strait of Haro was expressed by Bancroft in conversation with Lord Palmerston and by some congressmen in debates, but if Palmerston was aware of these implications he took no formal notice of them. Bancroft thought he detected some uncertainty in the attitude of the British Government in regard to the San Juan Islands. He believed that it was the Hudson's Bay Company, now entrenched in Victoria, which had designs on the islands, and that the Government might, once again, reluctantly be forced to advance the schemes of that grasping hydra.

Bancroft's doubts continued unabated until early 1848. In January the British Minister in Washington, John F. Crampton, had an interview with Secretary of State James Buchanan concerning the determination of the water boundary, and in response to Buchanan's request he submitted his views in a note. In it he stated:

> The Convention of the 15 June, 1846, declares that the line shall be drawn through the middle of the *channel* which separates the continent from Vancouver's Island; and upon this may be asked what the word 'channel' was intended to mean?
>
> Generally speaking, the word 'channel', when employed in treaties, means a deep and navigable channel. In the present case it is believed that only one channel — that, namely, which was

laid down by Vancouver in his chart — has, in this part of the gulf, been hitherto surveyed and used; and it seems natural to suppose that the negociators of the Oregon convention, in employing the word 'channel', had this particular channel in view.

The channel surveyed by Captain Vancouver was Rosario Strait, and the British interpretation would have given the San Juan Islands to Britain.

Crampton's note was an almost verbatim repetition of a dispatch he had just received from Foreign Secretary Viscount Palmerston. The dispatch had been some time in maturing. Even before the conclusion of the Oregon Treaty, the governor of the Hudson's Bay Company had addressed a private letter to the then Foreign Secretary Lord Aberdeen, in which he recommended Rosario Strait as the boundary, on the grounds that it was the only channel marked as navigable on Vancouver's chart. The Hudson's Bay Company continued to urge this view after the new Whig Government took office, and Sir George Simpson pressed it on Pakenham in Washington. Bancroft's hints therefore came as no surprise to Palmerston. Whether Palmerston would have adopted Rosario Strait without the Hudson's Bay Company's intervention is open to question, but it seems likely. It followed the imperial tradition of secure communication.

The possession of the San Juan Islands was probably a factor in the British decision, but a secondary one. The main consideration was no doubt the fear that if Britain did not obtain navigation rights in Rosario Strait it might find itself cut off from maritime access to the British Columbia mainland from Juan de Fuca Strait. Vancouver's chart did show Haro Strait (or "Canal de Arro"), but less distinctly, as Vancouver had not navigated it and could not vouch for it. The chart also showed that neither Rosario nor Haro Strait corresponded to the geometric middle line between Vancouver Island and the mainland. The geometric middle line ran straight through the San Juan Islands. If anyone had really wished to make the boundary run along a line equidistant from Vancouver Island and the continent, he would have had to choose the minor, meandering channel cutting through the archipelago. Had Palmerston made such a choice in 1847 the logic of the British position would have been wellnigh impregnable.

Many years later, when the Foreign Office realized the mess it had got itself into by opting for the "best navigable" channel, it did seek to fall back on the logical choice of the geometric middle. By that time it had become apparent that the "traditional" decision of 1847-48 had been a fatal error, for Rosario Strait turned out to be much shallower, narrower, and less useful to navigation than Haro Strait, and Palmerston's interpretation of the Treaty of 1846 was found to favour the United States claim. The Foreign Office now looked around for rectification and clarification, and it was Richard Pakenham's turn to write, in a memorandum in 1859, that neither Haro nor Rosario Strait

> could, as I conceive, exactly fulfil the conditions of the treaty, which, according to their literal tenor, would require the line to be traced along the middle of the channel (meaning, I presume, the whole intervening space) which separates the continent from Vancouver's Island.

Whether or not Pakenham had held such views consistently since 1846 is not known. The belated change in strategy succeeded only in impressing American negotiators with British shiftiness.

These somewhat dry considerations are essential to the understanding of the pivotal point of the San Juan boundary dispute.

The positions having been stated, nothing concrete came of talks to have the water boundary determined until 1856, when Congress passed an act for the survey and demarcation of the boundary between the territory of Washington and the British possessions (see also the preceding chapter). Early in 1857, Archibald Campbell was appointed United States commissioner. Britain had appointed its commissioner, Captain James C. Prevost, late in 1856, together with an assistant commissioner, Captain George Henry Richards. Unlike Campbell's commission, those of Prevost and Richards covered only the water boundary, *i.e.,* the line through the Straits of Juan de Fuca and Georgia. Prevost left England in command of the corvette *Satellite* late in 1856 and arrived at

Esquimalt, the naval station near Victoria, on June 12, 1857. Richards, commanding the auxiliary steam-sloop *Plumper,* had to cope with an engine failure and did not get to Vancouver Island until the end of that year. Commissioner Campbell, travelling on the *Active,* made his appearance at Victoria on June 22.

The two commissioners held their first joint meeting on June 27, 1857, exchanged commissions and settled down to wait for the *Plumper,* which had been expected earlier and was supposed to provide the commission with a marine survey on which to lay down the boundary line. When the *Plumper* still had not shown up by the middle of fall, Prevost told Campbell, on October 26, that he was prepared to use a United States Coast Guard chart of 1854 as the preliminary basis for discussion. The two commissioners then began a series of meetings at which they expounded their differing views as to the channel intended by the Treaty of 1846.

Before we proceed further with their arguments, however, we must take account of the events that had in the meantime taken place on the disputed islands — events that had much to do with the appointment of the commission itself.

When United States Minister George Bancroft wrote from London in 1846 that he suspected the Hudson's Bay Company of designs on the San Juan Islands, the Honourable Company had, for once, not been maligned. The situation was even more serious than Bancroft had thought.

The company's interest in the islands, and particularly in the Island of San Juan itself, dated from the days before the signing of the Treaty of 1846, when it was free to form posts anywhere between California and Alaska. San Juan Island was the closest of the larger islands to Victoria, and it had the best agricultural land, especially at its southern extremity, where there was also a sheltered harbour. The island, James Douglas explained later,

> was in the first place taken possession of by the Agents of the Hudson's Bay Company, in the month of July 1845, and a notice to that effect engraven on a wooden Tablet, was erected on an eminence, near the South east point of the Island; a record which is still in existence.

When the boundary was settled, the company assumed that the archipelago was on the British side.

The Hudson's Bay Company did not, however, follow up its symbolic taking of possession by any further act for several years. Only in 1850 did it establish a "fishing station," apparently a temporary post, on San Juan, which went unnoticed by either the United States or the British authorities.

At the same time, there were political and administrative changes on both sides of the new border. Vancouver Island was established as a British crown colony, and the first Governor, Richard Blanchard, arrived in Victoria on March 10, 1850. This meant that the exclusive jurisdiction of the Hudson's Bay Company on the island and its dependencies — presumably including San Juan — had been superseded by the direct control of the Colonial Office. Blanchard, however was Governor *de jure* only; just about all the inhabitants and all the power on Vancouver Island belonged to the Hudson's Bay Company, and after several months of frustration Blanchard resigned. The Colonial Office thereupon made the best of an awkward situation and appointed James Douglas, a chief factor of the Hudson's Bay Company, Governor of Vancouver Island. This political marriage of convenience, which had been recommended by the Hudson's Bay Company earlier, redounded entirely to the favour of the company. Douglas continued to hold his dual office until 1858, when the sudden immigration during the gold rush persuaded Whitehall to set up an independent and full-fledged colonial administration, and Douglas's connection with the Hudson's Bay Company was severed.

James Douglas (Sir James in later years) was born in 1816 in Demerara, British Guiana. He had what was described as a "swarty" appearance, and was said to have Creole blood from his mother. Douglas received a good education in Scotland, the home of his father, and immediately joined the North American fur trade. From 1830 he was stationed at Fort Vancouver, where he soon became the right-hand man of John McLoughlin. After the partition of Old Oregon between Britain and the United States, Douglas assumed the direction of Hudson's Bay Company activities at

Victoria. He was a man of resolute temperament, inclined to ostentation, and averse to compromise either with opponents or with popular assemblies.

South of the line, the American portion of Oregon was in 1853 divided into the territories of Oregon and Washington. A year before that the territorial legislature, assuming that the San Juan Islands were American territory, had included them in a county called Island County, which also embraced Whidbey Island at the entrance of Puget Sound.

This political action was of course noticed by Douglas and his colleagues of the Hudson's Bay Company, and in the fall of 1853 they determined to anticipate further American claims to the disputed islands by establishing a sheep farm on San Juan. The farm was set up in December.

They resolved on this course without notifying the Colonial Office. Perhaps Douglas feared that London would frown on a Hudson's Bay Company take-over of new agricultural lands; perhaps he feared that the Foreign Office would not wish to exacerbate British-American differences by such unilateral action.

At any rate, Douglas in his capacity as Colonial Governor wrote to the Colonial Office on November 21, 1853, complaining about American encroachments into British waters around southern Vancouver Island. He said that several of the intruders had attempted to establish themselves on the disputed islands, but had been "warned off." Since that time, "many parties of Americans have been rumbling about the Arro [San Juan] Islands, but no other attempt was made at actual settlement." He said it was his policy to keep all settlers off the islands so as to prevent conflicts of jurisdiction.

If it was Douglas's aim to keep his sheepish manoeuvre on San Juan Island out of the harsh international limelight, he was quickly disappointed. The watchful United States customs collector for Puget Sound, I. N. Ebey, had taken note of the landing of a large number of sheep on San Juan. Considering the island United States territory, he notified Griffin in midwinter 1853-54 that he intended to collect customs duty on the importation of British stock. In this Ebey was entirely in error, for the sheep had come from the Hudson's Bay Company farm at Nisqually in Washington Territory. If San Juan was in fact United States territory, as Ebey claimed, then the sheep had never left American soil.

It is quite possible that Ebey was aware of this contradiction, and that he was interested not so much in the collection of duty as in the assertion of United States sovereignty over San Juan.

In January, 1854, Douglas was obliged to complain to the Colonial Office of Ebey's threats, thereby revealing the presence of the sheep farm on San Juan. He took care, however, to say nothing about Griffin's connection with the Hudson's Bay Company, giving the impression that he was an independent British settler. At the same time he appointed Griffin a justice of the peace so that he could arrest anyone trying to interfere with his sheep.

In April it was reported to Douglas that Ebey had left Nisqually with two boats to seize Hudson's Bay Company property on the Island of San Juan for non-payment of customs duty. Douglas sent over the company vessel *Otter* with some men, whites and Indians, to support Griffin. Ebey, however, did not show up until May 3. Douglas, being notified, sailed to San Juan with several officials, among them the collector of customs for Victoria, James Sangster. Finding that Ebey was accompanied by only four men and did not present an immediate danger, Douglas contented himself with sending ashore Sangster and a constable, who were to warn Ebey off the island. Sangster also told Ebey that United States vessels were not to frequent the waters of San Juan. Ebey retorted that he would persist in exercising United States jurisdiction on the disputed island, and that he would install on it a resident deputy collector of customs. He declined Sangster's request to go on board the *Otter* for a conference with Governor Douglas. Sangster thereupon hoisted the Union Jack, and Ebey responded by unfurling the Stars and Stripes. The next day Ebey duly swore in his deputy, Henry Webber, while Sangster and Griffin looked on. After Douglas and Ebey had left, Sangster and a few of the Hudson's Bay Company men tried to evict Webber from the island; but he was prepared, having armed himself with four six-barrelled revolvers which he had hanging from his neck and waist, and a knife in his bootleg. The Britishers blew a retreat. The sheep continued unmolested for the time being.

Later that year, the Acting Governor of Washington Territory paid a visit to San Juan, accompanied by some United States troops and (wrote Douglas) "a large body of lawless followers." The official later told Douglas that he was being urged to take forcible possession of San Juan Island and British property thereon. The United States revenue cruiser *Jefferson Davis* "was the next and most formidable adversary we had to contend with." The *Jefferson Davis,* armed with six guns and commanded by officers of the United States Navy, nosed about the disputed islands, and her captain informed Governor Douglas that he did not wish British ships to touch at San Juan. This, however, appeared to be mere bluster. By Christmas, 1854, Douglas was able to report that the last "trial of strength" had ended favourably for Britain.

The trials were soon resumed. On March 30 the sheriff of Whatcom County, Washington Territory, with seven whites and two Indians, landed on San Juan Island and demanded eighty dollars in taxes. Griffin refused. The following morning the Americans seized thirty-four sheep, tied their legs, and proceeded to load them on their ship. Griffin, who had tried to prevent the seizure of his stock by dispersing it, happened on the harbour just as the raiders were loading the last of the sheep, which had been kept in an enclosure. A scuffle ensued, but being outnumbered and outgunned — the raiders were armed with "a brace of Revolver Pistols each" — Griffin and his lone helper had to give way. As soon as word of the affair reached Victoria, a sea-borne posse was sent to San Juan, where it arrived a few hours after the Americans had left. Having no taste for a naval battle, the Victorians did not take up the pursuit.

Douglas reported the affair to London in a letter dated April 19, 1855. The letter did not produce quite the effect Douglas desired. What sort of a sheep farm was this, the London bureaucrats wanted to know, that was always in trouble with the Americans, and how did it get to be on San Juan anyway — considering Douglas's assurance that he was keeping settlers off the disputed island?

The Governor's evasive reply that the Hudson's Bay Company had "taken possession" of San Juan as long ago as 1845 was not likely to remove from the minds of Whitehall officials the suspicion that they were being used as the poker wherewith Douglas tried to pull the company's chestnuts from the American fire.

Before any action could be expected from far-away London (return mail took from four to six months) the British Minister, Crampton — whom Douglas had also informed — had discussed the San Juan quarrel with Secretary of State William L. Marcy. They agreed that while the islands remained in dispute both nations should refrain from disturbing the peace. On July 14, 1855, Marcy wrote to Governor Isaac I. Stevens of Washington Territory, recommending that

> the officers of the Territory should abstain from all acts on the disputed grounds which are calculated to provoke any conflict, so far as it can be done without implying the concession to the authorities of Great Britain of the exclusive right over the premises. The title ought to be settled before either party should attempt to exclude the other by force, or exercise complete and exclusive sovereign rights within the fairly disputed limits.

The memorandum, though well conceived, had approximately the same effect on the attitude of the leading spirits of Washington Territory as the Fox-Forsyth agreement on that of Maine. It did, however, enunciate for the first time a bilateral hands-off policy that could serve as the basis for future international action at higher levels of government.

For the abducted sheep the Hudson's Bay Company claimed damages of fifteen thousand dollars — unsuccessfully, of course.

In the summer of 1855 Victoria received the visit of several ships of the British Pacific Squadron under Rear-Admiral H. W. Bruce. To entice the warships more frequently into his colonial waters, Douglas proposed to London — without success — that the naval-stores depot for the Pacific Station be transferred from Valparaiso to Victoria.

Still another development contributed to the relaxation of official American attempts to exercise jurisdiction on San Juan. The "northern" Indians were the scourge of the settlers and traders in Juan de Fuca and Georgia Straits, and in Puget Sound. Their raids were reminiscent of the Viking invasions of England and France during the Middle Ages, though the comparison should not be pushed too far. Among the tribes taking part in the raids were said to be the Haidas, Bella Bellas, Chimmesyans, Stikines, and Tongass. Some of them must have travelled close to a thousand miles from their tribal haunts in Alaska; since they used dug-out canoes and took their families along, this was no mean feat of endurance.

Unlike the Vikings, who relied on the sword alone, the northern Indians worked, begged, stole, lent out their women, robbed, and killed, according to temperament and opportunity. Their young women would often take up with settlers along the coast, forming a fifth column for their far-roaming kinsmen. In the spring of 1859, for example, the residents of Port Townsend passed a resolution

> that all men having northern women be notified that if they do not, on or before the first day of June, send the same out of the country, that legal action will be commenced against them, as by Act passed January 23, 1857.

Lonely farms, lighthouses, and traders were in particular danger, and among those murdered by Indians was the customs collector Ebey. In addition to these raids, Washington Territory was plagued in the middle eighteen-fifties by serious Indian uprisings in the interior, and the regular forces in the territory were not large enough to look after all the trouble spots.

In the fall of 1855 Governor Stevens asked Douglas for arms and ammunition to help his volunteer forces to fight the Indians, and Douglas immediately dispatched the *Otter* with the needed articles. Another request was made by Stevens in the winter of 1856, and yet another in spring. In addition to lead and powder Stevens also asked for sugar, coffee, pork, clothing, candles, soap, and tea. The only stocks on Vancouver Island from which these items could be supplied were those of the Hudson's Bay Company.

Since it was against company rules to supply merchandise without firm commitments as to payment, Douglas paid for the shipments out of his private funds, fully expecting to be reimbursed by either the British or the American Government, since he was "required to succour a Christian people in their peculiarly distressed circumstances; an act of kindness which they moreover may have it in their power, on some future occasion, to return with interest." He would soon have occasion to recall that statement with a bitter smile.

The total cost of the arms and other supplies sent to Governor Stevens amounted to seven thousand dollars; and after waiting in vain for repayment of his "loan" from Olympia, the Washington capital, Douglas began to appeal to the British Minister in Washington for intercession with the United States Government. After much delay and obstruction, the money was finally repaid by the United States Treasury with interest in the early summer of 1859 — just at the time Cutler killed the pig.

By that time Commissioners Prevost and Campbell had been carrying on their intermittent discussion of the boundary line for two years, without prospect of agreement. A recapitulation of their conferences would demonstrate merely to what exasperating length legalistic arguments can be carried. Basically, Captain Prevost claimed Rosario Strait because it was better suited to navigation, because it agreed with the words of the Treaty of 1846 which said the boundary should run in a "southerly" direction, and because it alone truly "separated Vancouver's Island from the continent," being the channel adjacent to the mainland. Campbell contended, on the contrary, that only Haro Strait, the channel running alongside Vancouver Island, truly separated that island from the continent; that the word "southerly" in the treaty meant merely the opposite of "northerly"; and that Haro Strait was better suited for navigation than Rosario.

Prevost then offered a compromise channel running through the disputed archipelago. More precisely, it ran between San Juan Island on the west and Orcas and Lopez Islands on the east. Campbell declined this proposal, and Prevost suggested that, agreement not having been reached, the dispute be referred to their respective governments.

Campbell now began to suspect that Prevost had never possessed true freedom to adopt any channel he chose, and that he had been secretly instructed not to agree to Haro Strait under any circumstances. In December, 1857, he asked for an unabridged copy of Prevost's instructions, saying:

> During our discussions in relation to the determination of "the channel" separating the continent from Vancouver's Island, I thought I perceived that your mind was subject to difficulties not inherent in the question; and this impression was strengthened when you informed me [this had been an undiplomatic slip on Prevost's part] that you had instructions for your guidance, in the event of our disagreement, which, according to my recollection, were not embodied in those you exhibited to me at our first meeting.

Prevost bristled with injured dignity and declared that he had full power to adopt any channel he judged proper; at the same time, however, he refused to let the United States commissioner have his full instructions. With that the talks broke down.

Campbell's suspicions were well founded. When the United States Government finally obtained Prevost's full instructions early in 1859 through its representative in London, it was revealed that Prevost had been really free only "to adopt any other intermediate channel" between Rosario and Haro, before referring the dispute to the two governments. This obviously excluded Haro Strait itself. The "secret" instructions came into Campbell's hands on July 25, 1859, and caused him to say that he could

> not well conceive of a more dishonest mode of attempting to evade the obligations of a treaty, or a greater outrage upon the confiding disposition of the Government of the United States, than is exhibited in these instructions for the guidance of the British Commissioner. Nor can I understand how an officer of the British navy could conscientiously undertake to carry a treaty into effect under such circumstances.

It is scarcely to be wondered at that official relations between Campbell and Prevost turned frigid, and that no further contribution to the preservation of peace in the San Juan Islands could be looked for from their association.

The question naturally arises why both Britain and the United States clung so stubbornly to their respective claims, since it had been shown that both Haro and Rosario Straits were well navigable. One reason was that national honour had been committed; another that the disputed islands, and especially San Juan, had been endowed with a worth that may seem pure rationalization, but which was no more subjective than that of other pieces of land over which wars have been fought.

Viscount William Fitzwilliam Milton, one of the few British parliamentarians ever to take a direct and personal interest in a North American boundary dispute, visited the area in 1864 and wrote about San Juan Island:

> The important colony of Victoria . . . with the harbours of Victoria and Esquimault, is situate at the southern and eastern coast of the Island of Vancouver; and the communication between these harbours and the eastern coast of the island, as well as with the mainland of British Columbia, is now carried on mainly by the Canal de Haro.
>
> The entrance to this strait or canal is, however, commanded by the Island of San Juan . . . and it will be seen that it is of the very last importance to the citizens of Vancouver's Island, and of the mainland of British Columbia, that in case of any disagreement with the United States they should hold possession of this key to the strait. . . . Should the Island of San Juan, commanding the Canal de Haro, fall into the hands of the United States, the inhabitants of Victoria and the inhabitants of the mainland of British Columbia could be cut off from intercourse with each other by the batteries of the United States erected on San Juan. . . .
>
> The Island of San Juan has, for the reasons given above, been aptly termed "the Cronstadt of the Pacific". [A reference to the island fortress commanding the entrance to the harbour of St. Petersburg.] Its conformation is such that a few batteries, skilfully placed, would render it almost impregnable. Imagine the position. Victoria, the capital, with the adjacent harbour of Esquimault, cut off from communication with British Columbia, and the Canadas, or "the Dominion", cut off from the seaboard of the Pacific!

The economic effects of this would be disastrous:

> Shut out from the Pacific, the [British] territory must perforce join its interests with those of the United States, and be added to the great protective federacy against the commercial energy of the people of Great Britain.

Such was the fate awaiting Canada if it lost the Island of San Juan.

The case for the United States was not so easily made out; even if it failed to gain San Juan Island, it still retained complete control of both sides of Rosario Strait. American military strategists therefore took a different tack, arguing that for the sake of military balance the island must be kept from falling into British hands:

> Possessing Esquimault harbor, the ownership of the San Juan Archipelago, or of that island alone, is not necessary to Great Britain for her own occupation, either for defensive or offensive purposes; because, while occupying Esquimault harbor, *and enjoying naval superiority,* she will command completely, so far as local position will enable her, the Straits of de Fuca, and all other waters within Cape Flattery, including Puget Sound, Admiralty Inlet, and all other channels and passages of the San Juan Archipelago. All our commerce and communications therein will be interrupted, or exposed to the greatest hazards . . . [Britain's] desire to retain the island arises, I am convinced, much less from a belief that . . . a military or naval station is necessary to her interest in that region, than from a knowledge that to us they will afford military advantages quite important, and not otherwise to be had.

So wrote General Tatten, Chief Engineer of the United States Army, in a report to the Government.

Actually, the danger of an enemy battery on San Juan Island was overrated by Milton. Ships hugging the opposite shore of Vancouver Island need not come closer to San Juan than within five nautical miles, well beyond the traditional three-mile cannon shot.

As to the island itself, another American official had this to say:

> San Juan Island is the most western of the Haro group, and has an area of about fifty-four square miles. Its greatest length is about fourteen and a half miles . . . its widest part is about six and a half miles. Low ranges of hills trend along its eastern and western shores, those on the western side being the highest, Mount

San Juan [Mount Dallas], in this range, having an elevation of about 1,000 feet. . . . There are extensive prairies in several localities, and from the south end of the island to within a short distance of its northern extremity, flocks can feed on green grass almost throughout the year. . . . The north end of the island contains much good land, now covered by a heavy forest. . . . Upon this island are at least four beautiful lakes. . . . A circumstance of great importance in connection with this island is the existence upon it of extensive deposits of limestone.

Apart from the San Juan Islands there was yet another small piece of territory on the Pacific coast which, for a while at least, aroused mutual suspicions — the peninsula of Point Roberts, jutting southward beyond the forty-ninth parallel on the mainland. The peninsula, which could be entered by land only from British territory, was an anomaly in British eyes, much like the United States enclave in the Lake of the Woods. Prevost therefore tried to delay the erection of a boundary marker on the Point, hoping to gain it entirely for Britain, but he was finally compelled to admit the logic of the American position that any portion of the mainland south of 49° belonged to the United States.

The suspension of talks by the two commissioners concerning the water boundary did not mean idleness for Campbell. He was, of course, also commissioner for the land boundary, for which Britain had appointed Captain (now Colonel) Hawkins, and was busy with that survey from 1857. Prevost had no such task to occupy him, but he took a hand in the maritime surveys that were being carried out by his assistant, Captain George Richards of the *Plumper*.

Things were pleasant in Victoria in 1857 and early 1858. Governor Douglas, the heads of the Hudson's Bay Company, and the ship's officers enjoyed the social life of country squires and cheerfully put up with the primitiveness of the new capital. One of the *Plumper's* officers reminisced:

All the half-dozen houses that made up the town were open to us. In fine weather, riding-parties of the gentlemen and the ladies of the place were formed, and we returned generally to a high tea, or tea-dinner, at Mr. Douglas' or Mr. Work's (another chief factor of the Hudson's Bay Company) winding up the pleasant evening with dance and song. We thought nothing then of starting off [from Esquimalt] to Victoria in sea-boots, carrying others in our pockets, just to enjoy a pleasant evening by a good log-fire. And we cared little for the weary tramp homeward to Esquimalt in the dark, although it happened sometimes that men lost their way, and had to sleep in the bush all night.

No one would lightly tramp the road alone at night, or bed down in the bush, a year later, when the gold-seekers and their hangers-on had turned Victoria into the brawling metropolis noted earlier in this chapter. The *Satellite* and the *Plumper,* being the only ships of the Royal Navy in the area, were now apt to be sent on a hurried expedition to the Fraser River to quell a disturbance or to enforce colonial revenue laws. Hawkins, too, followed the Governor's call and travelled up the river of gold to restore law and order in the "diggings."

In 1858 the mainland of British Columbia was created a colony, and Douglas appointed as its Governor, so that he now presided over two distinct political entities. His salary was increased substantially at the same time, enabling him to relinquish his post with the Hudson's Bay Company. He also acquired a proper staff and a heightened sense of power and dignity, an attitude that was looked on as foppish by the democratic newcomers to the city; it was said Douglas never went anywhere unless attended by his personal swordbearer.

In February, 1859, British military strength in Vancouver Island waters was increased greatly by the arrival of the thirty-gun frigate *Tribune,* Captain Geoffrey Phipps Hornby, carrying an extra complement of 150 marines, and the corvette *Pylades,* Captain Michael de Courcy. Captain de Courcy was a cousin of Magistrate de Courcy, whom Douglas later that year appointed to San Juan.

In the summer of 1859 the Hudson's Bay Company farm on San Juan was a prosperous establishment, having a flock of about five thousand sheep along with a fair number of cows and horses. It was an idyllic spot, and when A. G. Dallas married Jane, daughter of Governor James Douglas, in 1858, they chose San Juan Island for their honeymoon. (The respective ages of groom and bride were forty-one and eighteen.) Riding up the western slope of Mount Dallas they could see, across the blue waters of Haro Strait, the harbour of Victoria, twelve miles away as the crow flies. The sheep farm itself was located on the island's south-eastern peninsula, on an open piece of ground, within easy access of the landing in sheltered Griffin Bay. Apart from Griffin himself, there were three white and eighteen non-white farm-hands — Indians, half-breeds, or Hawaiians.

There were also on the island some twenty-nine American settlers, or squatters, men who had straggled from the stream of fortune-seekers that crossed from Victoria to the mouth of the Fraser River in 1858 and 1859. They occupied themselves with anything that might yield food, money, or amusement. Their houses or shacks also clustered on the southern extremity of the island, but they did not yet seriously inconvenience the Hudson's Bay sheep farm. Griffin's house served, in fact, as a rallying and rescue point for the settlers when Indian danger threatened, much as the manor-house in older days. Among the Americans was Paul K. Hubbs, the new customs collector, whose duties seem to have been decorative rather than practical.

In their midst appeared, on July 9, 1859, General Harney of the United States Army.

William Selby Harney was born in 1800, grew up in Tennessee, and entered the army as second lieutenant in 1818. He distinguished himself in the Seminole War in Florida under Jackson, whom he adopted as his mentor and ideal. In 1846 he was promoted to colonel and took part in the Mexican War, where his headstrong manner gained him martial renown and brought him into severe conflict with the commanding general (about which more will have to be said later). In 1858 General Harney was entrusted with the pacification of the recalcitrant Mormons in Utah. He proposed to solve the Mormon problem by hanging Brigham Young and the twelve apostles and turning the Temple of Latter-Day Saints into a barrack. His plan struck the United States Government as a bit too drastic, and the same year Harney was ordered to Oregon, where it was thought his fierceness would find a useful outlet in subduing the rebellious Indians. He was a man after the heart of the western frontiersmen, and he quickly became popular in Oregon and Washington. The feelings of the Indians about him are not recorded, but those of his superior and his British opposites are, and we shall come to them in due course.

Before proceeding to Victoria and to San Juan on his tour of inspection, Harney stopped off at the military posts along Puget Sound — Steilacoom (just south of the modern Tacoma), Port Townsend at the western entrance to the Sound, Bellingham east of the San Juan Islands. There he conferred briefly with the commanding officers, Colonel Silas Casey, Major Granville O. Haller, and Captain George Edward Pickett. At Bellingham he stayed at the house of Judge Fitzhugh. Harney, Pickett, and Fitzhugh were all Southerners, and they spent a congenial evening discussing the political situation along the boundary. There can be little doubt that Fitzhugh and Pickett knew about the state of things on San Juan — the island had been a bone of contention for many years — and that they told General Harney about the shooting of the pig two weeks earlier, and the altercation between Dallas and Cutler.

Haller, who was no Southerner and no friend of Harney, later stated that Harney had formed his plan to occupy San Juan while at Bellingham, *before* visiting Victoria and San Juan. Haller said that, after his stay in Bellingham, General Harney continued north to Semiahmoo (or Semiamoo) Bay, now called Boundary Bay, to pay his respects to Commissioner Archibald Campbell. While there, his adjutant confided Harney's intention of occupying San Juan to William J. Warren, Boundary Commission secretary. Warren did not pass the information on to his superior, as he took it for granted that the general had done so. This, Haller says, was not the case; when Campbell and Warren showed up at Fort Townsend a few days later to pick up their mail, Campbell was surprised to learn from Haller about the famous Special Order No. 72.

Haller's story has been discounted by some serious historians, especially as he coupled it with a highly speculative and dubious theory that Harney, Pickett, and Fitzhugh had attempted to cook up a military conflict between the United States and Britain so as to rally their nation and to prevent the impending rupture between North and South. Nonetheless, Haller was a man on the spot, and it does not seem likely that he would so far confuse the sequence of events as to reverse the order of Harney's decision to occupy San Juan, and the actual visit to that island. His account derives credibility from the subsequent behaviour of Commissioner Campbell, whose shadowy moves during the first days of the crisis were precisely those of a man who knows what it brewing and wishes to find out more about it, though without becoming personally involved. Also, Harney had no plausible reason to extend his inspection tour to San Juan — there were no troops on that island — and he probably knew as much about affairs on the island before his visit as he did after it. In this light, his trip to San Juan was made chiefly to elicit a petition that would provide him with an official excuse for his plan.

Be that as it may, General Harney issued, on July 18, 1859, instructions to Captain Pickett which said, in part:

> You are directed to establish your company on Bellevue, or San Juan Island, on some suitable position near the harbor, at the south-eastern extremity. . . . The object to be attained in placing you thus is two-fold, viz.:
>
> 1st. To protect the inhabitants of the island from the incursions of the northern Indians of British Columbia and the Russian possessions. You will not permit any force of these Indians to visit San Juan Island, or the waters of Puget Sound. . . .
>
> 2nd. Another serious and important duty will devolve upon you in the occupation of San Juan Island, arising from the conflicting interests of the American citizens and the Hudson's Bay Company establishment at that point. This duty is to afford adequate protection to the American citizens, in their rights as such, and to resist all attempts at interference by the British authorities residing on Vancouver's Island, by intimidation or force, in the controversies of the abovementioned parties.
>
> This protection has been called for in consequence of the chief factor of the Hudson's Bay Company, Mr. Dallas, having recently visited San Juan Island with a British sloop of war, and threatened

to take an American by force to Victoria for trial by British laws. . . .

In your selection of a position, take into consideration that future contingencies may require an establishment of from four to six companies.

The following day, Harney reported his action in a letter to the assistant adjutant-general of the United States Army at New York City. In that report, he repeated that Dallas had come to San Juan in a sloop of war, which he identified as the *Satellite,* to threaten Cutler. This complete fabrication was to be repeated several times by Harney, and the story got better with each telling. Harney claimed to have the information from Hubbs, the United States customs collector on San Juan. It is worth noting that in the petition the American settlers asked for protection only against Indians and mentioned the Hudson's Bay Company farm only to acknowledge its "timely aid." What the settlers communicated orally to General Harney is not known.

Harney's order took about a week to reach Captain Pickett at Bellingham. Griffin, the manager of the Hudson's Bay Company farm on San Juan, became aware of the landing of United States troops in Griffin Bay between eight and nine o'clock in the evening of Tuesday, July 26, 1859. Pickett's company numbered about sixty men, and he set them to tenting and positioning two brass field-pieces so that they overlooked the harbour. Griffin immediately sent word of the landing to Governor Douglas.

Douglas had meantime requested Captain Prevost to use his *Satellite* for transporting to San Juan the newly appointed stipendiary magistrate John F. de Courcy. When Prevost anchored in Griffin Bay on the evening of July 27, he noted with surprise the Stars and Stripes flying over an armed camp. He and de Courcy hesitated, but on July 28 the magistrate was installed with due ceremony in the presence of the British residents.

By that time the *Satellite* had been joined in the harbour by the *Tribune* under Captain Hornby. As soon as Douglas learned of Pickett's landing, he requested Captain de Courcy of the *Pylades,* who was the senior naval officer in the colony, to dispatch a powerful vessel of war to San Juan to (a) prevent the landing of further

United States troops, (b) prevent the troops already on the island from erecting fortifications. Geoffrey Phipps Hornby (born 1825), the son of a British admiral, was a stern disciplinarian who had taken over his ship in China. His strenuous efforts to whip his crew into shape had resulted in numerous desertions as soon as the *Tribune* cast anchor in Esquimalt Harbour. But Hornby was also an intelligent officer with a sense of humour, and he took Douglas's peremptory order with a grain of salt.

Soon after his arrival at the island, Hornby was told by Magistrate de Courcy that he, de Courcy, would probably have to issue a warrant for the arrest of Pickett and his soldiers. In this case it would be necessary to cut the Americans off from retreat into the northern woods. Once the soldiers and the squatters — who were also armed and would no doubt join their military compatriots — escaped into the forested interior of the island it would be practically impossible to catch them, and they would wreck havoc among the livestock. (The *Satellite* had meantime returned to Victoria.)

It did not take Hornby long to convince the British magistrate that any attempt to "arrest" the America force would be an unmitigated disaster. De Courcy nonetheless served his warrant on Pickett, who promptly ignored it. The magistrate let it go at that. It is also doubtful whether Griffin expected compliance when, on July 30, he requested Pickett to quit the island, which was the property of the Hudson's Bay Company, or be faced with civil action. Pickett replied that he did not acknowledge the right of the Hudson's Bay Company to dictate his course of action, and that he would obey only the orders of his Government.

The immediate danger of an armed collision was thus averted, but the Governor's orders not to permit fortifications or the landing of more American troops still kept Hornby in a quandary. It was obvious to the captain that Douglas had had no true conception of the situation that would confront the *Tribune* on San Juan. The only practical way to prevent the Americans from entrenching themselves was to loose a few broadsides. This would reduce Pickett's camp to shreds; it would also plunge the two nations into war. Fortunately, Hornby was accompanied on the *Tribune* by

Douglas's attorney-general, George Cary. Cary, though fully as militant as Douglas, was reluctantly persuaded that the Governor's orders had been too sweeping, and agreed to send word back to Victoria.

On July 31 Hornby went ashore for a man-to-man talk with Pickett, who had cautiously moved part of his camp across a ridge out of sight of the *Tribune*. While Hornby was away there steamed into Griffin Bay the United States Army steamer *Massachusetts,* carrying an extra complement of 120 men. The crisis which Hornby had feared and tried to avoid was now at hand, and the lieutenant left in charge of the *Tribune* was beside himself with anxiety, as the peace of the empire seemed to be in his hands. To his signals not to land troops the captain of the American warship retorted that he would land anything he pleased. At this moment the *Plumper* came sailing around the bend, signalling frantically to the *Tribune*: the Governor had rescinded his order.

As it turned out, the *Massachusetts* landed only provisions for Pickett's men, and, after lying in the harbour for three days, steamed off northward, troops still on board.

This is how Hornby described the development to his wife:

> San Juan, July 31, 1859. . . . The Governor's instructions say expressly we are to commit no act of war, and we are not allowed to bundle these fellows off neck and crop, so he takes a medium course. He sends over a magistrate, who is going to take legal steps to warn them off the land, and to issue a summons (!!) against those that won't go. I am sent to prevent any more troops landing, and to assist the civil power.
>
> 8 P.M. Everything has changed since I began my letter this morning. I have received fresh orders to take no steps against these men at present, or prevent others from landing.
>
> The Governor told me it would be as well if I called on the commanding officer, and told him what my orders were. When I called he was away, and before he returned my visit I had received my counter-orders, so I have not the disgust of having blustered, and then being forced to haul in my horns. He (a Captain Pickett) speaks more like a Devonshire man than a Yankee. His manner is more quiet than that of most of his countrymen, but he seems to have just the notion they all have of getting a name by some

audacious act. He dropped one or two things which may be useful to us to know, and, I hope, did not get much information out of me.

Evidently Hornby had talked to Pickett on board the *Tribune*.

Governor Douglas described the developments of the first few days of the crisis to the Colonial Office as follows:

> I lost no time in making a demand on Captain M. de Courcy the Senior Naval Officer in command of Her Majesty's Ships stationed here for a powerful Vessel of War to be despatched to San Juan, and requested him to instruct the officer in command to prevent the landing of further armed parties of the United States Soldiers . . . as well as the erection of fortifications of any description by the party already on the Island. . . . On the evening of the 30th July I received a Despatch from Mr. Attorney General Cary representing the American force as more powerful than had been reported to us and that the British force under the command of Capt. Hornby could not effect the object we proposed without a strong probability of resistance. I therefore immediately entered again into communication with Captain de Courcy, suggesting that another powerful vessel of War might be despatched to the spot trusting that the exhibition of an overwhelming force might prevent resistance and the probable effusion of blood. In a personal conference the same evening with Captains de Courcy and Richards RN they expressed a very strong opinion on the proposed employment of Her Majesty's forces against the Troops of the United States, and suggested that milder measures should be first tried. . . . Out of respect to the opinion of these officers, and especially as I felt assured that the measures of Government could not be carried into effect with the requisite spirit and vigor unless the officers intrusted with their execution were cordial in their support I agreed to a modification of the instructions issued to Capt. Hornby directing him to prevent the landing of armed parties of United States troops and the erection of military works by the party already on the Island, which part of his instructions was revoked and the magistrate Mr. de Courcy was directed not to issue any process against the United States detachment of Troops then on San Juan.

On July 30 the editor of the *Victoria Colonist,* a somewhat eccentric crusader who called himself Amor de Cosmos, visited the "seat of war" with several other citizens and reported as follows in his paper:

The Hudson's Bay Company station faces the Straits of San Juan de Fuca [*sic*] and comprises about 6 small one-story dwellings, of hewn logs, built around a small open square. Behind are several barns. The dwellings are situated within a hundred yards of the shore, on the side of a gentle slope, running back about half a mile to the summit of the peninsula. . . . A herd of 4,000 and odd sheep, with some 1,900 lambs, were quietly grazing a short distance below. [There followed a brief description of the house of the American customs collector Hubbs, flying an American flag, a few rods from the Hudson's Bay Company post.] Leaving Mr. Hubbs' residence, we passed on about half a mile south-easterly, and came to the centre of the dividing ridge of the peninsula — the southern side facing Fuca's Straits, sloping and extending to the shore, three-quarters of a mile distant. The whole of this side is prairie, extending to the end of the island. In the middle of it, near the springs, were 3 tents erected by Capt. Pickett's company, to which teams were hauling army stores. . . . On the northern side, there is an open piece of prairie, about a quarter of a mile, falling gently to the harbor, formed by the channel between San Juan and Lopez Islands. . . . In the centre of the space lay Capt. Pickett's company. . . . There were 18 tents pitched. Two brass field pieces were mounted in the centre of the camp, and sentinels posted. Immediately in front of the camp, on that fine sheet of water, lay HMS Tribune, with her fires burning, frowning on the invaders of British soil. . . . On entering the camp, we were very politely and hospitably received by Dr. Craig, surgeon to the forces, who invited us to be seated in his marquee. Refreshments being served, we passed a quarter of an hour very pleasantly in his company and Mr. Crosby's. Mr. Crosby is the American magistrate, who has come over from Whatcom [Bellingham] to supersede Mr. Hubbs. Capt. Pickett, having visited the Dr.'s tent, we had the pleasure of an introduction. After bidding farewell to our generous host, Capt. Pickett would not allow us to depart, without partaking of refreshments with him. Then we parted, feeling sorry that occasion had called these gallant men to visit our soil on other than the most friendly terms.

The imbibing of Pickett's refreshments did not, however, reconcile Amor de Cosmos to what he considered American aggression, and he continued to mount an editorial attack against it, as well as against the attitude of his rival newspaper, the *Victoria Gazette*. The *Gazette*, under American ownership, naturally found it hard

to condemn Harney's action outright, the more so as this would not
have sat well with most of its readership, being composed principally of American citizens, who then outnumbered British subjects
in Victoria. "An unscrupulous sheet published here," the *Gazette*
said, "has done its utmost to aggravate bitter feelings." Not to be
outdone by the *Colonist,* the *Gazette* reporter also paid a visit to
Pickett's encampment and came away with a high opinion of its
commander. "Captain Pickett raised the American flag at Chapul-
tepec in the Mexican war, is a brave and cautious officer, and will
go as far as duty and honor require."

Despite his brave front, Captain Pickett, too, was extremely
uneasy. On the same day that he entertained de Cosmos and companions he penned an urgent note to his immediate superior,
Colonel Casey in Steilacoom, asking that the *Massachusetts* be sent
over to restore some sort of naval balance and to bring additional
supplies. (This the *Massachusetts* did on July 31 — see above.)

In the Vancouver Island capital, Governor Douglas continued
to have a difficult stand with his pacific military advisers. Fearing
— rightly — that the Governor would before long devise new
measures for ousting or containing the United States troops on San
Juan, the officers and the small provincial council ganged up on
him at a war council on August 1, the outcome of which was a
memorandum calling for moderation and the solution of the dispute by diplomatic means. Any military action against San Juan,
the memorandum said, would bring massive retaliation from the
United States, and an invasion of Vancouver Island. There was also
the nasty possibility of internal rebellion:

> It appears also probable that if a collision takes place at San
> Juan insurrectionary and filibustering movements will ensue both
> in Vancouver Island and British Columbia, the great majority of
> the inhabitants being either United States citizens or embued
> with their feelings.

The memorialists did not forget the international situation,
which was then complicated by the war in Italy in which both
France and Austria were involved: "In the present state of European
politics it is extremely desirable that the Home Government be as

far as possible left unfettered by a war with the United States."
They recommended the withdrawal of British subjects (*i.e.,* Griffin
and his labourers) from San Juan as a safety measure. The
memorandum was signed by Captain Michael de Courcy, Colonel
Hawkins, four members of the provincial council, and Judge
Matthew Begbie. Only Attorney-General Cary withheld his signature.

The war council also determined, in line with its decision, to
send information to London by the quickest and most reliable
means. To this end, Colonel Hawkins (who could afford to leave
his boundary survey in subordinate hands) was to be taken to San
Francisco by Captain de Courcy's *Pylades,* where he would catch
the mail steamer about to leave for Panama. From Panama Hawkins would travel by the fastest ships available to New York and
England.

Douglas was embittered by the attitude of his advisers, notably
that of the military officers. "They do not know San Juan is their
country," he rumbled. The recommendation to withdraw the British
subjects he did not consider for a moment. As to the sending of
Hawkins as courier to London, there was nothing objectionable in
that, but Douglas protested against the use of the *Pylades* for the
errand; if the ship was to be sent anywhere, it ought to be San
Juan. Again he was overruled, and the *Pylades* set sail out of
Esquimalt, southward bound.

The two military signers of the anti-Douglas memorandum had
hardly disappeared over the horizon when Douglas bounced back
with a new scheme that would restore British honour on the Pacific
and preserve San Juan for the British Crown. On August 2 he
issued an order to Captain Hornby to land a body of troops on the
island to establish a joint occupation with Pickett, and the next day,
as if to make sure that there would be no back-tracking this time,
he announced the forthcoming landing of troops in a message to
the Vancouver Island legislature. Douglas was emboldened by an
interview between Captain Prevost and Captain Pickett, in which
the former had sounded out the American commander in regard to
British troop landings. Pickett had replied that he would prevent
any inferior force from landing, fight any equal force, and protest

against any superior force being landed. Douglas deduced that to prevent bloodshed he had merely to make sure that the British landing force was overwhelmingly superior. This was easily done, for in addition to the 150 marines brought from China by the *Tribune,* the *Satellite* and *Plumper* had taken on board a number of Royal Engineers from the British Columbia mainland.

Together with his order to land troops, Governor Douglas transmitted to Captain Hornby an official protest which Hornby was to hand to Pickett. The protest opened with the words: "By James Douglas, C.B., Governor and Commander-in-Chief in and over the colony of Vancouver's Island and its Dependencies, Vice-Admiral of the same, &c." In it Douglas protested against the occupation of San Juan Island and declared that sovereignty over it resided, and always had done, in Her Majesty Queen Victoria, and in her predecessors, kings of Great Britain.

On August 3, before attempting to carry out Douglas's order, Hornby consulted with Captains Prevost and Richards, whose ships were lying with his own in Griffin Bay, and the three officers decided to have another talk with Pickett and to see whether they could not crack the Virginian's dogged resistance by verbal assault.

Hornby accordingly sent a letter to Pickett, asking him to a meeting on board the *Tribune.* Pickett replied at once that he would be glad to meet Hornby in camp. The three captains were obliged to lower their boats and row across to the island. Round one had once again gone to Pickett.

The discussion was carried on chiefly between Hornby and Pickett. Hornby based himself on the Crampton-Marcy Agreement of 1855, and Marcy's injunction to the then Governor of Washington Territory. He proposed a joint military occupation, setting aside for its duration the authority of the civil powers on the island, each commander having jurisdiction over his own nationals. Should Pickett not agree to this, Hornby would reserve to himself full liberty of action and hold Pickett responsible for any collision. Pickett replied that he could, and would, do nothing that was not ordered by his commanding officer. "Any attempt to make any such occupation as you have proposed, before I can communicate with

General Harney, will be bringing on a collision which *can* be avoided by awaiting this issue."

Hornby and his fellow officers then withdrew, after agreeing to Pickett's suggestion that their oral declarations be repeated in writing. Round two had also gone to Pickett.

How Pickett himself viewed his situation is shown by a report of the meeting which he wrote the same evening for General Harney, and which is interesting enough to be quoted entire:

> I have the honor to report the following circumstances: — The British ships, the *Tribune,* the *Plumper,* and the *Satellite,* are lying here in a menacing attitude. I have been warned off by the Hudson's Bay Company agent; then a summons was sent to me to appear before a Mr. De Courcey, an official of Her Britannic Majesty. Today I received the enclosed communications, and I also enclose my answer to the same. [This refers to Governor Douglas's protest and the written declarations exchanged after the meeting.]
>
> I had to deal with three captains, and I thought it better to take the brunt of it. They have a force so much superior to mine that it will be merely a mouthful for them; still I have informed them I am here by order of my commanding general, and will maintain my position if possible.
>
> They wish to have a co-joint occupation of the island; I decline anything of that kind. They can, if they choose, land at almost any point on the island, and I cannot prevent them. I have used the utmost courtesy and delicacy in my intercourse, and, if it is possible, please inform me at such an early hour as to prevent a collision. The utmost I could expect today was to suspend any proceeding till they have had time to digest a *pill* which I gave them. They wish to throw the onus on me, because I refused to allow them to land an equal force, and each of us to have military occupation, thereby wiping out both civil authorities. I say I cannot do so until I hear from the General.
>
> I have endeavored to impress them with the idea that my authority comes directly through *you* from *Washington.*
>
> The *Pleiades* left this morning for San Francisco with Colonel Hawkins. [Pickett erred in the name of the ship and the date.] The excitement in Victoria and here is tremendous. I suppose some five hundred people have visited us. I have had to use a great deal of my *peace-making* disposition in order to restrain some of the sovereigns. Please to excuse this hasty, and I am almost afraid

unintelligible letter, but the steamer is waiting, and I have been writing under the most unfavorable circumstances. I must add that they seem to doubt the authority of the General commanding, and do not wish to acknowledge his right to occupy the island, which they say is in dispute, unless the United States Government have decided the question with Great Britain. *I have so far staved them off, by saying that the two Governments have, without doubt, settled this affair.* But this state of affairs cannot last; therefore, I must respectfully ask that an express be sent me immediately, on my future guidance. I do not think there are any moments to waste. In order to maintain our dignity we must occupy in force, or allow them to land an equal force, which they can do now, and possibly will do, in spite of *my* diplomacy.

The impression conveyed by Pickett that the occupation of San Juan had been ordered from Washington was of course false, and it was suspected from the beginning by his opponents.

As to Hornby, he wrote a long letter to Governor Douglas, in which he detailed the reasons against any attempt to land troops on San Juan in the face of Pickett's defiance. The letter was no doubt sincere and tinged by no shadow of cowardice. It must nonetheless be admitted that in this tug-of-war between Douglas and the military, represented chiefly by Captain Hornby, Douglas with his brinkmanship was not quite so dangerously out of line as might at first glance appear. He was a son of the frontier, as was Harney. Unlike his military advisers, Douglas had had long experience in dealing with Americans and their methods of expansion. He was keenly aware of squatter's rights.

Hornby and his fellow officers, on the other hand, could see the issue only as a choice between fight and standoff. To land on a disputed island merely for the sake of *being* there struck them as quixotic. Yet it was quite true, as Pickett emphasized in his report to Harney, that the British force could have landed almost anywhere on the island without his being able to prevent them. Hornby could, for instance, have landed a hundred men at the northwestern end, where there was a good harbour, well out of sight and sound of Pickett's camp. It seems that the Americans and the British could have glared at one another with just as much truculence, and as little harm, across a few miles of prairie as across a few hundred yards of water.

To leave no stone unturned in his attempts to remove the American force from San Juan, Douglas had, as soon as he heard of the landing, requested Commissioner Prevost to seek out his counterpart, Campbell, to protest Harney's action. Prevost immediately set out in the *Satellite* for Semiahmoo Bay, Campbell's headquarters, but could not find the United States commissioner. The *Shubrick,* a small steamer used by Campbell for his travels, was anchored in Griffin Bay, but to Prevost's inquiries the American sailors replied that Campbell was in Port Townsend. British sailors, however, claimed that they had seen him leave the island and board the *Shubrick.* Prevost himself reported to London that "Mr. Campbell the United States Boundary Commissioner was on board the Shubrick professedly on a deer shooting expedition." He also pointed to the "significant fact that Mr. Campbell has been absent from Semiahmoo for upwards of a fortnight, during which period these movements [of Pickett's company] have been matured and carried out."

Prevost surmised that Harney had engineered the occupation of San Juan to gain "political capital and notoriety," to help him along in his presidential ambitions. He also noted that Harney had been at Semiahmoo a few days before the landing of the troops. Not being able to meet Campbell personally, Prevost sent him a letter in which he requested the United States commissioner to bring pressure to bear on Harney to cause the troops to be removed from San Juan. Campbell, still fuming over Prevost's "secret" instructions, retorted with unwonted asperity that

> as the supervision of the movement and operations of the military forces of the United States forms no part of the duties of the Joint Commission . . . I cannot recognize your pretensions to catechize me thereupon, and therefore decline to return you either a positive or negative answer.

He also expressed his resentment at Prevost's attempt at "intimidation" — a reference to the British commissioner's warning of an armed collision if the American troops were not removed. There were several more notes of the same general tenor.

Campbell did not, however, agree with Harney's action — or at least not with its results. On August 14 he wrote a letter to the general (which supports the impression that Campbell knew beforehand about Pickett's landing):

> When I learned from Captain Pleasonton [Harney's adjutant] that Captain Pickett's company was ordered to San Juan, I thought it was a very proper movement for the protection of American settlers from northern Indians, and from the interference of the Hudson's Bay Company's agents, who had recently been threatening to take one of the settlers to Victoria for trial; and I did not anticipate from it any serious objection on the part of the British authorities. . . . But I happened to be making an exploration of the archipelago at the time Captain Pickett arrived, and for several days after he landed I was anchored in this harbor [San Juan] and I soon saw that it was going to produce great excitement. . . . I did not suppose that any resistance would be made by Captain Pickett to the landing of the British troops. . . . I shall be greatly relieved to learn that you have some authority from the Government for the decisive step you have taken.

Harney, of course, was in no position to afford this much-craved relief to the United States commissioner. He therefore evaded that question in his reply — except to say that he had submitted the whole matter to the President — and claimed that his action had not affected the problem of the boundary in the slightest. This did not entirely agree with his instructions to Pickett, in which San Juan was referred to as "the territory of the United States."

With these exchanges the participation of the two commissioners in the struggle over the water boundary came to an end, although Prevost was destined to play a certain role in the dispute many years later.

Hornby's pacific course and his politely hedged refusal to land troops on San Juan received favourable comment from yet another military source, the only one who had not so far been consulted in the matter — Colonel Richard Clement Moody, Royal Engineers. Colonel Moody had been sent from England early in 1859 to assume the duties of commissioner of lands and public works in mainland British Columbia, where he commanded a corps of Royal Engineers engaged in road-building and similar tasks. He did not get on well with Douglas, whose supervision he resented. The colonel wrote home:

> It is fortunate for Great Britain that Hornby of the Tribune is at San Juan. His sound sense may avert evil. He will avert war to the last without in any degree perilling the proper dignity of England. The Governor wrote him a very clever letter, indirectly ordering him to land troops, but throwing the responsibility on him. Hornby has far too much Motherwit to be caught that way — of course he did not land them. He is a fine fellow. . . . There can be no doubt . . . that a collision was desired. The embroglio would then have been inextricable.

But worse was yet to come for the embattled Governor of Vancouver Island and British Columbia. On August 5, before he had had time to react to the latest frustration of his policy, into Esquimalt harbour sailed HMS *Ganges* — last of the sailing line-of-battle ships of the Royal Navy — bearing the commander of the Pacific Station, Rear-Admiral Robert Lambert Baynes. Baynes took one look at the San Juan situation and whole-heartedly approved the course followed by Captains de Courcy and Hornby. Hornby could now breathe a vast sigh of relief, as the burden of responsibility was finally lifted from him.

On the same day the corvette *Pylades* returned to Esquimalt. On August 3, when the ship had covered about two-fifths of the distance to San Francisco, she encountered a strong south-easterly wind. Captain de Courcy calculated that he would be unable to make the Golden Gate in time for Colonel Hawkins to catch the mail steamer, and resolved to turn back. After consulting with Admiral Baynes and Governor Douglas, and bringing his dispatches up to date, Hawkins set out once more in the *Pylades* on August 13. He left San Francisco on August 20, was in Washington on September 13, where he informed the British Minister, and reached London two weeks later — certainly as fast a voyage as could be made at the time.

No written communications appear to have been exchanged between Douglas and Baynes until the second departure of Hawkins, and we can infer what was said between them only from subsequent letters. By then the situation on San Juan Island had changed radically.

General Harney received Pickett's cry for help on or about August 6. Harney immediately ordered Colonel Casey at Steilacoom to go to Pickett's assistance with all his troops — four companies — if necessary. Casey embarked on the steamer *Julia* on August 9, with his entire command. The steamer had travelled only a short distance when she was hailed by the *Active,* another American vessel bound from San Juan to Steilacoom. Her captain strongly and solemnly advised Casey not to attempt to land his troops on the island, as he was sure to meet resistance from the *Tribune.* Casey nevertheless continued on his course, his anxiety increasing as the *Julia* neared the disputed archipelago. The troopship spent the night at Port Townsend, intending to make San Juan early the next day.

In the morning, as they neared the island, Providence intervened in the shape of a dense fog. The *Julia's* captain declared that under the circumstances it would be hazardous, and unnecessary to boot, to attempt rounding the south-eastern promontory into Griffin Bay, and that it was just as simple to land the troops on the south side of the island, from where they could easily reach Camp Pickett. Casey heartily agreed, and the four companies and their howitzers were ferried ashore.

The fog lifted soon after, and the *Julia,* with Colonel Casey still on board, sailed around the spit and anchored near the *Satellite* and the *Tribune.* All that was left to be sent ashore was some equipment and ammunition, an operation with which the British warships did not interfere.

On going ashore, Casey found Captain Pickett reduced to near-hysteria by the two-week war of nerves. Gesticulating at the *Satellite.* Pickett declared his conviction that the warship was getting ready to shell him, and that this would be followed by the assault of the "several hundred" marines, engineers, and sappers the ships had on board. His plan, he told the colonel, was to fire on

the landing force with his howitzers, then spike the guns, deliver
fire with his musketry, and withdraw to the woods.

Casey, horrified by what he regarded as the imminent outbreak
of war between the United States and Britain, decided to make a
last-minute attempt to stave off the collision by proposing a conference. He was gratified when, after some hedging, Hornby and
Prevost came ashore, along with Archibald Campbell, who was
still anxiously hovering about the scene of the crisis. Casey informed
the Englishmen of his troop landing, chided them for frightening
Pickett, and asked who the top-ranking officer in the British colonies
was and where he could be found. Hornby told him it was Admiral
Baynes at Esquimalt. Casey then said that he intended to go and
see the admiral the next day.

On August 11 Colonel Casey and Captain Pickett put on their
gala uniforms and, accompanied by Campbell, travelled to Esquimalt in the *Shubrick*.

Casey's independent decision to seek an interview with Baynes
no doubt stemmed from his reservations about Harney's action.
Casey was a Northerner; he was a teacher of infantry tactics and
an outstanding mathematician, and accustomed to detached con-
templation rather than bravura; he had some reason to feel slighted
by the manner in which Harney had made him the auxiliary of
Captain Pickett. He intended to propose to Baynes that, if the
admiral gave his word of honour not to molest Pickett, the additional United States troops landed the day before would be withdrawn.

The meeting was, however, frustrated by Casey's sense of punc-
tilio. After reaching Esquimalt harbour, he expected Baynes to
visit him on board the *Shubrick*. Baynes (who happened to be
entertaining Governor Douglas on the *Ganges*) expected Casey to
visit *him* on his flagship. Casey did not go, but by using Pickett as
his herald he gave Baynes the unexpected opportunity of meeting
face to face the legendary American captain who was defying the
British Pacific Fleet. "I was of opinion," Casey wrote General
Harney, "that I had carried etiquette far enough in going twenty-

five miles to see a gentleman who was disinclined to come one hundred yards to see me."

Admiral Baynes was not impressed by Colonel Casey's attempt at intervention: "These officers had no authority whatever to treat, and it is extraordinary that they could have expected me, to descend from my position to meet them on board the United States steamer, when the Interview was sought by them." Another commander who was unimpressed, and let Casey know as much, was General Harney.

On August 12 the *Massachusetts* brought further reinforcements to San Juan in the shape of Major Haller's command from Fort Townsend. To beef up their artillery the American troops removed eight thirty-two-pounders from the *Massachusetts*. A few days later, four companies of artillery landed on the island. With this, almost the entire strength of the United States Army in the Puget Sound area had been concentrated on San Juan Island under the command of Colonel Casey. The number of men was 461. They had provisions for three months and were busy building entrenchments higher up on the slopes, so as to have some protection against fire from the warships.

On August 12 — two days after the reinforcement of the American garrison on San Juan — the Vancouver Island House of Assembly, consisting of seven members, debated the situation on the island and resolved to ask the Governor why his proclamation of August 3, promising that British troops would be landed on San Juan, had not yet been carried into effect. This seems to have brought the smouldering Baynes-Douglas differences to a head. On August 13 Baynes wrote a letter to the Governor telling him explicitly that he, Baynes, had revoked Douglas's orders to Hornby to land troops, "as I thought if carried out they could not but produce what I feel it my positive duty if possible to avert, a collision with the Forces of the United States." Furthermore, Baynes was gravely concerned about the presence of Magistrate de Courcy on San Juan. "The risk that he may at some moment overstep the line of prudence is great."

Douglas replied in a surprisingly mild tone, acquiescing in the decision not to land — which was perhaps inevitable now that the American force had been so greatly increased. He also promised to instruct the magistrate to consult with Hornby before acting. Baynes then rubbed in his advantage by attacking the idea of a joint military occupation as such, saying that it would do nothing to strengthen the British claim, and would only complicate the dispute. This impugning of his policy was a little too much for Douglas, and he vented his spleen on what he termed "a passive and retrograde policy," adding that had his measures been carried out, "no collision would have ensued, no bloodshed would have followed, tranquillity would now exist, and we should not be placed in the complicated and humiliating position which we hold this day."

To the Colonial Office the Governor wrote on August 22: "I confess with regret that my views differ essentially from those expressed by Rear Admiral Baynes, in reference to the maintenance of Her Majesty's rights to the Island of San Juan." He described the differences concerning the landing of troops, and said:

> My opinion on the subject remains unaltered. I feel assured that a bold and resolute stand, as I proposed in the first instance, would have nipped their project in the bud, increased the influence and dignity of this Government, and prevented collisions, which a policy of concession may precipitate.

No appeaser was Douglas.

The Governor was supported by his subjects who, on August 25, adopted a memorial at "a very numerous and highly respectable meeting" (as the *Colonist* had it) asking the Queen not to yield San Juan. "Without San Juan, communication with British Columbia would be cut off, the prosperity of Vancouver Island completely destroyed, and the magnificent project for connecting it with the British North American Provinces frustrated." The memorialists collected two hundred signatures.

During that period Douglas also carried on a verbal duel with General Harney, arising from Douglas's protest of August 2. Harney reiterated his charge that a British ship of war had been sent to San Juan to help Dallas seize an American citizen, and said he would leave the troops on the island until he heard from Washington. In reply Douglas wrote he was glad to learn Harney's action had not been taken with "direct authority from the Cabinet in Washington." He refuted the warship allegation, said that American citizens on San Juan had always been treated with consideration, and regretted that Harney had not conferred with him before embarking on his unilateral course. He called on Harney to withdraw the troops. To Douglas's veiled accusation of subterfuge, Harney replied that "on my late visit to Victoria I was without knowledge that any occurence had taken place on San Juan Island to outrage the feelings of its inhabitants" — a statement that is hard to swallow. He again refused to withdraw the troops.

In Washington Territory the action of General Harney was greeted with satisfaction. Both the *Puget Sound Herald* and the Olympia *Pioneer and Democrat* praised the occupation of San Juan, and the latter wrote:

> We suppose our neighbors may grumble a little at this summary way of settling the disputed title, but then it is the privilege of John Bull to grumble, and the motley crowd of native born British subjects congregated in these new colonies.

And, on another occasion:

> We thank God we have, in the commanding officer of the Department of Oregon, a man equal to any and all emergencies in the protection of American citizens in this north-west coast.

The new Governor of Washington Territory, R. D. Gholson, on August 21 wrote to Harney informing him that, in case of trouble with the British, the territory had available for the arming of its citizens 850 smooth-bore and 150 rifled muskets as well as four twelve-pound mountain howitzers, but no ammunition. Many of the arms had no doubt been supplied by the helpful Douglas.

Lord Lyons, the British Minister in Washington, learned about Pickett's landing on San Juan from Washington newspapers on or about September 3, 1859. The story had been carried to St. Louis, Missouri, by the forerunner of the pony express, and had been wired from that city to the eastern United States via the newly strung telegraph.

On September 3, Lyons addressed a query to Secretary of State Cass, asking for confirmation and explanation. The United States Government had by that time received Harney's first account of the landing, written on July 19, and Lyons's note merely added to the embarrassment and irritation felt by President James Buchanan and his Cabinet. On the same day that Lyons made his inquiry, the Acting Secretary of War, W. R. Drinkard, addressed a letter to Harney in which he said:

> Your despatch of the 19th of July last, addressed to the General-in-chief, has been forwarded to this department, and laid before the President for his consideration.
>
> The President was not prepared to learn that you had ordered military possession to be taken of the island of San Juan. . . . He had not anticipated that so decided a step would have been resorted to without instructions. . . . The President will not, for the present, form any decided opinion upon your course on the statement of facts presented in your despatch. He will await further details, which he expects to receive from you by the next steamer. He is especially anxious to ascertain whether, before you proceeded to act, you had communicated with Commissioner Campbell, who could not then have been distant from you.

To Lyons, who visited the State Department on September 5, Cass said that Harney had been asked for a detailed report, but that the troops had been left on the island for the time being.

Harney's later reports, however, were no more satisfactory to the United States Government than the first, even though the general elaborated on the threatening attitude of the strong British naval forces — "this force has been employed . . . in using every means in its power, except opening fire, to intimidate one company of infantry but sixty strong." His chief complaint — that Dallas, an official of the Hudson's Bay Company, had commandeered a British warship to take him to San Juan and to browbeat Cutler the pig-shooter — did not gain any more credence from being repeated and embellished. Toward the end of August Harney had worked himself into such a literary lather that he thought nothing of charging the Hudson's Bay Company at Victoria with all the atrocities which had flowed with such facility from the pens of expansionists a generation earlier, particularly with instigating the Indians to slaughter American men, women, and children.

Before these last reports could reach Washington, Buchanan had acted in a manner calculated to cut Harney to the quick: he had asked General Winfield Scott, Chief of the United States Army, to proceed to the scene of disturbance and to attempt an amicable settlement of the military dispute.

General Scott (whom the reader has already met in the first chapter) was then seventy-three years of age, and weakened by a recent fall. However, he could not resist one more chance to play the grand peacemaker and disciplinarian, and he accepted the mission to the Pacific with alacrity, the more so as it gave him the opportunity to even some ancient scores.

The fact was that the confrontation destined to take place between Scott and Harney was by no means the first such event in their lives. In the Mexican War, Scott had considered it necessary to relieve Harney of his command because of Harney's rashness. Harney yielded at first, but then his pride rushed back and he resumed command in defiance of General Scott. Scott then had Harney arrested and court-martialled. Harney was found guilty of disobedience, but the court was lenient with him and merely required him to apologize to Scott, which he did.

Harney, however, had an ace up his sleeve. As a Democrat, he had an excellent relationship with the Democratic administration in Washington; toward Scott, an ingrained Whig, the Government was definitely cool. Harney complained to Washington about his treatment, and President Polk put personal pressure on his Secretary of War, Marcy, to rehabilitate Harney and to reprimand Scott. Scott, recalling his 1859 mission in his memoirs, had this to say concerning Harney's political attitude:

> Brigadier-General Harney, who commanded our forces in that quarter, was a great favorite with the five Democratic Presidents [Jackson, Van Buren, Polk, Pierce, Buchanan]. Full of blind admiration for his patrons, he had before, in Florida, hung several Indians, under the most doubtful circumstances, in imitation of a

like act on the part of General Jackson, in the same quarter, and now, as that popular hero gained much applause by wrenching Pensacola and all Middle Florida from Spain, in time of peace, Harney probably thought he might make himself President too, by cutting short all diplomacy and taking forcible possession of the disputed island! . . . President Buchanan, however, well knowing the difference in power between Spain and Great Britain, kindly inquired of the autobiographer (now recently a cripple from a fall) whether, without injury, he could go on a mission to Puget's Sound?

Scott could, and did.

In his instructions dated September 16, 1859, he was told that he was to govern himself by the principle of the Crampton-Marcy Agreement, and that the President saw no objection to the plan proposed by Hornby to Pickett of a joint military occupation. As to the rest, Scott was given wide latitude.

Accompanied by two military aides as well as an army surgeon, Scott left New York on September 20 and, travelling via Panama and San Francisco, arrived at Fort Vancouver exactly one month later. He soundly snubbed General Harney by declining to see him when Harney first came to pay his respects. Without going ashore, Scott continued on past Olympia, the Washington capital, where he snubbed Governor Gholson by ignoring him completely. He had transferred to the *Massachusetts* for his trip to the northern waters, and the prosaic troopship promptly acquired the atmosphere of a Roman imperial pleasure barge. The correspondent of a California daily, who tried, and failed, to attach himself to Scott's retinue during the succeeding days, reported that "the Massachusetts proved a very comfortable and convenient conveyance. The General had fine and roomy quarters, and a glorious cuisine. Captain Fauntleroy [commanding the vessel] was assiduous in his attentions." Without ever leaving the steamer, Scott rapidly cruised about Puget Sound and the straits, all the while carrying on a busy correspondence with Governor Douglas in Victoria.

To facilitate these diplomatic exchanges, on October 26 Scott sent over to Victoria his adjutant, Lieutenant-Colonel George W. Lay, who was hospitably received by Douglas and installed in the gubernatorial mansion. To show his good faith, Douglas even placed his file of correspondence at Lay's disposal.

In his first letter, carried to Victoria by Colonel Lay himself, Scott suggested:

> Without prejudice to the claim of either nation to the sovereignty of the entire island of San Juan, now in dispute, it is proposed that each shall occupy a separate portion of the same by a detachment of infantry, riflemen, or marines, not exceeding one hundred men, with their appropriate arms only, for the equal protection of their respective countrymen in their persons and property, and to repel any descent on the part of hostile Indians.

This unexpected and unsolicited offer of joint occupation was no doubt a pleasant surprise for Douglas, and he poured out his sense of relief to Lay, who, on the very night of his arrival in the Vancouver Island capital, penned a hasty note to General Scott, in which he said that though Douglas had not yet considered the proposition in detail, "he is at a glance satisfied that no obstacle exists to a completely amicable and satisfactory adjustment."

A few days later Douglas had digested Scott's letter more fully, and he had probably also consulted with Baynes and some other advisers. Baynes was still afraid of the danger of collision in a joint occupation. Douglas was still without word from London (though he did have a letter from Lyons, brought along by Scott). He was no doubt apprehensive that he might overstep his authority by concluding an agreement with an official American representative that altered the *status quo* on San Juan. Also, he may have been disillusioned by the lackadaisical patriotism of the military and their annoying habit of frustrating civilian authority. At any rate, when he replied formally to Scott's proposal on October 29, he suggested a joint civil rather than military occupation, "composed of the present stipendiary magistrates, with such assistants as may be necessary, and that the military and naval forces, on both sides, be wholly withdrawn." For reasons that were probably the opposite of the Governor's, Admiral Baynes also thought a joint civil occupation was preferable to a military one. Douglas also assured Scott that Harney's allegations of British ill-treatment of American citizens were false, and that there was no intention to interfere with them under any circumstances. In the end, he invited Scott to Victoria.

Scott replied on November 2. He regretted that Douglas seemed to regard the withdrawal of troops as the *sine qua non* of a temporary settlement and expressed the opinion that even Lord Lyons had not made such conditions — otherwise he, Scott, would not have received the instructions he did. He pointed out, quite accurately, that a United States civil official would inevitably come under the control of the territorial rather than the federal Government, a highly undesirable arrangement, considering popular feeling in the Pacific North-west. He therefore elaborated his earlier proposal in a separate "Projet [*sic*] of a temporary settlement." This document provided for the occupation of San Juan by a British and an American detachment of soldiers "with their appropriate arms only" (*i.e.,* excluding artillery). As to jurisdiction, he took up Hornby's proposal and recommended that the two commanding officers should have the power

> to seize and confine, or to banish from the island, any person or persons, whatsoever, found or known to be engaged in fomenting any quarrel or misunderstanding between the officers or men of one of the detachments and the officers or men of the other, and further to treat in like manner all other offenders against the peace and good order of the island: — it being, however, expressly understood and enjoined that such measures of correction shall only be applied to American citizens or persons claiming to be such, by the American commander, or to British subjects or persons claiming to be such, by the British Commander.

Douglas answered the following day that he did not have authority to establish a joint military occupation, and that he must await instructions from London. In the meantime, however, he would direct the withdrawal of the British naval force (which now consisted of only one ship) from San Juan if Scott, in his turn, would "divest the large military force now on San Juan of its menacing attitude by removing it from the island."

Scott thereupon reduced the San Juan garrison to Pickett's original company.

The move was welcomed by Douglas, but there was one fly in the ointment, whose removal would require a delicate touch: Pickett. Douglas therefore instructed his colonial secretary to address a confidential note to Colonel Lay suggesting, in the most discreet terms, that General Scott be asked to substitute some other commander for Pickett, whose name and person were indelibly connected with Harney's first fateful proclamation. The note added:

> His Excellency has been informed (but with what shadow of truth he cannot judge) that Captain Pickett is of somewhat a hasty temperament and somewhat punctilious and exacting. . . . Governor Douglas feels sure that the General would desire to place such a man upon San Juan as would ensure a continuation of perfect harmony and tranquillity.

Scott acceded to the Governor's wish, and, rescinding his earlier order, placed on San Juan the company of Captain Lewis C. Hunt.

Having thus re-established, to his own satisfaction, tranquillity on San Juan and having pointed events in the direction of a bilateral policy, General Scott turned to deal with Harney. On November 15 he informed that unfortunate adventurer that the British would doubtlessly ask the United States to have Harney removed from the Pacific Coast; it might be wise to anticipate such a demand by Harney's transfer to the interior of the country, namely St. Louis, headquarters of the Army's Department of the West. Had not Harney himself once expressed a desire to be stationed in that city? Scott therefore transmitted an order to that effect. At the same time he hedged against the humiliation of seeing his order once more revoked by the Democratic administration in Washington by leaving it up to Harney himself whether he would comply with it or not.

General Scott then left for San Francisco and the East. His voyage, which must have cost the War Department a pretty penny, had a curiously theatrical quality. Since everything was done by letter, the only practical value of the trip was that it speeded up the mail. When Scott left the Pacific Coast, nothing had actually been settled. Douglas possessed no special powers to negotiate — which was perhaps not realized in Washington. What *was* realized was the dramatic effect the voyage of America's greatest living soldier must have on public opinion both in the United States and in England, and this was perhaps the main purpose of Scott's mission.

Harney, who had just started to build his dream house at Fort Vancouver, refused to obey the transfer order. In this he had the official backing of the population of Washington Territory, whose legislature passed a resolution on January 7, 1860, declaring that General Harney "deserved and secured the entire confidence of the people of this Territory" because of his action in the San Juan dispute as well as other matters, and requesting the President to leave Harney where he was. (The same year Harney was offered the candidacy for President by the Washington Democrats. The move did not succeed.) Both the territorial legislature and Governor Gholson were particularly incensed by Scott's entire suspension of civil authority on San Juan, an arrangement which seemed to them without precedent in United States constitutional practice.

> The late order of General Scott directing the military commander on San Juan Island to allow no person claiming to be a functionary of Washington Territory to interfere with any British subject residing or happening to be on the same was to me a matter of no small surprise or regret,

Gholson told the legislature on December 5, 1859, adding that he considered it "a usurpation of our rights." Here lay the seeds for future trouble.

Douglas did not escape criticism, either, though in the British tradition it was more subdued. Captain Hornby wrote to his wife on November 6:

> I hear from the Admiral, but in confidence, that General Scott (relieved General Hearney [sic]) has asked us to occupy San Juan jointly with 100 men each; that he and the Governor have suggested instead a civil occupation, which does not meet General Scott's views; that General Scott is very anxious to make some definite arrangement before the mail goes, so that he may send it to Washington in time for publication in the President's message to Congress, while our authorities wish to hold off to see what instructions the mail may bring from home, and further because

they think that General Scott ought at once to begin to remove his troops and guns from the island. The Admiral then went on to say that he considered we were indebted "to my [Hornby's] good judgment in not following the Governor's instructions" for not being involved in a war, and that he had written to that effect to the Admiralty.

On December 4 he went further:

I hear that the Governor got much praise in England for keeping the peace with the Yankees. That is rather good, when one knows that he would hear of nothing but shooting them all at first, and that, after all, peace was only preserved by my not complying with his wishes, as I felt he was all in the wrong from the first. I got the abuse for saying that San Juan was not more our island than the Americans', and that we should be equally wrong in landing troops there, and now they find that I was right.

Baynes's own state of mind was not, however, so assured nor that of Whitehall so unequivocal as Hornby's confident letters might suggest. On November 9, just after Scott's departure, Baynes wrote to the Lords of the Admiralty:

We have been perfectly passive exercising a degree of forbearance which their Lordships may not perhaps altogether approve. . . . [I hope that] the confidence in me as an officer holding so important a command has not been misplaced.

In London the first reaction of the new Colonial Secretary, the Duke of Newcastle, was that it was fortunate Douglas had not carried out his original intention of landing troops on San Juan. A little later, however, as disquieting news about the strengthening of the American garrison trickled in, he scribbled on the margin of one of Douglas's letters: "It is quite open to question whether Governor Douglas' plan would not have been best."

Lord John Russell, who was Foreign Secretary in the Palmerston Cabinet, took a harder line. Excoriating Commissioner Campbell for what he believed to be his complicity in the San Juan affair, he declared that "either the United States troops should be withdrawn from the island, or . . . a similar detachment of Her Majesty's Marines should jointly occupy the territory."

The British attitude in the dispute was growing militant just as on the other side of the world General Scott was casting oil on the troubled waters of the Pacific. Those were not happy days in the Foreign Office. Captain Richards's exhaustive surveys had shown that Haro Strait was by far wider and deeper than Rosario Strait. "It seems to me," Permanent Undersecretary Edmund Hammond noted confidentially in February, 1859, "that it goes to establish the American claim, and that the Canal de Haro is the best navigable channel."

On August 24, John Russell, still ignorant of Pickett's landing, inaugurated his assumption of the Foreign Office portfolio with a proposal to the United States Government, transmitted through Lyons. He said he had talked to the Earl of Aberdeen, who was Foreign Secretary in 1846, and Aberdeen "distinctly" remembered that, in conversation with United States Minister Louis McLane, it was assumed "that it was the intention of the treaty to adopt the *mid-channel of the straits* . . . without any reference to islands" as the boundary line. (It was odd how these distinct recollections of the middle channel were cropping up all over the place in London now that the selection of Rosario Strait had been shown to be ill-fated.) This, however, was definitely the limit of British concessions: "Whatever arrangement as to the boundary line is finally arrived at," John Russell warned in his dispatch, "no settlement of the question will be accepted by Her Majesty's Government which does not provide for the island of San Juan being reserved for the British Crown."

This stipulation had much the same effect on President Buchanan and Secretary Cass as Prevost's "secret" instructions had had on Commissioner Campbell. It aroused their righteous wrath. "If this declaration is to be insisted on," Cass notified John Russell, "it must terminate the negotiation at its very threshold." The United States Government refused to submit to any limitation of what was negotiable; the more so as its view of Haro Strait as the proper boundary remained unchanged.

Livelier still were the private exchanges. Lord Clarendon, who had got to know President Buchanan when the latter was United

States Minister in London in 1853-56 and when Clarendon was Foreign Secretary, wrote to the President that he ought not to underestimate British preparedness to fight for San Juan:

> John Bull's usual habit is to take things quietly, but his dander has been roused by the high-handed proceedings of General Harney more than I ever remember upon occasions of the kind, and this miserable business might be productive of the most disastrous consequences. May God of his infinite mercy avert from us all responsibility and guilt of such a disaster!

Buchanan's reply was in the same vein:

> You may judge our astonishment when we found that Lord John, in his first diplomatic note, gives us fair notice that Great Britain never will surrender the subject in dispute. . . . Should he act upon this principle, and take possession by force, I say with you, "May God of his infinite mercy . . ."

John Russell himself wondered whether Britain should not seize, and hold hostage, some other island to which it had as little right as the United States had to San Juan. The *Manchester Guardian* demanded that the United States disavow the action of General Harney, one of the "licensed ruffians of the Federal army," and declared that the Americans must be shown they could not "appropriate British Territory as coolly as if they were merely cutting off another slice of Mexico." The Admiralty sent two more warships to the Pacific Station in October.

But San Juan was not Oregon, and these dire predictions and veiled threats lost their sharpness when the outcome of the Scott-Douglas correspondence — imprecise though it was — became known in the capitals. Buchanan, in his annual message, praised Scott for his negotiating skill, but also Admiral Baynes for his forbearance.

On January 16 Douglas notified Admiral Baynes that he had that day received instructions from the Colonial Office to place on the Island of San Juan a force equal to that of the United States, and asked the admiral to lend him his assistance. Baynes, who did not consider himself the Governor's subordinate, wanted a copy of the instructions. Douglas demurred: "The instructions alluded to are conveyed to me as Her Majesty's Representative in this part of the world and it would not be proper for me, without express direction, to delegate those instructions to others." He condescended sufficiently, however, to let Baynes *read* the instructions.

This was not enough for the admiral. Muttering about Douglas's deplorable "lack of confidence" he sat back to wait for his own direct instructions from the Admiralty, which finally arrived on February 29. (Douglas was reprimanded by the Colonial Office for his haughtiness.)

Baynes determined that the British garrison on San Juan should consist of a company of Royal Marines commanded by Captain George Bazalgette and having two first lieutenants, one colour sergeant, four sergeants, four corporals, one bugler, one assistant surgeon, and seventy-three privates. Governor Douglas, who was loath to find himself suddenly deprived of all influence on San Juan, made a feeble attempt to retain some of it by proposing to set up Magistrate de Courcy "in residence" at the British camp. Baynes replied, coolly, that de Courcy could "reside" wherever he pleased, but that he wished it to be understood that he considered "Mr. de Courcy's appointment as a Magistrate in abeyance during the Military occupation." Douglas, having no legal leg to stand on, was forced to agree, contenting himself with bestowing on the unemployed but not unpaid magistrate (whose appointment had from the start been denounced as a sinecure by the irrepressible Amor de Cosmos) the nebulous title of "Government Agent."

There still had to be chosen a suitable location for the British camp. At least half a dozen spots around the perimeter of the island were being considered, and Colonel Moody, who fancied himself an astute military strategist, was asked to comment. Moody took the matter rather more seriously than Douglas and Baynes intended, and sent a captain of engineers to survey the island. He also volunteered the opinion that the other nominally disputed islands — Lopez and Orcas — ought to have British garrisons as well. He was thoroughly miffed when his efforts were rebuffed. The location finally chosen by Baynes was near a sheltered bay on the northwestern end of the island, *i.e.,* diametrically opposite from the

American camp. The erection of the barracks for the British garrison cost between fifteen hundred and two thousand pounds.

The British contingent was landed from the *Satellite* on March 21, 1860. Captain Bazalgette carried with him instructions from Admiral Baynes, according to which each of the two commanders was to have jurisdiction exclusively over his own nationals.

> American citizens have equal rights with British subjects on the island. Should the officer commanding the United States troops bring to your notice offences committed by any of Her Majesty's subjects, you will use your best judgment in dealing with the case, and I authorize you, if you deem it necessary, to send them off the island by the first opportunity.

Banishment was to be the supreme punishment. Bazalgette immediately established contact with his American counterpart, Captain Hunt, and amicable co-operation ensued.

With these developments the British military show of force on the Pacific Coast was gradually disbanded. Captain Hornby, who had whiled away the winter by taking a hand in provincial election campaign high-jinks and helping to defeat Amor de Cosmos ("a miserable, Radical newspaper editor"), took the *Tribune* back to England around the Horn. Prevost also left for England in the *Satellite*. He was discharged from his duties as boundary commissioner in 1862. Admiral Baynes too was to leave in 1860. Before that, however, General Harney provoked one more crisis.

As his excuse he took once more a petition from American "settlers" on San Juan, drawn up on March 7 (*i.e.,* two weeks before the arrival of the British garrison) and signed by nine persons. The petition, addressed to Harney himself, said:

> We, the undersigned citizens of this island, beg respectfully to call your attention to the gross and ungentlemanly conduct of Captain Hunt, the officer in command at this station. We ask if he is justified, as a military man, to infringe on the rights and privileges of American citizens? Is he justified in stopping trade, and endeavoring to drive the inhabitants from the island? Such conduct he is guilty of. . . . By his recent conduct the whole of the inhabitants of this island have been insulted, their position as tradesmen and citizens lowered, and he himself become an object of contempt. We,

therefore, respectfully ask your attention to this appeal, and trust that either a more sane and proper officer may replace the one now in command, or steps may be taken to prevent any further inquisitorial and injust interference on his part.

Hunt, queried by Harney, had his own side of the story, which could be summed up in one word: bootlegging.

It is unnecessary, I am sure, for me to deny that I have interfered with "trade" or "tradesmen" beyond the fact of taking action *in behalf* of the citizens of San Juan Island against a number of transient persons, illicit liquor dealers, who had been complained of in the strongest terms by the real settlers, who lived by dealing poison to my men, and who all without exception, I believe, have no other stake upon the island than that arising from their ill-gotten gains.

His actions had been confined to driving bootleggers off the military reserve and helping in the search for stolen property. Most of the wrongdoers were not Americans at all, but "a German Jew" and several Englishmen. (The "petition" does have a British ring to it.)

Harney, however, saw his chance, and on April 10 he directed Captain Pickett to replace Captain Hunt on San Juan. More remarkable yet than this change in command were the instructions he issued to Pickett:

You will be obliged . . . to acknowledge and respect the civil jurisdiction of Washington Territory in the discharge of your duties on San Juan, and the General commanding is satisfied that any attempt of the British commander to ignore this right of the Territory will be followed by deplorable results.

Pickett arrived on San Juan on April 30.

General Scott, as soon as he learned of the change, submitted a memorandum to the Secretary of War dated May 14, 1860, in which he praised Captain Hunt and condemned Harney's action. "Harney considers San Juan Island *as a part of Washington Territory.* . . . If this does not lead to a collision of arms it will again be due to the forbearance of the British authorities." He reminded the

Secretary that it might be well to relieve Harney of his command. Scott had also some harsh things to say about Harney's treatment of his own subordinates. Another matter that may have contributed to the Government's dissatisfaction with Harney was the latter's feud with the Hudson's Bay Company in Fort Vancouver, arising from military encroachments on the company's properties. Lieutenant Wilson of the Boundary Commission, one of Colonel Hawkins's staff, visited the fort at about this time and wrote:

> The Fort is now surrounded by the garrison of the American troops of General Harney of San Juan renown; alas the poor old fort once the greatest depot of all the western fur trade is now shorn of its glories, General Harney having taken forcible possession of nearly all the ground and confined the H.B.C. people to the Fort itself. . . . It is most annoying to them to see all the fields and lands they have reclaimed from the wilderness and savage gradually taken from them.

On June 8 an order went out from Washington directing Harney to turn over his command to his next-ranking officer and to repair to the capital without delay. His sojourn in the North-west had come to an end.

Harney's instructions to Pickett were of course revoked, and good relations continued between the two commanders on San Juan. Colonel Casey, too, was forgiven for his presumptuous attempt at negotiation in August, 1859. On June 5, 1860, when Casey, Archibald Campbell, and a group of male and female companions dropped in on Admiral Baynes, they were hospitably entertained and all was friendly. Not so General Harney; although he passed through Victoria by express steamer on July 14, he did not send his card to Admiral Baynes, and Baynes preferred not to take official notice of a man who had been known to use "coarse and unwarrantable language."

With this both Scott and Harney passed from the scene as far as the San Juan dispute was concerned. Harney was posted to St. Louis. At the outbreak of the Civil War he found himself in the midst of agitation by opposing Union and Confederate factions, and aroused suspicions in Washington by entering into a non-aggression pact with the pro-Confederate Missourians. No active command was given to him, and he was finally retired in 1863.

Winfield Scott, despite his Southern origin, remained loyal to Lincoln. When he resigned in 1861 he received great honours from the Cabinet.

The American Civil War put British-American negotiations over the water boundary on the shelf. Occasionally the file was taken down, dusted off, and looked at, and notes would pass back and forth. A term that turned up in nearly all of them was "arbitration," that stand-by panacea of British diplomacy.

The proposal to refer the dispute to a third party for arbitration was first broached by John Russell in a note he had Lyons submit to the Secretary of State on December 10, 1860. In that note, and in every note thereafter, the British Minister endeavoured, unobtrusively but persistently, to obtain United States agreement to arbitration on terms that would leave the arbitrator free to choose any channel for the boundary that he pleased. Well knowing the tendency of arbitrators to "split the difference," as Albert Gallatin had put it many years ago, the Foreign Office calculated that such freedom of choice would inevitably result in the adoption of the middle channel. For the same reason the State Department, just as unobtrusively and persistently, kept shying away from unlimited arbitration. Various arbitrators were discussed — the Tsar (ideal with the United States, frowned on by Britain), the President of Switzerland or the King of Sardinia (favoured by Britain, less so by the United States).

The breakthrough for Britain came in October, 1868, when Reverdy Johnson, a special United States envoy, and Lord Stanley concluded a protocol converted into a convention on January 14, 1869. According to the convention, the two nations agreed

> to refer to some friendly sovereign or state to determine the line which, according to the aforesaid treaty [of 1846], runs southerly through the middle of the channel which separates the continent from Vancouver's Island, and of Fuca's Straits, to the Pacific Ocean. . . . If such sovereign or state should be unable to ascertain and determine that precise line intended by the words of the treaty, it is

agreed that it shall be left to such sovereign or state to determine upon some line which, in the opinion of such sovereign or state, will furnish an equitable solution of the difficulty.

To come into force, the convention had to be ratified within one year. British ratification followed as a matter of course, but the United States Senate proved difficult, as usual. After some unsympathetic debate, the Senate put off final consideration. Edward Thornton, the British Minister, could only watch in quiet despair as January 13, 1870, slipped by, and with it the chance for Britain to gain control of Haro Strait.

The dispute was thus thrown open again and joined the list of British-American claims and grievances to be dealt with by the Washington Conference of 1871.

On San Juan, after the forced departure of General Harney, Captain Pickett's days, too, were numbered by fate. At the outbreak of the Civil War he and his company received orders to withdraw from the island because it seemed that the soldiers were more urgently needed elsewhere. A few days later, however, after Pickett had packed his bags and exchanged cordial farewells with his opposite number Bazalgette ("the acquaintance formed during our sojourn on this Island will ever be remembered with very pleasant reminiscences both by myself and officers," Bazalgette wrote), the order was countermanded. War or no war, there was to be no hint of yielding to Britain.

Pickett, however, had already made up his mind. On June 25, 1861, he resigned from the United States Army, leaving the island one month later. On his arrival in his home town of Richmond he was commissioned captain in the Confederate forces, rising within a few months to brigadier-general. He survived several encounters to lead his division in the famous suicidal attack of July 3, 1863, at Gettysburg. Although he lost three-fourths of his men, Pickett himself lived through it and became an insurance agent after the war.

After Pickett, one United States commander succeeded another on San Juan, which had become the remotest of backwaters. (Governor Douglas, of course, did not consider it such. When

British-American relations were strained over the removal, by the United States, of Confederate diplomats from a British ship, he suggested to the Colonial Office that the Marines on San Juan and the Royal Engineers be used to occupy Puget Sound. If another regiment or two were then sent, the Columbia River could be seized as well. His martial ardour, worthy of a Harney, was quickly cooled by Whitehall.)

Affairs on the island, however, were far from quiet. The causes of trouble were the grasping factionalism of the representatives of Washington Territory, and the morals of the civilian inhabitants. We have already noted Captain Hunt's difficulties with bootleggers and thieves. This was merely the beginning, for it became obvious very soon that San Juan Island, so solicitously protected by the two powers, was nothing less than a den of smugglers, robbers, and murderers.

On February 20, 1860, the store of United States postmaster I. E. Higgins was broken into by "pirates" cruising among the islands and five hundred dollars' worth of merchandise was stolen. In March the *Victoria Colonist* reported four more robberies. So it went, month after month. Bodies of men and women were found washed up on the shore, in abandoned canoes drifting in the gulf, at camp sites after a night of drinking and fighting. Pickett had hardly resumed command on the island when he found that he could control the unruly element no better than Hunt, and appealed to the civil authorities on the mainland to help him deal with debaucheries. The civilians, he complained, "were constantly importing quantities of *northern women* from Victoria for their nefarious purposes."

The Hudson's Bay Company sheep farm soon became a mere shadow of its former solid and prosperous self. In 1863 Chief Factor W. F. Tolmie complained to company headquarters that "all the Sheep Stations on San Juan are squatted over and only the Homestead of Bellevue with about sixty acres of enclosed land remains."

In April, 1863, Captain Lyman Bissell, United States commander on the island, drew a vivid picture of the chaotic conditions prevailing in the "town" on the fringe of his camp. "Mr. Higgins is a postmaster," he wrote to his commanding general, "but lives by dealing out his poisonous liquor to my men, thereby destroying them for usefulness." Several traders, he went on, were selling whisky to Indians, and an Indian had been killed in a drunken brawl. When Captain Bazalgette complained about the whisky seller, Bissell had the man arrested and put off the island. The Americans were jumping the claims of British settlers, and when one of them objected the Americans convened a court to try the case: "The court was held in the night session in a bar-room in the town, where the men were allowed to drink, smoke, and play cards at the same time." To no one's surprise, the Britisher was convicted, but his eviction from San Juan was prevented by Bissell.

When a complaint was made by respectable American settlers that liquor was being sold without the requisite licence, the bootleggers, treating the affair as a huge joke, again convened their court in the bar, and, with jurymen and witnesses freely imbibing around the counter, the court found (a) the case had been proven, (b) the defendant was not guilty of violating the laws of Washington Territory.

In their dealings with the civilians on San Juan the American commanders themselves were sometimes handicapped by misunderstanding the terms of their own jurisdiction. Having been reared in a society which thought of laws only in geographical application, they were trying to devise some sort of demarcation line between their own and the British camp and began to speak of "our half" and "their half" of the island. It took a search for General Scott's "Projet" and a careful reading of the same to re-establish the principle spelled out clearly in a letter from the commanding general in September, 1864:

> It is a mistake to speak of our exercising authority over the Southern half, and of the British exercising authority over the Northern half, as if the Island were in fact divided between them, — separated by some undefined line! and to give warning to the inhabitants in the Southern, as if they, and none others, were all under our jurisdiction!

The authority to be exercised is not as to territory, for that is the matter at issue, but as to individuals and, on the part of each military commander so far as his countrymen are concerned, extends over the whole island.

In this legal twilight it was not long before the commander of the United States garrison himself was called before the bar of justice by the civilian authorities. The affair once more involved postmaster-barkeeper Higgins. Higgins occupied land between the military reserve and the harbour, and in 1866, when he became displeased with the supervision of the current commander, Captain Thomas Grey, he decided to bring the latter to heel by building a fence across the road leading from the harbour to the camp. As the camp depended on the road for hauling its supplies, Grey had the fence torn down and banished Higgins from the island.

Following charges brought by Higgins, the United States District Court in Washington Territory then ordered Grey's arrest. But when the sheriff's posse appeared on San Juan, Grey had his men run them off. He and a fellow officer were summonsed several times to appear before the judge, but, as far as can be ascertained, they never complied, even though the commanding general reported that Grey had been fined five thousand dollars. The *Washington Standard* complained that the citizens of San Juan were being denied all justice and were "objected to the force of the bayonet to obey the caprices of a petty military officer." It is hard to imagine a more absurd relationship between protector and protected.

Captain Bazalgette, too, ran into trouble, though of a different sort. In 1866 he learned that one of his former deserters, the bugler, had enlisted in the United States Army and was now actually serving with the American garrison on San Juan, flaunting his infidelity at his former comrades. When Bazalgette informed his superior officer at Esquimalt he was told to ask the American commander to extradite the fugitive. Bazalgette did so, in a formal note. The request was rejected, and thus came to the notice of the authorities in London. Bazalgette's undiplomatic "demand" was severely censured, and, although his admiral put in a word for the unfortunate officer and the American commanding general obligingly had the bugler transferred from San Juan, Bazalgette was replaced by another commander, Captain W. F. Delacombe.

The legal position of the island also caused headaches in Victoria. The maintenance of the British claim to San Juan meant, naturally, that traffic between it and Vancouver Island had to be free of customs duty; but since the Americans followed a parallel policy, the island had all the makings of a smuggler's paradise. Governor Frederick Seymour of British Columbia complained in 1867 that if all the goods entering Victoria from San Juan were to be allowed in duty-free, "the whole trade of Puget's Sound and probably of San Francisco would centre in the island." He invented the expedient of having the British commander certify all produce of San Juan destined for shipment to Victoria.

There is no record of how the men of the two garrisons spent their time, but it is a safe guess that a posting to San Juan was not one that was eagerly sought after either in Britain or, for that matter, war-torn America.

In 1870 the United States included the disputed islands in its national census and found a population of 550. This number consisted of 295 Americans, 196 British subjects, 29 Germans, 11 Danes, 10 Hawaiians, 5 Swedes, 2 Chinese, 1 Frenchman, and 1 Swiss. Most of them lived on San Juan.

In the spring of 1871 a joint British-American commission met in Washington to consider a number of claims and grievances, headed by the so-called *Alabama* Claims, which arose from the Civil War exploits of the British-built Confederate raider of that name. Also on the agenda was the San Juan dispute. Most of the other questions pertained to Canada, and for this reason Sir John A. Macdonald, the Canadian Prime Minister, was appointed as one of the five British commissioners, all of whom were directly responsible to the Foreign Office.

Strictly speaking, Macdonald had no special right to plead in the matter of San Juan, since the union of British Columbia with Canada, hotly debated for years, did not become effective until July 20, 1871. Such legalities did not embarrass Macdonald; as early as December, 1868, just after the signing of the Stanley-Johnson arbitration protocol, his two emissaries to the Colonial Office, George E. Cartier and William McDougall, had notified Whitehall of Canadian interest in the affair:

> Our experience of past diplomacy in the settlement of boundaries in North America in which the disposition on the one side to concede, and on the other to encroach, was always present and always resulted disastrously for Canada, admonishes us, that a similar disposition and similar results may be feared in the future. . . . We cannot help feeling, when we look at the Map of Canada, and observe that on our Eastern frontier, the State of Maine, by a recent treaty has been thrust like a wedge between the Provinces of Quebec and New Brunswick, intercepting direct communication . . . and that on the West, through ignorance of the natural features of the Country in 1773 [1783?] and under the spirit of concession in 1818, a vast territory was surrendered, and the boundary carried so far north . . . we say, we cannot help feeling, when we recall these unhappy, and as we now find, costly blunders of the past, that we are only discharging a solemn duty when we add our earnest warning . . . to prevent a similar, and in some respects, a worse blunder, in reference to our position on the Pacific Coast.

It was a note that was soon to reverberate clangorously throughout the breadth of the Dominion.

The conference at Washington had not proceeded very far when it became evident that the San Juan dispute, in Macdonald's own words, presented "more difficulties than all the other cases put together." The arguments again turned on Haro versus Rosario Strait, and one of the American commissioners, Senator G. H. Williams of Oregon, was adamant against any concession. Macdonald himself was not at all optimistic, and confided to his friend and colleague, Charles Tupper:

> This matter offers great difficulties, and between ourselves, I think the United States have a very strong case; stronger in equity than ours which can only be maintained by the most technical construction of the actual words of the Treaty. However, we are fighting the battle stoutly and do not intend to give up San Juan.

In the face of an apparent deadlock, Macdonald suggested that the island ought to be jointly occupied for another twenty-five years. He was going to make that offer palatable to the Americans, he wrote jokingly, by pointing to the widespread belief in the United States that all of Canada was destined to be absorbed long before that by its southern neighbour.

Finally, however, the commission agreed on arbitration, but only after the British side accepted the proviso that the arbitrator be given a choice only between Haro and Rosario Strait. The treaty, finally signed on May 8, 1871, also named the arbitrator — Emperor William I of Germany.

Formal notes requesting arbitration were submitted by the British and American envoys to Prince Bismarck on July 29, 1871. On September 1 the Emperor signified his acceptance of the office. The case for Britain was prepared by Admiral Prevost, the former boundary commissioner, and the American case by the historian George Bancroft, United States Minister in Berlin. The two cases were submitted to the German Government in mid-December. Each side then drew up a rebuttal, and these were submitted in June, 1872.

The German Government put the arbitration in the hands of three experts. They were Dr. Ferdinand Grimm, vice-president of the Prussian Supreme Court, Dr. Levin Goldschmidt, professor of law and a member of the German Supreme Trade Court, and Professor Heinrich Kiepert, a famous geographer and cartographer. Both the international position of Germany in 1872 and the qualifications of the arbitrators ensured that the question would be decided impartially and competently. In fact, no charges of bias, such as those following the Netherlands Award of 1831, were ever made against the German award, which was delivered in Berlin on October 21, 1872. It sustained the United States claim. It did not say that Haro Strait was the channel intended by the Treaty of 1846. It merely said that of the two channels in question, Haro Strait was "most in accordance with the correct interpretation of the Treaty (*am meisten im Einklang . . . mit der richtigen Auslegung*)."

The award was not unanimous, however. Dr. Goldschmidt submitted a dissenting opinion. He declined to subscribe to the majority view, on the ground that it was quite obvious that the line described by the Treaty of 1846 must run through the middle of the entire space between Vancouver Island and the continent (*i.e.,* the British compromise line) and that by being prohibited from choosing it the tribunal had been presented with an impossible task. If Britain had claimed the middle channel from the beginning and the choice had been between that channel and Haro Strait — is it not possible, or even probable, that at least one of Dr. Goldschmidt's colleagues would have joined him and that San Juan Island would have become British?

Admiral Prevost was deeply aggrieved by the award, but he and the British Government acquiesced in it gracefully, and orders went out from London to give effect to the German decision. On November 16, 1872, telegrams via the newly laid transatlantic cable were sent to the admiral commanding the Pacific Station and to the senior officer at Esquimalt, Captain R. P. Cator, informing them of the award and ordering them to withdraw the British garrison from San Juan forthwith.

Rumours about the impending award had been flying about Victoria, the capital of the province of British Columbia, for some weeks, but the first accurate statement, evidently derived from the Admiralty telegram, was published in the *Victoria Colonist* on November 19, oddly enough without comment. Times had changed on the Pacific seaboard, as elsewhere. No longer was war with the United States so easily imaginable as thirteen years ago; no longer were the British subjects in British Columbia a beleaguered minority in a flood of American adventurers; the militant, empire-building Douglas had long since retired, and his authority had devolved on the elected Premier of the Province — an office about to pass to the "miserable Radical" Amor de Cosmos.

When the *Colonist* commented, after several days' silence, on the San Juan award it bewailed — of all things — the "death blow to the profitable trade" between Victoria and the islands. Since the population of the islands was too small to account for any appreciable trade, the reference appears to have been to trans-shipped contraband. Only on December 15 did the paper finally come out with a full-blown editorial on the loss of the islands, and found a silver lining: the world-wide publicity stirred up by the arbitration had helped to put British Columbia on the map. "The result of all this is that British Columbia is more favourably thought of and more widely known to-day than could possibly have been the case had the Archipelago been awarded, as it ought to have been . . . to the Dominion of Canada." The voice of the booster had replaced that of soldiers and politicians.

The wire ordering the withdrawal from San Juan had said nothing about the disposal of the British camp buildings, which had been thoroughly renovated at considerable expense in 1867. Captain Cator and his garrison commander on San Juan, Captain Delacombe, were in a quandary.

On November 21 at sunset the Union Jack was hauled down for the last time over the British camp at Roche Harbor. The general commanding United States forces in the Department of the Pacific, Harney's former post, politely sent his regrets that the short notice had not allowed him to send a ship "to pay the honours due our Colours on the Withdrawal of the British Garrison," as Cator put it. But the American garrison on the island lined up and gave three cheers. The flagstaff from which the British flag had floated for twelve years, was cut into pieces to be distributed among the men, and a longer piece was taken to the Esquimalt dockyard as a souvenir. This caused vindictive residents of Washington Territory to complain the pole had been cut down to prevent the hoisting thereon of the Stars and Stripes.

The British garrison embarked on November 22, but Captain Delacombe with a few men stayed behind to watch the buildings until Cator received an answer to his telegram requesting instructions as to the disposal of the property. The transcontinental wire, however, appeared to be broken, and when no answer had been received by Sunday, November 24, Cator ordered Delacombe to leave. The squatters were restless that night, and as the camp fires burned low shadowy figures were seen lurking among the trees around the camp, waiting to rush in and take over. To prevent such an unworthy end Delacombe sent a message to the American camp, and Lieutenant Epstein and an orderly arrived that evening, stayed the night, and stood on the landing the following day at two o'clock as H.M.S. *Peterel,* drawing a lazy wake, pulled out of the harbour.

The Royal Marines and their three officers were sent home to England by passenger steamer via San Francisco and Panama. Of the eighty-two men, four chose to remain with the Pacific Station and two bought their discharge.

Remnants of the two camps have been preserved to this day. The United States camp is marked by a square obelisk and the British one by a large tablet, which recites briefly the circumstances of the joint occupation and ends with the words, "In October of that year [1872] the British garrison was abandoned," erring by one month.

As excellent charts of the straits were available, there appeared to be no need for a survey to lay down the boundary. On March 10, 1873, Secretary of State Hamilton Fsh for the United States, and Edward Thornton and Admiral Prevost for Britain, signed a protocol and four identical charts on which the water boundary through Haro Strait had been traced.

Lyman Cutler, whose well-aimed shot had served as the signal for the crisis of 1859, survived the settlement of the dispute by five years, and died in 1877 — the same year as Sir James Douglas, C.B., ex-Governor and Commander-in-Chief in and over the colony of Vancouver's Island and its Dependencies, and Vice-Admiral of the same.

CHAPTER FIVE

Panhandle Problems

The river Stikine (or Stickeen, Stachine, Stakene, Stikene — you could still have your choice in the year 1876) has its source in the Cassiar Mountains of British Columbia. Fed by numerous tributaries from both north and south, the river flows in a deep canyon through the dry mountainous interior, its course generally southwesterly, until it breaches the coastal range in a series of spectacular cuts, to emerge, wide and placid, on the rain-shrouded, darkly forested, island-strewn coast of the Alaska Panhandle. Just south of its mouth sits the town of Wrangell, on the island of the same name.

Down the Stikine River in the middle of September, 1876, there travelled in one of the large canoes typical of the region an oddly assorted party. There were several Indians with their women, or "klootchmen" as they were called in the lingua franca of the Pacific, some white passengers, and two special constables, Francis Beegan and Henry Richardson, with a handcuffed prisoner whom they were conveying from the gold-mining centre of Laketon, on Dease Lake, to jail in Victoria.

The prisoner's name was Peter Martin, but he was better known in the Cassiar gold-fields as "Bricktop," because of his flaming-red hair. Bricktop was a tough character. He had been arrested in Laketon for some minor offence, and had broken out of jail, assaulting the jailer in the bargain. For this he was tried on September 6, 1876, before Justice J. H. Gray, who had travelled to Laketon from Victoria for just such a purpose, and sentenced to three months for "escape from custody and prison breach," and twelve months for "assaulting an officer in the execution of his duty." The sentences were to run consecutively, and had to be served in the provincial jail in Victoria, there being no suitable prison accommodation in primitive Laketon or, for that matter, anywhere else in the wilds of northern British Columbia.

On September 11, Beegan, Richardson, and Martin set out from Laketon on their long trip south. Beegan was in charge. Neither of the two guards, who had been sworn in expressly for the trip, appears to have had any experience in police work, and Beegan made up his own rules and regulated his behaviour in the spirit of the gold-fields — which was not a civilized spirit.

The branch of the Stikine which curves down from Dease Lake is not navigable, and the three men travelled the pack trail from the lakehead to Glenora on horseback. The trail was busy that year, and there were crudely put up stopping places every few miles, with a bar for the travellers to fill up on the fiery liquor and bunks to bed down after. While drinking away the evening hours the men would gather round for their favourite card game of "whisky cinch," more commonly known as twenty-one. Beegan and Richardson saw no need to depart from this agreeable routine merely because they had a prisoner along who had bluntly informed them that he would make a break and that there were not enough men in all of Cassiar to take him to Victoria. On the second day of their trip Martin did attempt to ride off into the bush, and Beegan fired his pistol after him. This stopped Bricktop. "You came pretty near combing my hair, didn't you?" he demanded.

They had a room to themselves at Telegraph Creek, a little town deep down in the Stikine River canyon, dwelling in almost perpetual shadow by the side of the swiftly flowing water. Curious visitors would drop in from time to time to look at Bricktop, whom many of them knew, or to have a word or a drink with the two constables. At one point the company broke into the song "Whisky, you're the devil drunk or sober," but it is not certain whether Beegan joined in the singing or the drinking. Finally Beegan told the visitors to leave. He was nervous and apprehensive; it was quite possible that some of the men hanging about the place might help Martin to make a break. He and Martin kept up a constant patter of recriminations.

On September 18 they arrived at Glenora, the common head of steamship navigation. There Beegan was given a letter by J. B. Lovell, justice of the peace, addressed to Captain Jocelyn, officer commanding at Wrangell in the American coastal strip. The letter stated Beegan's mission and requested Captain Jocelyn's co-operation in the conveyance of the prisoner through United States territory.

The party set out from Glenora in a canoe on September 19. They camped that night on the shore, and the following night they bedded down at a store run by an old sourdough named Alexander Choquette, familiarly known as "Buck." Buck Choquette had been one of the first men to discover gold on the upper reaches of the Stikine; "Buck's Bar" was a well-known barrier between Glenora and Telegraph Creek. Again there were drinking and card-playing.

The next morning they left on their final run to Wrangell. They could tell that they had passed through the coast range by the steady rain that began to fall soon after they left and continued without let-up. They were cold, hungry, and miserable. The boat was gliding rapidly down-river, borne on the strong current. So smooth was the ride that the Indians could pass liquor back and forth in a cup on a paddle. Just before noon they decided to put to shore for a quick lunch. While the others huddled about in the rain, the Indians got a fire going and Richardson heated up some tea and canned meat. After Richardson had eaten, Beegan, who had been watching the manacled Martin with a shotgun borrowed from one of the Indians, leaned the gun against a tree and told Richardson to stand guard while he got some food.

What then happened is not clear in all details, owing to contradictory stories told by the participants, but the main sequence of events is undisputed. Martin, disregarding his handcuffs and the revolver in the hands of Richardson (whom he obviously feared much less than Beegan), seized the shotgun and began backing off into the trees, shouting that he was now in American territory, and that they would never get him. To Richardson he said: "Harry, I don't want to kill you, but I want to kill that son of a bitch Beegan."

Richardson, instead of firing or taking up the pursuit, went over to Beegan and told him their prisoner was making a break. Beegan told him to go after Martin. Richardson replied that it was Beegan's fault Martin had got hold of the shotgun, and he could try to recapture him himself.

While they were talking both were moving in Martin's direction, Beegan brandishing an axe. When he saw that Richardson did not intend to use his revolver, Beegan took it out of the hand of his fellow constable, and the latter immediately retreated to a safer distance. Beegan then fired twice at Martin, who kept dodging away behind the trees. Martin waited until he had the constable squarely in his sight, then blasted away. But Beegan was partially hidden behind a tree trunk, and most of the birdshot went into the wood, though Beegan was hit by a few pellets.

Beegan then yelled at Martin to lay down the gun, or he would shoot him. "Shoot, shoot, you goddam son of a bitch!" Martin shouted. "Shoot and be damned, I'm never going to let you have this gun till I kill you." Beegan pulled the trigger — he knew it was the last bullet in the gun — but there was only a small click. Enraged, he rushed Martin, but just before he came up with him he tripped and fell. At the same time the revolver discharged, the bullet passing through Beegan's cheek.

The next instant Martin was upon him, bashing away at the fallen guard with the butt of his gun, and breaking both it and Beegan's shoulder. Beegan the while hung on to one of Martin's legs until Richardson came up belatedly together with the other men, and Martin was once more in custody.

Beegan, bleeding profusely, comforted himself with a whisky bottle until they reached Wrangell harbour. There Bricktop Martin was transferred directly from the boat to the British ship *Grappler*, Victoria-bound. Beegan had his wounds bound up by a Wrangell physician, after which he boarded the steamer *Gussie Telfair*, arriving at Victoria on the same day as the *Grappler*, September 30, 1876.

A preliminary hearing on a charge of assault against Martin opened in Victoria on October 5, and after two days of testimony the prisoner was committed to jury trial, which opened on December 16. The judge was Henry Pellew Crease.

Martin pleaded not guilty on the grounds that he was an American citizen, and that the alleged assault took place on United States territory. He could not, however, produce evidence of his citizenship, and Justice Crease doubted his statement on account of Martin's "fresh Irish accent."

Far weightier was the question of national jurisdiction. The witnesses disagreed widely as to the distance from the place of the assault to the sea coast, some estimating that it was eight miles, others that it was nearer twenty. Perhaps the nearest estimate was fifteen miles. But even if the distance had been established exactly it would not have removed all doubt as to territorial sovereignty, because the boundary between British and American possessions long the Alaska Panhandle had never been determined.

Justice Crease was, of course, keenly aware of the international implications of the case, and to forestall false rumours he invited the United States consul at Victoria, D. Epstein, to sit in on the trial. He also consulted with, as he termed it, "higher powers." Perhaps as a result of this consultation he instructed the jury that "for the practical purposes of this trial you must consider the occurrence either to have taken place in British territory, and that the custody of the prisoner in British hands was unbroken, or as if it had taken place in British territory."

The jury thereupon returned a verdict of guilty, and Martin was sentenced on December 20 to twenty-one months in prison, in addition to his earlier term imposed at Laketon. After the judge pronounced the sentence, Bricktop bowed and said, "Thank you, sir."

The case was over, but its repercussions were only beginning to be felt in Ottawa, Washington, and London, where the problem of the Alaska boundary had just penetrated to the top levels of government.

The Alaskan Panhandle had its origin in the voyages of Vitus Bering, a Danish seafarer in Russian services, who in 1741 discovered the southern coast of Alaska, notably Mount St. Elias. For the next thirty years or so, Russian hunters and traders cruised among the Aleutian Islands and some parts of the Alaska coast, collecting furs from the natives, often by cruel means. In the late eighteenth century, traders and explorers of other nationalities — Spanish, British, American, and even French — began to nose about the southern coasts of Alaska, and the Russian traders became alarmed. To present a united front to the intruders, the Russians formed a trading concern clearly modelled on the Hudson's Bay Company and known as the Russian-American Company. It obtained imperial consent in 1799 and, after some misadventures, established its headquarters and central trading post of Novo-Arkhangelsk, or Sitka, on Baranof Island, in latitude 57°.

The formation of the company, however, did little to help the Russians in their competition with the British and American traders and whalers. The Russians were handicapped by three factors: the enormous length of their overland supply route, their weak navy, and the inherent superiority — by experience and temperament — of the Anglo-Saxon traders. Before long the directors of the Russian-American Company began to importune St. Petersburg for political or military measures to aid them in their struggle, and in 1821 the Imperial Government obliged by promulgating its famous ukase which barred ships of other nations from Alaska and Alaskan waters. Specifically the decree forbade foreigners to pursue "commerce, whaling, and fishery, and all other industry, within an area extending from Bering Strait south to 51° of north latitude on the American coast," or to approach this coast closer than one hundred Italian miles.

This had an almost electric effect on the governments in London and Washington, for if there was anything to which these seafaring nations reacted with utmost fury it was their exclusion from any part of the seven seas.

The Imperial Court at St. Petersburg quickly realized that it had gone too far, and that Russia had no means of enforcing the ban. To save face and, at the same time, to substitute some sort of trilateral guarantee for its unilateral threat, Russia entered into separate negotiations with the United States and Britain (see also Chapter III). The result of this was an extensive modification of the maritime prohibitions, and the delimitation of Russian possessions on land. The Russian-American treaty of 1824 stipulated that American citizens would not form settlements north of 54°40' latitude, and Russian subjects would not form settlements south of that line. The Russian-British treaty, signed in 1825, was more elaborate in its definition of the boundary, since it needed to define not merely the southern but also the eastern extent of Alaska. The negotiations between Britain and Russia stretched over several years, from 1821 to 1825, and every scrap of correspondence, every draft and memorandum was later dug up from musty archives and scrutinized backward and forward by whole battalions of lawyers, linguists, diplomats, and historians in a feverish quest for a phrase, a word perhaps, that would vindicate or demolish (as the case might be) a single contention. None was found. None was found because the issue was so obvious to the negotiators themselves that to spell it out would have been a banality which no diplomat in his right senses would commit.

I shall not, therefore, go into these negotiations very deeply, and I shall take up the consideration of the contentious point where the chronology demands it.

For the time being it is important only to emphasize once more that the sole aim pursued by the Russian Government in its negotiations with Britain was to secure a fishing and fur-trade monopoly to the Russian-American Company, by protecting it against rival encroachments both from seaward and from landward. Since the company had its base and its chief field of operations on and around the offshore islands and was not interested in the interior of the mainland, all it required for its landward protection against the agents of the Hudson's Bay Company was a coastal strip.

This strip, to the delighted surprise of the British, turned out to be even narrower than London had first been willing to concede. Foreign Secretary George Canning instructed the British Minister in St. Petersburg, Charles Bagot, to limit the Russian strip on the mainland to a width of fifty to one hundred miles, but under no circumstances to allow it to extend to the Rocky Mountains. The Russian Foreign Minister, Count Nesselrode, proposed instead a strip limited by the mountains bordering the coast (*montagnes qui bordent la côte*). On the other hand, the Russians wished to extend the strip much farther south than the British — to 54°40'. "Without a strip of land on the coast of the continent from Portland Canal," they informed Bagot, "the Russian Establishments on the adjoining islands would be left unsupported, they would be left at the mercy of those Establishments which foreigners might form on the mainland." Nesselrode added that "as for us, we restrict our demands to a small strip (*lisière*) of coast on the continent . . . only as a means to enhance the value, nay more, not to lose, the adjacent islands."

After much fruitless bargaining aimed at pushing the Russians farther north, the British were finally compelled to accede to their demand, with minor modifications. Instead of limiting northern Alaska at the 139th meridian, the British succeeded in pushing the boundary westward to the 141st meridian; along the Panhandle, they managed to incorporate a recommendation from Hudson's Bay Company Governor J. H. Pelly that the Russian strip limited by the crest of the coastal mountain range was not to exceed under any circumstances the width of ten marine leagues (or about 34.5 statute miles); and they obtained for British traders the right to navigate the rivers crossing the Russian strip. (If the Russian Government was in effect negotiating on behalf of the Russian-American Company, the Foreign Office was performing the same service for the British fur and fishing interests. The coldly brilliant Canning wrote humorously to Bagot that the proposed convention "had been submitted to both the furry and the finny tribes — the Enderbys, the Pellys, and the Barrows. . . . In addition to the claims of science, there is very nice 'bobbing for whale', they tell me, *ipsis*

Behringi in faucibus [in Bering Strait itself], which must be guarded.")

The Treaty of 1825, signed at St. Petersburg on February 28, described the boundary of Alaska as follows:

> *Commencing from the southernmost point of the island called Prince of Wales Island, which point lies in the parallel of 54 degrees, 40 minutes, north latitude, and between the 131st and 133rd degree of west longitude (meridian of Greenwich), the said line shall ascend to the north along the channel called Portland Channel, as far as the point of the continent where it strikes the 56th degree of north latitude; from this last-mentioned point the line of demarcation shall follow the summit of the mountains situated parallel to the coast as far as the point of intersection of the 141st degree of west longitude (of the same meridian); and, finally, from the said point of intersection, the said meridian line of 141st degree, in its prolongation as far as the frozen Ocean, shall form the limit between the Russian and British possessions on the continent of America to the northwest.*

The foregoing was qualified by another article, which read as follows:

> *1st. That the island called Prince of Wales Island shall belong wholly to Russia. 2nd. That whenever the summit of the mountains which extend in a direction parallel to the coast, from the 56th degree of north latitude to the point of intersection of the 141st degree of west longitude, shall prove to be at the distance of more than 10 marine leagues from the Ocean, the limit between the British possessions and the line of coast which is to belong to Russia, as above mentioned, shall be formed by a line parallel to the windings [sinuosités] of the coast, and which shall never exceed the distance of 10 marine leagues therefrom.*

It may be well for the reader to fix these phrases in his memory, for they were destined to form the basis of an argument so bitter and exhaustive that it overshadows even the quarrel over the highlands line between Maine and New Brunswick.

The treaty also contained other clauses, mainly designed to limit British maritime access to Russian establishments in Alaska, and conceding to British subjects the perpetual right of navigating all rivers crossing the Russian strip from the British interior to the sea.

The troubles started early. The directors of the Russian-American Company found soon after the signing of the treaty that even its stringent and explicit provisions were inadequate to keep out the wily and energetic agents of the Hudson's Bay Company. In 1832 the governor of the Russian company, Baron Wrangell, reported that ships of the English company were cruising the passages between the Russian islands and would probably seek to penetrate the mainland strip. He added:

> In a year or two the English will occupy a post there also undoubtedly in prejudice of our commercial relations with the Kolosh [Indians]. For the excellent quality and abundance of the merchandise of the English constitute an attraction to the Kolosh which we have no means to compete with. . . . [The Hudson's Bay Company's] blankets are better than those of the Americans, weigh 10½ pounds, and are dyed in dark blue, green, light blue, also striped, but no white ones; [they have] moreover a large quantity of old men's and women's woolen clothing of pretty good material, old officer's uniforms, coats, swallow tails, trousers, waistcoats, theatrical costumes, renovated by tailors and bought very cheap in London.

It must have been an unnerving experience for unsuspecting explorers to put into a remote Indian village and be confronted with an assemblage of swallow-tailed, barefoot dandies, British admirals, war-painted replicas of Lady Macbeth, and sundry other weirdly attired characters.

Wrangell's hunch proved correct. In 1833 Peter Skene Ogden from Fort Vancouver on the Columbia River rowed up the Stikine and did a little trading with the up-river Indians, exchanging, among other things, gun-powder. His main mission, however, was the selection of a site for a trading post, just far enough from the coast to be outside the Russian strip.

The Russians were greatly alarmed. If the Hudson's Bay Company did form its trading post, there would be nothing to stop it from capturing the trade of the entire Panhandle, for the coastal Indians were just as capable of paddling thirty or forty miles up the Stikine to sell their furs as they were of rounding Baranof Island to Sitka. Wrangell had also heard about the horribly efficient

French-Canadian trappers employed by the Hudson's Bay Company. There was nothing else to be done — the English had to be stopped. The local heads of the Russian company were, of course, aware that in doing so they might run afoul of the treaty provisions, but it was either that or the collapse of the Russian fur business in America. The best thing would be to change the treaty itself:

> Should any other convention be signed [Wrangell wrote to St. Petersburg in April, 1834] you should solicit that free navigation of the rivers should at least be limited by the condition that free navigation to the British from the interior to the sea should not be forbidden, while free navigation from the sea up the rivers should be prohibited. Of course it would be best not to allow any navigation whatever. . . . Until further instructions I will hinder the British by force from sailing up the Stachin river.

To give effect to his decision, the governor had a fort built at the mouth of the Stikine in the summer of 1834, and left it in charge of a twenty-man garrison. The fort was named after one of the Orthodox saints, Dionysios.

It was completed none too soon, for on June 18 the fort's lookout spied a sail approaching. A boat party was immediately sent out to intercept it, and found that it was the Hudson's Bay Company brig *Dryad* under the command of Chief Trader Ogden. The ship was loaded with goods and equipment for the establishment of a post on the Stikine River. The Russian officer who boarded the ship spoke no English or French: none of the Hudson's Bay Company people spoke Russian, and they could understand nothing of what their visitor said. But he came armed with a proclamation (presumably in French) which he left with Ogden. The proclamation, signed by Baron Wrangell, merely said that two Russian ships were stationed "in the straits within the territories of Russia, that is to say northward of 54° 40′ latitude, where no foreign ship or vessel has now the right to trade with the Indians." Ogden, who later reported the encounter to his superiors, continued:

> About two hours later, as we were casting anchor, another Russian boat with a Russian officer boarded us, and by signs and with the assistance of an Indian interpreter gave us to understand, we

must not cast anchor, but immediately depart. To this order I paid
no attention. Having invited him down to the cabin, all I could
comprehend from him was, that they were determined to use force
against us.

Ogden decided to stand pat while messages were sent to Baron
Wrangell at Sitka. During the wait Ogden went ashore to visit the
commander of the fort, who bore the sonorous name Denis Fiodoro-
vitch Zarembo. Zarembo gave Ogden "directly to understand that
if we attempted to proceed up the river in our boats, he would use
force against us." To reinforce his words, Zarembo pointed at the
Russian trader *Chichagov,* riding at anchor before the fort, armed
with fourteen cannon. Ogden then began to fear that if he persisted
in his intention there would be loss of lives, the more so as he had
to ascend the river in open row-boats.

On June 29 answer came back from Sitka (from the deputy
of Baron Wrangell, who was temporarily absent) that the Russians
were merely acting according to the treaty provision that "the
subjects of His Britannic Majesty shall not land at any place where
there may be a Russian establishment." The Russian word for the
French *aborder,* "to land", was *pristavat'.* Literally it means "to
accost," "to come into contact," or "to dock," but the Russians now
claimed that it also meant "to pass by," and that the British were
therefore prohibited by the treaty from entering any river near
whose mouth there was a Russian post. Confidentially, Zarembo
was instructed "to prevent with all your might" the British from
ascending the Stikine.

Ogden, who knew his treaty as well as anyone, still determined
to beard the lion in his den and gave orders to sail to Sitka. There
he had a personal interview with Wrangell on September 15.
Wrangell merely repeated the claim that the Stikine River was now
occupied by Russians and therefore out of bounds for the British.
Ogden had to return with his cargo to Fort Vancouver, where he
told his tale of woe to John McLoughlin.

The reaction from London was predictably prompt and sharp.
The Foreign Office, on information supplied by the Hudson's Bay
Company, charged the Russian Government with flagrant violation

of the Treaty of 1825 and demanded compensation for the *Dryad* misadventure of no less than £22,150. (Wrangell's action had given the Hudson's Bay Company just the incident it needed to press home the attack on its rival.) The Russian Foreign Minister twisted and squirmed under the accusing verbal barrage from the British Minister, throwing up every possible excuse and obfuscation his staff could think of, including the countercharge that the Hudson's Bay Company men were illegally arming the natives. When St. Petersburg ran out of evasions, Count Nesselrode was forced to admit, privately, that

> we shall be obliged ultimately to give in because the clear provisions of the treaty are not calculated to strengthen the side we have defended until now. . . . As the matter now stands, we are not likely to have any more plausible pretexts for further evading the claim for indemnity.

However, the Russian-American Company did not have the kind of money the British demanded, and Nesselrode recommended to its directors compensation in some other form, perhaps territorial rights. The result was that in 1839 representatives of the two rival fur companies met on the neutral ground of the Free Hanse City of Hamburg to conclude an agreement whereby the Hudson's Bay Company leased from the Russian-American Company most of the Alaska Panhandle mainland, except for a small piece in the north, in return for an annual payment of two thousand otter skins plus the guaranteed sale of a variety of provisions from the Oregon farms. This odd symbiosis, which was to continue for ten years, was from time to time renewed, until it was automatically severed by the acquisition of Alaska by the United States in 1867. Long before that, however, the vitality of the Russian-American Company had been sapped, and it was slowly drifting toward bankruptcy.

After the *Dryad* case the next immediate danger for the Russian-American Company was the Crimean War of 1854-56. Fully aware that Russia was incapable of defending herself against the navies of Britain and France in the Pacific, the directors of the company at the outbreak of the war planned to resort to deception in order to save their trading vessels from capture. They wrote to the governor at Sitka:

> The Board of Directors intends to send to the Colonies, for your use in this year's navigation, a screw steamer belonging to the Company, but furnished with Hamburg papers and flag. In addition to this, the Board of Directors, for the purpose of supplying its vessels with neutral flags, has sold (according to their papers) the vessels Nicholas, Sitka, and Kamchatka.

The three ships were to be sent to San Francisco, evading enemy patrols, where they would receive neutral flags and papers. It was not the first time that fur merchants were to cruise the Pacific coast under false flags; the practice had been initiated by the English in the late eighteenth century.

The ruse, however, was unnecessary. An informal agreement was reached by Britain and Russia that their fur-company holdings should not be involved in the war. A Franco-British naval squadron visited Sitka in June, 1855, and spotted the masts of the Russian trading vessels behind some islands, but when the admiral was told that there were no warships among them he was satisfied and sailed away without molesting the settlement.

The economic troubles of the Russian-American Company caused a good deal of soul-searching in St. Petersburg, and it was at length agreed by the foreign-policy specialists that Alaska was becoming more and more of an economic and political liability rather than an asset, and that something would have to be done about it. In 1862, when the charter of the company came up for renewal, the Government insisted on tougher terms than the company considered bearable. In order to continue in business, the company needed an annual subsidy of 200,000 rubles.

In the search for a decent way to rid itself of its colonial white elephant the thoughts of the Russian Government naturally turned to the United States. The United States was expansionist — in North America; also, it was known to have paid for the acquisition of territory with real money, a peculiarity in European eyes, where territory was normally won with the sword. Confidential hints were dropped to Washington as early as 1857, but not until after the

American Civil War did negotiations seriously get under way between the two capitals. They were conducted in utmost secrecy between Secretary of State William Seward and the Russian Minister, Baron Eduard de Stoeckl, during early 1867. No written communication concerning the sale passed between them until they were ready to consummate the deal, at the end of March. The treaty of cession was signed at four o'clock in the morning on March 30, 1867, and provided for the payment to Russia of $7,200,000. The treaty was ratified by the Senate on May 28. Public opinion in the United States was decidedly lukewarm toward the new territory, which became known by such names as "Seward's Folly," "Seward's Ice Chest," and similar uncomplimentary labels. Congress showed itself no more willing to grant funds for developing Alaska than the Russian Government before the cession.

The sale of Alaska took the British Government by surprise. Of all nations, Britain was naturally most concerned with the transaction, since it was the only one having a border with Alaska. On April 2, 1867, the British Minister in Washington, Frederick Wright-Bruce, wrote to the Foreign Office:

> The Russian Government have entered into a Treaty ceding the whole of their possessions in North America to the United States for seven million dollars.
>
> The Negotiation was conducted with the greatest secrecy, nor was it known until the Proclamation of the President appeared summoning an extra Session of the Senate to consider it. . . . The Russian Minister states the motives of the sale to be the little value and unproductive nature of the Territory, the expense of the force necessary to protect it and preserve order, and the desire of getting rid of a possession which may ultimately involve them in questions with the United States. — But considering the condition of the Turkish Empire and the ambitious views of Russia in that quarter, the aggressive policy of the United States undisguisedly bent on ruling North America without a rival — And recollecting that Great Britain is the opponent common to both, it seems not unreasonable to infer that the object of Russia is to provide the means of neutralizing the efforts of Great Britain in the event of antagonism in the East.

Wright-Bruce thought that Alaska would be held by the United

States as a club over the head of Britain to force it to settle American grievances arising out of the Civil War, such as the *Alabama* Claims, perhaps by the cession of British Columbia, with Russia as the laughing third. The Minister added: "Unless a great change takes place in public opinion, I regret to say that this policy will meet with general support in the United States."

The letter had been preceded by a telegram via the Atlantic cable laid in 1866, and on April 1 the Foreign Office wired the British Minister in St. Petersburg for confirmation and amplification. He replied also by telegram and followed it up with a letter on April 4. The sale, he said, was confirmed by the Foreign Ministry.

> The reason given to me for the sale was that the Russian American Company though receiving an annual subvention of two hundred thousand rubles from the Government, was almost in a state of bankruptcy. . . . It [Alaska] would be entirely incapable of being defended during war, if measures were taken for its conquest by a maritime Power. . . . I said it might have been considered a friendly act on the part of the Russian Government if She had afforded her Majesty's Government or the Government of Canada an opportunity of purchasing the territory which has been sold, but that their not having done so was materially unimportant as I felt it would not have been bought.

That last assumption was later confirmed by the British Government.

During the first days of April the British Minister in St. Petersburg found himself in a peculiar position, being the only person outside a tight top-level clique to know about the sale of Alaska, and meeting with disbelief and bewilderment whenever he mentioned it. When the news drifted in from Western Europe, Russian newspapers reacted angrily, denouncing the reports as the typical slanderous and provocative fabrications of the Western press. What would they dream up next — the sale of the Crimea, the Caucasus, or the Baltic Provinces? When the Russian Government was obliged to announce that the rumours were true, "the impression produced . . . was of a most painful character."

Painful also was the impression produced in the British province adjacent to the new United States possession — British Columbia. The *Victoria Colonist,* which only a few years before had declared that the Panhandle "must eventually become the property of Great Britain," now saw the Alaska Purchase as another link in a chain that would ultimately strangle British North America. All that was needed now was that the United States be put in possession of San Juan Island "and Great Britain will have scarcely a foothold of Coast on the Pacific that she can call her own or with which in case of war with our neighbor she would not find it next to impossible to communicate."

The formal transfer of Alaska from Russia to the United States took place at Sitka on October 18, 1867. Both nations had sent special commissioners, and there were military honour guards. As the blue Cross of St. Andrew began to descend the flagstaff, Russian and American ships in the harbour began to boom out twenty-one-gun salutes, firing alternately. "When the flag had descended one-third of the distance," an American newspaper correspondent on the scene reported, "it caught fast upon the yardarm. One of the governor's marines ascending disengaged it, and it dropped down upon the heads of the Russian soldiers, as if seeking a home with those who were its appointed defenders." The Stars and Stripes was then attached to the halyard, and the fifteen-year-old son of the American commissioner raised it to the head of the staff, again to the accompaniment of a double twenty-one-gun salute. Such cannonading had not been heard on those misty shores since Alexander Baranov had shot up the Sitkan Indians' fort in 1804.

After that resplendent act, Alaska quickly dropped out of sight as far as the American political scene was concerned. Most of the pure-blooded Russians departed, and the institutions they had built up in Sitka languished. There were almost no white settlers in the territory, whose administration was shifted around from department to department in Washington. For a while it was administered from a small warship anchored in Sitka harbour. Once, when an Indian uprising seemed to threaten, the residents appealed to the British authorities to the south, and a warship was sent from Victoria to calm their fears.

In this lack of immigration to Alaska there was an advantage not only to the Canadian side in the boundary dispute that followed, but also to the United States Government, for it left both sides relatively free of the aggressive pressures of an American organized local community. Throughout the dispute, the only local opposition to Canadian claims came from appointed representatives of the United States Government, and any problems they raised could be dealt with quickly and exclusively in Washington. In later years, it is true, the larger regional interests of the American Pacific seaboard — Seattle, San Francisco — made themselves felt, but in Washington, not in Alaska.

In a curious turnabout, it was the British side that was embarrassed by having to reconcile the claims and actions not just of two but of three political entities, claims and actions that varied in aggressiveness and, quite often, in interpretation. The entities were represented by the Imperial Government in London, the Dominion Government in Ottawa, and the British Columbia Government in Victoria.

For five years after the Alaska Purchase the Panhandle boundary remained calm, but the fuse had already been lit that would soon shatter the jurisdictional peace. In 1861, Buck Choquette and another miner had discovered gold on Buck's Bar in the Stikine in British Columbia. Sporadic panning went on for several years, but the erstwhile discoverer, Choquette, found that the diggings in miners' pockets, in barroom and store, promised a better income than the hazards of the gold-fields. He retired to become a shopkeeper on the lower Stikine, where he soon established a profitable monopoly on the trade of the traffic passing up and down the river.

The real gold-rush to the Cassiar district of British Columbia started in the early eighteen-seventies. On July 11, 1872, the Lieutenant-Governor of British Columbia forwarded to Ottawa a request by his legislature for the demarcation of the boundary between British Columbia and Alaska. This was necessary, the petition said, to maintain peace, order, and good government in the boundary region during the expected influx of gold-seekers. The Lieutenant-Governor added that although the boundary was defined in the Treaty of 1825 the definition was impractical and "some more clearly marked or definitely ascertained line" should be substituted.

Ottawa passed the matter on to the British Ambassador in Washington, Sir Edward Thornton. The United States Government was sympathetic to the determination and demarcation of the boundary. It asked the United States Engineers for an estimate of the cost of a boundary survey. The estimate was $1,500,000. At this tremendous sum Congress threw up its hands and refused to consider the survey.

The Canadian Government, on its part, requested a report, with estimate, on the proposed boundary survey from the man whom its ruling Cabinet members considered most qualified to pass judgment on this subject — Her Majesty's North American Boundary Commissioner Captain Donald Roderick Cameron, Royal Artillery. Captain Cameron, as readers will no doubt remember, was then in charge of the survey of the Prairie boundary. Although he received the request for the report in November, 1873, it was not until February 18, 1875, that he submitted his views and calculations to the Dominion Government. He had gone into the matter with his customary thoroughness, and estimated that the Alaska boundary survey would cost "not less than $425,000 nor more than $2,230,000, and that the time for its completion will be from two to seven years" depending on various enumerated circumstances. The bewildered Government merely put the report on file. An abridgement found its way into the Sessional Papers of 1878, after a request for the tabling of Alaska boundary documents had been made in the House of Commons by Amor de Cosmos, M.P. from British Columbia.

In 1874 the British Columbia Government again petitioned to have the boundary defined. The petition is worth noting only because it referred to the Panhandle as "the 30-mile belt of American territory running along a part of the seaboard." Apparently the leading minds at Victoria had given up trying to arrive at a simple interpretation of the Treaty of 1825 and were now content to follow the easy habit which had grown up among the local people of taking the Panhandle boundary as being everywhere thirty miles from the coast. This was of course inaccurate. The Treaty of 1825 would make the boundary run ten marine leagues (34.5 miles) parallel to the coast only where the parallel mountain range receded beyond that distance. In other words, although there was a maximum width for the Panhandle, there was no theoretical minimum width. The boundary could conceivably run within three miles from the coast if the crest of mountains came as close as that. These considerations were entirely abstract; no one had attempted to designate the boundary range or ranges, and the boundary was not marked anywhere at all, not even where it crossed the Stikine River.

Boundary markers or not, the customs men on both sides could not let such a promising stream of goods go untapped. By 1875, a United States customs officer had established himself at Wrangell, six miles below the mouth of the Stikine, and a Canadian customs officer had pitched his tent some twenty-odd miles up the river, just below Buck's store. The choice of the spot was more or less arbitrary, but the United States representative raised no objections, and throughout the long rainy winter of 1875-76 the Canadian official levied duty on all American goods carried past him into British Columbia. The American customs men, on the other hand, made certain that no British goods were dropped off while ships were in transit through the Panhandle, by accompanying each steamer on its up-river voyage. This surveillance annoyed the passengers, who objected strenuously to the American customs man's practice of locking up the bar and pocketing the key the moment he stepped aboard, not to release it until the ship was out of American territory.

During 1875 and 1876 the annual yield of gold in the Cassiar district exceeded a million dollars, and some one thousand miners were busy in the diggings each summer. For the winter they would descend on Victoria or Wrangell, where they spent their time playing cards, drinking, and making love to their Indian concubines.

In the spring of 1876 the Canadian customs officer, having found winter in his temporary shelter unpleasant and being worried about possible robbery, folded his tent and quietly moved up the river to

Glenora, far beyond the utmost limits of the Panhandle. He left behind him a Union Jack as mute guardian of the *ad hoc* boundary line.

The American customs men now saw their chance. They had long been annoyed by the lucrative trade of Buck Choquette, who was a thorn in the side of the merchants of Wrangell. The removal of the Canadian customs post, they calculated, had left Buck high and dry, and fair game. On September 19, 1876, after communicating his intention to Washington, the chief United States customs collector for Alaska, at Sitka, wrote to Choquette that he would either have to vacate his store, or pay duty on all British merchandise, as his place was found to be on American territory. He gave Choquette until the spring of 1877 to comply.

Choquette was extremely loath to lose his booming business. He was popular with both whites and Indians, and claimed to have sold as many as twelve hundred blankets to an Indian in a single transaction. He sent appeals for help to Ottawa, and he also found a sympathetic listener in Judge J. H. Gray, who passed by Choquette's store on his return trip from Laketon, where he had just sentenced Bricktop Martin. Gray lost no time in bringing Choquette's plight to the attention of both the Victoria and the Ottawa authorities.

The news about the customs quarrel and the Martin affair thus reached Ottawa almost simultaneously in the late fall of 1876, strongly emphasizing the need for boundary demarcation at least on the Stikine River.

The preliminary hearing of Martin in Victoria was naturally reported to the State Department by the American consul, and on November 2, 1876, Secretary of State Hamilton Fish wrote to the British Minister that Martin claimed to be an American citizen, that the alleged assault had taken place only a few miles from the mouth of the Stikine, "within the territory of Alaska," and that Martin should therefore be set at liberty.

The Colonial Office thereupon requested a report from Ottawa. Ottawa in turn requested the Colonial Office to bring pressure to bear for the demarcation of the boundary. On January 10, 1877,

Secretary Fish, having received the report of Martin's conviction, again pressed the British Minister for his release. His recapture on, and removal from, American territory had been "an illegal, violent, and forcible act."

London and Ottawa were growing anxious, and communications were flying back and forth at an increasing rate. London was worried about its relations with the United States; Ottawa was worried about loss of face. On February 5 the Canadian Minister of Justice produced a long report on the Martin affair. It contained the following admission:

> In my opinion, there was, on the trial, no evidence to show in which of the two countries the act was committed. . . . There is, therefore, in my judgment, a fatal defect in the evidence for the Crown. . . . I think the conviction at Victoria not sustainable, and I should be disposed to advise that the sentence of the prisoner on that conviction be remitted.

This would not mean the immediate freeing of Martin, who would still have to serve the two sentences imposed at Laketon. The Canadian Government, however, found immediate compliance with the Justice Minister's report distasteful. Instead, it commissioned a civil engineer in the employ of the Canadian Pacific Railway, Joseph Hunter, to survey the lower Stikine River with a view to ascertaining the boundary as defined by the Treaty of 1825. No doubt the Ottawa politicians still entertained a distant hope that the Martin affair could be shown to have taken place on Canadian soil. Hunter was to get in touch with Beegan in Victoria to find the exact location of the escape attempt.

Hunter executed his task with great dispatch, and in June, 1877, he was able to report from Victoria that he had found the crest of the coast range, marking the boundary, to be at a distance of 19.13 miles from the coast in a straight line, or 27.74 miles along the windings of the river. He also found that the Martin affair had taken place thirteen miles from the mouth of the river, well within the territory of the United States.

There was now no excuse left for detaining Martin, the less so as the Colonial Secretary himself, on August 16, 1877, urged

Ottawa to release him, regardless of whether the assault had taken place in American territory or not: "The unauthorized conveyance of a prisoner through the territories of a foreign Power is an infraction of the rights of sovereignty of such Power." Even though the Treaty of 1825 had given British subjects the right to navigate the rivers for any purpose whatsoever, this unlimited right had inadvertently been lost through the Treaty of Washington of 1871, where free navigation was conceded for purposes of commerce only.

The Canadian Department of Justice accordingly advised the British Columbia authorities that Martin be released, remitting even the sentences of Laketon. Bricktop had triumphed.

But Hunter's survey also had its agreeable consequences for Canada. On February 20, 1878, the United States Government accepted Hunter's line as the temporary boundary on the Stikine. This not only saved Buck Choquette, but it also strengthened the principle that the coastal mountain range, rather than the thirty-mile line, marked the boundary.

This marked the end of the first serious quarrel over the Panhandle boundary, and for several years thereafter nothing was heard on the subject.

In 1883 Lieutenant Frederick Schwatka of the United States Army made an extensive exploration of Alaska, which helped to revive public interest in the forgotten territory. One of the men especially interested in Alaskan affairs was Professor William H. Dall of the United States Coast and Geodetic Survey. Dall (born 1845) was the son of a well-known writer and reformer, Caroline Wells Healey Dall, and he seems to have inherited some of his mother's crusading zeal. He studied under Louis Agassiz the naturalist, and made the acquaintance of Alaska in 1865-68 when he was in charge of an expedition to ascertain the possibility of telegraphic communication with Europe via Bering Strait. Since 1871 he had been with the Coast and Geodetic Survey.

In the line of his work Dall frequently exchanged information with his Canadian counterparts, especially Dr. George Mercer Dawson of the Geological Survey of Canada. Dawson, whom we have already met in his capacity as geologist and naturalist with the Prairie boundary survey of 1872-74, had built up a respectable reputation in geology, geography, cartography, and similar disciplines. On April 24, 1884, Dall made the following suggestion in a letter to Dawson:

> The matter of the boundary should be stirred up. The language of the Treaty of 1825 is so indefinite that were the region included for any cause to become suddenly of evident value, or if any serious international question were to arise regarding jurisdiction, there would be no means of settling it by the Treaty. There being no natural boundary and the continuous range of mountains parallel to the coast shown on Vancouver's charts, like a long caterpillar, having no existence as such, the United States would undoubtedly wish to fall back on the "line parallel to the windings of the coast and which shall never exceed the distance of ten marine leagues therefrom" of the Treaty. It would of course be impracticable to trace any such winding line over that "sea of mountains". I should think that the bottom of the nearest valley parallel to the coast might perhaps be traced and its stream form a natural boundary; even then it would be difficult to determine the line between one valley and the next. Before the question has attained any importance, it should be referred to a committee of geographers, a survey should be made, and a new treaty should be made stating determinable boundaries. Perhaps at some time you may be able to set the ball in motion on your side, and it would be only a matter of time when it would follow here.

It was Dall, however, who set the ball in motion by impressing his views on Thomas F. Bayard, who became Secretary of State in 1885. Bayard had them elaborated in a note to the British Government. "In the judgment of the President," the note said, "the time has now come for an understanding between the Government of the United States and that of Her Britannic Majesty." It repeated Dall's argument about the virtual impossibility of surveying a boundary in accordance with the Treaty of 1825, whose framers had been fooled by Vancouver's imaginary caterpillar of mountains. As to the ten-league line parallel to the coast, it would be just as difficult to survey as the mountain line. The note concluded:

> It is of evident advantage to both countries to agree upon some boundary line capable of survey at a reasonable cost, yet so precisely

and practically described, that in case of need any given point thereon may be readily determined in advance of a general survey.

Regardless of the practical (and quite innocent) motivations, this tampering with the letter of the Treaty of 1825 was a fateful strategic error on the part of the United States. It was an invitation to Canada to follow suit, and this the Canadians did — by tampering not with the letter but with the spirit of the treaty. They advanced a fantastic and momentous claim, which for the sake of convenience I shall call the Coast Doctrine.

To trace its origin we must return briefly to the report on the Alaska boundary submitted by Captain Cameron in February, 1875. When this report was printed in the Sessional Papers of the Canadian House of Commons in 1878, and thus became public, the official responsible for it had deleted those portions of the elaborate document which he considered unimportant. Among them were some theoretical musings about the precise interpretation of the Treaty of 1825. What, for instance, was the meaning of "coast" in the phrase "the limit . . . shall be formed by a line parallel to the windings of the coast"? "Do the words 'winding of the coast'," Cameron asked rhetorically, "imply that the line is to be parallel to the ocean low or high water mark following indents in bays and long tortuous inlets?"

This train of thought was not followed up or, it seems, even noticed by anyone of authority in Ottawa. In 1886, after Dall and and Bayard had raised the question of redefining the Panhandle boundary, the Canadian Government cast about for expert advice. The Conservatives were again in power, and Sir Charles Tupper, Cameron's father-in-law, was Canadian High Commissioner in London. Cameron himself, then a colonel in the Royal Artillery, was stationed at Sheerness. Tupper seized the opportunity for rescuing his daughter's husband from his humdrum garrison duties by obtaining his appointment as an adviser to the Canadian Government. Cameron plunged into the boundary problem with his customary single-mindedness. During his long years in exile from international policy-making he had had opportunity to ruminate about the deeper meaning of the issues which had first presented themselves to him during the exciting middle eighteen-seventies. On February 10, 1886, Cameron wrote to Tupper:

> The Mountain summit line may be found for very long distances to be more than ten leagues from the coast line. This difficulty might be met by determining a succession of points not exceeding ten marine leagues from the coast line, measured, however, from neither promontory nor inlet, but instead from successive straight lines along the coast intersecting approximately alike both promontories and inlets.

On April 9 he followed up with a more detailed memorandum in which he said:

> A suggestion that the shore lines of the deep narrow inlets which occur in the Alaskan Coast should be considered "windings of the Coast" referred to in the Convention is negatived by a universally admitted law of nations and by the language of the Convention itself. Inlets of which the mouths are less than six miles in breadth are territorial. They cease to be part of the ocean.

Here was the Coast Doctrine in all its mad beauty: if the "coast" did not include the shores of the inlets, then a line drawn along the crest of the "coastal" mountains would leave the heads of several of the longer inlets in Canada, thus giving the interior of British Columbia access to salt water right through the Alaska Panhandle. Even if the boundary was drawn everywhere at 34.5 miles from the "coast," it would still cut through one inlet — the ninety-mile-long Lynn Canal, the most important inlet of them all.

All authors whom I have consulted on this subject treat the Coast Doctrine, with fine deterministic insouciance, as the natural product of nascent Canadian nationalism. If they mention Cameron, he appears to be merely the instrument, the spokesman for ideas that were in the air at the time. Yet the Coast Doctrine — the doctrine that the Treaty of 1825 spoke of an abstract, political ocean coast rather than the physical limit of salt water — was no more "in the air" than Newton's theory of gravitation or Columbus's voyage to America. It was the brain child of a man whose unquiet, almost mystical, yet oddly narrow mind condemned him ever to look for a meaning behind each meaning, and to whom *überspitzte Formulierungen* were the only ones worth striving for. The bounds between practicality and impracticality, reality and fantasy, solemnity and farce had no existence for him.

In another time and place he would perhaps have been a great success. It is not hard to picture him among the casuistic courtiers of a medieval papal curia, such as that of Gregory VII or Innocent III. But in the position in which life had placed him every project he undertook seemed doomed to failure. It was typical that on the eve of wireless telegraphy's triumphant conquest of communications he should succeed in convincing the Canadian Government that its most urgent need in that field was a messenger pigeon service. The pigeon service, duly installed as a means of communication between Sable Island and the Nova Scotia mainland, failed miserably.

In 1888, after his retirement from active service with the rank of major-general, Tupper secured him the directorship of the Royal Military College at Kingston, Ontario. During his eight years in that post, until removed by the incoming Liberal Government, Cameron's mismanagement almost brought about the demise of that once proud and hopeful institution. (His foibles on the Prairie boundary survey have been described in the second chapter.) There are of course many such men as Donald Cameron, but few of them marry the daughters of powerful and durable politicians.

His other mistakes and misadventures blew over more or less harmlessly, without leaving much of a trace, but the Coast Doctrine debacle was of a very different dimension, large enough to provoke almost revolutionary changes in Canadian political attitudes. The causes of revolutions are seldom truly noble, even by the revolutionaries' own standards. They become ennobled only by the roseate glow of retrospect. So it was with the Coast Doctrine and its effect on Canadian emancipation from the Empire. To give credit for this change to Cameron is a bit of a left-handed compliment; but it is the best we can offer prospective apologists.

Cameron embodied his views in a formal report which was published in September, 1886, by the Colonial Office.

In 1885, the year before, the British Columbia Government

added to the confusion by bringing forward its own interpretation of the Panhandle boundary. It claimed that the words "Portland Channel" in the Treaty of 1825 were an error and should be disregarded, and that the southern limit of the Panhandle ran along Clarence Strait to strike the mainland at 56° latitude, thus leaving on the British Columbia side the island of Revilla Gigedo and a large piece of the mainland. The claim was based on two things: First, the treaty said that the boundary should run in a northerly direction from the southern point of Prince of Wales Island; but to reach Portland Channel it had to run due east. Second, the treaty said the line should ascend Portland Channel to latitude 56°; but Portland Channel does not quite extend to 56°.

This claim was a palpable perversion of the explicit meaning of the treaty. It originated with a circle of superpatriots in Victoria, notably Judge Gray and an amateurish and sycophantic historian named Alexander Begg. The Cabinet at Ottawa vacillated in its attitude toward the British Columbia claim.

In 1887 the Dominion Government dispatched to the Yukon River the surveyor William Ogilvie, who was to determine the point at which the 141st-meridian boundary crossed the river. Ogilvie took twenty-two moon transits over the meridian during the winter of 1887-88. He wrote in his memoirs:

> This was the first direct attempt to fix with any degree of precision the boundary line. . . . When I say that some of my observations were taken when the temperature was lower than fifty below zero . . . one can appreciate the difficulty of getting the most accurate work from even such limited appliances as the transportation facilities at that time afforded. . . . One must be very warmly clothed indeed to remain standing still in an open-roofed observatory for two hours in such temperatures, but it also seriously interfered with the instruments used and impaired their delicacy.

Ogilvie had left the heavy stand for his transit telescope behind in hopes of basing his instrument on a thick and solidly rooted tree stump, but the best tree he could find in the vicinity of the boundary was twenty inches in diameter. When Ogilvie's line was checked around 1906 by telegraph, his longitude determination was, as he put it, only "a few score yards out." (The 141st-meridian boundary never caused disputes. It was a question of survey only.)

In 1887-88 a British-American conference was held in Washington to settle various disputes over fishing rights. It was attended by a Canadian delegation headed by Sir Charles Tupper, who brought along Donald Cameron as his secretary. At the suggestion of the British negotiators, George Dawson was brought in from Ottawa to discuss informally with William Dall the technicalities of determining the Panhandle boundary. (Dall had transferred to the United States Geological Survey.) Dawson on his arrival in February, 1888, discussed the boundary with his old chief Cameron and other members of the Canadian delegation.

There is no doubt, however, that he was already familiar with the Coast Doctrine. A boundary line in accordance with that doctrine had already made its appearance on maps published by the Department of the Interior — to which Dawson belonged — in 1887. One such map, dated January 16, 1888, shows a line cutting off four inlets and following the general trend of the coast at an average distance of eight miles. It is designated "Line approximately following summits of mountains parallel to coast." Another line, sweeping around the heads of inlets at a distance of forty miles, is designated "Line approximately as shown on U.S. Coast Survey Map of Alaska 1884. N.B. This line disregards both the Treaty reference to mountains and that to the ocean coast." The term "ocean coast" is a clear reference to the Coast Doctrine. This map was shown by Dawson to Dall.

Cameron himself would probably have liked to represent the British side in the boundary discussion, but he was not considered a professional expert such as Dall and Dawson.

The two men held a series of conferences, but failed to reach agreement. Dawson reported on the conference to Sir Charles Tupper, apparently in the latter's capacity as head of the Canadian delegation. At the beginning of his talks Dawson wrote, *inter alia*:

> Such a line as that which it is believed was intended is by no means impossible of survey [as had been asserted by Dall and Bayard], nor should it even be very difficult to define, as the sum-

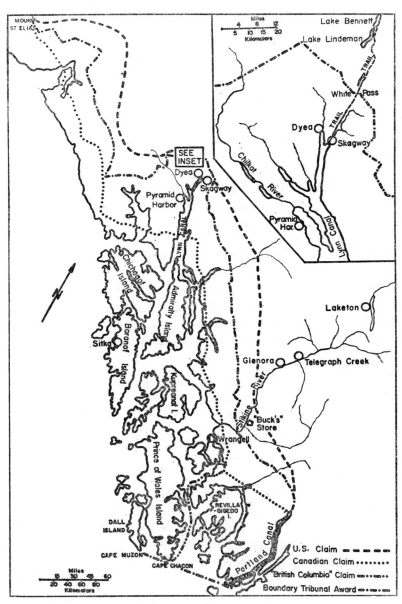

Alaska Boundary Dispute.

mits of the mountains are, as a matter of fact, found to be everywhere visible from the coast, and are probably at an average
distance of considerably less than five miles from it. In respect to
the important question as to what is intended by the expression
la côte, Major-General D. R. Cameron's view, as expressed in a
report on this point, may be substantially adopted.

He then repeated, without quotes, Cameron's thesis: "The word
ocean is wholly inapplicable to inlets; consequently the line, whether
marked by mountains or only by a survey line, has to be drawn
without reference to inlets."

The Coast Doctrine had cleared its first important hurdle; it had
won the adherence of Canada's No. 1 scientific expert. Whether
Dawson in his heart believed in the doctrine or whether he adopted
it out of political expediency will probably never be known.

Dawson also gave qualified approval to the British Columbia
claim.

It is not surprising that Dall rejected all of these claims. He also
rejected Dawson's suggestion of a mutual cession of territory to
straighten the Panhandle boundary. Dall coupled his rejection of
the Coast Doctrine with the sarcastic comment:

> As those of a venerable and gallant officer, however unversed
> in history or logic, General Cameron's views deserve attention; and
> in showing their irrationality, I wish to repudiate once for all any
> intention of reflecting upon him personally.

The reports on the Dall-Dawson talks were published by the
Unted States Government along with the proceedings of the Atlantic
Fisheries Commission.

It would be a mistake to assume that the Coast Doctrine had
now become the practical policy of the Canadian Government.
Rather it had become the credo of a small but influential coterie in
the Department of the Interior, which kept it alive through the
succeeding years by seeing to it that it appeared on maps published
by the department after 1887. The group was headed by Deputy
Minister A. M. Burgess, Dr. Dawson, and William Frederick King,
the chief astronomer. The view most commonly held by the Cana-

dian public, in so far as it was aware of these matters, was that of the United States. On January 20, 1886, for example, the commissioners of the Hudson's Bay Company at Winnipeg — generally a knowledgeable group — petitioned the British Government for the demarcation of the Panhandle boundary, saying: "The present boundary, giving to the United States all the islands, and on the mainland 10 marine leagues from the coast, seems to be a boundary easily ascertained."

The Coast Doctrine was not taken into account by William Ogilvie in February, 1889, when he wrote of the boundary near the head of Lynn Canal: "If the Boundary is the summit of the coast range of mountains, it is distant 15 miles from the *head* of tidewater." (Italics supplied.) It was tacitly rejected by the Foreign Office in September 1888, when the British Minister to the United States passed on a Canadian complaint (drafted by Cameron and based on the Coast Doctrine) to the State Department with the deliberate deletion of the operative portion, so that it became meaningless.

An atlas published in 1890 in London by "The Geographer to the Queen" followed the American line. A map of the Panhandle published by the Canadian Pacific Railway in early 1896 showed the boundary running around the inlets at about thirty miles. Even after the Dall-Dawson talks the problem of the boundary was still treated by Ottawa as one of survey rather than interpretation. In 1890 a government spokesman told the House of Commons: "No difficulty is likely to arise in regard to the boundary." Not once before 1898 did the Canadian or the British Government make a formal statement to the United States Government sustaining the Coast Doctrine, although opportunities were not lacking. Not once was a token occupation of the heads of inlets attempted by Canada to test the new treaty interpretation, although this, too, would have presented no practical difficulties.

At the Alaska Boundary Tribunal in 1903, where the Canadians did their utmost to endow the Coast Doctrine with authority and antiquity, their efforts were satirized by the United States counsel. Speaking of Cameron's report, he said:

He was a pioneer of thought in that direction, but his views were not adopted by the Government; . . . it never followed it up by any demand upon the American Government or by any question of its right of occupation. On the contrary, from that time, with its mind thus addressed to the subject matter, it continued to issue its maps as it had hitherto issued them, drawing the boundary line all around that territory that is now in controversy . . . thereby making a public declaration to the world that it was American territory. So far from being able to predicate anything upon the act of Dr. Dawson [in 1888] the record shows that this act was in effect disavowed.

On July 22, 1892, Great Britain and the United States concluded a convention for the "survey of the territory adjacent to that part of the boundary line" separating British Columbia and Alaska. The survey was to be completed in two years. When it was found in 1894 that two years was not enough, the time limit was extended to the end of 1895. The survey was simply a mapping operation; it was not connected with the determination of the boundary. It was carried out jointly by Canadian and American personnel. The Canadian operations were under the direction of W. F. King, the American, of T. C. Mendenhall and later of W. W. Duffield. The surveyors produced the first accurate maps of the Panhandle region.

The survey had no special political significance, except for one point: by agreeing to having the survey start at 54°40′ on the mainland, the Canadian Government implicitly disavowed the British Columbia claim, which would make the mainland part of the Panhandle start at 56°. It took a little while for this to sink in at Victoria, but when it did the proponents of the British Columbia claim reacted angrily. To forestall further "concessions" the British Columbia Government on February 19, 1895, formally requested to be "directly represented in the negotiations for the settlement of the boundary line," a weak echo of Maine's attitude more than half a century earlier. After considering the request briefly the Dominion Cabinet turned it down.

Cameron, who appears to have learned about the British Columbia pretensions a year later, estimated, correctly, that their adoption by the Canadian Government would discredit the whole Canadian claim, and above all his Coast Doctrine. He entered a strong protest against the British Columbia claim with the Department of the Interior, and was reassured by the Deputy Minister, Burgess:

> I entirely concur in your views . . . and have advised my Minister to abstain from any public discussion of this question in any form. I have further taken very strong objection to what some of the Ministerial papers in British Columbia have been saying, chiefly at the instigation of Alex. Begg, who is an old ass. . . . To say the least expectations will be created in the minds of the Canadian people which can never be realized.

Public interest in the Panhandle boundary may be gauged from the debates and questions in the Canadian House of Commons. After a flurry of excitement over the Martin case and the customs dispute on the Stikine River in 1875-76, interest died down, and during the next two decades there would be many years when the Alaska boundary was not mentioned in the House at all. Then, in 1897, the storm began to break.

The nuggets which started the great Klondike gold-rush were found in August, 1896, but it was not until almost a year later that the first steamers filled with frenzied gold-seekers steamed up to the head of Lynn Canal. There, where the towns of Skagway and Dyea sprang up, was the starting-point of the gruelling climb over the mountain passes leading to the Yukon watershed and its gold-fields.

The big strike in the Yukon district coincided very nearly with a change of government in Ottawa. In 1896, for the first time since 1874, the Liberals won a general election, and Wilfrid Laurier became Prime Minister. With him into the new Cabinet went a bright young man, the "representative" of expansionist western Canada, thirty-five-year-old Clifford Sifton. Sifton was given the Interior portfolio, and he immediately set about infusing his department with his own aggressive, adventuresome spirit. Before he took it over, he said scornfully, "it was a department of delay, a department of circumlocution, a department in which people could not get business done." One subject on which there would be no more circumlocution was the Alaska boundary.

The first official and reliable information about the Klondike gold finds arrived in Ottawa in the winter of 1896-97 from William Ogilvie, who happened to be in Fort Cudahy on the Yukon River at that time, not far from the mouth of the Klondike. On September 6, 1896, he wrote: "I am very much pleased to be able to inform you that a most important discovery of gold has been made on a creek called Bonanza creek, an affluent of the river known here as the Klondike." Later he reported in more detail:

> We have every reason to assume that this part of our territory will in a year or two contain 10,000 at least. . . . Prospecting has only begun, and up to date of mailing, November 22nd, very rich prospects have been found on the few claims prospected on; from one dollar to the pan of dirt up to twelve dollars are reported and no bedrock yet. This means from $1,000 to $12,000 per day per man sluicing. The excitement is intense. . . .

In the first week of April, 1897, Sifton got a hastily scribbled note from his director of the Geological Survey, George Dawson. Pasted on it was a small clipping from the *Victoria Colonist* which said:

> The Alaska Searchlight publishes the following letter from W. F. Cornell, dated Fort Cudahy, Jan. 15, 1897: 'As to the richness of the Clondyke region . . . I may as well tell you that in my 42 years' experience on the Pacific coast so much gold has never been found in the same extent of country. In fact you may believe anything you hear; it can hardly be exaggerated. I have concluded that we may as well have a rush here the coming season as at any future time.'

The old-timer ended his report with a stern warning of the sufferings awaiting men who rushed into the rugged Yukon district without adequate provisions and equipment. Underneath Dawson wrote: "The attached clipping has reference to the trouble likely to occur in Yukon District should the anticipated 'rush' occur."

The political implications of a gold-rush to the Yukon were plain. The shortest route from salt water to the Kondike started at the head of an inlet that was claimed both by Canada and the United States. Somewhere there would be customs houses and a dividing line —

but where? Was there to be a repetition, on a more dangerous scale, of the Stikine troubles?

It was now too late to plant the Union Jack at the forked head of Lynn Canal. That region had been pre-empted by United States officials at least since 1891, when one of the American residents was appointed honorary customs inspector. But to maintain law and order in the gold-fields and to guard against further American encroachments, Sifton had the Cabinet appoint a government commissioner for the district and organized a large force of North-West Mounted Police to accompany him.

While Sifton was engaged in these preparations complaints had started to pour in from Dyea and Skagway, the two new shack-towns at the head of Lynn Canal, that American customs agents refused Canadian vessels permission to discharge goods and passengers. Action had to be taken at once, for more ships from Victoria and Vancouver were under way. On July 22, 1897, the Canadian commissioner of customs at Ottawa wired Washington, requesting that arrangements be made for bonding British goods through the Panhandle without payment of duty, provided that the owners paid for a United States customs officer accompanying the goods. The request was granted at once for Dyea, and a little later for Skagway, but by making it the Canadian Government had implicitly recognized American jurisdiction over the head of Lynn Canal.

Sifton was painfully aware of this further setback to the Canadian claim. He had adopted the Coast Doctrine with great enthusiasm, and every complaint from British Columbia merchants, gold-seekers, and members of Parliament served to strengthen his, and his colleagues', determination to leave nothing undone that might help to break through the barrier of the American Panhandle, which threatened to channel the profits of the Yukon trade — trade with a Canadian territory — into American hands.

Sir Charles Tupper, now out of office and leader of the Opposition, was also aware of these problems, and in June, 1897, he told the House of Commons that he had asked General Cameron to give him a statement concerning the Alaska boundary situation, and that he was now passing the statement on to Sifton so that Sifton could have it published for the enlightenment of the House. It was the second such back-door attempt that year to get Cameron re-established as government expert on the boundary — at the very time that he was being removed from his post at Kingston. Some time later, when nothing further was heard of the document, Tupper made an inquiry in the House. Sifton replied that he had refrained from publishing the report because he did not want to give the appearance of government endorsement to a statement that contained errors. He added: "The difference between the boundary line as claimed by the British authorities and the boundary line as claimed by the United States authorities is very considerable." It was the first public indication that the official policy of Canada on the Alaska boundary had taken a new direction since 1890, when, as we noted, the Government maintained that the boundary would cause "no difficulty."

Sifton did not say in what respect Cameron was in error, but it is not difficult to guess, for on February 28, 1898, Sifton exhibited before the Cabinet a map of the Panhandle whose boundary not only followed the Coast Doctrine but also included the British Columbia claim in its most extreme form. (Deputy Minister Burgess, who so vigorously opposed the British Columbia claim, had been replaced in April, 1897.) Where Dawson's map of 1887 had the boundary running across four inlets, Sifton's new boundary cut across no fewer than eighteen. It was this map which formed the basis of the Canadian claim before the British-American conference later that year.

There could be no irony more bitter than in the fate which now befell Donald Cameron. Dismissed from his office in disgrace at the end of an (outwardly) distinguished career, his reputation torn to shreds by the merciless attacks of government supporters, he finally saw his Coast Doctrine proclaimed boldly and defiantly as official policy. But he and his advice were no longer wanted; he who had once been too extreme was no longer extreme enough. His lovingly fashioned sophistries were now hurled into battle by other men while there was nothing left to him but to watch from afar, a prematurely old man whom history was passing by.

To learn about conditions on the United States-Canada frontier above Skagway at first hand, Sifton accompanied the first troop of North-West Mounted Police to Alaska. With him were the commissioner for the Yukon District, James Morrow Walsh; W. F. King, William Ogilvie, and other officials. Ogilvie had just returned from the Klondike, where he had laboured throughout the winter of 1896-97 surveying claims. Although he was literally walking on gold some of the time, he had never joined in the digging himself.

The group travelled via Vancouver and reached the head of Lynn Canal on October 8. There the policemen had to organize a relay system to get their supplies across the precipitous White Pass, through a struggling mass of men and beasts, all bent on reaching the gold-fields before the onset of winter — an utterly hopeless undertaking. Commissioner Walsh wrote later in his first report:

> The cost of packing had reached a high point, 3,200 horses lay dead on the Skagway trail, the rain was falling incessantly. . . . The Skagway trail is all that it has been described to be, such a scene of havoc and destruction as we encountered through the whole length of the White Pass can scarcely be imagined. Thousands of pack horses lay dead along the way . . . often, I regret to say, exhausted but still alive, a fact that we were unaware of until after the miserable wretches turned beneath the hoofs of our cavalcade. . . . The inhumanity which this trail has been witness to, the heart-breaking suffering which so many have undergone, cannot be imagined.

The White Pass, with the nearby Chilkoot Pass, marked the watershed between Alaska's south coast and the Yukon River basin. In a straight line it was only fourteen miles from Skagway and salt water, though the winding trail to its summit was much longer than that. After passing the summit, the travellers descended to Lake Lindeman and Lake Bennett, where they built boats on which they hoped to float down by stages and portages to Dawson City (named in honour of the geologist), but all of them were sooner or later caught by the freeze-up. Commissioner Walsh himself did not reach Dawson City until May, 1898, but some of his troop pushed on across the ice. The policemen set up headquarters on Lake Bennett and posts along the route to Dawson City.

Lake Bennett was twenty-eight miles in a straight line from the nearest salt water, and it was to be expected that the United States would claim a portion of it in accordance with its view that the parallel mountain range of the Treaty of 1825 could not be found and that the boundary must everywhere keep a distance of ten marine leagues from salt water. The situation on the frontier was detailed in an inquiry made in January, 1898, by the admiral commanding the Pacific Station, H. Bury Palliser. From the N.W.M.P. Palliser received the following information:

> The Government of this district [the Yukon] is being administered by the Federal Government at Ottawa, and immediately by the Minister of the Interior. An Administrator has been appointed with large and extensive powers. . . . The [police] force at present in the country consists of 150 officers, non-commissioned officers, and men. . . . Of these 45 are at Dawson City and the remainder between Skagway and Selkirk, about 245 miles inland. Dawson City is 600 miles. The Administration is now in winter quarters on the Yukon. It is proposed to raise the strength of the force to 250 men. . . . The Mounted Police have posts at short distances, starting from the summit, about 18 miles from Skagway. . . . On the Skagway and Dyea passes there is a dispute as to the boundary lines. United States authorities claim that the Boundary is 30 miles from the tide water on the Lynn Canal, which takes the line to the head of Lake Bennett and places Lake Lindeman . . . in United States territory. The Canadian Government claim that the summit of the Mountain is the Boundary, without doubt, although under a different reading, the Towns of Skagway and Dyea would also belong to Canada. [The Coast Doctrine was apparently not yet accepted "without doubt" by the N.W.M.P.] United States authorities have exercised authority on Lake Lindeman, and also on the head of Lake Bennett. Canadian officers have also exercised jurisdiction on Lake Lindeman.

Another brief submitted to the admiral said:

> A party of Americans went just below the Police Station [at the southern end of Lake Bennett] where the Union Jack is floating and hoisted the Stars and Stripes. The Police immediately went down and . . . after some parleying the flag was lowered and an apology tendered.

The effect of United States customs procedures was described by Inspector S. B. Steele of the N.W.M.P. in his memoirs:

> An iniquitous practice was instituted by the United States officials in Skagway of sending escorts with all parties who had Canadian goods in bond. Those unlucky people, although they had only about 19 miles to go, and no place where they could hide or sell the goods en route, were forced to pay five dollars a day, and as they had to pack their goods and it took some days to do that, the expense was ruinous. The American customs officer endeavoured to force them to take escorts as far as Bennett, 25 miles inside British territory, but as soon as I heard of it, I gave orders that the escorts should come no farther than the summits of the Pass.

Sifton's own version of how he forestalled an American attempt to push the boundary beyond the pass was contained in a letter to Commissioner Walsh dated April 1, 1898:

> The difficulty was that the officers of the United States Government asserted their jurisdiction down to and including the lower half of Lake Bennett, and a military force of the United States army was already detailed to go to Skagway. This force was gathered at Portland, and in another ten days would have taken possession of the territory down to Lake Bennett, and it would have taken twenty years of negotiating to get them out, in fact I doubt if we would ever have got them out. To prevent the loss of this territory I sent secret orders to Major Perry to send up Steele and forty more men, and plant out posts in the Passes just under the Summit, and had them there with a supply of provisions before the other party knew what we were doing. It is a case of possession being ten points in the law, and we intend to hold possession. The United States authorities have now been communicated with through diplomatic channels, and we intend to hold the territory if we possibly can.

It was a very small victory, more of a symbolic nature than of practical value. The only "possession" which would really have meant something to Canada was that of a salt-water port. Walsh lamented:

> The only product this district will have for some time to come, perhaps for ever, is gold. All that Canadians can or ever will get of this is what may come to them through the channels of trade . . . and if the trade goes we might better give the district with it than

to retain it and pay the cost of government and development. Let us find a harbor. Let us do it even if we have to go to Fort Simpson.

Fort Simpson was a harbour just south of the Alaska Panhandle, and between it and Lake Bennett there was five hundred miles of wilderness.

Officially Sifton maintained a diplomatic stance in order not to prejudice forthcoming negotiations with the United States. To the clamour for retaliatory measures against the United States (there were even suggestions that Canada should stop an American relief expedition to Dawson City, most of whose residents were American citizens) he replied in the House of Commons in February:

> So far as the Government of the United States is concerned . . . we have met with every courtesy at their hands. . . . It was an act of the greatest possible friendliness on the part of the Secretary of the Treasury of the United States to amend their regulations and provide such regulations at Dyea and Skagway, as are calculated to facilitate and promote Canadian trade. . . . Dyea and Skagway, at the entrance to this Yukon district, are nearly a thousand miles from Vancouver, and we could not send in an officer, we could not send a rifle or a revolver or a single charge of ammunition or a pound of provisions without leave of the United States.

As to getting a foothold at Dyea and Skagway, the opportunity had long since passed:

> I believe our contention is that Skagway and Dyea are really in Canadian territory, but as the United States have had undisputed possession of that territory for some time past, we are precluded from attempting to take possession. . . . There have been no protests made.

Prime Minister Laurier confirmed this: "So far as I am aware no protest has ever been entered against the occupation of Dyea by the American authorities."

The difficulties of passing Canadian goods through the Panhandle at Skagway, despite the "act of the greatest possible friendliness" of the United States in allowing the trans-shipment in bond, were outlined a few years later in the *Empire Review* by one of the officials sent to the Yukon in 1897:

Canadian goods shipped from, say, Vancouver to Dawson require to be accompanied by a certified invoice and copy of the bill of lading consigned to the Pacific and Arctic Railway and Navigation Company, to enable it to execute a bond for twice the value of the goods, required by the United States Government before the goods can be loaded on the cars. The cost of the bond and the charge for preparing the necessary papers is paid by the Canadian shipper. Should there be a shortage in goods consigned . . . the Canadian shipper must pay the duty. If stock dies in transit full duty must be paid, and be added to the loss of the shipper. Even should a cow calve while en route the shipper must pay excess.

As a practical measure to circumvent the American quasi-blockade, Sifton came up with a far-fetched scheme: build a government-subsidized railway from the head of navigation on the Stikine River to the head of navigation on the Yukon. (Passing Canadian goods through the Panhandle on the Stikine apparently presented less difficulty than the land route at Skagway.) The railway, which was estimated to cost four million dollars, would be useful during the navigation season on the rivers only. The railway bill passed the House of Commons but was killed by the predominantly Conservative Senate, which for once lived up to its avowed purpose of being a place of "sober second thought."

But Canadian efforts for breaking the American stranglehold on all salt-water ports north of the fifty-fourth parallel went further than that. On August 23, 1898, a British-American Joint High Commission convened at Quebec City to deal with an omnibus agenda of Canadian-American relations. The conference was similar in purpose to the Washington Conference of 1871, but in recognition of greater Canadian stature in international affairs the first half of the sessions was to take place in Quebec, and the second in Washington. Canada was also given equal representation with the mother country in the make-up of the British delegation, the two British commissioners being Sir Julian Pauncefote, British Ambassador to the United States, and Sir Louis Davies, Canada's Minister of Marine and Fisheries. The chief topics of the conference concerned fishing and sealing rights and Canadian-American trade policies. But the Alaska Panhandle boundary was also to be considered. Contrary to common misconception, the British delegation did not aim at a final settlement of the boundary but rather at a *modus vivendi* at the head of Lynn Canal more in keeping with the Coast Doctrine; in other words, an arrangement that would give Canada access to salt water.

The United States was already at war with Spain, but peace-time elegance surrounded the proceedings of the conference. The American delegation, headed by John W. Foster and John A. Kasson, began to arrive in Quebec's largest hotel, the Château Frontenac, where it had reserved thirty-five rooms, in July. "The entertainment of the commissioners will be on a scale worthy of Canadian hospitality," a newspaper correspondent reported.

The Canadian boundary claim was presented by Lord Herschell of England, aided by a flexible array of Canadian experts and politicians, including, on occasion, Prime Minister Laurier himself. They had persuaded Herschell to put forward the entire Canadian line as formulated by Sifton, embracing the British Columbia claim. The idea behind this was that the greater the Canadian maximum demand, the more likely the United States would be to grant the minimum demand, a port on Lynn Canal. Some time before, Cameron had cautioned Ottawa against tipping its hand early in boundary negotiations, a warning that had been repeated in the spring by W. F. King.

Herschell was willing to put his best effort into the Coast Doctrine, but he was unhappy about the British Columbia claim. He wrote home at the beginning of September:

> I thought it well to put forward fully the contention which has found much favour in Canada, that the boundary ascends to the north along the channel on the east side of Prince of Wales' Island and not along the channel marked on Vancouver's maps as Portland canal, but I may as well observe that I regard the contention as hopelessly untenable.

After the American delegation had been introduced to the Coast Doctrine, the hard bargaining began. But if the sessions were tough and tiresome, the evenings and holidays were filled with an unending round of festivities as Quebec's hostesses vied with one another in lavish and exotic entertainments, and the various governments were not to be left behind. There were balls and receptions, moonlight cruises on the St. Lawrence, and excursions into the mountains. One hostess had the feudal idea of staging a "living chess" game for the amusement of the delegates, but an untimely rainstorm came up and the colourfully costumed chess pieces broke ranks and scurried for shelter. The high point in ostentation was the unveiling, on September 21, of the statue of Samuel de Champlain on Quebec's Dufferin Terrace. The occasion was marked by a parade of British and American warships on the river and the attendance of all the delegates, with the Consul-General of France, Sir Wilfrid Laurier, the Lieutenant-Governor and the Premier of Quebec, and Canada's Governor-General, Lord Aberdeen, together with their wives. The *Toronto Globe* special correspondent reported:

> To-night the city is a blaze of electric light, the warships are decorated, a great ball is in progress at the City Hall, at which the city is host and the International Commissioners are the guests, and the officers of the fleet are dining with the Governor-General at the Citadel. The city is given over to rejoicing, and the jackies who predicted "a hot time in the old town to-night" have their prediction fulfilled.

With so much nocturnal revelry, some of the gruff repartee at the morning conference table may have been due as much to upset stomachs and aching heads as to reasons of state. Indeed, so pressing were social engagements that the secretaries of the commission were sometimes compelled to compose bogus protocols of discussions that were never held. We owe the revelation of this and other interesting sidelights to the uninhibited reports of one W. C. Cartwright, a Foreign Office man who was acting as secretary to the British delegation (and who is not to be confused with Sir Richard Cartwright, the Canadian Minister of Trade and Commerce). On October 10 Cartwright wrote to his confrères in London:

> The Alaska Boundary looks fairly promising, but even on that question I don't feel quite so optimistic as his Lordship. . . . Our friend King, who is our sole mainstay, is addicted to whisky and has no power of speech; we have to drag his sentences out of him, and

old [Joseph] Pope is called in, as he says, like Aaron to help Moses, not knowing much of the question but being indispensable to make King open his mouth, or to speak for him.

One cannot help wondering what Cameron's feelings would have been had he read these lines.

After the theoretical preliminaries had been disposed of, Herschell proposed that the United States cede to Canada the small port of Pyramid Harbor south of Dyea and Skagway, and a strip of territory to connect it with the Yukon District, presumably along the Chilkat valley. On December 9 Cartwright reported that the proposal had been rejected by Senator Charles Fairbanks, representing the American delegation.

> Instead of giving us Pyramid Harbour and keeping Dyea & Skagway, he suggests making all three places free ports and allowing the Canadians certain special privileges at Pyramid Harbour, such as the maintenance of a Customs establishment.

On December 16 he added:

> The American proposal is that they should have the whole of Lynn Canal, but give us certain privileges at Pyramid Harbour and engage that British Vessels should have absolutely the same rights as American Vessels both there and at Dyea and Skagway. This proposal has actually been formulated and seems to secure us every possible right as regards access.

By that time the conference had moved to Washington, where its arrival was marked by a ball given by President McKinley and followed, as the *Globe* correspondent wrote, by so many social functions that he could no longer keep track of them. He also noted that the climate for Canadians was chillier in the American capital:

> The people of Canada can scarcely understand the feeling of absolute indifference toward Canadian affairs that one continuously encounters here. . . . To the average American in public life the Dominion does not exist.

Herschell did not consider the granting of privileges at Pyramid Harbor a satisfactory solution of Canadian needs. He was adamant in maintaining the Canadian claim to territorial possession. On December 23 Cartwright noted:

> Lord Herschell is in the depth of despair about everything but he was a little cheered by his talk with the President. It is however very doubtful whether the President can help us; he is not famous for strength of character, and even if he were he has not the power to bring the Commissioners into line. McKinley has always talked in the optimistic strain to Lord Herschell, but we have never yet seen any good result.

The American commissioners, in their turn, regarded Herschell as the main stumbling-block on the road to a boundary settlement. Senator Henry Cabot Lodge wrote:

> Mr. [Joseph] Chamberlain gave me clearly to understand that Lord Herschell was sent out to mollify and . . . to bring to reasonable terms the Canadians who are difficult to deal with. . . . But Lord Herschell goes far beyond them. He is making most of the trouble in the Commission; he is sharp, often violent . . . and if it had not been for him we might have done something ere this with the Canadians.

Secretary of State John Hay was told by several American delegates that

> by far the worst member of the Commission to deal with is Lord Herschell, who is more cantankerous than any of the Canadians, raises more petty points, and is harder than any of the Canadians to get along with. In fact, he is the principal obstacle to a favorable settlement.

On December 22 the *Toronto World* published a cartoon showing Herschell atop a bicycle, pedalling full speed down a steep slope and towing a small wagon wherein sat Laurier and "Dickey," presumably Sir Richard Cartwright. Laurier to Cartwright: "We'd better let go — now — Dickey before it's too late." W. C. Cartwright thought the cartoon "describes rather well the Canadian sentiment." Such was the light in which Canadian public opinion saw the strenuous efforts of Lord Herschell.

There can be no doubt that there was a good deal of truth in the American imputation that the Canadian politicians at the conference were not whole-heartedly behind the Coast Doctrine. This applies with special force to Sir Wilfrid Laurier himself. His attitude throughout the ensuing struggle for the boundary betrays a lack of inner conviction, a merely formal commitment to a popular but unrealistic cause. On February 1, 1899, Cartwright was moved to exclaim:

> Why . . . have the Canadians allowed their excellent case to lie in darkness so long? Why did they not at once ask (after the survey [of 1892-95?] was completed) that the line should be drawn? They have wasted so much time that it is now quite impossible to get the Americans out of Dyea and Skagway.

Herschell himself wrote on February 7, 1899:

> The members of the Canadian Government who are my colleagues on the Commission have exhibited a very reasonable disposition, but from what I have heard from themselves, as well as from conversations I have had with other members of the Dominion Government, it is evident to me that all the members of that Government are not actuated by an equally reasonable spirit.

And Cartwright again:

> Whatever irresponsible writers may have said, the Canadian officials and Govt. never realized till now that there was any backbone in their contention [*i.e.,* the Coast Doctrine]. They vaguely asked for a great deal more than they were entitled to, but they did not believe in their right to the Lynn Canal. It is even now difficult to persuade some of their men here that they have a good claim there, although the balance of the Cabinet at Ottawa, having heard of the windfall brought by Lord Herschell in the shape of a sound argument, are clamouring for absolute sovereignty at Pyramid Harbour.

The aggressive faction back in Ottawa appears to have been led by Justice Minister David Mills, who wrote to Laurier in January that "a concession which falls short of sovereignty is not worth taking," and by Clifford Sifton.

The Coast Doctrine was not, of course, so firmly supported as W. C. Cartwright, in his emotional loyalty to Lord Herschell, makes out. There was an amusing slip-up in the early stage of the conference, when an Interior Department expert was sent to Europe to search in the archives for historical evidence to confirm Cameron's theory. The choice fell on Otto Julius Klotz, born 1852, the son of a German immigrant. On his return the honest Klotz reported to W. F. King:

> My researches in various London Government Offices, as well as in St. Petersburg, confirm me in the conviction that the Convention of 1825 never intended to convey to Great Britain any foothold on the sea northward of Portland Canal, and the subsequent action and words of Great Britain as well as of the Hudson's Bay Company, who were at the time more interested in the question of territorial rights than the Government, show such to be the case. — In short, the boundary runs somewhere behind all the inlets.

It can be imagined that this statement was not greeted with cries of delight in Sifton's circle.

To meet British demands for territorial rights at the head of Lynn Canal, Senator Fairbanks on Christmas Eve, 1898, unwrapped what he considered a generous present — a memorandum proposing that

> there shall be granted for a period of fifty years to the British Government the occupation, use and control of the port or harbor in the Territory of Alaska known as Pyramid Harbor, on Chilkat Inlet of Lynn Canal, occupying a shore frontage of not exceeding two statute miles in width, extending from said port or harbor in a north-westerly direction along the Chilkat River and Pass to the boundary line fixed between the territory of the United States and the Dominion of Canada. The said port and strip of territory . . . shall be subject to the exclusive jurisdiction of the civil and criminal laws and authorities of the British and Canadian Governments.

Herschell countered with a demand for a hundred-year lease, or, better yet, an indefinite lease on certain conditions. The Canadians told him they were not willing to take the risk of building up a town and port and then have them fall into American hands. "The rest of the cabinet at Ottawa are urging very strongly upon Laurier that we should insist on getting the absolute sovereignty," Cartwright wrote.

Somehow the American proposal concerning Pyramid Harbor leaked out, and protests were made by the shipping interests on the

Pacific coast. On February 2 they sent a joint telegram to Senator George C. Perkins of California saying they were "very much exercised over a report that the Joint High Commission has conceded to Canada a waiving of the boundary line between Alaska and British Columbia which gives Canada a Port on Lynn Canal." President McKinley received about a hundred protest telegrams. The press in the Pacific states raised a hue and cry against concessions in the Panhandle, which echoed in Congress. "One dubious consolation," Laurier wrote, "is that if the Senate sometimes irritates us, it irritates the Secretary of State still more."

Fairbanks's proposal and Herschell's rejection of it marked the end of compromise attempts on the Panhandle boundary, and caused the breakdown of the conference. The first definite indications that the conference was foundering reached the public in the middle of February, 1899, when Sifton was hurriedly called to Washington. Until then the Alaska boundary had been almost ignored by the press in favour of other and, it seemed, weightier points on the agenda, particularly the "reciprocity" of tariffs. Suddenly the Lynn Canal and the Coast Doctrine leaped into prominence, and for the first time the Canadian public learned in detail what the Canadian claim was all about.

Writing to a friend after the breakdown of the conference on February 27, Laurier said:

> Our chief efforts . . . were directed to three subjects: The Atlantic fisheries, the Pacific seal fisheries, and the Alaska boundary. . . . The stumblingblock was the Alaska boundary. In this, our American fellow Commissioners were at first and almost to the last disposed to come to a reasonable compromise. I may tell you confidentially that the compromise was that they gave us Pyramid Harbour on the Lynn Canal with everything but the official sovereignty in name; in other words, the arrangement which we had practically concluded was that we should have Pyramid Harbour under our jurisdiction, our laws and our administration, but that if, at any moment we chose no longer to occupy it, it would revert to the United States. This arrangement provoked such a storm in the Pacific states that our fellow Commissioners withdrew their consent.

Herschell himself telegraphed to London on February 13:

Our negotiations are approaching a crisis. We seem near an agreement as to Alaska Boundary, but owing we believe to pressure from interests on Pacific Coast of America proposals as to port on the Lynn Canal have become such as require from us practical surrender of all our claim thereon.

These and similar statements gave rise to the belief that a British-American accord on Pyramid Harbor had been practically in the bag when it was torpedoed by the selfish shipping interests of San Francisco and Seattle. But it is also possible that if Herschell and Laurier had accepted Fairbanks's proposal, it would have been torpedoed by the more militant faction in the Canadian Cabinet. The question remains one of the enigmatic might-have-beens of history. Lord Herschell, recapitulating British-American differences for Senator Fairbanks, wrote on February 15:

> The American Commissioners offered us certain rights in ports on the Lynn Canal in consideration of our giving up our territorial claims around a portion of it, which however seemed insufficient.

Fairbanks himself reported to Secretary Hay:

> There would be no difficulty in agreeing upon a boundary line at all points if a harbor were ceded to the British Government at the head of Lynn Canal. . . . The British Commissioners demanded practically the perpetual occupancy of the harbor and territory mentioned. . . . However . . . if they failed to maintain peace and order, or ceased to use the territory for the purpose indicated, or should attempt to fortify or use it as a basis of military operations, it would revert to the United States. They were unwilling to put any restrictions upon the coastwise trade, and insisted the port should, for all purposes of commerce, be an English port. To this we could not agree.

The British Government was not happy with Ottawa's intransigent attitude. In the summer of 1899 the Foreign Office, at the instance of Prime Minister Lord Salisbury, wrote a long letter to Laurier describing a British enclave at the mouth of the Zambesi River in Portuguese Mozambique which gave Britain freedom to unload, store, and trans-ship its goods between the coast and British Rhodesia. It suggested that this be used as a model for a Canadian enclave at the head of Lynn Canal. Laurier, in his reply of August 17, turned the recommendation down.

> Under the terms of that treaty [of 1825] Canada has a very strong case to claim that under the most favourable construction which can be set forth by the United States, her jurisdiction over the Lynn Canal cannot extend more than ten marine leagues from the coast, and that consequently all the upper portion of the Canal, which portion is not less than fifty miles, belongs to Canada. . . . The concession suggested could hardly be held sufficient to engage Canada to surrender pretensions which, in her opinion, are tantamount to positive rights.

Secretary of State Hay made the following revelation about the situation:

> It is far more to Canada's advantage than ours to be on good terms with us. Lord Salisbury, in a private conversation the other day, compared her to a coquettish girl with two suitors, playing off one against the other. I should think a closer analogy would be to call her a married flirt, ready to betray John Bull on any occasion, but holding him responsible for all her follies.

When the conference was stalemated the British delegates proposed that the Alaska boundary be referred to arbitration by a tribunal of three, one of whom should be a neutral. Arbitration now held a particularly strong appeal for Britain, because it had only recently been forced by the United States to submit to arbitration its boundary dispute with Venezuela and thereby lost the mouth of the Orinoco. What was good for Britain and Venezuela was good for the United States, London argued. Its arguments fell on unreceptive ears. The boundary dispute between British Guiana and Venezuela was at least fifty years old, whereas the Coast Doctrine had only just been proclaimed, the American negotiators said. The only thing open to arbitration was the exact location of the inland boundary; the heads of inlets were not negotiable. The Americans also disliked the idea of a neutral arbitrator; they suggested a tribunal composed equally of American and British experts. Privately, Secretary of State Hay admitted that, after compelling Britain to submit to arbitration in regard to Venezuela, he did not feel "entirely easy" in refusing to submit to similar treatment over Alaska.

The breakdown of the conference of 1898-99 ended compromise attempts. Henceforward each side stood on its basic claim — the United States asserting that the boundary should run approximately thirty miles from the actual coast, and Canada (and Britain) asserting that it should cross every inlet that broke through the coastal mountains. The most extreme views, however, were quietly abandoned. The United States no longer suggested, as it had in 1886, that it was impossible to survey the treaty line and that the boundary would have to be redefined; and Ottawa quietly dropped the British Columbia claim. This was not noted publicly until May, 1901, when a British Columbia Member of Parliament asked in the House why a map of Canada exhibited in Paris showed the boundary running along the Portland Canal. Laurier replied that "in view of the advice we have received from our law officers, it is very hard to maintain that the boundary runs up Clarence Channel. The treaty says in so many words 'the Portland Canal'."

For Lord Herschell the conference proved fatal; shortly before it ended he slipped on a snow-covered sidewalk and fractured his hip. The illness, which did not seem serious at first, suddenly took a turn for the worse, and he died on March 1, 1899.

Canada's failure to obtain territorial possession at the head of Lynn Canal led to a *modus vivendi* established by an exchange of notes on October 20, 1899, that fixed White Pass and Chilkoot Pass as the temporary boundary.

The next few years were taken up with British-American negotiations concerning the arbitration of the boundary dispute. Two distinct problems had to be dealt with: how was the arbitration tribunal to be constituted, and what questions would it have to answer?

Washington favoured a six-man tribunal, to be composed of three "impartial jurists of repute" from each side. Ottawa, which was hampered in the negotiations by having to go through London, was prepared to agree to the six-man tribunal only if there was at least one neutral on each side, but preferred a neutral umpire in addition.

The questions to be decided presented less difficulty. The Americans at first tried to keep the head of Lynn Canal out of the arbitration by saying it would be cruel to play with the fate of the established American communities there, but when they saw that the Canadians would never agree to such a proposal they dropped it. The Americans also maintained that the tribunal should "decide" the questions, and not "compromise" them — a clear departure from the Venezuelan example. To this the British-Canadian side agreed.

The truth was that England found the time unpropitious for a quarrel with the United States, its hereditary enemy. The cautious, faltering movement toward an Anglo-German understanding had come to a halt and been reversed by irreconcilable colonial ambitions. The British-French *entente cordiale* was yet to be born. Widespread condemnation by European nations of Britain for its callous conduct of the Boer War had sent shivers down the backs of Foreign Office experts and persuaded them that it was time for Britain to leave its isolation and prepare the ground for future alliances.

The Canadians, however, were not impressed by such exigencies. They reasoned that Britain had had, in the Clayton-Bulwer Treaty, an excellent card for bargaining with the United States. This British-American compact, concluded in 1850, stipulated that neither of the two powers would seek exclusive control of any ship canal built across the Isthmus of Panama. To build the proposed Panama Canal the United States needed to be released from this obligation — a release it obtained in 1901. Ottawa could not readily forgive London for not having exacted a *quid pro quo* in favour of Canada.

As luck would have it, the White House, for the first time in history, was occupied by a genuine Anglophile, Theodore Roosevelt. Roosevelt took great personal interest in foreign politics, and it was partly due to him that the negotiations over arbitration were conducted at a leisurely pace during his first year as President to the fall of 1902. "I don't want [the Alaska boundary dispute] reopened," he wrote to a friend, "because I am friendly to England, and while the South African War is unfinished I don't want to give the

American pro-Boers a chance." His sympathies did not, however, cover what he considered the cession of indisputably American territory, and in March, 1902, he instructed the Secretary of War to send additional troops to Alaska.

The negotiations speeded up in the summer of 1902. Laurier and Lord Minto, the Governor-General of Canada, were attending a colonial conference in London and were seeking ways and means of extricating Canada from the difficult position into which it had manoeuvred itself. They sought out the American Ambassador and urged him to press in Washington for early agreement to arbitration. In return they seem to have promised Canadian acquiescence in an evenly composed tribunal. Clifford Sifton confided to John Dafoe, the editor of a newspaper Sifton owned, that before Laurier's departure for London he and some other Cabinet members had called on the Prime Minister and extracted a pledge that Laurier would not be inveigled into agreeing to a tribunal without neutral umpire. But when Laurier returned from London he admitted that he had given in to British pressure. This version, however, contrasts somewhat with subsequent Canadian Government declarations.

Be that as it may, in October, 1902, Secretary of State Hay proposed to Britain that the tribunal should merely record its "reasoned opinion" and that it should be left to both sides to implement it or not. Ottawa, being consulted, said it would consider the proposal favourably. On December 8 the British Ambassador called on Hay and went away with the impression that the United States would be willing to consider the decision of the tribunal as final and binding. This accorded with the British view. The Ambassador added in his report:

> In discussing the composition of the tribunal I expressed the hope that all the American members would be judges of the Supreme Court of the United States. . . . Mr. Hay agreed with this view, but feared it would be difficult to carry out owing to the pressure of business before the Supreme Court.

Ottawa was immediately asked by London to give its view on this new development, and replied that it needed more information. London then transmitted a draft treaty provisionally agreed on by

Britain and the United States. The draft outlined the composition
of the tribunal and the questions to be put. The Canadian Government found the questions satisfactory, but still demurred against
the tribunal, holding out for a neutral arbitrator.

Pressure now began to mount from London, to the effect that
the moment was favourable, and that "if the question is further
postponed, the Senators' attitude may change." From January 18 to
20 Governor-General Lord Minto, the official link between Ottawa
and London, received four telegrams, two from the British Ambassador and two from the Colonial Secretary, urging acceptance of the
treaty. On January 21 the Canadian Cabinet gave in.

On February 18, 1903, there arrived from London, like a bomb-
shell, the information that President Roosevelt intended to appoint
to the tribunal Secretary of War Elihu Root, Senator Henry Cabot
Lodge of Massachusetts, and Senator George Turner of Seattle,
Washington.

The Canadian Government was thunderstruck. None of the three
men could by any stretch of the imagination be considered an
"impartial jurist of repute." Their legal qualifications were on the
whole unexceptionable, but their positions and offices precluded
impartiality. Secretary Root, as an executive officer of the United
States Government, was naturally sworn to obey the directions of
the President; Senator Lodge had already publicly declared that the
Coast Doctrine was "manufactured and baseless," and for Senator
Turner to vote against the American claim was tantamount to
political suicide.

But it would be quite wrong to suppose that these appointments
constituted a gratuitous and arbitrary act on the part of President
Roosevelt. The American Cabinet was painfully aware that the
treaty of arbitration faced a great deal of opposition in the Senate.
Lodge, who acted as go-between in the matter, reported that the
senators from the Pacific North-west had called on him and told
him that they would make their assent to the treaty dependent on
satisfactory appointments to the tribunal. Roosevelt then told Lodge
he might inform the opposition, in confidence, that the American
arbitrators would be Root, Turner, and Lodge himself. On this

condition the Senate was won for the treaty.

Secretary Hay was as much shocked by the appointments as Ottawa. According to Lodge,

> When Mr. Hay heard of the three men whom the President had selected he was extremely displeased, and protested in the strongest way to the President against Mr. Root, and even more strongly against me, taking the ground that our opinions were already well known, which was also true of Senator Turner.

The Canadian Government immediately protested against the proposed American appointments, saying they would be regarded as "a violation of an important article in the treaty," and the whole situation would have to be reconsidered. London allowed that the situation was indeed "full of difficulty" but that arguments against the appointments could have no practical results.

While the Canadian Government was still steaming it learned, as Lord Minto said, "from the public press" that the treaty had been ratified by the British Government. Sifton, the man most intimately concerned, was plunged into a veritable sea of bitterness and frustration. He wrote to John Dafoe:

> As you have no doubt already sized the matter up, the British Government decided about a year ago to sacrifice our interests at any cost, for the sake of pleasing the United States. . . . The United States would not recede, and England would not take any chances of a quarrel.
>
> It is, however, the most cold-blooded case of absolutely giving away our interests, without even giving us the excuse of saying we have had a fight for it, which I know of, and I do not see any reason why the Canadian press should not make itself extremely plain on the subject. My view, in watching the diplomacy of Great Britain as affecting Canada for six years, is that it may just as well be decided in advance that practically whatever the United States demands from England will be conceded in the long run, and the Canadian people might as well make up their minds to that now.

The treaty of arbitration, which was signed in Washington on January 24, 1903, placed the following questions (here simplified) before the tribunal:

(1) Where does the boundary line start?

(2) What channel is the Portland Channel?

(3) How does the line run from the starting-point to the entrance of Portland Channel?

(4) How does the line run between the head of Portland Channel and the fifty-sixth parallel?

(5) Was it the intention of the Treaty of 1825 that there should remain in the possession of Russia a *continuous* strip of coast not exceeding ten marine leagues, separating British possessions from all inlets and waters of the ocean?

(6) If the strip was not to be continuous, how should its width be measured — from the general direction of the coast, from a line separating ocean and territorial waters, or from the heads of inlets?

(7) What, if any exist, are the mountains referred to as parallel to the coast, intended to form the boundary?

The treaty said that the decision of the tribunal would be binding on both sides, who would have to appoint scientific experts to lay down the boundary line.

As will readily be seen, the crucial question was the fifth. If it was answered in the affirmative, then the sixth question became irrelevant; if in the negative, the break-up of the strip could still be nullified by measuring it from the heads of inlets.

Roosevelt's behaviour during 1903 has made him the *bête noire* of Canadian writers, who have dwelt with relish on his shameless string-pulling and blatant bullying of the British and American statesmen involved in the arbitration. He let it be known to one and all that he expected to win the case for the United States and ordered the American members of the tribunal not to yield "on the principle." Should the tribunal fail to settle the question he would move troops into the Panhandle and would get authority from Congress "to run the line as we claim by our own people." So vehement was he that Secretary of State Hay, who favoured a more diplomatic approach, offered his resignation, which was not accepted.

Nothing, however, could be more damaging to the understanding of the Alaska boundary dispute than to confuse the lurid froth surrounding the arbitration proceedings with the solid substance.

It is all too easy to whip up emotions with selected quotations from deeply committed and biased politicians. The feelings of the participants in a historical drama are not without interest, since they may help to explain their actions. But the actions of the men of 1903 were not on trial at the arbitration. On trial were the words and actions of men who had gone before them, and nothing that the politicians of 1903 said or did can alter by one iota the issues over which they fought and which still occasionally agitate their descendants.

When Ottawa found that it would have to live with the arbitration treaty, it set about obtaining the best possible representation on the tribunal. London had previously suggested one member from Canada, but it now had to accept two. The men chosen by Laurier were Sir Louis Jetté, a retired judge of the Quebec Superior Court and now Lieutenant-Governor of the province, and Justice John Douglas Armour of the Supreme Court of Canada. When Armour died shortly after, he was replaced by Allen Bristol Aylesworth, a Toronto lawyer. Each side was also to have an agent who was to prepare and present its case, and Canada's obvious choice for that post was Clifford Sifton.

Britain named as its sole member of the tribunal Lord Alverstone, formerly Richard E. Webster. Alverstone was born in 1842 and had been a lawyer all his life, rising successively to the highest honours reserved for that profession in Britain. In 1903 he was Lord Chief Justice of England. He had eminent official qualifications for his new task, having represented Great Britain in the Bering Sea arbitration of pelagic sealing rights in 1893 and in the Venezuela boundary arbitration of 1899. The British *Dictionary of National Biography* says of him:

> It is unlikely that in thirty-two years at the bar any man ever had more work to do, or earned more money. . . . Perhaps the truest, and most modest, remark in Alverstone's *Recollections* is that throughout his life he had been favoured by good fortune. He was not a very clever man, nor a learned lawyer, nor a good speaker — either in the courts or in parliament. His equipment as an advocate consisted mainly in a splendid physique, a forcible personality, and

immense industry. As a judge he was dignified, and sitting with a jury was satisfactory, though not distinguished; but the reports will be searched in vain for judgments of his that are valuable as expositions of the law. Socially he displayed a somewhat boisterous geniality which his detractors sometimes regarded as artificial.

Throughout the spring and summer of 1903 both the American and the British-Canadian delegations to the tribunal laboured at assembling their evidence. The tribunal was scheduled to meet early in September in London, and the Canadians, finding the time insufficient, applied for a postponement, but without success. All this time the press on both sides of the Atlantic, and especially in Canada, kept arguing and prejudging the issues.

On September 3, 1903, the tribunal assembled in the diplomatic reception room of the Foreign Office. The British and American cases and counter-cases had already been delivered to it, together with atlases, and the six arbitrators were thoroughly familiar with the various issues. It remained for the counsels on both sides to explain and elaborate on the evidence, and for the members of the tribunal to ask for elucidation of obscure or contradictory points. The sessions took up eighteen days, and ended on October 20.

The transcript of the hearings forms part of the tribunal's proceedings. It contains roughly 600,000 words and makes extremely dull reading. Semantic arguments about the true or intended significance of words and phrases, in and out of context, took up a disproportionate share of the tribunal's attention. The following exchange relating to the Russian words for Portland Channel is fairly typical.

> Mr. Aylesworth: "I am told that the Russian pronoun is feminine, and might be attributable to 'land' as well as to 'line'."
> Sir Robert Finlay [British counsel]: "I am told that is so, but then the channel is masculine."
> Mr. Lodge: "The inlet is masculine."
> Sir Robert Finlay: "Yes."

Essentially, the British case was based on hermeneutics, and the United States case on history. The British — meaning the Canadians and their English associates — relied chiefly on what they considered the internal evidence of the Treaty of 1825; they were therefore accused by the Americans of playing with words and disregarding the common-sense explanations furnished by the historical circumstances. The Americans relied chiefly on the history of the treaty negotiations and the subsequent acts and statements of Russian and British diplomats, map-makers, fur-traders, and historiographers; they were therefore accused by the British of trying to obscure the language of the treaty by dragging in irrelevant and meaningless matter.

On the crucial coast question the British maintained that the inlets along the Panhandle were not considered part of the ocean by the treaty, since these terms were differentiated and not used interchangeably; that the treaty contemplated the possible and not the impossible, and since it was impossible to draw a line parallel to the deep indentations it must be drawn parallel to the general trend of the coast, disregarding deep inlets; that the principle that Britain should not have access to salt water was nowhere stated in the treaty; that, if the Russians did seek a "barrier" against the British interior, this was just as effectively provided by an interrupted strip as by an uninterrupted one; that according to universally acknowledged international usage the ocean "coast" does not include territorial waters; that the Russians wanted to guard not against British access to salt water but against British trading posts too near their own; and that there were mountains fulfilling the requirements of the treaty along which the boundary could be drawn without recourse to the ten-league limit.

British counsel also maintained that ever since the first tentative statement of the Coast Doctrine by Cameron in 1875 the inlets had been officially in dispute. He said:

> I think the Tribunal will agree with me that Major Cameron in that report showed very great prescience, because the questions I have just read out touch really upon the vital points to which so much attention has been devoted in the course of the present discussion.

Another counsel said of the same statement: "Acquiescence is impossible after that."

The Americans maintained that the chief aim of Russia in seeking a mainland strip was to create a territorial barrier against the British possessions; that the British had explicitly been given free use of rivers because no other waterways were intended to cross the strip; that Russia and the United States had exercised continuous sovereignty over the shores of all inlets; that the coastal mountain range meant to furnish the boundary did not exist and that the line must therefore run everywhere at ten marine leagues from the coast, including the heads of inlets; that the words "coast" and "ocean" were used in their common, physical sense in the treaty and not in their modern political sense; that Cameron's statements of the Coast Doctrine in 1875 had not been made known even to the Canadian Parliament, let alone the United States Government; that the Dall-Dawson conference was an informal exchange of personal views between technical experts and did not constitute an official notification of the United States Government; that the United States Government had first been notified of the Canadian claim to the heads of inlets in August, 1898.

The two sides also disputed the possession of four islands at the entrance of Portland Channel — Sitklan, Kannaghunut, Wales, and Pearse. The first two were very small, but the last two were of fair size. Their possession hinged on the question whether the channel south or north of the islands was the Portland Channel referred to by the treaty. Canada considered the islands important chiefly because they "commanded" Port Simpson, a prospective railroad terminus.

From the beginning it was widely assumed in Canada and the United States that the three Americans on the tribunal would vote in a body against all British claims, and that the two Canadians would with like unanimity vote against the American claims. The question mark was Lord Alverstone. If he voted with the Canadians there would be a draw, and no decision. If he voted with the Americans, there would be a four-to-two decision in favour of the American claims. It followed that the best Canada could hope for was a draw.

In July, 1903, Lodge had written home that nothing reasonable could be expected from the Canadian members of the tribunal, who were "perfectly stupid" and failed to see "that a disagreement deprives them of their only chance to get out of the matter creditably." As to Alverstone, he might very possibly go along with the Americans, but England being "in such mortal terror of Canada" it was more than doubtful. On September 13, after the tribunal had been sitting some days, Lodge again vented his fear that England would give in to Canada. The Canadians were "filling the newspapers with articles of the most violent kind, threatening England with all sorts of things if the decision should go against Canada."

Under the circumstances, Lord Alverstone's attitude and behaviour throughout the proceedings were of the greatest importance. He had an active social life and saw at least some of the members of the tribunal or the Canadian or American delegation almost every evening. The two opposing sides watched these comings and goings and whispered corner conversations with greedy anxiety, and the intrigues surrounding the Chief Justice would have done credit to the court of a Renaissance prince. Unfortunately it cannot be said that Alverstone was equal to the situation. Where he should have maintained Olympic detachment and reticence, he was vacillating and indiscreet. He allowed himself to be drawn into conspiratorial speculations and negotiations.

It was therefore soon evident which way the wind was blowing. On September 13, for example, Alverstone took one of the members of the Canadian delegation aside and asked him in confidence (as if any member of the delegation could be counted on to keep anything confidential from the other members) what the real attitude of the Canadian Government was. Would Canada be satisfied with a "mountain line" going around all the inlets? Would it be satisfied if the four disputed islands were compromised, with the two smaller ones going to the United States and the larger ones to Canada? Or would Canada rather see the arbitration end in a draw? The Canadian replied that he would personally prefer the mountain line and the division of the islands, but that "people were as unreasonable in Canada as elsewhere and that the inlets were the question."

On October 8 Laurier received a telegram from Sifton:

I think that Chief Justice intends joining Americans deciding in such a way as to defeat us on every point. We all think Chief Justice's intentions are unjustifiable and due to predetermination to avoid trouble with United States. Jette and Aylesworth are much exasperated and considering withdrawing from Commission.

But the participants were not the only ones in the know. Word had also leaked out to the press. On October 12 a Member rose in the Canadian House of Commons to ask the Government to comment on a dispatch in that day's *Ottawa Citizen,* which said:

> I am informed on what may be accepted as high authority that a majority of the Alaskan commission will shortly give judgment adverse to the Canadian contention. It is understood that Great Britain's representative on the commission, Lord Alverstone, has privately intimated to diplomatic and Colonial Office officials that he is convinced that a stronger case is made out by the United States, and that he intends to give judgment accordingly.

Laurier reserved comment until the next day and sent off an urgent wire to London. On October 13 he was able to inform the Commons:

> I have received a telegram from Lord Alverstone . . . : "London, October 13, 1903. There is not the slightest foundation for statement attributed to me. . . . I have made no communication of any kind to any diplomatic or colonial officials, or to any person respecting the case. The report is an absolute fabrication."

The dire predictions were confirmed on October 17 by Clifford Sifton, who telegraphed the complete decision to Laurier, three days before it was announced officially. The three Americans and Alverstone had agreed on a mountain line — a line skipping from peak to peak rather than along the legendary ranges parallel to the coast — and running around the heads of all inlets. They had also agreed on splitting up the four contested islands at the entrance of Portland Channel.

There is fairly conclusive evidence that Alverstone had intended to award all four islands to Canada — a draft to that effect had already been prepared and is still in existence — but that at the very last moment he yielded to American pressure and agreed on the split. It was rumoured that the three Americans told him that without the split they could not face their Government or their public. In this connection a letter written by the American Ambassador to Hay on October 20 is of interest:

> Our Commissioners, agent and counsel are entitled to the highest possible praise for the manner in which they have performed their duties. They have all done their very best, and the dignity and courage of Lord Alverstone's conduct must be fully appreciated by the President. On Wednesday last [October 14], when there seemed to be a tendency to a dead-lock between the Commissioners, I had an interview with Lord Lansdowne in which I pressed upon him very urgently the views of the President. . . . I left satisfied that he and Mr. Balfour would, if they had not already done so, tell Alverstone what they thought as to the necessity of agreeing upon that line, and that the present chance of settling the controversy ought not to be lost.

It is obvious that more was expected of Alverstone than dignity and courage.

The small and essentially trivial compromise over the four islands was nonetheless Alverstone's Achillean heel. The division of the islands was not supported by the documents and had not been advocated by either side. It was an obvious compromise — and the arbitration tribunal had not been set up to make compromises but "judicial" decisions. It was an accommodation, a sacrifice in the name of British-American amity; and the deduction was instantly made by most Canadian politicians and journalists that the rejection of the Canadian claim to the inlets was also a sacrifice to the superior interests of Britain.

Laurier, replying to Sifton's telegram, dwelt only on the islands, saying that these should certainly have gone to Canada, thereby revealing his doubt as to Canada's claim to the inlets.

When the award was published on October 20, it was signed only by Alverstone and the Americans. Aylesworth and Jetté had refused to sign, and submitted dissenting opinions. Aylesworth stated that the majority decision concerning the four islands was not a decision on judicial principles, but a compromise, and "a grotesque travesty of justice." Jetté wrote that the division of the islands was "totally unsupported either by argument or authority, and was, moreover, illogical."

The phrases with which Aylesworth and Jetté rejected the majority decision on the inlets were moderate by comparison, and although they submitted lengthy arguments on that point they never suggested that the decision was not "judicial."

Alverstone was deeply offended by the vehement language with which Aylesworth and Jetté had condemned his decisions. He wrote to them about it, and they wrote back. Aylesworth told him: "I believe that your only motive in it all was the one you gave us — that you knew unless you did these things there could be no award, and you could not view such a result as other than an international calamity." The two Canadians also issued a press release, in which they said: "We have been compelled to witness the sacrifice of the interests of Canada, powerless to prevent it."

Strong as their language was, it was nothing but a *moderato* prelude to the *molto furioso* clamour raised by the Canadian politicians and the press. The latter in particular indulged in an orgy of Anglophobia that is still unsurpassed in Canadian history. The *Toronto Globe* said, "Canadian interests have been sacrificed by Lord Alverstone." The *Vancouver Province* wrote, "Led like a lamb to slaughter." "Canadian independence may eventually be arbitrated away," was the premonition of the *Halifax Herald*. "Surrender our rights on the altar of expediency," proclaimed the *Winnipeg Tribune*. The *Victoria Colonist*, closest to the territory affected, spoke for most Canadian newspapers when it expressed

> ungovernable rage that the commission should have come to a decision in which . . . the rights of the contending parties have been entirely overlooked, and the diplomatic relations between Great Britain and the United States alone regarded. . . . This unfortunate commission, unfortunate in its inception, unfortunate in its constitution, and doubly unfortunate in its result, has raised questions of the gravest and deepest import which Canada will meet overflowing with loyalty to Canada.

A theatre audience in Vancouver drowned out the playing of "God Save the King" with jeers and catcalls, and "Alverstone" became a dirty word. (Aylesworth himself, however, went out of his way to reassert his loyalty as a British subject.) Summing up these feelings, Sifton wrote: "It is beyond a question that the cold-blooded and somewhat supercilious conduct of our English friends has had a profound effect upon Canadian public opinion." And he drew a conclusion which was being made by many others: "I regard it as out of the question that the representation of Canada as it exists to-day will be content to do business in the way in which it has been done . . . a somewhat radical adjustment will have to be made."

In the House of Commons, Laurier was measured and restrained, but his words had a heavy import.

> I have often regretted also that we have not in our own hands the treaty-making power, which would enable us to dispose of our own affairs. . . . We have no such power, our hands are tied to a large extent owing to the fact of our connection — the fact of our connection with the mother country making us not free agents. . . . The difficulty, as I conceive it to be, is that as long as Canada remains a dependency of the British Crown the present powers that we have are not sufficient for the maintenance of our rights.

This was heady, almost rebellious stuff. Although the English press showed a good deal of sympathy with Canada's plight, Laurier's statement was difficult to swallow. It was, the *London Globe* huffed, "not compatible with that perfect loyalty to England which the Mother Country has a right to expect from all Colonial Prime Ministers." The *Manchester Guardian*, refraining from outright criticism, pointed out that though the emancipation demanded by Canada might still be compatible with strong imperial ties, "it would involve something of a constitutional revolution and the setting up of a colonial ideal in opposition to the Imperial ideal." The London *Times* thought it could not but lead in the end to separation.

Lord Alverstone, who was as garrulous after the award as before, sent a long explanation of his decision to Sir Wilfrid Laurier. (This contrasted somewhat with his declaration that if the judges of England had to "explain and justify their conduct by public utterances and by public argument, a death-blow would be struck at the confidence in judicial decisions.") Laurier replied that while he did not doubt Alverstone's good intentions he still could not view the award as a judicial one. This irritated the Chief Justice, and he retorted that Laurier had no right to make such imputations.

The American press, with the exception of the Pacific Coast papers, had throughout 1903 shown a tolerant if condescending attitude, on the theory that Canada could not win, and that politeness cost nothing. This carried over after the announcement of the award. The *New York Times,* the *New York Sun,* and the *Baltimore Sun* thought that Lord Alverstone had acted fairly and courageously, and that the Canadian members of the tribunal were being unfair — a feeling expressed in one way or another by many other papers.

President Roosevelt in his annual message to Congress welcomed the award as "satisfactory in every way. . . . It has furnished a signal proof of the fairness and goodwill with which two friendly nations can approach and determine issues involving national sovereignty, and by their nature incapable of submission to a third power for adjudication."

Such were the effects of the Alaska boundary dispute. The questions on which it turned are a different matter. They must be answered on the basis of the Treaty of 1825, and there is no doubt whatever that the United States was right when it claimed that the treaty had conceded to Russia, and thus to the United States, an unbroken strip of mainland coast from the mouth of Portland Channel to the 141st meridian. When the treaty-makers of 1825 spoke of "sinuosities of the coast" they meant just that; and when they spoke of the "coast" they meant the physical coast and not the abstract, artificial construct of the Canadian claim. The maps on which the treaty-makers relied are known and have survived; chief among them are Captain Vancouver's charts and some Russian Admiralty charts. They show the legendary mountains, supposed to form the boundary, running at a distance of about twenty miles from the coast around the heads of all inlets. All British maps up to 1887, at least, show the boundary sweeping around all inlets.

To imply, as the Canadian claim did, that the map-makers had for over sixty years misinterpreted the Treaty of 1825 without being corrected by anyone; that Russia had bargained so tenaciously for the longest possible mainland strip only to leave in the hands of Britain every desirable harbour on that coast and to content itself with the useless promontories; that the Hudson's Bay Company expedition of 1834 was prepared laboriously to work its way up the Stikine in open boats lowered from the *Dryad* when the ship could have sailed freely up any inlet into British territory; that the treaty would make a special point of conceding to Britain the right to navigate the rivers without mentioning the "territorial" inlets — all this deserves only one description: it was absurd.

Alverstone, despite his human frailties, had rendered a just judgment on the land boundary; and that, after all, was all that could reasonably and fairly be expected of him. The same cannot with like assurance be said of the United States. True, its stand was just — but was it wise? Was it necessary to wound Canadian sensibilities by so much gratuitous overkill?

These are intangibles, and factual analysis alone cannot answer them. Theodore Roosevelt behaved according to his character. There is no indication that he or his close advisers felt any particular animosity toward Canada. One certainly shudders to think how he would have behaved had his opponent in Alaska been William II of Germany. It was a time of unabashed imperialism, and America, fresh from the glorious battlefields of Cuba and the Philippines, lusted for larger rings to throw its hat in. It would not have long to wait.

And Canada? It fought a brave fight at the conference tables, and a tenacious one, and through it all it gained in stature and maturity. But the sympathetic observer cannot help wishing that on this first jousting in the international arena its lance had borne aloft a worthier oriflamme than that odd thing of gall and gossamer which Donald Cameron had woven in the cabalistic laboratory of his mind.

CHAPTER SIX

The Long, Long Vista

The sun rises over Turning-point 15. Turning-point 15 is in 44°46'36.11" north latitude and 66°54'11.32" west longitude. It is the eastern terminus of the Canada-United States boundary.

From the time the sun rises over Turning-point 15 until it first shines on Monument No. 1, where the 141st meridian strikes the Arctic Ocean, almost five hours pass.

In the first of those five hours day comes to the St. Croix River and tiny Dochet Island in that river, where the remnants of de Monts's camp still bear witness to his voyage of discovery four and a half centuries ago, and to the true identity of the river. No longer are there any doubts about which of the two — Schoodic or Magaguadavic — is the true St. Croix, and the name "Schoodic" no longer appears on maps. Up the meandering St. Croix the boundary runs, always through water, until it comes out on dry land at the river's source. That is the start of the north line, a long arrow pointing northward still toward some legendary highlands it was destined not to reach, for it is cut short by the St. John River.

The boundary follows the middle of the river to the mouth of its tributary the St. Francis. This is one of the world's most beautiful river valleys, but not one of the richest. The excitement of history-in-the-making is gone, and the ghostly memories of Sir John Harvey the impetuous Lieutenant-Governor, the puritanical politicos of Maine, and that flamboyant peacemaker General Winfield Scott are ignored by the staid potato farmers on both sides of the river. The French tongue is still heard, not only on the north but also on the south bank, and in the plain Roman Catholic churches on the United States side the plaques honouring the war dead are heavily French.

Up and down the barren highlands wanders the boundary, until it drops into the head-waters of the Connecticut River. This remote and picturesque corner, once the plaything of land speculators and narrow-eyed politicians, is now proclaimed "a fisherman's paradise." On the Canadian side the French tide has come down from the St. Lawrence, lapping across the border, but in the valleys of the old Indian Stream territory and in the town of Canaan, Vermont, descendants of the stalwart pioneers of 1835 still live and chuckle occasionally over the picayune passions of their ancestors.

Rouses Point on Lake Champlain, for whose sake the false forty-fifth-parallel boundary was retained, never came to serve its military purpose and is now a tourist attraction. Soon after that the water boundary begins at St. Regis, through the St. Lawrence River, carefully avoiding all islands. Here, where boundary commissioners and their surveyors once fêted the local gentry, grain and ore carriers now glide in and out of the locks and channels of the St. Lawrence Seaway.

An hour after the sun has risen over Grand Manan it touches the waters of western Lake Erie and shores once polluted with fever, and now with industrial waste. The islands in the Detroit River over which Peter Porter and Anthony Barclay haggled are now used for recreation by visitors from both shores. The channel east of Sugar Island in the St. Mary River — a channel demanded and finally obtained by the United States because it was the navigable one — has long since been abandoned by shipping in favour of the western dredged channel.

The boundary runs up the Pigeon River, snakes through a maze of lakes and watercourses, and descends gently with the Rainy River to the Lake of the Woods with its American enclave. It is an area of flour and lumber mills and summer people, bearing no resemblance to the old French enclave of Chandermagore in India, as Cameron feared it would, where thieves and refugees organized "illegal proceedings."

In its third and fourth hour the sun follows the sweep of the boundary across the Prairies and the Rockies to the Pacific. If a man stands on an elevation in the Rocky Mountains he can see the gentle arc of the boundary rising and dipping with the land. From then on there are mountains all the way, cut by north-south valleys, until the alluvial plain of the Fraser River meets the Strait of Georgia. Here the people of British Columbia and Washington have done their best to erase the line drawn under Polk and Peel. A Peace Arch overlooks the boundary where the big highway between Vancouver and Seattle passes, carrying an unending stream of visitors north and south. Point Roberts, the American peninsula cut off from the Canadian mainland by the forty-ninth parallel, is inhabited chiefly by Canadian cottage owners.

The San Juan Islands, where Harney, Douglas, Baynes, Hornby, Pickett, and Scott measured each other's mettle, advertise themselves as "the marine wonderland of the North-west". The Island of San Juan itself boasts a population of eighteen hundred, 150 miles of road, one liquor store (licensed), a high school, churches, lodges (including a branch of the Western Washington English Springer Spaniel Club), a year-round open season on domestic rabbits gone wild, a scenic drive for the tourist that takes in the remnants of the British and American camps, and, thanks to its "sea level altitude, temperate climate, relatively high humidity, and quiet natural surroundings," proclaims itself "an ideal place for victims of heart disease, high blood pressure and diseases of tension." Its inhabitants are noted for longevity.

The fifth hour of the sun's travel belongs wholly to the Alaska boundary, from Cape Muzon on the southern tip of Dall Island to the Beaufort Sea. The Stikine River, now secure in its spelling, still serves as an entrance to the British Columbia interior, but Laketon of Bricktop Martin fame is no more. Where once the North-West Mounted Police stood guard on chilly, wind-swept White Pass, entrance to the fabled Yukon, the trains of the White Pass and Yukon Route now roll past, their tourist passengers gazing at the steep climb from Skagway to the pass and trying vainly to re-create in their imagination the struggling line of men and beasts that made the area memorable in the late eighteen-nineties. But if the gold-rush is now but a nostalgic memory, the boundary dispute which it fed is still capable of rousing strong feelings in many Canadians, and Alverstone has not been forgotten or forgiven.

The length of the Canada-United States boundary is 5,526 miles (8,893 kilometers). Of this, 3,145 miles are on land, and 2,381 on water. The boundary is marked and referenced by approximately 8,100 monuments and range marks, the number changing slightly from year to year. It consists of 10,311 straight courses; there are no curves in the boundary. These courses vary greatly: the shortest, in the Quebec-Maine highlands, is 23½ inches long; the longest is 647.1 miles. That, of course, is the 141st-meridian boundary separating Alaska and the Yukon Territory. Wherever the boundary runs through wooded areas — 1,353 miles — a twenty-foot strip, or "vista," is kept open.

This orderly state of boundary delimitation and demarcation did not come about by happenstance, nor would it long endure if it did not receive constant professional care at the hands of the International Boundary Commission.

The commission was created pursuant to the Treaty of February 24, 1925. A bilateral boundary commission had actually existed since 1908, but it was temporary. It was in 1925 that it was made permanent. The treaty said:

> . . . Whereas boundary monuments deteriorate and at times are destroyed or damaged; and boundary vistas become closed by the growth of timber;
> And whereas changing conditions require from time to time that the boundary be marked more precisely and plainly by the establish-

ment of additional monuments or the relocation of existing monuments;

The Contracting Parties . . . hereby agree that the Commissioners appointed under the provisions of the Treaty of April 11, 1908, are hereby jointly empowered and directed: to inspect the various sections of the boundary line . . . at such times as they shall deem necessary; to repair all damaged monuments and buoys; to relocate and rebuild monuments which have been destroyed; to keep the boundary vistas open; to move boundary monuments to new sites and establish such additional monuments and buoys as they shall deem desirable; to maintain at all times an effective boundary line between the United States and the Dominion of Canada and between Alaska and the Dominion of Canada, as defined by the present Treaty and Treaties heretofore concluded, or hereafter to be concluded; and to determine the location of any point of the boundary which may become necessary in the settlement of any question that may arise between the two Governments.

Since that time, there have been boundary commissioners in Ottawa and Washington, each with a small office and survey staff. And since that time, the boundary monuments and the boundary vista have been kept in repair.

The commission grew in stages.

Early in 1904 — a few months after the Alaska Boundary Tribunal had given its award — commissioners were appointed by Britain and the United States for the "delimitation" of the boundary. They were W. F. King for Britain and Otto Hilgard Tittmann for the United States. Tittmann, born in Illinois in 1850, was on the staff of the United States Coast and Geodetic Survey. He was a highly skilled surveyor and invented various instruments and methods. Lord Alverstone and his three American colleagues on the tribunal had designated a number of mountain peaks as defining the boundary of the Alaska Panhandle (or, more exactly, Alverstone had designated the peaks and the Americans had accepted them). The peaks were each marked with the letter "S" on maps drawn up after the survey of 1892-95. In this series of peaks there was, however, a 120-mile gap in the approximate middle of the Panhandle, where the surveys had not been carried far enough east to provide sufficient information. This gap was filled by King and

Tittmann, who then proceeded to survey and mark the boundary on the ground.

The survey and demarcation of the Panhandle boundary took approximately ten years, and was essentially completed in 1914, although an additional survey was undertaken in 1920 north of the head of Portland Canal because of mining activity in that area. The work was done by Canadian and American parties working separately, though usually accompanied by attachés, or observers, from the opposite side. In comparison with earlier boundary surveys the parties working on the Alaska boundary were small, usually from one to two dozen men. Had there been more of these parties in the field the survey and demarcation would have been finished sooner, but time was not pressing. The Klondike gold-rush had already burned itself out by the time the survey started, and expected rushes into adjacent areas did not develop. The Alaska survey thus turned out to be not only the last but also the longest of all Canada-United States boundary surveys, even if the survey of the Great Lakes boundary under Articles 6 and 7 of the Treaty of Ghent is reckoned as a single operation.

In 1906, two years after the establishment of the Panhandle Boundary Commission, Britain and the United States agreed to charge that commission also with the survey and demarcation of the 141st-meridian boundary from Mt. St. Elias to the Arctic Ocean. This task was completed in 1913, earlier than the Panhandle survey.

The smallness of the parties labouring on the two sections of the Alaska boundary was due not only to the lack of pressure for early completion, but to the extremely rugged terrain and climate, in which it would have been dangerous to let loose larger numbers of generally inexperienced men. The entire course of the boundary was mountainous; the mountains were high, their sides steep and usually covered with snow or ice; there were practically no roads, and the swiftly rushing rivers were in most cases the only transportation routes from the coast to the boundary.

The hardships and dangers the survey parties had to face and overcome read almost like a catalogue of terrors culled from an adventure story for boys. Canoes overturned in the creeks and rivers, usually with the loss of the entire cargo, though not, fortunately, of lives; one such accident might wipe out the labour of many weeks. Horses brought in from "the outside" had to winter in the open; sometimes the entire stock perished, sometimes it survived. Rock-slides would thunder down unexpectedly from the mountainsides, and on one occasion a party saved itself only by pressing close to the rock face, watching its canoe and all its equipment being buried under tons of rock.

Where glaciers came down to the seashore, great care had to be taken in navigation, for enormous blocks of ice would sometimes break off from the glacier face and tumble into the sea, setting off veritable tidal waves. One such wave washed away a canoe secured on a ledge fully thirty-five feet above high water. Another danger to small craft navigating the inlets was thawing icebergs. These placid-looking masses of ice floating in the water might at any moment shift their center of gravity and turn over, sending out tremendous waves.

The surveyors and their helpers had to become alpinists; they equipped themselves with spiked boots, rope, and alpenstocks and traversed glaciers and scaled peaks never before seen by man. They started up the rivers as soon as the ice had broken up — sometimes there would still be ice in August. In one case a canoe party, caught in swirling ice that barred access to either shore, had to stand in the frigid, swiftly flowing water for two hours, hanging on to their boats and warding off ice floes, until they managed to drag themselves and their equipment to shore.

The weather was nearly always miserable right through summer, with drizzle, fog, overcast, and unseasonable snowstorms. One such storm caught a party in the middle of August, and although there were three men huddling in a tent with a brightly burning oil lamp the temperature would not rise above freezing. In 1912 parties working at the northern end of the Panhandle were showered with fine volcanic dust from an eruption of Mount Katmai, six hundred miles to the west. The dust not only interfered with visibility, but aggravated skin irritation caused by scratches and mosquito bites. Parties nearing the Arctic coast were bedevilled by marvellous and awesome mirages, and one pack train made a detour of many miles along a lake that was not there.

Considering all this it is something of a surprise that only three men lost their lives during ten years of surveying. All three were Canadians. The first fatality occurred in June, 1909, on a glacier east of Endicott Arm. The Boundary Commission report describes the accident as follows:

> At the summit of Bird Mountain, on the north side of Brown Glacier, the drifting snow had formed a cornice that overhung a precipice above the South Sawyer Glacier. During the progress of the observations the recorder, Joseph Shepard of Nanaimo, despite previous warnings, walked too close to the edge of the cornice. The cornice broke, carrying Shepard with it to the glacier 2,000 feet below. Although the body was seen on the glacier there was no way to get down to it from the mountain. Later a party reached the locality from Tracy Arm, but more snow had broken off Bird Mountain and swept the body into a very deep crevasse.

Shepard's body was never recovered.

In 1913 a Canadian party was surveying the water boundary from Cape Muzon to the entrance of Portland Canal. Lights were set up at the stations to be observed, one of them at Cape Chacon, the southern tip of Prince of Wales Island. Two men, G. R. Roberts and C. H. Bode, were left to tend the light, and were apparently surprised by a large landslide in their tents, during the night of September 6-7. It took some time before the accident became known, and efforts to dig out the dead men failed. Cruel Alaska claimed its victims in death as well.

There was one curious geographical discovery: the survey teams found that the design of excluding Canada from salt water along the entire Panhandle was being foiled by a quirk of nature. In Tarr Inlet, the Grand Pacific Glacier, which descends into the sea from the north-westernmost corner of British Columbia, was retreating across the border, permitting the sea to flow into Canada. The glacier has been retreating and advancing ever since, but no practical use has yet come to Canada from this uncertain breach in the Panhandle barrier.

The Panhandle survey started from the area north of Lynn Canal and gradually spread to other areas. The 141st-meridian survey started from the Yukon River and worked its way north and south. The point where the meridian crosses the Yukon was determined by telegraph in 1906, and it was found that William Ogilvie's determination in the winter of 1887-88, made by observations of the moon, was in error by only 218 feet — less than one-third second of time, a remarkable achievement. The Arctic Ocean was reached in the summer of 1912, and the occasion was ceremoniously observed on July 18. Mount St. Elias, which had been considered the point of juncture of the two parts of the Alaska boundary, turned out to be east of the 141st meridian.

The boundary parties placed bronze cones and plaques to mark the boundary wherever convenient and practicable, and cut vistas through the forests in the valleys. Some peaks defining the boundary could not be climbed, and the surveyors had to content themselves with fixing their co-ordinates through triangulation and photographs. Photography played an extremely important role in the boundary surveys, and many mountains could be identified only from photographs.

While King and Tittmann were still directing the Alaska surveys, new tasks had been given to them. On April 11, 1908, a treaty was signed in Washington by representatives of Britain and the United States providing for the re-survey and demarcation of the entire Canada-United States boundary from the Atlantic to the Pacific. The treaty also provided for the extension of the boundary through Passamaquoddy Bay. King and Tittmann were placed in charge of all sections, except that from the forty-fifth parallel through Lake Superior, *i.e.*, that portion covered by Articles 6 and 7 of the Treaty of Ghent, with the exception of the line west of Lake Superior. This section was to be covered by the existing International Waterways Commission.

The Waterways Commission had been created in 1905 to regulate the use, by Canada and the United States, of the Great Lakes system for transportation, fishing, and other purposes. It was headed by two co-chairmen, George C. Gibbons for Canada and

O. H. Ernst for the United States. They in turn delegated the work of boundary survey and demarcation to two commissioners, William J. Stewart and Eugene E. Haskell. Stewart was then head of the Canadian Hydrographic Survey, and Haskell was dean of the College of Civil Engineering at Cornell University. They carried out their task from 1908 to 1913. The International Waterways Commission rendered its report on the boundary survey in 1915, when it became defunct, being replaced by the International Joint Commission. The maintenance of the Great Lakes boundary was taken over by the commissioners for the other sections of the Canada-United States boundary.

The Treaty of 1908 stated that the sections of the boundary through Passamaquoddy Bay, through the Great Lakes system, and through the Gulf of Georgia and Juan de Fuca Strait should consist of straight courses. The surveyors therefore eliminated all curves from the boundary line in those sections, substituting straight lines and angles. They adhered as closely as possible to the old line, and for all practical purposes the elimination of curves involved no change in the boundary itself. A boundary of straight courses had the great advantage of being definable and recoverable entirely without maps.

Although they were not required to do so by the Treaty of 1908, they also eliminated the curves on the other sections of the international boundary, with the exception of the prairie boundary from Lake of the Woods to the Rocky Mountains, where Cameron's stubborn legacy of absolute curvature still held good.

The field work under the Treaty of 1908 was completed by the early nineteen-twenties. The last section to be finished was that from the source of the St. Croix River to the St. Lawrence River.

By that time both King and Tittmann had been succeeded by other men, starting a line of succession that continues to this day.

In the course of their work the boundary commissioners and their surveyors had arrived at certain definite conclusions, which they communicated to their governments. They had experienced at first hand the perishability of boundary monuments, and the rapidity with which forest growth obliterated boundary vistas. (In

1890, for instance, an inspection of the Quebec-New York boundary showed that of 130 monuments set in 1845 by Estcourt and Smith, only ten still remained firmly in place.) They had also had to cope with the carelessness and cupidity of settlers along the boundary, and their efforts to obliterate the line.

The outcome of this was the Treaty of 1925, which has already been cited. Apart from establishing a permanent International Boundary Commission, that treaty also eliminated two awkward hold-overs from the days of Cameron and Archibald Campbell on the prairie boundary.

In a belated official repudiation of Cameron's idealized curve, the treaty said that

> whereas the average distance between adjacent monuments as thus established or re-established along the 49th parallel of north latitude from Lake of the Woods to the summit of the Rocky Mountains by the Commissioners acting under . . . the Treaty of 1908 is one and one-third miles and therefore the deviation of the curve of the 49th parallel from a straight or right line is . . . only one-third of a foot, and in no case does the actual deviation exceed one and eight-tenths feet;
>
> And whereas it is impracticable to determine the course of a line having the curvature of a parallel of 49° north latitude on the ground between the adjacent monuments,

the boundary between adjacent monuments should consist of straight lines.

In a little tit-for-tat the United States agreed to the elimination of its two useless water areas just south of the North-west Angle of the Lake of the Woods, created by the intersection of the meandering north line by the straight south line. The two areas measured only 2½ acres. This had the effect of moving the North-west Angle 4,800 feet to the south. (It did not, of course, in any way affect the American peninsula in the Lake of the Woods.)

The Treaty of 1925 was the last important international agreement concerning the Canada-United States boundary. It was also the first such instrument negotiated and concluded by the Canadian Government itself, rather than by the British Government on behalf of Canada. Since that time, London has been out of the picture as far as the boundary is concerned, and all boundary matters are dealt with entirely between Ottawa and Washington.

Each of the two governments appoints its own commissioner, who in turn is in charge of his own office and staff. At this writing, the Canadian boundary commissioner is A. F. Lambert, and the United States commissioner is E. J. King. Lambert, who graduated in mathematics and physics from Queen's University, Kingston, Ontario, spent several years as a surveyor with the Geodetic Survey of Canada and with the International Boundary Commission before being appointed commissioner in 1957. King was a labour-union official before his appointment in 1961.

The staff of each commissioner is small. That of the Canadian commissioner consists of three engineers, one draftsman, and one typist. It is augmented every summer by several student surveyors, cooks, and some sixteen labourers. The United States commission employs approximately the same number of persons. The Canadian commission is incorporated administratively into the Surveys and Mapping Branch of the federal Department of Mines and Technical Surveys, but is politically responsible to the Secretary of State for External Affairs. The United States commission is entirely responsible to the Secretary of State. The administrative expenses and the salaries of each commission are paid separately by each government, but boundary maintenance expenses are shared equally.

Every summer the two commissions go into the field. Their main task is the clearing of the boundary vista of young tree growth. The commission has found that to keep the vista reasonably clear it is necessary that the wooded portion be gone over every ten years, *i.e.,* 10% per year, or thirty miles per crew. Since 1958 the commission has experimented with various growth-retarding chemicals, sprayed from the ground or from the air. It expects that these innovations will make it possible to cover the boundary every four years, each crew clearing one hundred miles in one season.

Another of the commission's tasks is the maintenance of monuments. Although the commissioners have in recent times tried to standardize monuments, there is still great variety in shapes, sizes, and materials. This will no doubt continue for a long time, and reflects the piecemeal definition and demarcation of the boundary. Most monuments now consist of a concrete base bearing a shaft of reinforced concrete, granite, cast iron, or aluminum-bronze, four to five feet tall. At official border crossings the commissioners have set up twin monuments 5½ feet high with a washed pebble finish. Where monuments are impractical, as on international bridges and in international tunnels, the boundary is marked by bronze plaques.

Although the Treaty of 1908 made many references to buoys along water boundaries, it was soon found that demarcation of the boundary in the water was impractical. At present the boundary is marked by buoys only at the western end of Lake Erie, where it cuts through busy fishing-grounds.

One of the commission's most irksome problems has been the encroachments of settlers and public utilities on the boundary. Contrary to fairly common belief, the land immediately adjoining the boundary does not constitute a "neutral" strip. Until recent years no restrictions whatever were placed on its use. The results were often curious, and sometimes dramatic.

East of the Great Lakes, for example, where both the boundary and the settlements are relatively old, numerous properties straddled the line, and there were a good number of "line houses" — farms, homes, stores, and other buildings that were partly in Canada and partly in the United States. A number of monuments had to be placed in farmyards, on or beside porches, in fences, and other unlikely spots, and their fatality rate was high. Residents of line houses were well aware of their special opportunities as far as customs duties were concerned, and did not hesitate to take advantage of them. They did, however, have to contend with a law which made the house subject to confiscation if smuggled goods were found in it. Strictly interpreted, this might mean that a family was precluded from moving an American refrigerator from its American kitchen into its Canadian pantry.

In 1908 the United States Government, by presidential proclamation, reserved all public lands within sixty feet of the Canada-United States boundary from any use other than public highways, and various Canadian provinces took similar action. This did not affect lands already in private hands, and this was the case with most of the land east of the Great Lakes.

Line houses were in their heyday during the period of prohibition in the United States, when many of them would contain bars, with the liquor on the Canadian side and the thirsty customers lining up on the American side of the room.

In 1935 the commission made a survey of the situation and found that there were still over a hundred line houses. They included "dwelling houses, sheds, barns, stables, henhouses, storehouses, garages, stores of various kinds, factories, hotels, post offices, and even one building which has been and perhaps still is used as a jail." There were no legal provisions for preventing anyone owning land on the boundary from erecting any sort of structure thereon or from putting it to any lawful use. In so far as line houses were concerned, the provision of the Treaty of 1925 concerning the boundary vista was inoperative.

This state of affairs was remedied in 1960 when the Canadian Parliament passed an Act which prohibited the erection of line houses or any similar obstruction in that half of the vista belonging to Canada. The act, entitled International Boundary Commission Act, states:

> Except with the permission of the Commission, no person shall
> (a) construct or place within ten feet of the boundary any work or any addition to a work, or
> (b) enlarge any work that is, at the time of the coming into force of this Act, within ten feet of the boundary.

The Act defines "work" as "any ditch, earthwork, building or structure of any description or any lines of telephone, telegraph or power, including posts, piers, or abutments for sustaining or protecting the wires or cables of those lines."

The Act also authorizes the Boundary Commission to enter upon private property to carry out its lawful work, and to remove and destroy any work erected contrary to the provisions of the Act. Anyone who contravenes these provisions, or who damages a boundary monument, is liable to a fine of five hundred dollars or six months' imprisonment, or both.

It will be noted that the Act does not affect line houses that were in existence in 1960.

Probably the most substantial and impressive line house still standing is a combined theatre and library in the twin Canadian-American city of Rock Island-Derby Line, straddling the boundary between Quebec and Vermont, an area where the boundary is so cluttered with buildings that it is difficult to tell whether one is in Canada or the United States. The library and theatre has its front entrance in the United States, while most of the books are in Canada. The theatre, on the upper floor, has its stage in Canada and its audience in the United States. During World War II a rope was strung through the theatre to mark the boundary, but such unneighbourly restrictions have since disappeared.

Too much international co-operation and fraternization still pose the odd problem for the Boundary Commission. Service clubs in cities along the boundary are fond of erecting "friendship monuments" in the boundary vista, a practice that is discouraged, and flying clubs in the Prairies see the boundary as the ideal location for landing-fields, if only a few boundary monuments were razed.

The International Boundary Commission possesses 255 large-scale maps of the boundary. The history of the boundary, the pertinent treaties, a description of field work, and tables of co-ordinates for monuments and other points are contained in eight volumes. Seven of them, bound in green cloth and handsomely printed on glossy paper with numerous illustrations, were compiled and published by the International Boundary Commission itself; one volume, much more modest and containing little beyond technical information, was published by the International Waterways Commission. It covers the boundary from the St. Lawrence River through Lake Superior — a section which is, in a sense, the stepchild of boundary history. (The books referred to will be found in the bibliography.)

The Canadian and United States commissioners each year submit reports on their operations to the Canadian Secretary of State for

External Affairs and the United States Secretary of State, respectively. The Canadian commission's activities are also briefly described
in the annual reports of the Department of Mines and Technical
Surveys. Here, for example, is the report for 1963:

> The Commissioners for Canada and the United States made a
> joint inspection of various points on the international boundary
> along the provinces of New Brunswick, Quebec, Ontario, and
> Manitoba. They also inspected the work of two United States
> parties and two Canadian parties carrying out maintenance oper-
> ations along the boundary.
>
> A Canadian party working along the New Brunswick-Maine
> and the Quebec-Maine boundaries applied chemicals to retard
> growth, on 100 miles of 20-foot boundary vista. The Commission
> eventually expects to maintain much of the boundary vistas through
> the use of chemicals.
>
> A second Canadian party was engaged on the Manitoba-North
> Dakota boundary, where 40 miles of 20-foot boundary vista were
> recleared and chemically treated through the Turtle and Pembina
> Mountains. A number of boundary monuments found disturbed by
> construction work along the Manitoba boundary were relocated.
>
> Tests were again carried out on the control of vista growths
> through the use of chemicals applied by helicopter. These tests were
> applied on mountainous sections of the British Columbia-
> Washington boundary, where ground operations are difficult.
>
> Inspections of reference monuments along the St. Clair and St.
> Lawrence rivers, and position checks of boundary buoys in Lake
> Erie, were also carried out during the season.
>
> In all, 220 miles of boundary and 440 monuments were
> inspected, 40 miles of boundary vista were recleared, 160 miles
> chemically treated to retard growth, and 12 monuments repaired
> or relocated during the 1963 field season.

And there the Canada-United States boundary rests, as definite
and durable as the minds of men can make it — which is to say, as
definite and durable as the minds of men.

SELECTED BIBLIOGRAPHY

Readers who wish to learn more about the genesis of the Canada-United States boundary can obtain a good grasp of the subject from the publications listed below. For a more detailed study, original sources, such as unpublished correspondence and published British and United States state papers, will have to be consulted. It should be noted that the publications listed under "General" may in some cases contain more detail than those listed under the chapter headings.

GENERAL

Bemis, Samuel F., (ed.), *The American Secretaries of State and their Diplomacy*. New York, 1928.

Miller, Hunter, *Treaties and Other International Acts of the United States of America*. Washington, various years.

Moore, John Bassett, *History and Digest of the International Arbitrations to which the United States has been a Party*, Vol. I. Washington, 1898.

Nicholson, N. L., *The Boundaries of Canada, Its Provinces and Territories*. Ottawa, 1954.

Paullin, C. O., *Atlas of the Historical Geography of the United States*. Washington, 1932.

White, James, *Boundary Disputes and Treaties*. Toronto, 1914.

CHAPTER I
(From the Atlantic Ocean to the St. Lawrence River)

Bemis, S. F., *John Quincy Adams and the Foundations of American Foreign Policy*. New York, 1949.

Brown, Roger Hamilton, *The Struggle for the Indian Stream Territory*. Cleveland, 1955.

Burrage, Henry S., *Maine in the Northeastern Boundary Controversy*. Portland, 1919.

Ganong, William F., "Monograph on the Evolution of the Boundaries of the Province of New Brunswick," *Trans. Royal Soc. Canada*, 1901, Section II, pp. 139-449.

International Boundary Commission, *Joint Report upon the Survey and Demarcation of the Boundary between the United States and Canada from the Source of the St. Croix River to the Atlantic Ocean*. Washington, 1934.

————, *Joint Report upon the Survey and Demarcation of the Boundary between the United States and Canada from the Source of the St. Croix River to the St. Lawrence River*. Washington, 1925.

Lowenthal, David, "The Maine Press and the Aroostook War," *Can. Hist. Rev.*, 32:315-36, December, 1951.

Reid, R. L., "The Indian Stream Territory," *Trans. Royal Soc. Canada*, 1940, Section II, pp. 143-71.

Scott, Winfield, *Memoirs*. New York, 1864.

Sprague, J. F., *The North-Eastern Boundary Controversy and the Aroostook War*. Dover, Maine, 1910(?)

CHAPTER II
(From the St. Lawrence River to the Rocky Mountains)

Anderson, S., "The North American Boundary from Lake of the Woods to the Rocky Mountains," *Royal Geogr. Soc.*, Vol. 46, pp. 228-62.

Bemis, S. F., "Jay's Treaty and the Northwest Boundary Gap," *Amer. Hist. Rev.*, 27:465-84, April, 1922.

Bird, W. A., "Reminiscences of the Boundary Survey between the United States and British Provinces," *Publications of the Buffalo Historical Society*. Buffalo, 1896.

Delafield, Joseph, *The Unfortified Boundary*, edited by R. McElroy and T. Biggs. New York, 1943.

Department of State, *Reports upon the Survey of the Boundary between the Territory of the United States and the Possessions of Great Britain from the Lake of the Woods to the Summit of the Rocky Mountains*. Washington, 1878.

Featherstonhaugh, A., *Narrative of the Operations of the British North American Boundary Commission 1872-76*. Woolwich, 1876.

Howard, J. K., *Strange Empire*. New York, 1952.

International Boundary Commission, *Joint Report upon the Survey and Demarcation of the Boundary between the United States and Canada from the Northwesternmost Point of Lake of the Woods to Lake Superior*. Washington, 1931.

―――, *Joint Report upon the Survey and Demarcation of the Boundary between the United States and Canada from the Gulf of Georgia to the Northwesternmost Point of Lake of the Woods*. Washington, 1937.

International Waterways Commission, *Report upon the International Boundary between the Dominion of Canada and the United States through the St. Lawrence River and Great Lakes*. Ottawa, 1916.

Jefferson, Thomas, "The Limits and Bounds of Louisiana," *Documents Relating to the Purchase and Exploration of Louisiana*. New York, 1904.

Parsons, John E., *West on the 49th Parallel*. New York, 1963.

CHAPTER III
(From the Rocky Mountains to the Strait of Georgia)

Baker, Marcus, *Survey of the Northwestern Boundary of the United States 1857-61*. Washington, 1900.

Bancroft, Hubert Howe, *History of Oregon*. San Francisco, 1886.

Galbraith, John S., *The Hudson's Bay Company as an Imperial Factor, 1821-69*. Toronto, 1957.

International Boundary Commission, *Joint Report upon the Survey and Demarcation of the Boundary between the United States and Canada from the Gulf of Georgia to the Northwesternmost Point of Lake of the Woods*. Washington, 1937.

Johnson, Patricia M., "Boundary Journal," *The Beaver*, Winter, 1955-56.

Merk, Frederick, *Manifest Destiny and Mission in American History*. New York, 1963.

―――, "British Government Propaganda and the Oregon Treaty," *Amer. Hist. Rev.*, 40:38-62, October, 1934.

―――, "British Party Politics and the Oregon Treaty," *Amer. Hist. Rev.*, 37:653-77, July, 1932.

Polk, James, *Diary*, edited by Allan Nevins. New York, 1929.

Rich, E. E., *The History of the Hudson's Bay Company 1670-1870*, Vol. II (Vol. 22 of the Publications of the Hudson's Bay Record Society). London, 1959.

Rich, E. E. (ed.), *The Letters of John McLoughlin from Fort Vancouver to the Governor and Committee 1839-44* and *1844-46* (Vols. 6 and 7 of the Publications of the Hudson's Bay Record Society), 1943 and 1944.

Schafer, Joseph, "Documents Relative to Warre and Vavasour's Military Reconnoissance [*sic*] in Oregon 1845-46," *Quarterly of the Oregon Hist. Soc.*, Vol. X, March, 1909.

CHAPTER IV
(Through the Straits of Georgia and Juan de Fuca)

Bancroft, Hubert Howe, *History of British Columbia.* San Francisco, 1890.

Haller, Granville O., *San Juan and Secession.* Seattle, 1896.

International Boundary Commission, *Joint Report upon the Survey and Demarcation of the Boundary between the United States and Canada from the Western Terminus of the Land Boundary along the Forty-Ninth Parallel, on the West Side of Point Roberts, through Georgia, Haro, and Juan de Fuca Straits, to the Pacific Ocean.* Washington, 1921.

Milton, William F. (Viscount), *A History of the San Juan Water Boundary Question.* London, 1869.

Shippee, Lester B., *Canadian-American Relations 1849-74.* Yale Univ. Press, 1939.

CHAPTER V
(The Alaska boundary)

Alaska Boundary Tribunal, *Proceedings.* London, 1903; Washington, 1903 and 1904. (Containing British and United States cases and counter-cases, appendices, protocol, arguments, atlases, etc.)

Dafoe, John W., *Clifford Sifton in Relation to his Times.* Toronto, 1931.

Hopkins, J. Castell, *The Canadian Annual Review of Public Affairs, 1903.* Toronto, 1904.

International Boundary Commission, *Joint Report upon the Survey and Demarcation of the Boundary between Canada and the United States from Tongass Passage to Mount St. Elias.* Ottawa, 1952.

———, *Joint Report upon the Survey and Demarcation of the International Boundary between the United States and Canada along the 141st Meridian from the Arctic Ocean to Mount St. Elias.* n.p., 1918.

Pope, Joseph, *Public Servant: The Memoirs of Sir Joseph Pope.* Edited and completed by Maurice Pope. Toronto, 1960.

Skelton, Oscar D., *Life and Letters of Sir Wilfrid Laurier.* New York, 1922.

Tansill, Charles C., *Canadian-American Relations 1875-1911.* Yale Univ. Press, 1943.

CHAPTER VI
(Surveys and maintenance after 1903)

Detailed information on operations of the International Boundary Commission in the definite survey and demarcation of the boundary will be found in the reports of the commission listed under the preceding five chapters. Brief reports on the work of the Canadian commission appear each year in the annual reports of the Federal Department of Mines and Technical Surveys.

INDEX

373

DATE DUE

NOV 2 8 1989

AUG 10 2010